LEADING RUSSIA: PUTIN IN PERSPECTIVE

Leading Russia: Putin in Perspective

Essays in Honour of Archie Brown

Edited by

ALEX PRAVDA

OXFORD

UNIVERSITY PRESS

OXFORD

UNIVERSITY PRESS

Great Clarendon Street, Oxford OX2 6DP

Oxford University Press is a department of the University of Oxford.
If furthers the University's objective of excellence in research, scholarship,
and education by publishing worldwide in

Oxford New York

Auckland Cape Town Dar es Salaam Hong Kong Karachi
Kuala Lumpur Madrid Melbourne Mexico City Nairobi
New Delhi Shanghai Taipei Toronto

With offices in

Argentina Austria Brazil Chile Czech Republic France Greece
Guatemala Hungary Italy Japan Poland Portugal Singapore
South Korea Switzerland Thailand Turkey Ukraine Vietnam

Oxford is a registered trade mark of Oxford University Press
in the UK and in certain other countries

Published in the United States
by Oxford University Press Inc., New York

© Alex Pravda 2005

The moral rights of the author have been asserted
Database right Oxford University Press (maker)

First published 2005

British Library Cataloguing in Publication Data
Data available

Library of Congress Cataloging in Publication Data
Data available

Typeset by SPI Publisher Services, Pondicherry, India
Printed in Great Britain on acid-free paper by
Biddles Ltd, King's Lynn, Norfolk

ISBN 0-19-927614-5

1 3 5 7 9 10 8 6 4 2

Preface

This volume of essays is a present from colleagues and friends to Archie Brown on the occasion of his retirement as Professor of Politics at the University of Oxford and Professorial Fellow of St Antony's College. In an academic career spanning four decades, Brown has gained international recognition for his scholarship on the politics of Communist and post-Communist states, particularly Soviet and post-Soviet Russia.

Archie Brown's interests are extensive, ranging from the Scottish and Russian Enlightenments of the eighteenth and twentieth centuries to British politics to political culture in Communist states, and leadership and political change in the USSR and Russia.

All those embarking on editing a Festschrift face a difficult choice. Do they put together a collection of essays that touches on as many areas as possible of the work of the scholar being honoured, or do they give priority to thematic coherence? In this case, the difficulty of the choice was eased by two factors. First, the subject that stands at the centre of Archie Brown's work, political leadership, relates directly to most of the other large questions with which he has been concerned, including the role of culture and institutions in the process of political change. Second, Archie has such a large and distinguished circle of close colleagues and friends that it was possible to assemble from among them a team of leading specialists on leadership and political change in contemporary Russia.

All responded with enthusiasm to the invitation to join the Festschrift team. I am indebted to the contributors for the admirable efficiency with which they met editorial requests, even when these coincided with unusually busy periods in their lives. My thanks go to Dominic Byatt and Claire Croft of Oxford University Press for their encouragement, patience, and support in the process of producing the volume. For invaluable help with ensuring that the final typescript was in good order I am indebted to Jackie Willcox, the Secretary and Librarian of the Russian and Eurasian Studies Centre of St Antony's College. Helen Belopolsky and my wife, Riitta Heino, provided much appreciated editorial and research assistance. I am very grateful to Pat Brown for helpful biographical information about her husband, and for compiling the index for this book, as she has done for so many others connected with his name.

In policy circles as well as in the academic world, Archie Brown's name is associated with outstanding analysis of Russian politics. Some of the qualities of that analysis, and of his scholarship in general, are highlighted in the review and appreciation of his work which precedes the Introduction to this volume. At the end of the book, readers will find an annotated bibliography of Brown's work over the last four decades. The body of the volume consists of essays on key dimensions of Putin's leadership and the changes in the Russian political system over which he has presided. The early chapters set Putin's presidency in historical and comparative post–Communist context. Detailed studies consider the impact of Putin's leadership on elections, the legislature, popular attitudes towards democracy, personnel policy, and the Kremlin's relations with business tycoons as well as regional authorities. Finally, two Russian analysts consider the directions in which Putin has taken their country in the domestic and the international arena. By investigating Putin's policies from different thematic and interpretive perspectives, the volume seeks to provide a textured analysis of leadership problems in contemporary Russia. In doing so, we hope to shed some light on the larger questions of political leadership which Archie Brown has done so much to illuminate over the last forty years. This book is a small token of our appreciation of his scholarship, collegiality, and friendship.

Alex Pravda
St Antony's College, Oxford

Contents

Contents

Notes on Contributors

George W. Breslauer is Chancellor's Professor of Political Science and Dean of Social Sciences at the University of California, Berkeley. He is author of *Gorbachev and Yeltsin as Leaders* (Cambridge: Cambridge University Press, 2002) and editor (with Victoria E. Bonnell) of *Russia in the New Century: Stability or Disorder?* (Boulder, CO: Westview, 2001). His earlier publications include *Khrushchev and Brezhnev as Leaders* (London: Allen & Unwin, 1982).

Paul Chaisty is a Lecturer and Tutor in Politics at the University of Oxford. He received his Ph.D. in Politics from the University of Leeds. He has written a number of publications on Russian parliamentary politics, including articles in *Legislative Studies Quarterly*, *Party Politics*, and *Europe-Asia Studies*, and is the author of *Legislative Politics and Economic Power in Russia* (Basingstoke: Palgrave, forthcoming).

Timothy J. Colton is Morris and Anna Feldberg Professor of Government and Russian Studies and Director of the Davis Center for Russian and Eurasian Studies at Harvard University. He is the author of *Moscow: Governing the Socialist Metropolis* (Cambridge, MA: Harvard University Press, 1995); *Growing Pains: Russian Democracy and the Election of 1993* (Cambridge, MA: Harvard University Press, 1998); and *Transitional Citizens: Voters and What Influences Them in the New Russia* (Cambridge, MA: Harvard University Press, 2000).

Andrei Grachev is Chairman of the Scientific Committee of the World Political Forum and foreign affairs correspondent of *Moscow News* and *New Times*. He was a senior research fellow at the Institute of World Economy and International Affairs, Moscow from 1992 to 2001. In 1990–1 he was President Gorbachev's official spokesman. He is the author of *Final Days: The Inside Story of the Collapse of the Soviet Union* (Boulder, CO:Westview, 1995); *L'Exception russe. Staline est-il mort?* (Paris: Ed. du Rocher, 1997); and *Le Mystère Gorbatchev. La terre et le destin* (Paris: Ed. du Rocher, 2001).

Leslie Holmes is Professor of Politics at the University of Melbourne. He is the author of *Post-Communism: An Introduction* (Oxford: Polity Press, 1997) and co-author (with John Dryzek) of *Post-Communist Democratization: Political Discourses Across Thirteen Countries* (Cambridge: Cambridge University Press, 2002).

Eugene Huskey is William R. Kenan, Jr. Professor of Political Science and Russian Studies at Stetson University, Florida. He is the author of *Presidential*

Power in Russia (Armonk, NJ: M.E. Sharpe, 1999) and editor of *Executive Power and Soviet Politics* (Armonk, NJ: M.E. Sharpe, 1992).

Neil Melvin is Senior Lecturer at the Institute for Politics and International Studies at the University of Leeds, currently on leave serving as Senior Adviser to the OSCE High Commissioner on National Minorities. He is the co-author (with Charles King) of *Nations Abroad: Diaspora Politics and International Relations in the Former Soviet Union* (Boulder, CO: Westview, 1998) and has published several journal articles and book chapters on regional politics in Russia.

Julie Newton is Assistant Professor in the Department of International Affairs at the American University of Paris and a Senior Associate Member of St Antony's College. She is the author of *Russia, France and the Idea of Europe* (Basingstoke: Palgrave, 2003).

Alex Pravda is Director of the Russian and Eurasian Studies Centre at St Antony's College and Lecturer in Russian and East European Politics at the University of Oxford. He is the co-author (with Neil Malcolm, Margot Light, and Roy Allison) of *Internal Factors in Russian Foreign Policy* (Oxford: Oxford University Press, 1996) and co-editor (with Stephen White and Zvi Gitelman) of *Developments in Russian Politics* (Basingstoke: Macmillan, 2001) and (with Jan Zielonka) of *Democratic Consolidation in Eastern Europe: International and Transnational Factors* (Oxford: Oxford University Press, 2001).

Robert Service is Professor of Russian History at the University of Oxford and Fellow of St Antony's College. He is the author of *A History of Twentieth-Century Russia* (Basingstoke: Macmillan, 1997); *Lenin: A Biography* (Basingstoke: Macmillan, 2000); *Russia: Experiment with a People: From 1991 to the Present* (Basingstoke: Macmillan, 2002); and *Stalin: A Biography* (Basingstoke: Macmillan, 2004).

Lilia Shevtsova is Senior Associate in the Russian and Eurasian Program at the Carnegie Endowment for International Peace. She is the author of *Putin's Russia* (Washington, DC: Carnegie Endowment, 2003) and *Yeltsin's Russia: Myths and Reality* (Washington, DC: Carnegie Endowment, 1999), and co-editor (with Archie Brown) of *Gorbachev, Yeltsin, and Putin: Political Leadership in Russia's Transition* (Washington, DC: Carnegie Endowment, 2001).

William Tompson is Reader in Politics at Birkbeck College, University of London. He is the author of *Khrushchev: A Political Life* (Basingstoke: Macmillan, 1995); *The Soviet Union under Brezhnev* (London: Longmans, 2003); and numerous journal articles on Soviet and Russian politics and on the political economy of the Russian transition. He is currently on secondment to the Organization for Economic Cooperation and Development (OECD), where he heads the Russia desk in the Economics Department.

Stephen Whitefield is Fellow in Politics at Pembroke College, Oxford. He is the author of *Industrial Power and the Soviet State* (Oxford: Oxford University Press, 1993) as well as numerous journal articles and book chapters on popular support for democracy in Russia and other post-Communist states. At present he is in receipt of a Leverhulme Foundation Major Research Fellowship.

Note on Transliteration

The British Standard System has been used to transliterate Russian words that appear in italics as well as non-italicized ones which figure in the titles of articles. Elsewhere, and especially where proper nouns are concerned, modifications have been made in order to ease the task of the reader unfamiliar with the Russian language (hence Yeltsin rather than Yel'tsin, and Khodorkovsky rather than Khodorkovskiy).

1

Archie Brown

Alex Pravda

Archie Brown is the doyen of British specialists on Russian politics. Over the last forty years he has established an unrivalled international reputation for his scholarly work, particularly on leadership and political change in Soviet and post-Soviet Russia. His research in the decade preceding *perestroika* alerted Western policy-makers, as well as academics, to the significance of forces for change within the Soviet system. *The Gorbachev Factor* (1996) is the most authoritative study of the crucial role the last Soviet leader played in the reform and transformation of Communism. While Russia has remained central to his interests, Archie has also made an important contribution to the field of comparative Communist and post-Communist studies. His research has greatly advanced our understanding of the cultural, institutional, and leadership factors that shaped the political evolution of states under Communism, and have defined their post-Communist transition. Brown's scholarship is distinguished by judicious use of comparative analytical insight, meticulous attention to empirical data, keen sensitivity to cultural and historical context, and sound judgement. As a result, his work has been of great value to the politician and political observer as well as to the student and academic researcher.

I

Archibald Haworth Brown was born in Annan in the south of Scotland on 10 May 1938, the son of Mary Yates Brown and the Reverend Alexander Douglas Brown. His father, who had been an outstanding student in classics and divinity at Glasgow University, was a minister in the Church of Scotland. Archie left school at the age of sixteen, determined to become a newspaper reporter. His work on local papers, in Lockerbie and Annan, was cut short in 1956 by National Service. Most of the following two years were spent in London, where the tedium of army duties was relieved by the opportunity to see West End plays as well as observe political theatre from the Strangers' Gallery of the House of Commons. The enforced break from journalism also gave Archie a chance to reconsider his career plans. He stayed on in the capital and a year later entered the London School of Economics; in 1962 he graduated with a first-class B.Sc. (Econ.), specializing in Government. Archie continued at the LSE as a Ford Foundation research student, working under the supervision of Professor Leonard Schapiro. Although his interests lay in contemporary Soviet politics, he agreed with his supervisor that there were major obstacles to doing serious research in the USSR in this area, and that it would be preferable to analyse political questions in a historical context. Archie began work on the Russian followers of Adam Smith and the links between the Scottish and the Russian Enlightenment. After two years as a research student, he was appointed in 1964 to a Lectureship in Politics at the University of Glasgow. Archie returned to Scotland with his wife Pat (née Patricia Susan Cornwell), whom he had married in 1963; their daughter, Susan (an Oxford City Councillor since the age of twenty-five and a young parliamentary candidate in the general election of 1997) was born in 1969 and their son, Douglas, in 1971. After an initial stint of teaching, Archie spent the academic year 1967–8 on study leave in Moscow. While KGB surveillance was sometimes obtrusive, he encountered no serious problems while in Moscow, though he witnessed at first hand the pressures to which the Soviet security services could subject British graduate students.[1]

Once back in Glasgow, Archie continued research on eighteenth-century themes and worked on British politics and comparative Communist studies, which were to continue to interest him in following decades. He published a substantial analysis of the British prime ministerial powers, based on historical as well as contemporary material, the first foray into the field of leadership to which he was to contribute so much, especially in the context of Russia.[2] Brown was among the first Western scholars to appreciate the significance of reformist trends in Czechoslovakia, well before 1968. On study visits to Prague, he met a number of notable reformist Communist intellectuals, including Zdeněk Mlynář, who had been Gorbachev's closest friend when a student in Moscow and became the leading theoretician of the liberalizing reforms of the Prague Spring. The insights Archie gained in the course of these visits helped him to produce incisive analyses of the sources and significance of pluralizing change in Communist Czechoslovakia.[3]

[1] Archie alerted British embassy officials to particularly unsavoury KGB attempts to blackmail a fellow student into spying for Moscow; see Archie Brown, 'Glasnost at the FCO', *Prospect*, (July 1998), 68. As all subsequent references, unless otherwise specified, are to works by Brown, only title and location are given. Full references to Brown's published work, as well as summaries of selected items, may be found in Julie Newton's annotated bibliography at the end of this volume.

[2] 'Prime Ministerial Power', *Public Law*, Part I (Spring 1968), 28–51; Part II (Summer 1968), 96–118. This long article was written before the Browns left for Russia.

[3] 'Pluralistic Trends in Czechoslovakia', *Soviet Studies*, 17/4 (April 1966), 453–72; and 'Political Change in Czechoslovakia', *Government and Opposition*, 4/2 (Spring 1969), 169–94. Archie first met Mlynář in Prague in 1965 and kept in touch with him and his then wife, Rita Budínová, who later, as Rita Klímová, became the first post-Communist Czechoslovak ambassador to Washington; see 'Introduction' to Mikhail Gorbachev and Zdeněk Mlynář, *Conversations with Gorbachev: On Perestroika, the Prague Spring, and the Crossroads of Socialism* (New York: Columbia University Press, 2002), viii–xiv. Brown returned to Czechoslovakia in 1968, 1969, 1976, and 1983.

This period also saw his first analyses of a subject that was to dominate his academic activity over the following decades—the Soviet political system.

In 1971 Archie moved to Oxford, where he was appointed to a Lectureship in Soviet Institutions and to the fellowship at St Antony's College that he was to hold for over three decades. The first years at Oxford saw the publication of a book assessing interpretations of the Soviet political system. The first systematic study of its kind, *Soviet Politics and Political Science* was praised as 'a model of common sense as well as disciplined academic argument . . .' and soon became a staple item on reading lists.[4] So did the volume *The Soviet Union since the Fall of Khrushchev* (1975), which he edited with his economist colleague Michael Kaser. This brought together a team of leading British specialists and provided the most systematic and comprehensive coverage available of recent Soviet developments. The sequel, *Soviet Policy for the 1980s* (1982), succeeded in maintaining this high standard.

The years between the publication of the two studies saw Brown turn his attention to a complex and important subject, in which he has maintained an active interest ever since: political culture. *Political Culture and Political Change in Communist States* (1977), which he edited with Jack Gray, a China specialist at Glasgow University, broke new ground in the comparative analysis of political culture in countries under Communist rule. It sparked widespread interest and lively debate, some of which was reflected in the later volume Archie edited, *Political Culture and Communist Studies* (1984).

As the Brezhnev era drew to a close, Brown began to focus more closely on the powers of the General Secretary and his role in political change. He made a shrewd assessment of Andropov's reform programme and produced prescient analyses of likely leadership developments, identifying Mikhail Gorbachev as the most impressive and promising candidate for the top job.[5] The influence of Archie's insights extended well beyond academic circles. His views made an important impact on British decision-makers, most notably Mrs Thatcher. At a seminar held at Chequers on 8 September 1983, attended by the Prime Minister and leading members of her Cabinet, Brown described Gorbachev as probably the most 'open-minded' member of the Politburo and the most 'hopeful choice from the point of view of both Soviet citizens and the outside world'. After listening attentively to Brown's carefully argued presentation, Mrs Thatcher asked her Foreign Secretary, Sir Geoffrey Howe, whether they should not invite Mr Gorbachev to Britain. According to Sir Anthony Parsons, the prime minister's foreign policy adviser at that time, the seminar 'changed British foreign policy'. It

[4] Review by A. L. Reid, *Political Studies*, 23/4 (December 1975), 549.
[5] 'The Power of the General Secretary of the CPSU' in Archie Brown, T. H. Rigby, and Peter Reddaway (eds.), *Authority, Power and Policy in the USSR: Essays Dedicated to Leonard Schapiro* (London: Macmillan, 1980), 135–57; 'Leadership Succession and Policy Innovation' in Archie Brown and Michael Kaser (eds.), *Soviet Policy for the 1980s* (London: Macmillan), esp. 240–1; and 'Andropov: Discipline *and* Reform?', *Problems of Communism*, 32/1 (January–February 1983), 18–31.

Alex Pravda

is rare that academics get an opportunity to make a critical contribution to developments that alter the course of international relations. On the eve of Gorbachev's visit in December 1984, Brown was one of four invited to Downing Street to brief Mrs Thatcher and senior colleagues.[6] Gorbachev made a very favourable impression on his British host, who famously declared that she liked him and thought they could do business together. Her positive judgement about the man, who within three months became General Secretary, in turn influenced Ronald Reagan, helping to open his mind to the new qualities of the young Soviet leader. And it was Gorbachev's distinctive attributes—intelligence, flexibility, and a strong disposition to take ideas and reform seriously—that Brown highlighted in a substantial analysis published soon after the new leader had come to power.[7]

As early as May 1985, Archie Brown defined Gorbachev unequivocally as a 'reformer'.[8] When, nearly two years later, many still remained sceptical about the real significance of *perestroika*, Brown berated those observers who dismissed as trivial anything that fell short of transforming the system into something akin to a Western liberal democracy.[9] He reminded them that reform and evolutionary change had considerable merits which Western specialists and politicians were well advised not to undervalue. The momentous importance of Gorbachev's reforms and their transformative effects on the political system emerged clearly from the large number of important analyses Brown published during the halcyon years of *perestroika*.[10] Recognition of the outstanding scholarly quality of this and earlier work was reflected in his appointment as Professor of Politics at Oxford in 1989 and, two years later, in his election as a Fellow of the British Academy. Brown's magisterial study of leadership and political change, *The Gorbachev Factor*, was published in 1996 and received wide critical acclaim. It won two major academic awards: the W. J. M. Mackenzie prize and the Alec Nove prize.[11]

[6] For these meetings, see 'The Leader of the Prologue' in Ferdinand Mount (ed.), *Communism* (London: Harvill, 1992), 296–7; Archie Brown and Alec Cairncross, 'Alec Nove: An Appreciation', *Europe-Asia* Studies, 49/3 (1997), 495–6; and *The Gorbachev Factor* (Oxford and New York: Oxford University Press, 1996), 77–8. Among the other specialists who took part in the September 1983 Chequers seminar were Ronald Amann, Michael Kaser, Alec Nove, and Alex Pravda. Archie participated in a further seminar at Chequers on 27 February 1987; *The Gorbachev Factor* 335, n. 125.

[7] 'Gorbachev: New Man in the Kremlin', *Problems of Communism*, XXXIV/3 (May–June 1985), 1–23.

[8] 'Can Gorbachev Make a Difference?', *Détente*, No. 3 (May 1985), 4.

[9] See 'What's Happening in Moscow?', *The National Interest*, No. 8 (Summer 1987), 10; 'Soviet Political Developments and Prospects', *World Policy Journal*, 4/1 (Winter 1986–7), 85; and 'The Soviet Political Scene: The Era of Gorbachev?', in Lawrence W. Lerner and Donald W. Treadgold (eds.), *Gorbachev and the Soviet Future* (Boulder, CO: Westview, 1988), 38.

[10] See Julie Newton's annotated bibliography at the end of this volume, 275–94.

[11] The W. J. M. Mackenzie Prize is awarded by the Political Studies Association of the UK for the best political science book of the year; the Alec Nove prize is given by the British Association for Slavonic and East European Studies for the best book or article in any discipline on Russia, Communism, or post-Communism. The *Gorbachev Factor* was also published in German as *Der Gorbatschow-Faktor* (Frankfurt: Insel-Verlag, 2000).

Brown, characteristically, did not rest on his laurels. He continued to write on the *perestroika* period, taking account of new primary sources as they became available, and tackled the difficult task of interpreting the fast-changing and often chaotic story of post-Communist Russia. He was critical of those Western analysts who exaggerated the ease with which Russia's transition from Communism would lead to liberal democracy. He saw Russia under Yeltsin in terms that were more sober and complex, and proved to be more realistic.[12]

The policy establishment proved less open to unfashionably realistic views of Russia than it had been a decade earlier. To the surprise of many Labour supporters within the academic community, Mr Blair seemed to pay less attention to the assessments of Russia by country specialists than had Mrs Thatcher. Even so, Archie had an early opportunity, in the mid-1990s, to brief the Labour leader on developments in Moscow, and over the last decade has continued to be consulted by government and parliament alike. His contacts with members of the House of Commons have developed well beyond the realm of Russian affairs, largely as the result of a link between parliament and the academic world which Archie initiated in 1994. The Visiting Parliamentary Fellowship scheme makes possible the association each year with St Antony's College of two MPs, from different parties, who take part in the life of the College and help organize a major seminar series. The scheme has become now a permanent feature of College life, and the seminar firmly established as an important forum for exchanges of views between academics and parliamentarians.

This is just one of the many contributions Archie Brown has made to St Antony's, where he has spent most of his academic life (a total of thirty-four years by the time he retires in 2005). He is a natural team player, whether on the cricket pitch or in the committee room. He has always been a Fellow who can be relied on to accept College jobs and do them well, whether as General Editor of the Macmillan/St Antony's monograph series or as sub-warden of the College. He has done an enormous amount over the years for the Russian and East European Centre (since 2003, the Russian and Eurasian Studies Centre). It is Archie who made the Monday seminar (which has run weekly during term since 1953) into one of the most important forums for the discussion of Russian politics in Britain, and indeed anywhere in the academic world. Those who attended the seminar in the late 1970s and early 1980s will recall the climate of intellectual and political excitement which Archie helped foster with his inimitable combination of enthusiasm and equanimity. The hot-house atmosphere was made all the more intense by the capacity crowds, with latecomers listening attentively while seated on central-heating pipes. Just as at St Antony's, so in Oxford University as a whole, Archie has provided intellectual and organizational leadership in the development of Russian and East European studies.

---

[12] See, for instance, 'Political Leadership in Post-Communist Russia' in Amin Saikal and William Maley (eds.), *Russia in Search of its Future* (Cambridge: Cambridge University Press, 1995), 28–47.

Never one to limit his activities to the geographical area which he studies, Archie has always played a full part in the political science community, within Oxford and beyond. He has been on the editorial board of the *British Journal of Political Science* for twenty-six years and served for a decade on the Standing Committee of the Political Studies section of the British Academy, including a three-year period as chair. He continues to be a member of the British Academy's International Policy Committee. In 1999 he was elected a founding academician of the (UK) Academy of Learned Societies for the Social Sciences.

Archie Brown has also given a great deal to the wider academic community engaged in Russian and Communist studies. His many published reviews are distinguished by thoroughness and balance.[13] He has been very effective in organizing and facilitating scholarly collaboration. Archie has edited or helped to edit no fewer than fifteen collaborative volumes, aided by the indexing skills of his wife Pat. He has made his considerable contribution to collective research in a spirit of academic altruism that reflects his professional as well as personal kindness and generosity. Countless numbers of younger scholars have benefited from his advice and help in participating in collaborative research and getting their work published. While most of the beneficiaries have belonged to the British scholarly community, many have come from the two countries Archie has made his second academic homes: the United States and Russia.

Brown's links with the United States go back nearly a quarter of a century when he held visiting professorships at Yale University and the University of Connecticut. In the course of the following decade, he spent a semester at Columbia University and an academic year as holder of the Frank C. Erwin Jr. Centennial Chair in Government at the University of Texas at Austin. Fortunately for the British academic community, Brown, unlike many who have had the chance to enjoy North American research facilities, did return to the United Kingdom. He continues to visit the United States regularly, and is held in high regard by the Slavic studies and Political Science communities alike. A signal mark of recognition came in 2003 when Archie Brown was the only foreign scholar to be elected that year as a Foreign Honorary Member of the American Academy of Arts and Sciences from its Political Science, International Relations, and Public Policy section.

Connections with Russia stretch back still further, starting with a study visit to Moscow and Leningrad in 1966, soon followed by a full academic year's research attachment at Moscow State University. During the 1970s and 1980s, Brown was one of a minority of serious and critical analysts of the Soviet system who were willing to contend with the practical hazards and intellectual challenges of regular study visits. The authorities' deep suspicion of foreign specialists—a trait that seems resurgent in present-day Russia—made obtaining visas an uncertain business. Some Western analysts tried to ensure visa access by tempering their

---

[13] For selected reviews, see Julie Newton's annotated bibliography, p. 294.

published views, often, in fact, to no avail. Brown always maintained his academic integrity and was fortunate not to fall victim to the British–Soviet diplomatic spats that put leading scholars on blacklists for extended periods. Quite apart from the practical hazards involved, visits to Moscow were also intellectually challenging as they meant confronting a complex political reality that did not square easily with Western social science theories and models. Brown used the visits to get to grips with the intricacies of Soviet politics, and it was his success in doing so that gave his analysis its depth and insight.

In the course of his regular stays in Moscow, Brown established contacts across a broad spectrum, ranging from social scientists close to inner Communist Party circles to academics who held radically critical views and had great difficulty holding on to their academic posts. Some became personal friends and greatly valued Archie's loyalty and help, especially in difficult times. His extensive network of professional colleagues much appreciated the trouble Archie took to help them develop international academic contacts and get their work published in the West. In the three decades since political science first emerged as an embryonic academic discipline in Russia, he has been one of the most attentive Western observers of that community's professional activities. In the years since the end of Communism, he has been able to become more directly involved in helping to develop this academic community. He has helped to make the work of outstanding scholars on Russian politics better known in the West. For instance, a third of the contributors (thirteen out of thirty-eight) to his unusually comprehensive *Contemporary Russian Politics: A Reader* were Russians. And some of the Russian research students he has taught at Oxford in recent years have returned home and become leading members of the new generation of Russian political scientists.

As well as being a first-rate scholar, Archie has always been an outstanding teacher. He has managed to realize in practice the oft-trumpeted yet seldom achieved symbiosis between teaching and research. His ability to explain complex issues in a systematic and lucid manner have made him an effective and popular lecturer. Dedication, conscientiousness, and patience have made him the ideal tutor and supervisor. He has successfully guided over a score of research students through the travails of graduate work. Most of the resulting doctoral theses have been turned into books through a process of revision in which he has also played a highly supportive role. He remains in close touch with large numbers of former students. Several, including James Blitz, Owen Bennett-Jones, and Bridget Kendall, have made their mark in the media; others, such as Joel Hellman, Jeffrey Kahn, and Tiffany Troxel, have distinguished themselves in the fields of economic policy, law, and finance; and many have gone on to successful academic careers. They include Charles King, Tomila Lankina, Alexander Lukin, Stephen Welch, and several of the contributors to this volume: Neil Melvin, Julie Newton, William Tompson, and Stephen Whitefield. All have benefited from Archie's ability to impart the qualities which his own work and teaching exemplify:

painstaking research and respect for empirical evidence; analytical rigour and clarity; and, perhaps above all else, open-mindedness and intellectual honesty.

II

Archie Brown's research has embraced the most important elements in politics—institutions, interests, ideas, culture, and leadership—and grappled with the fundamental and complex matter of political change. Over the last four decades, he has explored the ways in which culture, ideas, institutions, and leaders interact to bring about reform and transformation. The Communist and post-Communist states, and Russia in particular, have provided him with a remarkably fruitful context within which to conduct his investigations. Those who dig deep in interesting regions often unearth a great deal of important material without using it to construct the kind of analysis that feeds into the disciplinary mainstream. It is precisely this type of analysis that Archie has succeeded in providing over the years.[14]

What distinguishes his scholarship is the very high quality of the empirical research, an open-minded approach to analytical models and methods, and exceptionally sound judgement.

Brown has always been painstaking in collecting material and scrupulous in using it: a combination that perhaps reflects both the investigative instincts that fired his initial interest in journalism, and the archival skills he acquired in his early work on the Russian followers of Adam Smith. Thoroughness occasionally brings unexpected rewards. In the first half of the 1960s, Archie came across an interesting item of correspondence between Hume and Smith 'filed' in an empty Kellogg's Cornflakes packet, otherwise empty apart from some old photographs of River Clyde steam-boats. Intuition and textual skills enabled him to identify an entry in the Commonplace Book of a Glasgow professor as an important set of notes of Adam Smith's lectures on Jurisprudence. The leading Smith scholar to whom Brown sent the material conceded, after initial scepticism, that the young researcher's 'original intuition was well founded'.[15] The combination of a forensic eye for detail and excellent intuition has served Brown well in identifying and interpreting a range of material bearing on Russian politics, from the details of

[14] See, for instance, the appreciative references to Archie Brown's work on political culture and pluralism by the leading political scientist Gabriel Almond in *A Discipline Divided: Schools and Sects in Political Science* (Newbury Park, CA: Sage Publications, 1990), 77, 88, 106–7.

[15] Ronald L. Meek, 'New Light on Adam Smith's Glasgow lectures on Jurisprudence', *History of Political Economy*, 8/4 (Winter 1976), 441. Professor John Anderson, who had made the notes, had had an altercation with Semyon Desnitsky, the main subject of Brown's own research; see 'Adam Smith's First Russian Followers' in A.S. Skinner and T. Wilson (eds.), *Essays on Adam Smith* (Oxford: Clarendon Press, 1975), 256–7.

careers to the nuances of official speeches and esoteric specialist debate. The range of sources which he has used may be unusually broad for a political scientist, but essential for anyone seeking to comprehend the political realities of Russia, especially in Soviet times when economists produced novels and political scientists wrote plays. Keen awareness of historical and cultural developments has long enriched Brown's understanding of the intellectual climate in which politics operates. His 'feel' for the context and spirit of Russian politics comes through in the insight and balance with which he has interpreted the mass of evidence thrown up by the dramatic changes of the last four decades. And that interpretation is made all the more convincing by his practice of setting out (often in substantial notes) the evidence and the reasoning supporting key points, so that readers can make their own informed assessments.

This practice is typical of the open and fair-minded approach Brown has always taken to the enterprise of scholarly analysis. He has consistently opposed methodological dogmatism, whatever its source. In the Cold War years, Soviet and Communist studies were adversely affected by ideological differences. The effect on French and Italian scholarship was particularly marked, that on the British academic community less acute and shorter-lived.[16]

The post-Cold War years have seen dogmatic tendencies of another kind. Since the collapse of Communism, most Western leaders and many of those who have written on Russia, often with little knowledge of the country, have been all too ready to see developments there through the prism of an inevitable and 'natural' process of market democratization. Such views have led to wrong-headed assessments and policies and reflect the kind of culture-bound narrowness which Brown has long disliked.[17]

More generally, he is sceptical about the unicausal and mechanistic theories and explanations that from time to time engulf political science, in wave-like succession. Brown has always been alert to the dangers of all too readily dismissing the value of old approaches and exaggerating the explanatory reach of the new. Instead, he has long favoured 'discriminating eclecticism' and made careful use of a selection of analytical tools so as to do justice to the complexities of the problems under scrutiny.[18] He makes ample and rigorous use of social science

[16] 'The Study of Totalitarianism and Authoritarianism' in Jack Hayward, Brian Barry, and Archie Brown (eds.), *The British Study of Politics in the Twentieth Century* (London: Oxford University Press, 1999), 263.

[17] For critical comment on Western understanding, see 'The Russian Crisis: Beginning of the End or the End of the Beginning?', *Post-Soviet Affairs*, 15/1 (January–March 1999), 57. Long before, Brown had drawn unfavourable comparisons between the culture-bound nature of twentieth century theories of development and those of the eighteenth century; see '"Political Development" and the Study of Communist Politics', *Studies in Comparative Communism*, 15/1 (Spring–Summer 1982), 133.

[18] *Soviet Politics and Political Science* (London: Macmillan, 1974), ch.1; and 'Political Power and the Soviet State: Western and Soviet Perspectives' in Neil Harding (ed.), *The State in Socialist Society* (London: Macmillan, 1984), 53 .

concepts, never allowing them to skew or obscure the empirically based analytical story. The clarity with which Brown tells this story is helped by the fact that his writing is mercifully free from jargon; he has the ability, all too rare among social scientists, to make complex points in clear and plain language.

Brown's insistence on methodological rigour and dispassionate analysis does not reflect a dry scholastic approach to research. His work has never been simply about trying to resolve difficult intellectual puzzles; there is a concern with the moral dimension of politics as well as with its scholarly analysis. What comes through in his writing is an appreciation of the merits of peaceful and evolutionary change, especially when this process helps to develop democratic pluralism and to advance the cause of social justice.

III

To do justice to the outstanding scholarly contribution Archie Brown has made would require far more space than I have at my disposal. I hope that the following pages give some flavour of his insights into the sources of within-system reform; the role of Gorbachev in the transformation of Soviet Communism; and leadership and democratization in post-Communist Russia.

Within-system Reform

In the three and a half decades that separated the death of Stalin from the demise of the system he had created, our understanding of change within that system was hampered by conceptual stereotypes. Brown has always been even-handedly rigorous in his criticism, reminding the proponents of both totalitarianism and pluralism of the dangers of conceptual 'stretching'.[19] From the late 1960s on-wards, he took to task those who applied totalitarianism as a model rather than employing it as a useful ideal type.[20] Those claiming that totalitarianism captured political reality exaggerated the monolithic uniformity of post-Stalin Communist states, and contributed 'virtually nothing to an understanding of

---

[19] 'Pluralism, Power and the Soviet Political System' in Susan Gross Solomon (ed.), *Pluralism in the Soviet Union: Essays in Honour of H. Gordon Skilling* (London: Macmillan, 1983), 61–107 (for discussion of Giovanni Sartori's criticism of 'conceptual stretching', see 64–5); 'Political Power and the Soviet State' (n. 18); and 'Political Science in the USSR', *International Political Science Review*, 7/4 (October 1986), 473.

[20] Brown's study of radical reform in Czechoslovakia brought home to him the pitfalls of misapplying the totalitarian model; see 'Political Change in Czechoslovakia' (n. 3), esp.179; 'Political Power and the Soviet State' (n. 18), 55–6. He has made sparing use of the concept even as an ideal type; see, for instance, 'Soviet Political Development and Prospects' (n. 9), 83.

political change'; rather, they helped to obscure its sources. He also pointed out that such inaccurate use of terms had damaging effects on Western policy as well as scholarship, blinkering observers to the possibility of gradual change.[21]

Brown applied equally exacting standards to those at the other and more fashionable end of the analytical spectrum, who, in the late 1970s and early 1980s, depicted Communist politics in pluralist terms. In trenchant reviews of their work, he called for the rigorous use of the concept of political pluralism to denote relatively autonomous organized activity, of which there was no evidence in Brezhnev's USSR.[22] Nor did Brown consider it appropriate to use the term 'interest group' in the Soviet context.[23] What did exist in the Soviet system, he maintained, were institutional interests and 'opinion groupings' of specialists, and the innovative debates of the latter were well worth examining.[24]

Most Western observers paid little attention to these specialist debates as a possible source of political change. They looked instead to the far more radical ideas and challenges coming from the dissident community. Brown was one of the very few analysts who appreciated the far greater importance of specialist debates as a crucible of innovative political thinking.[25] He realized that the very features that inclined most observers to discount these discussions—their 'esoteric' nature and the proximity of the participants to centres of power—were actually keys to their political significance. While there was some room for debate, it remained highly circumscribed, and the only way of getting new ideas into print was to dress them in doctrinal camouflage.[26] His pioneering work detailed how Soviet political scientists were breaking away from traditional legalistic approaches and putting 'the real political process' on the scholarly agenda by

[21] 'Transnational Influences in the Transition from Communism', *Post-Soviet Affairs*, 16/2 (April–June 2000), 185–6; and 'Political Power and the Soviet State' (n. 18), 55–7. For an early measured review of totalitarianism, see *Soviet Politics and Political Science* (n. 18), 35–41.

[22] 'Governing the USSR' *Problems of Communism*, 28/5–6 (September–December 1979), 107–8; 'Pluralism, Power and the Soviet Political System' (n. 19), 68–9.

[23] 'Problems of Group Influence and Interest Articulation in the Soviet Union', *Government and Opposition*, 7/2 (Spring 1972), 229–43; and *Soviet Politics and Political Science* (n. 18), ch. 3.

[24] 'Policy-making in Communist States', *Studies in Comparative Communism*, 11/4 (Winter 1978), 433–4. Brown also referred to usefulness of other terms, such as 'issue networks'; see 'Andropov: Discipline and Reform?', *Problems of Communism*, 32/1 (January–February 1983), 19.

[25] While fully recognizing the courage of the dissidents and the indirect influence of some of their ideas, Brown has never regarded them as having played a major role in bringing about political change; see 'Mikhail Gorbachev: Systemic Transformer' in Martin Westlake (ed.), *Leaders of Transition* (London: Macmillan, 2000), 23; and 'Gorbachev and Reform of the Soviet System' in Jon Bloomfield (ed.), *The Soviet Revolution: Perestroika and the Remaking of Socialism* (London: Lawrence and Wishart, 1989), 71.

[26] 'Policy-making in Communist states' (n. 24), 433; 'Political science in the USSR' (n. 19), 470; and 'Introduction' in Archie Brown (ed.), *The Demise of Marxism-Leninism in Russia* (London: Palgrave, 2004), 5.

discussing concepts such as political culture, checks and balances, and competitive elections.[27]

Most of the ideas discussed by the Russian specialists were drawn from Western sources, because, as Brown put it, they 'had seen the future (in Western Europe) and it appeared to work.'[28] There were parallels here with other instances of the transnational flow of ideas which he had studied: the migration of Adam Smith's ideas to Catherine's Russia, and, more to the point, Western influences in the intellectual ferment that preceded the Prague Spring. There were parallels, too, at least with Czechoslovakia, in the way that the debates in the Soviet Union became increasingly open and far-reaching. By 1987–90, the more radical of the Soviet specialists had helped bring about 'a conceptual revolution' in the form of New Thinking, which legitimated notions of political pluralism and electoral contest at home and promoted 'humanistic universalism' abroad.[29]

The impact of innovative specialist debate on official doctrine was due not so much to the intellectual novelty of the ideas, in a universal sense, as to their political appeal for reformist officials in the Communist Party establishment. In his work on the role of new ideas in Soviet political change, Brown has rightly stressed the importance of political access and acceptability. The most influential specialists were Party intellectuals, 'insiders' who belonged to policy-making circles, or who moved in and out of them, and were therefore sensitive to changes in the climate of thinking at the top of the Party hierarchy.[30]

Climatic change depended crucially, as Brown underscores, on the ultimate insider, the General Secretary himself. In Gorbachev, the supporters of reform finally found 'a standard-bearer who actually came to power and opened up hitherto-unheard-of space for political innovation'.[31] In the event, the combination of intellectual ferment among Party intellectuals and support from the top made possible something neither the 'totalitarians' nor the 'pluralists' anticipated but for which Brown's interpretation set the scene: an evolutionary process of reform from within that led to the transformation of the system. Indeed, as he persuasively contends, 'a process of ever more radical reform was the only way in which the Communist system could have been peacefully transformed in a country where . . . Communist institutions and norms were deeply entrenched'.[32]

[27] 'Political Science in the Soviet Union: A New State of Development?', *Soviet Studies*, 36/3 (1984), 317–44; 'Political Science in the USSR' (n. 19); 'Political Power and the Soviet State' (n. 18), 73–5. For an early reference, see *Soviet Politics and Political Science* (n. 18), 54 .

[28] 'Introduction' (n. 26), 11. For the influence of foreign visits on Gorbachev before he came to power, see *The Gorbachev Factor* (n. 6), 41–3.

[29] 'Introduction' in Archie Brown (ed.), *New Thinking in Soviet Politics* (London: Macmillan, 1992), 1, 8; and 'New Thinking on the Soviet Political System', in ibid. 15–25; and *The Gorbachev Factor* (n. 6), 121–9, 221–5.

[30] Ibid. 18–22, 48–9; and 'New Thinking' (n. 29), 31–2.

[31] *The Gorbachev Factor* (n. 6), 57.   [32] Ibid. 317.

Leadership, Reform, and Systemic Transformation

All students of Russia would agree that the leader in the Kremlin exercises extraordinary influence on the direction and complexion of political development. Few, though, have shed as much light as Archie Brown on the sources, nature, and exercise of leadership power in the Soviet and post-Soviet periods. None has produced as authoritative and penetrating an analysis of how the last Soviet leader came to reform the Communist system out of existence. In examining leadership politics in Moscow, Brown has long drawn on his knowledge of leadership issues in the Western, and particularly the British, context. His early work on prime ministerial power brought out the complexity of factors affecting its historical development, and identified no simple and clear trends over time. Similarly, he found, there was no linear pattern in the personal power of the General Secretary of the Communist Party of the USSR over the whole post-Stalin period. From the perspective of the late Brezhnev years, there appeared to be a secular decline in the power of the Soviet leader. But even Andropov's short rule indicated an upward shift in the exercise of personal power, and one that rose steeply under Gorbachev.[33] At the core of Brown's interpretation of *perestroika*, both at the time and in retrospect, lies the argument that Gorbachev made a crucial difference—to how reforms began; to how they took on radical content; and to how they evolved into a peaceful transformation of the Communist system and the Cold War world.[34]

Why did the Kremlin embark on a course of radical reform in the mid-1980s? Unlike many Western analysts, Brown has never seen the move to reform as an unavoidable response to a crisis that threatened the survival of the system. He views as myth the notion that Reagan's intensification of the arms race induced the changes in Moscow. Nor does he think that adverse social and economic indicators, however important a stimulus to change, in any sense pre-ordained radical reform. He makes a persuasive case: in 1985 the USSR was in 'slow and relative decline' but 'had not yet reached crisis point ... whereby it was faced by imminent death or recovery'.[35] There was nothing ineluctable about the choice of a radical way forward. The members of the Politburo, including those who

[33] For discussion of the patterns identified for different time periods, see 'Conclusions' in Archie Brown (ed.), *Political Leadership in the Soviet* Union (London: Macmillan, 1989), 222–4, 230, n. 9. Archie Brown's observations on patterns up to 1980 (see 'The Power of the General Secretary' (n. 5), 136) were referred to as 'Brown's Law' by Thane Gustafson, *Slavic Review*, 43/4 (Winter 1984), 684. For Brown's observations on the complexity of British patterns, see 'Prime Ministerial Power' (Part I), *Public Law* (Spring 1968), esp. 33, 117.

[34] *The Gorbachev Factor* (n. 6). For Gorbachev's decisive role in bringing about the radical transformation of foreign policy, see ch. 7; and 'Mikhail Gorbachev and the End of the Cold War', in Ned Lebow and Richard Herrmann (eds.), *Ending the Cold War* (London: Palgrave, 2004), 31–57.

[35] *The Gorbachev Factor* (n. 6), 90–1. As Brown notes, it was the 'unintended consequences' of Gorbachev's attempt to reform the system 'that turned dire problems into a real crisis of the system'. Also see ibid. 134–5, 225–30; and 'Mikhail Gorbachev and the Transformation of Russian Politics', in *A Millennium Salute to Mikhail Gorbachev on his 70th Birthday* (Moscow: Valent, 2001), 100–2.

belonged to the post-Brezhnev generation, combined an uneasy awareness of declining performance with a reluctance to face up to the existence of any fundamental problems, let alone far-reaching change. Of the possible candidates to succeed Chernenko, only Gorbachev, as Brown has shown, favoured serious reform.[36]

How, then, did the notoriously cautious and conservative Soviet Communist Party establishment come to choose such an unusually reform-minded individual as General Secretary? Brown has provided a full and convincing account of how Gorbachev rose rapidly to high office, by dint of outstanding ability and the support of powerful patrons, including Andropov. An energetic supporter of new ideas, Gorbachev abided by the rules of the game and was 'as pragmatic an innovator as the conservative temper of the times allowed'.[37] By 1980 he had become a 'senior secretary', one of the small pool from which the 'selectorate' typically co-opted one of its members as leader. Blocked by the Brezhnevite old guard from succeeding Andropov, Gorbachev emerged as the most energetic and effective member of the leadership under the ailing Chernenko. There being no other strong contenders for the succession, good political groundwork ensured that the choice of Gorbachev was a unanimous one. Most of the Politburo, including Gromyko who proposed his candidature, selected him as 'a modernizer who would give dynamism to Soviet policy, not radically transform it.'[38]

That the new General Secretary proceeded to surprise his colleagues and take the Soviet system far beyond the bounds of reform is clear and uncontroversial. Far more contentious and difficult are questions of how Gorbachev helped to bring about such transformative change and what led him to do so. It is by providing 'richly textured answers'[39] to such questions that Brown has made such a major contribution to our understanding of *perestroika* and Gorbachev's key role in the momentous changes it brought.

Brown sets little store by what he calls the 'Pandora's Box' interpretation, according to which the Soviet leader was simply swept along by a rising tide of forces he had inadvertently set free. Brown's own interpretation highlights two strands of the story, one to do with the evolution of Gorbachev's thinking, the other with the changing balance of power within the Communist Party and the political system.[40]

---

[36] 'Gorbachev: New Man in the Kremlin' (n. 7); 'Can Gorbachev Make a Difference?' (n. 8); 'Soviet Political Developments and Prospects' (n. 9), 83, 86–7; *The Gorbachev Factor* (n. 6), 81, 90–1; and cf. 'The Soviet Union: Reform of the System or Systemic Transformation?', *Slavic Review*, 63/2 (Fall 2004), 496 n. 21, 497 n. 23.

[37] *The Gorbachev Factor*, 45.

[38] Ibid. 61, 81–8, 229; for succession and the 'selectorate' under Brezhnev, see 'Postscript' in *Soviet Policy for the 1980s* (n. 5), 268–9.

[39] Robert Legvold, review of *The Gorbachev Factor* in *Foreign Affairs* (November–December 1996), 161.

[40] *The Gorbachev Factor* (n. 6), 13–14.

Many have identified a process of learning as the key to Gorbachev's increasingly radical policies; they portray him as a leader whose ideas underwent wholesale change while he was in office. What distinguishes Brown's reading of this strand in the story is that he sees Gorbachev as far more advanced in his intellectual journey by 1985, as well as travelling far further in the following six years, than most analysts have appreciated. Brown makes a good case for seeing Gorbachev as a reformed Communist, with liberal inclinations, who evolved into a social democrat in all but name. Gorbachev arrived in the Kremlin deeply dissatisfied with the 'flawed' nature of Soviet socialism, committed to serious reform and optimistic about its feasibility, if unclear as to its precise content.[41] Over the following three to four years, he gradually came to embrace a social democratic conception of socialism, defining it with a qualitatively new emphasis on freedom; he moved from 'being a Communist reformer to a socialist of an essentially West European social-democratic type'.[42] In 1987 Gorbachev endorsed the notion of 'socialist pluralism' and 'before long reached the view that the system had to be comprehensively transformed and that meant nothing less than its pluralization'.[43]

When and how Gorbachev translated his evolving intellectual agenda into policy was crucially conditioned by the balance of power, both within the executive and within the political system as a whole. Back in the Brezhnev era, Brown had pointed out that the power of the General Secretary in relation to his colleagues tended to grow within his period in office. Unlike their Western counterparts, Soviet leaders enjoyed neither institutionalized appointment rights nor early policy 'honeymoon' periods. In order to change the composition of the leadership and build sufficient power to get policies through, they had to do deals with senior colleagues.[44] Gorbachev had to adjust the pace of innovation to what

[41] On Gorbachev's optimism, see 'Transformational Leaders Compared: Mikhail Gorbachev and Boris Yeltsin', in Archie Brown and Lilia Shevtsova (eds.), *Gorbachev, Yeltsin, and Putin. Political Leadership in Russia's Transition* (Washington, DC: Carnegie Endowment for International Peace, 2001), 35–6. Brown sees Gorbachev's political ideas as evolving in the course of his career 'from dogmatic Communism to Communist reformism (or revisionism) to a social democratic understanding of socialism' ('Introduction' (n. 2), vii).

[42] 'Mikhail Gorbachev: Systemic Reformer' (n. 25), 7; and *The Gorbachev Factor* (n. 6), 119, 314. Cf. Gorbachev in conversation with Mlynar: 'We have . . . provided freedom of choice and democratic pluralism, and that is the main thing for the cause of socialism, which is inseparable from democracy' (in *Conversations with Gorbachev* (n. 3), 200).

[43] *The Gorbachev Factor* (n. 6), 96, 127; and 'The Rise of Non-Leninist Thinking about the Political System' in *The Demise of Marxism-, Leninism in Russia* (n. 26), 32–6. Brown explains that Gorbachev reconciled this shift in thinking with his respect for Lenin by reading into him what he wanted to find. By 1989, he 'had ceased to be a Leninist, without consciously rejecting Lenin' (*The Gorbachev Factor* (n. 6), 119–20).

[44] 'The Power of the General Secretary' (n. 5), 136; 'Conclusions' (n. 33), 221–4; and 'Leadership Succession and Policy Innovation' (n. 5), 228, 230–1. Brown distinguishes between the personal honeymoon of Western leaders and the 'group honeymoon' which the leadership as a whole tended to enjoy in the Soviet setting.

seemed politically feasible, especially as he found himself in 'the uncomfortable position of being simultaneously both Pope and Luther'.[45] It is in terms of power factors and tactical calculation in difficult circumstances, rather than lack of reformist zeal, that Brown explains both the initial caution of Gorbachev's early moves and the twists and turns in his last two years. Similarly, Gorbachev's growing power within the Politburo is seen as enabling him to change gear in 1988–9 from liberalization to democratization, and to move from reform of the system to its transformation. After 1989, when the system had become different in kind, the Soviet leader found himself increasingly buffeted by conservative resistance within the Party, as well as by pressure for more radical change from the politicized society he had helped to animate. He made some tactical retreats, notably in winter 1990–1, to accommodate the former, yet continued, in line with Brown's interpretation, strategically to favour the latter and to pursue a course of far-reaching transformation.[46]

In Archie Brown's eyes, the fact that Gorbachev lost power, and *perestroika* came to a dramatic end, does not diminish his historic role. In much of Brown's evaluation of Gorbachev one can see a concern to set the record straight about a 'great reformer' who has been misunderstood and maligned, especially in his own country.[47] And Brown has managed to do this with a vigour and scholarship that has impressed even those with reservations about the role Gorbachev played. For, while his assessment of Gorbachev is highly positive, it is realistic and far from unqualified. He notes specific instances of what in retrospect appears faulty judgement, notably Gorbachev's failure in 1990 to split the Communist Party and to hold direct elections for the federal presidency.[48] He also identifies general areas of relative weakness—in making appointments, designing economic reforms, and dealing with nationality problems.[49] He recognizes Gorbachev's underestimation of 'the potentially explosive strength of national sentiment' but makes a persuasive case for the critical role of contingency and elite power play, especially on the part of Yeltsin, in the demise of the USSR. Brown argues that the timing and course of this were far from inevitable. He maintains that 'a smaller, voluntary union could have survived', and questions assumptions that disintegration necessarily advanced the cause of democracy.[50]

[45] *The Gorbachev Factor* (n. 6), 93.
[46] *The Gorbachev Factor* (n. 6), 160–211.
[47] 'Mikhail Gorbachev: Systemic Transformer' (n. 25), 5; and 'Gorbachev' in Joel Krieger (ed.), *The Oxford Companion to Politics of the World* (Oxford: Oxford University Press, 1993), 360.
[48] *The Gorbachev Factor* (n. 6) , 202–7, 271–2; and 'Mikhail Gorbachev and the Transformation of Russian Politics (n. 35), 105–6; and especially, 'The Soviet Union' (n. 36), 498–500, 501–3.
[49] 'Political Change in the Soviet Union', *World Policy Journal*, 6/3 (Summer 1989), 86–7; *The Gorbachev Factor* (n. 6), 307, and chs. 5 and 8.
[50] 'The Soviet Union' (n. 36), 500. Cf. his critical view of insistence on symmetrical federalism, 'Asymmetrical Devolution: The Scottish Case', *Political Quarterly*, 69/3 (July–September 1998), 215, 222.

In evaluating Gorbachev, Brown insists that one must take a large historical view. On the scales of history, policy flaws and failings have to be set against Gorbachev's remarkable achievements in tackling the 'virtually insuperable task' of simultaneous transformation of the economy, the political system, centre–periphery relations, and foreign policy. The systemic nature of these changes makes Gorbachev what Brown terms a 'transformational' leader, distinct from 'transforming' leaders associated with qualitative changes in policy only.[51]

Gorbachev's most clearly spectacular successes came on the international front, where he played a decisive personal role in bringing an end to the Cold War. In domestic politics, his role and achievements were more complex, but no less important. Brown shows that Gorbachev took the Soviet system further beyond Communism and towards democracy than is generally appreciated. In 'a breakthrough of breathtaking speed', Gorbachev brought about a transition from 'an orthodox Communist regime to one of mixed government (a mixture of authoritarianism and democracy), of which the most important characteristic was political pluralism.'[52] He began with a programme of liberalizing measures designed to improve the system and in the process made the USSR 'safe for dissent'.[53] When liberalization started to strain the limits of adaptive reform, Gorbachev did not try to stop the qualitative shift to systemic transformation.[54] Instead, he accelerated it by allowing contested elections and removing the Communist Party's constitutional monopoly of power. Brown sees electoral competition and the existence of 'relatively autonomous political organizations' as marking the end of the Communist system and the beginning of a transition from Communism.[55] In assessing how far transition under Gorbachev advanced along the road to democracy, Brown is sensibly measured. He describes the Soviet political system at the end of the 1980s as 'substantially pluralist and partially democratized'.[56] But it is clear from his analysis that Gorbachev set the USSR firmly on the path towards democracy. And he did this not only by accepting political pluralism but by the general way in which he carried through democratizing change. The remarkably peaceful and civilized means by which Gorbachev transformed the domestic (and international) political scene were as important for democratization as the ends which defined the social democratic orientation of his agenda.

---

[51] 'Introduction' in *Gorbachev, Yeltsin, and Putin* (n. 41), 6–7; and *The Gorbachev Factor* (n. 6), 157–60.

[52] 'The Soviet Union' (n. 36), 495; *The Gorbachev Factor* (n. 6), 95.

[53] 'Mikhail Gorbachev: Systemic Transformer' (n. 25), 15;

[54] On the limits of reform, see 'The Soviet Union' (n. 36), 503; and *The Gorbachev Factor* (n. 6), 317.

[55] Ibid. 315. For Brown's discussion of the defining characteristics of a Communist system, see 'Communism' in Neil Smelser and Paul B. Baltes (eds.), *The International Encyclopedia of the Social and Behavioral Sciences* (Oxford: Pergamon, 2001), 2323–4; and *The Gorbachev Factor* (n. 6), 310–5.

[56] Ibid. 307; more recently Brown has described the transition from Communism under Gorbachev as 'less than a transition to democracy; see 'The Soviet Union' (n. 36), 498.

Indeed, it was Gorbachev's awareness of the importance of means as well as of ends in politics which distinguished him from all of his Communist predecessors as well as from his *de facto* successor, Boris Yeltsin. Gorbachev's mind-set was far removed from the Bolshevik psychology of *kto-kogo* (who will crush whom). He did not see politics as a zero-sum game. Whether in foreign policy or domestic politics, he combined consensus-seeking with pushing forward increasingly fundamental change.[57]

This is a point of cardinal importance. It was Gorbachev's rejection of the Bolshevik approach to politics, and especially his antipathy to the use of force, that made it possible for him to accomplish a transformation of revolutionary proportions through a process of peaceful evolution. As Brown fittingly concludes, Gorbachev has 'strong claims to be regarded as one of the greatest reformers in Russian history and as the individual who made the most profound impact on world history in the second half of the twentieth century.'[58]

Post-Soviet Leadership and Democratization

The contrast between this verdict on Gorbachev and Brown's evaluation of Boris Yeltsin could hardly be greater. Though, like Gorbachev, a 'transformational' leader, Yeltsin is seen as having done far less for democratization. What praise Brown finds for the first Russian president is of the fainter variety: 'Yeltsin is not the worst leader Russia could have had in the 1990s ... '.[59] Those of Yeltsin's qualities that Archie views as leadership assets, including strength in crisis and an intuitive sense for power, appear as deficits from the perspective of building democracy. He considers that the president's handling of the 1993 crisis, for which extremists on both sides bore responsibility, did 'more harm than good to the cause of freedom, democracy and the rule of law in Russia'.[60]

Brown's critical fire also extends to political leaders in the West for turning a blind eye to this and subsequent instances of presidential arbitrariness. He censures them, along with Western businessmen and advisers, for being more concerned with securing stability and interested in building capitalism than in building democracy.[61] Such priorities reflect the mistaken belief, which Western free-marketeers helped instil in the minds of susceptible Russian reformers, 'that capitalism inevitably leads to democracy'.[62] Misconceptions of this kind are also seen to have complicated the generally positive influence of the West on developments in many of the East and East-Central European transitions from

[57] *The Gorbachev Factor* (n. 6), 308–9.

[58] *The Gorbachev Factor* (n. 6), 317.

[59] 'The Russian Crisis' (n. 17), 71.

[60] 'Political Leadership in Post-Communist Russia' in Amin Saikal and William Maley (eds.), *Russia in Search of its Future* (Cambridge: Cambridge University Press, 1995), 39.

[61] 'The Russian Crisis' (n. 17), 57.

[62] 'Is Russia Becoming a Democracy?' in *Beyond Transition: Ten Years after the Fall of the Berlin Wall* (New York: Regional Bureau for Europe and the CIS, United Nations Development Programme, 1999), 61; and 'The Russian Crisis' (n. 17), 61.

Communism, which Brown convincingly argues should be seen as constituting a distinct Fourth Wave of democratization.[63] But in the case of Yeltsin's Russia, imported misconceptions did considerable harm. Western neoliberalism helped to legitimate self-serving greed and to divert attention from the need to build state institutions to regulate the market and make both business and political elites legally and democratically accountable. What emerged was a weak and 'bloated' state and a 'pseudo-market', both riddled with corruption and manipulated by narrow and selfish interests.[64] To capture the overlapping links among major politicians, financiers, captains of industry, and media barons, Brown coined the term 'diamond quadrangles'. If compatible with political pluralism, this kind of political geometry is hardly conducive to democratization. Rather, the 'symbiotic' relationship between political leadership and business 'oligarchs' which emerged under Yeltsin helped make for a 'hybrid' political system which Archie has described as 'a mixture of arbitrariness, kleptocracy, and democracy.'[65]

Evaluating the democratic content of that mixture is an exercise to which Brown has devoted considerable effort. Rather than following the pendulum swings of fashionable analysis, from early optimism about the inevitability of democratization to more recent gloom about ineluctable reversion to authoritarian tradition, he has based his judgements on a careful appraisal of what has actually happened. He has taken as systematic an approach to appraising the fortunes of democratization in transition as he adopted when assessing the development of pluralism in the Communist period. To Dahl's widely accepted list of requirements for democracy, Brown has added two that are particularly important and telling in the Russian case: political accountability and the rule of law.[66] He finds the record under Yeltsin ambiguous at best for Dahl's requirements and very weak as far as accountability and law are concerned. Yeltsin bequeathed to his successor 'a skewed and flawed pluralistic system, not a democracy'.[67] Most Western observers were far more sanguine about Yeltsin's legacy and generally optimistic about the outlook for democratization under a new president, who stressed the need for consensus, moderation, and stability. Brown welcomed Putin's apparent flexibility and leanings towards political inclusion, but was rightly concerned from the start about some of the methods the president was

[63] Brown considers it 'an oversimplification' to include them in the Third Wave; see 'Transnational Influences' (n. 21), 181 and 181–6.

[64] 'The Russian Crisis' (n. 17), 63–6.

[65] 'Ten Years After the Soviet Breakup: From Democratization to "Guided Democracy"', *Journal of Democracy*, 12/4 (October 2001), 37. 'Is Russia Becoming a Democracy' (n. 62), 60–2; and 'Vladimir Putin and the Reaffirmation of Central State Power', *Post-Soviet Affairs*, 17/1 (January–March, 2001), 48.

[66] 'Is Russia Becoming a Democracy?' (n. 62), 51–60. The list of eight requirements is that in Robert Dahl, *Polyarchy: Participation and Opposition* (New Haven: Yale University Press, 1971), 3, as cited on p. 51. For Brown's subsequent reduction of Dahl's points to four, see *Contemporary Russian Politics: A Reader* (Oxford: Oxford University Press, 2001), 546–7.

[67] 'Ten Years After' (n. 65), 39.

using to stabilize the chaotic system he had inherited. Neither the lack of consultation on federal reform nor the politically selective use of the law to pressure troublesome oligarchs augured well for democratization.[68]

At the same time, public support for these moves and the very high approval ratings Putin continued to enjoy suggested a popular legitimacy that would normally be reckoned as positive in the democratic balance. In this case, however, approval for a forceful chief executive ran alongside both a continuing decline, evident since the mid-1990s, in positive evaluations of what passed in Russia for democracy, and weakening identification with democratic values.[69]

For many observers, ranging from Western right-wingers to Russian democrats, these trends have signalled the resurgence of authoritarian values embedded in the traditional culture. Archie Brown takes a less pessimistic view, as he has long rejected tendencies to cultural determinism of this kind.[70] In his extensive work on political culture, including pioneering volumes published in the late 1970s and early 1980s, Brown has long seen the perceptions, values, beliefs, and foci of identification and loyalty involved as being resilient rather than immutable. He takes the view that cultural values develop in complex and reciprocal interaction with institutions.[71] His own analyses have shown that political experiences can leave long-lasting cultural imprints. The democratic experience of the inter-war Czechoslovak First Republic, for instance, had a cultural after-life in the 1960s and beyond. Brown contends that *perestroika* 'facilitated and produced substantial belief change' that strengthened the democratic content of Russian political culture.[72] By the same token, the arbitrariness, disorder, social injustice, and extremely limited accountability of 'real existing democracy' under Yeltsin may well be responsible for triggering the apparent weakening in popular attachment to democratic values. For Brown, the future trajectory of current trends in cultural values depends crucially on developments in the political system. And here he sees Putin's emphasis on increasing control and strengthening the state taking priority over the strengthening of democracy. In Putin's Russia, the

---

[68] 'Vladimir Putin' (n. 65), 48–51; 'Ten Years After' (n. 65), 39–40.

[69] 'Is Russia Becoming a Democracy?' (n. 62), 62–3; 'Vladimir Putin' (n. 65), 47–8; 'Ten Years After' (n. 65), 38; and 'Cultural Change and Continuity in the Transition from Communism: The Russian Case', paper presented at the conference 'Culture Matters' held at Tufts University, 26–8 March, 2004, 14–16.

[70] 'Cultural Change' (n. 69), 9–10. Brown has noted the need to guard against views of the Russian political culture as 'irredeemably authoritarian'; see 'Reconstructing the Soviet Political System' in Abraham Brumberg (ed.), *Chronicle of a Revolution: A Western-Soviet Inquiry into Perestroika* (New York: Pantheon, 1990), 47–8.

[71] 'Cultural Change' (n. 69), 6–7. For the 'narrow' or 'subjectivist' definition of political culture Brown has consistently favoured over 'omnibus' ones, see 'Introduction' in Archie Brown and Jack Gray (eds.), *Political Culture and Political Change in Communist States* (London: Macmillan, 1977), 1; 'Conclusions' in Archie Brown (ed.), *Political Culture and Communist Studies* (London: Macmillan, 1984), 153 and *passim*.

[72] 'Cultural Change' (n. 69), 5–6; and Archie Brown and Gordon Wightman 'Czechoslovakia: Revival and Retreat' in *Political Culture* (n. 71), 159–96.

political system remains a hybrid of the democratic and the authoritarian, and may be moving further in the latter direction.[73]

Whether Russia, in its uncertain transition, turns towards the consolidation of democracy depends on its citizens and, crucially, its rulers. But Brown thinks that the West can still make a difference, by drawing attention to the paramount importance of building democratic institutions and a rule of law, instead of acting as if it considered them mere by-products of a market economy and political stability.[74] To be able to make any positive contribution to Russia's development, the Western community policy needs to combine a sophisticated understanding of existing political realities with an intuitive sense for the sources of change. It is precisely this combination that has made Archie Brown such an incisive analyst of Russia in the Communist period and in the first decade and a half of democratization. His insight and judgement will continue to guide and inspire all those seeking to comprehend Russia in the decades to come.

[73] 'Introduction' (n. 26), 13; 'Is Russia Becoming a Democracy?' (n. 62), 70; 'Vladimir Putin's Leadership in Comparative Perspective' in Cameron Ross (ed.), *Russian Politics under Putin* (Manchester: Manchester University Press, 2004), 12–13.

[74] 'Cultural Change' (n. 69), 24.

2

Introduction: Putin in Perspective

Alex Pravda

Russian leaders, like Russia itself, often appear to be either too weak or too strong. For a time it seemed that Putin was a rare Kremlin incumbent who could avoid both extremes. His measured and cautious use of executive power to steer a steady middle course was greeted as a welcome contrast to Yeltsin's leadership. The mixture of executive weakness and erratic presidential intervention had helped give the country the worst of all political worlds in the 1990s: a bloated and chronically weak state floundering in a sea of special interest politics. Putin's more prudent and consistent approach seemed to augur well for the stabilization of Russia's fragile democracy and market economy. Such optimism became increasingly sober as the prosecution of Mikhail Khodorkovsky and Yukos revealed a more arbitrary and coercive side to Putin's leadership. The landslide victory of United Russia in the parliamentary elections of December 2003, and the plebiscitary nature of the president's election to a second term in March 2004, reinforced concerns about the future of Russian democracy. With the Kremlin's moves to tighten central executive control in the wake of the autumn 2004 wave of terrorist actions, Western concern about the frailty of democracy turned into widespread anxiety about the authoritarian direction in which Putin was leading the country.

Political leadership matters to a remarkable extent in Russia. To be sure, chief executives play a key part, and often a dominant one, even in liberal democratic systems, let alone authoritarian ones.[1] In few countries, though, has the role of a leader remained as enduringly important as in Russia. There has been a striking continuity in the salience of political leadership through all the ideological and institutional mutations of the last century. The notionally anti-leadership ideology of Marxism-Leninism was used initially to underpin dictatorial rule and then, after Stalin, to sustain a highly authoritarian system in which the leader retained considerable sway and prominence. Such was the authority of the General Secretaryship within the Party–State executive hierarchy that incumbents, once

---

[1] Taketsugu Tsurutani and Jack B. Gabbert 'Introduction' in Tsurutani and Gabbert (eds.), *Chief Executives. National Political Leadership in the United States, Mexico, Great Britain, Germany, and Japan* (Pullman, WA: Washington State University Press, 1992), xi–xvii and *passim*; and Robert Elgie, *Political Leadership in Liberal Democracies* (Basingstoke: Palgrave, 1995).

securely established in office, were able to drive through changes that challenged powerful institutional interests. Even where, as in Gorbachev's case, the leader turned out to be a 'genetic error' of the system, the power and authority of his office made it possible for him to reform the Communist system out of existence.[2]

In post-Communist Russia the central role of the leader is more formally legitimate even if the powers of the president are more institutionally circumscribed. Even after the success of forceful action against a strongly assertive parliament in 1993, Yeltsin found himself more limited than his predecessors by representative bodies, notably the legislature. And he had to contend with far stronger regional and corporate interests. Not that even the more powerful Communist leaders were able in practice to exercise unbounded executive power. As Robert Service reminds us, they typically faced non-compliance and illegal practices; both were pervasive features of totalitarian regimes. Still, the restrictions that departmental and regional interests imposed on the Soviet General Secretary were less powerful and constraining than the bureaucratic, regional, and business interests that conditioned the executive actions of the first Russian president. In the later years of his presidency, Yeltsin's standing was also weakened by low and declining levels of popular support. Yet the authority inherent in being leader enabled even a debilitated Yeltsin to behave in a super-presidential manner within a constitutional structure that remained formally semi-presidential. He managed to bring about a quasi-monarchical transfer of power to a designated successor who found it relatively easy to secure the imprimatur of electoral confirmation.

The rapid rise in the power and authority of Putin underscores the capacity of the office of chief executive to bestow authority on an incumbent with little previous political standing or support. The recovery of the presidency after the weakness of the late Yeltsin years testifies to its resilience as the dominant institution in the Russian political system.[3] In the post-Communist period as in the Soviet era, the office of leader remains of paramount political importance. It is the office that attracts by far the highest levels of popular recognition and respect as the most important focus of political power. Many look to the holder of power in the Kremlin for the kind of leadership traditionally associated with paternal authority.[4] As the repository of popular expectations and the holder of supreme executive power, the leader in the Kremlin has always played an important role, and often an excessively crucial one, in Russia's political development.

[2] Archie Brown, 'Mikhail Gorbachev: Systemic Transformer' in Martin Westlake (ed.), *Leaders of Transition* (London: Macmillan, 2000), 3–26; Archie Brown, *The Gorbachev Factor* (Oxford: Oxford University Press, 1996).

[3] Eugene Huskey, *Presidential Power in Russia* (Armonk, NJ: M.E. Sharpe, 1999), 6.

[4] Caring, discipline, and strength are qualities that resonated with many respondents in one survey conducted in April–May 2003; see E.B. Shestopal, T.N. Pishcheva, E.M. Gikavy, and V.A. Zorin, 'Obraz V.V. Putina v soznanii rossiiskikh grazhdan', *Polis*, 3 (80), 2004, 7–8, 12.

To point to recurrent patterns and the enduring prominence of leadership through Russia's historical convulsions is not to equate either the way in which individual leaders have ruled or the impact they have had on the system. The topography of the Russian historical landscape is a varied one, its volcanic periods associated with high leadership impact and its plateaux of relative stability linked with lower profile and less influential chief executives. The different roles played by leaders, and especially the variation in kind among the changes they help bring about, provide the basis for the distinction drawn by James MacGregor Burns between transactional and transforming leaders. The former are 'foxes', who introduce incremental change by means of expedient political brokerage; the latter are 'lions' who provide inspiring and visionary leadership and make bold moves to bring about policy change of a qualitative kind. In the Russian context, it is useful to add Archie Brown's further category of 'transformational' to describe leaders, including Gorbachev and Yeltsin, who preside over change of a systemic nature.[5]

Putin initially struck most observers as a transactional leader. He appeared as somebody installed in the Kremlin by Yeltsin to safeguard the fortunes of his family and political legacy. Putin seemed intent on stabilizing the status quo by carefully balancing interests and seeking consensus through give-and-take negotiation, all hallmarks of a transactional leader. With his practical and even technocratic approach to fixing problems, Putin appeared to be less of a political leader than a prudent manager. A year or so into his first term, he began to develop a more independent leadership profile. The programme of administrative and organizational reforms, initiated soon after coming to office, was pressed more assertively, and there began to be more 'take' than 'give' in the Kremlin's political bargaining. As a leader, Putin remained a transactionalist fox but there were occasional signs of leonine potential, as in his commitment to unprecedented cooperation with the United States in the wake of the events of 11 September 2001. Such shifts in leadership style were accompanied by innovative policy moves altering the Kremlin's relations with regional and business elites.[6] Reforms to stabilize the system assumed an increasingly prominent place in Putin's presidency as he finished his first term and embarked on his second.

Putin as Consolidator

The mixture of caution and boldness in style, and of reform and stabilization in purpose, make it difficult to define Putin in terms of transactional and

---

[5] Archie Brown, 'Introduction' in Archie Brown and Lilia Shevtsova (eds.), *Gorbachev, Yeltsin, and Putin: Political Leadership in Russia's Transition* (New York: Carnegie Endowment for International Peace, 2001), 6–7; and James MacGregor Burns, *Transforming Leadership. A New Pursuit of Happiness* (London: Atlantic Books, 2003), 22–7.

[6] Archie Brown, 'Vladimir Putin's leadership in comparative perspective' in Cameron Ross (ed.), *Russian Politics under Putin* (Manchester: Manchester University Press), 4–5, 14.

transforming leadership. One helpful way to portray him is as a consolidator. In his contribution to this volume, George Breslauer places Putin in historical context as one of a number of Russian leaders who have sought to bring about political consolidation following a period of convulsive transformation. There are of course various kinds of consolidation and different ways of leading the process. Putin's approach to consolidation contrasts with the adaptive stance exemplified by Brezhnev and exhibited by the rather passive Yeltsin of the later 1990s.[7] In actively using administrative measures to try and stabilize the system, Putin more closely resembles Yury Andropov. There are also echoes of Andropov in the statist and centralizing thrust of the Russian president's approach. Archie Brown has written of Putin's commitment to 'reaffirming central state power'.[8] And it is in terms of 'strengthening the instruments of state power' that Breslauer defines the principal task of Putin's consolidative regime. He notes that consolidation has other core aims, such as bringing back into the democratic fold groups alienated by the turmoil of the Yeltsin era. This is just one dimension of the restoration of normality to which Putin has given much prominence. Another is repairing the social fabric rent by the economic convulsions of the Yeltsin years. Such 'normalizing' measures require the kind of economic growth and prosperity that Putin reiterates can be delivered only by a modern market economy. And only through modernizing itself, he insists, can Russia become globally competitive and play a leading role on the world economic and political stage. Putin's consolidation project is about building a strong centralized state, a unified democratic society, and an efficient modern economy.[9]

The emphasis placed by the president on all three components of his project has led some observers to remark on his policy ambiguity, symptomatic of a leader trying to appeal to a wide range of constituencies. What adds to the puzzle for many Western observers is that the elements of his three-fold consolidation project seem difficult to reconcile.[10] Putin's commitment to a strong central state seems at odds with his championing of democracy and a market economy. The tripartite programme is less of a puzzle if we look more closely at the ordering principles and logic that underpin it. The perspective is a top–down one, informed by a concept of rule that sees state and society as a corporate entity, administered by the executive.[11]

---

[7] Huskey (n.3), 50

[8] Archie Brown, 'Vladimir Putin and the Reaffirmation of Central State Power', *Post-Soviet Affairs*, 17/1 (2001), 47.

[9] See for instance his Annual Address to the Federal Assembly, 8 July 2000 and 18 April 2002, both available in Russian and English on http://president.kremlin.ru

[10] For a good discussion of these issues and an interpretation of Putin's approach as a coherent 'third way' strategy, see Richard Sakwa, *Putin: Russia's Choice* (London: Routledge, 2004), especially ch.3.

[11] This is the essence of Michael Oakeshott's 'universitas' concept which he contrasts from 'societas' in which society appears as a plurality of interests kept together by relatively permissive

In Putin's consolidation programme, a strong state figures as a means as well as an end. It is crucial in four respects. State strength is first, and self-evidently indispensable at a fundamental level to ensure territorial integrity and security. Second, a strong state provides the organizational framework and unity of purpose required to sustain an effective democracy and a robust civil society. Third, state guidance is needed to ensure that market-driven modernization works to strengthen rather than undermine social harmony, stability, and national vigour. And finally it is the state that has the clearest interest in making sure that national resources work for the national good and maximize Russia's competitive strength in the international arena.

The strong statist thread running through Putin's programme can be traced to systemic factors as well as to circumstances more closely connected with Putin's outlook and experience. Given the stage in Russia's historical cycle at which Putin came to office, one might say that he had consolidation thrust upon him.[12] Yeltsin had presided over the convulsive emergence of a new system and had tried to consolidate the situation by encouraging self-regulation. As the major actors failed to regulate themselves, Putin, it could be argued, had to bring in the state. But there were also leadership power incentives for Yeltsin's successor to move in this direction. As a leader who had gained power by defeating the August putschists and demolishing the Soviet Union, Yeltsin had drawn legitimacy from combating the Communist challenge; he had enlisted any ideas and forces—marketization, oligarchs, regional fiefdoms—that could help him in this contest. However such forces might weaken the central state, what mattered is that they kept Yeltsin in office, even if they also circumscribed his power.[13] For Putin, by contrast, the causes of state and leadership power have coincided. By the time he became president, the Communists were a spent political force and the main challenge was disorder in the economy and in the federation. It was on a platform of restoring order in the south, and reining in the excesses of business and regional bosses, that Putin received electoral approbation and high approval ratings. From the outset, it has been in his interest to appear as the guardian of state order and stability. This is a role to which he also has a personal predisposition.

All incumbents bring to the exercise of office a set of beliefs and a way of thinking, a cognitive style, which distinguishes their leadership.[14] Putin's general outlook and professional experience give him a pragmatic, institutionalist, and statist bent. He is a double realist. He takes pride in recognizing realities

rules; see James Malloy, 'Contemporary Authoritarian Regimes' in Mary Hawkesworth and Maurice Kogan (eds.), *Encyclopedia of Government and Politics*, vol. 1 (London: Routledge, 1992), 232.

[12] In Sidney Hook's terms, Putin is an 'eventful' rather than 'event-making' leader; see Robert Tucker, *Politics as Leadership* (Columbia and London: University of Missouri Press, 1981), 27.

[13] Eugene Huskey has pointed out that the weakness of Yeltsin's leadership sometimes helped to maintain a 'relatively stable equilibrium' (n.3), 218.

[14] Alexander L. George and Juliette L. George, *Presidential Personality and Performance* (Boulder, CO: Westview, 1998), 210–12.

and dealing with them practically. He is a realist, too, in the Hobbesian sense of seeing the world as an arena where the weak lose out to the strong.[15] While he may extol the merits of cooperation and compromise, Putin's actions testify to an understanding of politics as ultimately a zero-sum game in which determination and power decide conflicts. This kind of thinking was of course central to the Bolshevik tradition and the Soviet security culture in which Putin spent his formative professional years. One must be careful not to exaggerate and oversimplify the 'KGB effect' on his style of leadership. At the same time, one should not overlook features of his approach to problems that might well have been reinforced by training and experience in the intelligence community. Prominent among these is Putin's inclination to frame problems as threats and challenges to state power.

Putin has depicted the Yeltsin period as a very costly one for the Russian state. He sees its permissive policies as having brought about a dangerous loss of state control over developments in the national economy as well as over the activities of regional authorities.[16] Business tycoons ('oligarchs') were able to shape key areas of government policy to suit their narrow interests and in doing so caused disruptive effects that further undermined the authority of the state. Vertically, the fabric of state power was strained by the autonomy, verging on self-rule, achieved by many regions and republics of the Russian Federation. The resulting 'neo-feudal fragmentation' produced separatist tendencies in the North Caucasus which posed a real threat to territorial integrity.[17]

Both 'lateral' and 'vertical' threats to the power of state within Russia are linked to a weakening of its international position. The influence of commercial groups, Putin argues, exposed the country to international financial speculators; that of separatism made it vulnerable to penetration by hostile forces interested in its fragmentation.[18] While the overweening influence of the 'oligarchs' has, over the last five years, declined somewhat as a direct threat—becoming more of a challenge to state power—the separatist problem, identified increasingly with that of international terrorism, has become ever more menacing.

The way in which Putin tends to frame major problems is connected with his diagnosis of the factors shaping them. Two lines of diagnosis offer interesting insights into his general approach. One follows from his Hobbesian view of politics. He sees the problems surrounding the degradation of the state as flowing from the Kremlin's relaxation of the reins of power, its encouragement of economic and political devolution, and its acquiescence to the extreme forms

---

[15] See, for instance, Annual Address to the Federal Assembly, 8 July 2000 (n.9).

[16] Annual Address to the Federal Assembly, 26 May 2004; and Speech at Moscow State University, 12 February 2004, http://kremlin.ru.

[17] Ibid; and Vladislav Surkov, deputy head of the presidential administration, *Komsomol'skaya Pravda*, 29 September 2004.

[18] Speech at Moscow State University 12 February 2004 (n. 16); and speech on Russian television 4 September 2004, translated in BBC Monitoring Service, reproduced in *Johnson's Russia List*, 8353.

these processes assumed under Yeltsin. One can easily think of plausible alternative interpretations that would highlight the weak legitimacy of political institutions, poor executive accountability, or the corrosive effects of informal rules on law. Needless to say, Putin is aware of such factors. Yet he gives diagnostic priority to zero-sum game politics, to the basic dynamics of a power tug-of-war: if the centre allows any slack on the rope this is immediately taken up by other actors, and the Kremlin is kept off balance.

Alongside this zero-sum logic runs a line of diagnosis that attributes threats and challenges to more general pathologies affecting the state. These embrace a wide range of factors, including social divisions, ethnic conflicts, and corruption, all of which are seen as damaging the immune system of the body politic. With its immune system impaired, Russia has little resistance to 'infections', which tend to flare up into more serious illnesses. If Putin has typically reserved references to 'life-threatening' disease to the threat of terrorism, he appears to apply a similar line of diagnosis to other problem areas, portraying the major problems of state weakness as symptoms of an infirm political organism.[19]

Both lines of diagnosis lead to the prescription that lies at the centre of Putin's project: putting the state in charge. This involves two overlapping strategies: reassertion of central control and moves to organize civil society. The more urgent and straightforward, though by no means simple, has been the attempt to reassert state control over business and regional elites. As this loss of control is attributed to the Kremlin's unwise relaxation of its grip on power in the 1990s, remedial moves have consisted of efforts to pull the tug-of-war rope back in the centre's direction. The task of fashioning a more unified and responsive civil society is less urgent, though just as important to the enterprise of revitalizing the Russian system and creating a national sense of moral purpose.[20]

The means chosen to administer these remedies have come mostly from the traditional sections of the state armoury. Putin has tended to rely on 'hard power' instruments, ranging from the security forces to the tax police and the prosecutor's office to enforce the centre's authority. 'Softer' power resources and techniques, such as information management, have been bought into play, especially in efforts to shape political society. But even in dealing with civil society, the Kremlin seems to have given priority to organizational and administrative approaches. The strong preference for institutional mechanisms to regulate society and politics is consistent with the Hobbesian approach traditionally taken by Soviet leaders.[21]

---

[19] Speech at the Enlarged Government Meeting, Russian television, 13 September 2004, translated in BBC Monitoring Service, reproduced in *Johnson's Russia List*, 8365.

[20] Surkov (n. 17) refers to the need for a 'moral majority'.

[21] John Miller describes Soviet leaders as Hobbesians because they sought 'the bulwark against social breakdown in an institutional arrangement'; see 'The Communist Party: Trends and Problems', in Archie Brown and Michael Kaser (eds.), *Soviet Policy for the 1980s* (London: Macmillan, 1982), 1.

There is also a marked neo-Soviet element in the steps taken to tighten hierarchical lines of command within government and in Moscow's relations with regional authorities. In time-honoured fashion, Putin has sought to tighten central control over administrative appointments. As Eugene Huskey shows in his contribution to this volume, the president has revived many features of the Soviet *nomenklatura* system in moves to increase his powers of patronage. One new feature is that the Kremlin has used its powers to appoint a significant number of officials with military and security backgrounds. The promotion of these *siloviki*, as they are often labelled, presumably reflects calculations that they will be statist-minded as well as more disciplined in executing the orders of hierarchical superiors. Certainly, the mentality and skills fostered in their earlier professional training may make such officials feel more at home with the spirit of tough dirigisme that infuses Putin's consolidation project.

How far such neo-Soviet administrative methods, heavy on sanctions and light on incentives, have proved effective in strengthening state control remains far from clear. As the chapters in this volume show, Putin has made considerable headway but progress has varied considerably across the major problem areas. Corruption is perhaps the most diffuse and intractable problem on which Putin has set his sights. As Leslie Holmes notes, Russia has the unenviable distinction of being among the most corrupt post-Communist states. Like many of his post-Communist counterparts, Putin has declared combating corruption a high priority but found it difficult to make more than a modest impact.[22] Part of the problem may lie in the level of commitment to combating corruption and in the methods used to reduce its incidence. Putin appears to have taken the problem more seriously than Yeltsin, whose own behaviour belied the numerous anti-corruption campaigns launched in his presidency. Putin has set a somewhat higher standard of probity, but corruption remains rife in the bureaucracy. Higher levels of recruitment from the security agencies, perhaps among the less corrupt parts of the administration, may have some impact on the machine as a whole. But the effects will remain marginal without substantial increases in civil service salaries; so far these have been awarded only to small numbers of higher officials. Sanctions are a cheaper option and more in line with Putin's administrative approach. The Kremlin may well hope that one of the side effects of its high-profile prosecution of leading magnates for illegal and corrupt practices will be to intimidate the thousands of smaller businessmen and officials involved in illicit transactions on a daily basis.

A concern with corruption is of course only one of several factors involved in Putin's crackdown on selected members of the class of corporate tycoons, known colloquially if misleadingly as oligarchs. Driving the campaign is the Kremlin's

---

[22] Such assessments are shared by the Russian public which gives Putin very low performance ratings in this area. One poll, conducted in spring 2003, found that only one in ten respondents thought Putin had definitely made inroads into corruption; nearly half considered his adminstration had made no difference; see Shestopal et al (n. 4).

determination to counter the 'lateral' challenge to state supremacy posed by the influence of the tycoons in the media, the legislature, and even the government bureaucracy. In his early 'transactionist' phase, Putin used political consultation and negotiation to redefine his relationship with big business. But when tacit understandings about mutual restraint proved ineffective, the state put such pressure on Gusinsky and Berezovsky, the most assertive of the Yeltsin-era moguls, that both left the country. The imprisonment of Khodorkovsky, and the prosecution of his company Yukos from late 2003, marked a new ruthlessness in the Kremlin's determination to show that even the most powerful magnate could be cut down to size. Putin has stood above the fray, allowing the 'hard power' instruments of the state to do the work, on occasion calling for moderation and keeping all in a state of nervous uncertainty. As William Tompson's chapter shows, this strategy has enabled the president to redefine the power relationship with the tycoons in his favour, taming the most assertive of them without alienating the rest. Business leaders have accepted that they are dependent on the Kremlin and have adjusted their involvement in public life accordingly. Rather than attempting, like Khodorkovsky, to gain influence by funding a broad portfolio of political parties, in the 2003 elections they concentrated their investments in the presidential party, United Russia.[23] The relative ease with which Putin has established sway over the tycoons points up the underlying asymmetry in the relationship. As Tompson notes, Russia's business magnates, even under Yeltsin, lacked the independent standing and the corporate solidarity of true oligarchs. When Putin chose to apply the full power of the state, the tycoons adjusted to the new situation. There was no corporate protest; all were too eager to further their particular interests by proving their loyalty to the president. The authority inherent in the office, plus Putin's display of strength, seem to have been enough to emasculate what once appeared as a powerful 'lateral' challenge to state supremacy.

Strengthening the Kremlin's grip on vertical power, its control over the regions, has been at the centre of Putin's consolidation project since he came to power. As Neil Melvin details in this volume, there have been two waves of institutional reforms and extensive use of tough administrative methods to fashion a system of more centralized control from the messy tangle of bargains that defined Yeltsin's relations with the regions. Putin's supra-regional district plenipotentiaries have not been able to ensure that the centre's writ runs throughout the federation. The process of harmonizing laws is far from complete, despite claims to the contrary. Still, Moscow has eliminated some of the most glaring anomalies and shifted the overall balance of legal and financial power towards the centre.[24] The Kremlin

---

[23] Michael McFaul and Nikolai Petrov, 'What the Elections Tell Us', *Journal of Democracy*, 15/3 (July 2004), 27.

[24] In addition to Neil Melvin's chapter, see Peter Reddaway and Robert W. Ottung (eds.), *The Dynamics of Russian Politics. Putin's Reform of Federal-Regional Relations*, vol. 1 (Lanham, MD: Rowman and Littlefield, 2004); and Cameron Ross, *Federalism and Democratization in Russia* (Manchester: Manchester University Press, 2002).

has used an armoury of administrative methods to influence gubernatorial elections, with mixed if increasing effectiveness. Such interventions, combined with institutional centralization, have increased Putin's hold over once-assertive regional elites. Putin's decision in September 2004 to revive the presidential appointment of governors will clearly tighten the Kremlin's political and administrative grip and move the federation closer to becoming a de facto unitary state. Pointing in the same direction are the plans, noted by Melvin, to create larger units and restructure the federation so as to decouple ethnic and territorial identity.

Reorganization along these lines, it is reckoned, might make it easier to prevent ethnic tensions from flaring up into the kind of separatism seen in Chechnya. It was in large part to deal forcefully with this threat that Putin was initially selected as prime minister, and it was on a platform of bringing the situation in the North Caucasus under control that he later stood for election as president.[25] Chechnya has remained central to Putin's image as a strong and martial leader. He waged war to gain a hold over the republic and has used coercive administrative means to maintain central control, steadfastly refusing to negotiate with any part of the Chechen opposition, whom he calls 'bandits'. The uncharacteristically emotional tone in which Putin has defended his policies suggests a strong personal commitment to impose order on the republic. In 2003, his claims that Chechnya's troubled times were over were belied by the persistence of large-scale opposition activity. In 2004, the president sought to redefine the problems of the North Caucasus in terms of a war being waged against Russia by international terrorism.[26] The wave of terrorist attacks in Moscow and the south in August–September catalyzed a nationwide tightening of security controls across the board, including over the media. Taken together with the package of centralizing measures announced at the same time, this may be seen as marking a significant milestone along the road to a security state.

Towards Authoritarianism

The upward curve in Putin's assertion of executive power as he moved towards and into his second term, prompted observers to reappraise his leadership and its significance for Russia's political development. Some who had initially taken a relatively optimistic view of the prospects for democracy saw Putin's later moves as a possible turn towards dictatorial rule.[27] In autumn 2004, alarms were sounded

[25] See Matthew Evangelista, *The Chechen Wars. Will Russia Go the Way of the Soviet Union?* (Washington, DC: Brookings Institution Press, 2002).

[26] Annual Address, 26 May 2004 (n. 16); and speech on 4 September (n. 18).

[27] See, for instance, Michael McFaul, Nikolai Petrov, and Andrei Ryabov (eds.), 'Introduction' in McFaul, Petrov, and Ryabov (eds.), *Between Dictatorship and Democracy. Russian Post-Communist Political Reform* (Washington, DC: Carnegie Endowment for International Peace, 2004), 1–22.

singly and collectively by Western politicians and observers.[28] Specialists such as Lilia Shevtsova, who had long depicted Putin as a leader hesitating between democratic and authoritarian options, detected a move towards the latter before the end of his first term in office.[29] As her contribution to this volume argues, Putin appears to have chosen the authoritarian path. Many analysts still find it difficult to apply clear-cut labels to Putin's leadership and the regime over which he presides. The more optimistic of the Western specialist community favour applying adjectival qualifications of democracy. Others consider it misleading to use as a point of departure a destination which Russia never reached. In his contribution to this volume, Leslie Holmes sensibly suggests that we should think in terms of Russia's position on an axis between poles of ideal types, with liberal democracy at one end and authoritarianism at the other. To assess location and movement along the axis, we need to look at issue areas such as the concentration and transfer of executive power; political accountability; the strength of political pluralism and opposition; the quality of political participation; and institutional and legal restraints on the exercise of executive power.[30] All these issues are touched on in the course of the chapters that follow. The overall picture which emerges is one of an ever more consolidated and extensive system of executive power that has become ever less subject to external accountability and constraint. Putin's moves to strengthen state power have taken Russia in an increasingly authoritarian direction.

Even a brief review of developments in a few key areas reveals what might be described as a process of authoritarianization. Take, for instance, the conduct of elections and the workings of the legislature. The decline in the real political choice available to voters and the growing role of the state in determining electoral outcomes contribute to what Timothy Colton in his chapter identifies as an 'attenuation of democratic contestation'.[31] The landslide victory of United Russia in December 2003 made possible the tightening of executive control over the Duma, as a majoritarian system was consolidated into what amounted to one-party rule. As Paul Chaisty notes, conflicts over legislation have effectively become confined to the presidential coalition. The move to elect the Duma solely on the basis of party lists will make it easier still for the executive to manage the lower chamber and further reduce its capacity to constrain the government, let alone the

---

[28] For concern expressed in a letter addressed to Western leaders by 115 politicians (including Vaclav Havel) and specialists, see C. Lynch, *Washington Post*, 29 September 2004, reproduced in *Johnson's Russia List*, 8386.

[29] Lilia Shevtsova, *Putin's Russia* (Washington, DC: Carnegie Endowment for International Peace, 2003).

[30] For discussion of democratic characteristics in the context of Russia, see Archie Brown, 'Is Russia Becoming a Democracy?', *Beyond Transition: Ten Years after the Fall of the Berlin Wall* (New York: Regional Bureau for Europe and the CIS, United Nations Development Programme, 2000), 51–70. For characteristics defining authoritarian regimes, see Juan Linz, *Totalitarian and Authoritarian Regimes* (Boulder, CO: Lynn Riener, 2000), 54, 159–68; and James Malloy (n. 11), 231–5.

[31] McFaul and Petrov, (n.23), 31, aptly refer to elections as being of 'limited consequence'.

Kremlin. The ability of the upper chamber, the Federation Council, to hold the executive to account, very limited in any case, might well disappear altogether as a result of the shift from elected to appointed governors. Presidential appointees will be concerned to nominate to the Council senators acceptable to the Kremlin. Moving from elected governors to what may amount to a new system of presidential plenipotentiaries means further weakening constraints on the central executive and further impoverishing political pluralism.

The overall environment for political pluralism in Russia has steadily deteriorated. Wary of the disruptive effects of allowing a free play of political interests and activity, Putin has sought to make pluralism more manageable by moves to consolidate institutions of civil society.[32] Not all such moves are necessarily antidemocratic. The law on political parties, designed to reduce numbers and fragmentation, might well as Holmes points out bring some democratic benefits, as it has in other post-Communist systems. But the Kremlin's plans to foster a small multi-party system bear all the hallmarks of the concern for control that have distinguished its policy towards the media. Repeated commitment to press freedom has been accompanied by a tightening of state controls over its expression. As Holmes notes, Putin's leadership has seen Russia decline significantly in international rankings in this area. With security interests invoked increasingly to justify curbs on political criticism, the pressure on journalists to toe the official line has become ever more intense, reinforcing the self-censorship that has plagued media freedom over the last decade.

The stifling climate in which the media and political organizations function helps breed the kind of popular indifference to the political process one associates with authoritarian regimes. Turnout in most elections remains respectable by international standards but popular regard for multi-party elections seems worryingly low.[33] Political parties command little popular trust or loyalty and there is widespread dissatisfaction with the performance of representative institutions. Yet Putin continues to attract very high levels of support and confidence. How are we to explain this? Timothy Colton argues that the key to Putin's popularity and electoral dominance lies in widespread positive prospective assessments of his capacity to cope with major policy problems. For most Russians, even those who think that things have got worse, Putin appears as the only leader available who is capable of dealing with the situation. Performance capacity also figures prominently in Stephen Whitefield's analysis. He interprets the president's standing as reflecting an appreciation of performance rather than any growing

[32] Harley Balzer, 'Managed Pluralism: Vladimir Putin's Emerging Regime', *Post-Soviet Affairs*, 19/3 (2003), 189–227.

[33] One August 2003 survey found that only 29% thought that the elections were useful while 40% of respondents considered the elections did more harm than good; see Yuri A. Levada, 'What the Polls Tell Us', *Journal of Democracy*, 15/3 (July 2004), 45.

illiberalism.[34] His data suggest a robust popular commitment to democratic values, notwithstanding deep disappointment with what passes for democracy in Russia. The question of the 'real existing' democratic system does not appear to figure as a divisive issue in elections. There seems to be widespread and perhaps growing popular indifference to the very flawed practice of democracy in Russia, at least in the short term. Most Russians give priority to effective rule that ensures order and prosperity—very much in line with Putin's statist consolidation programme. And Whitefield's data suggest that the president has ample scope to use authoritarian means without losing popular support.

As we have already noted, and as many of the chapters show, the Kremlin has relied increasingly on command methods to further consolidation, with little regard either for democratic consultation or for legal process. Putin seems concerned to enforce the law only when he thinks it serves the purposes of the state. The politically selective use of the law against leading tycoons, especially Khodorkovsky, has made clear that the Kremlin does not consider itself bound by formal norms or procedures (whether Putin adheres to his commitment to abide by the two-term constitutional limit on his tenure of the presidency remains to be seen). Informal and frequently arbitrary administrative methods typically trump due process. Their use tends to be self-reinforcing. As Tompson observes in the context of relations between the Kremlin and the tycoons, the absence of effective constraints on state behaviour has undermined the credibility of any understandings reached and created a commitment problem for both sides. In this case as in others, authoritarian methods have helped create a climate of mutual suspicion which makes more likely the repeated use of administrative means to reassert state will. A self-perpetuating cycle of this kind is reinforced by the command mentality and material interests of the bureaucracies acting in the name of the state. It is the prominence of these bureaucracies in Putin's consolidation that prompts Shevtsova, in her chapter, to apply the term bureaucratic authoritarianism to the regime emerging under his leadership.

Are there any countervailing factors that might moderate the authoritarianizing trends we have identified? Two stand out: the requirements of market-driven modernization, and the imperatives of global competitiveness. To operate efficiently, market capitalism needs a resilient and reliable framework of enforceable laws. A state which stands above the law creates uncertainty about basic issues such as property rights. As Tompson points out, some of the state bureaucracies have an interest in perpetuating that uncertainty. The Russian state still regards all property rights as a conditional gift. Putin is aware of such problems but remains determined to meet the requirements of political consolidation as well as

---

[34] Assessment of Putin's performance is mixed; see Shestopal (n.4), 8–10. Levada presents evidence that much of the confidence in Putin is founded on hopes of effective performance; see 'Ramki i varianty istoricheskogo vybora: neskol'ko soobrazhenii o khode rossiikskikh transformatsii', in *Monitoring obshchestvennogo mneniya: ekonomicheskie i sotsial'nye peremeny*, 63 (January–February 2003), 11.

those of market consolidation. The way in which the state has prosecuted Yukos, and increased its control over the natural resources sector, suggests that Putin may be willing to risk some efficiency losses in the economy—in any case impossible to calculate—for the sake of gains in political control.

More tangible are the pressures that come from the international arena. Putin wants to make Russia a globally competitive economy and a major player in world affairs. The need to meet international business concerns is certainly an incentive for the authorities to ensure legal compliance. Yet the Yukos case underscores the Kremlin's determination to give priority to Russian ways of doing business. Putin remains intent on integration into the Western-managed international system system, but wishes to do so on Russia's terms. As Andrei Grachev shows, the president has conducted an increasingly flexible and assertive foreign policy, aimed at demonstrating Russia's independence of action. A growing emphasis on self-reliance has gone hand-in-hand with a heightened sensitivity to Western criticism of Russian policy, particularly on issues of security and domestic politics. In autumn 2004, the Kremlin drew links between such criticism and Cold War attitudes in the West. There was much in Moscow's reactions to the wave of terrorist attacks that echoed traditional 'fortress' thinking, with its emphasis on external and internal enemies.[35]

Such defensive stances do not necessarily indicate any trend towards isolationism. Putin continues to want cooperation with the West, not least in the common struggle against terrorism. Yet, there is a tendency towards greater insulation of the regime against what the Kremlin sees as domestic and international threats to the consolidation of state power. The more insulated and inward-looking Russia becomes, the more likely is it to continue to develop in an authoritarian direction. Whether the country follows this course depends on Putin—to an excessive extent. The way in which he has gone about consolidating the state has produced an ever greater convergence of power and responsibility in a presidency whose tasks exceed its capacities. Once again, as so often before in Russian history, too much hinges on an overloaded leadership.

---

[35] Putin's speech, 4 September 2004 (n. 18). Vladislav Surkov (n. 17), deputy head of the presidential administration, referred to a fifth column of left- and right-wing radicals.

3

Regimes of Political Consolidation: The Putin Presidency in Soviet and Post-Soviet Perspective[1]

George W. Breslauer

When we think of most Soviet and post-Soviet leaders, our tendency is to focus attention on the dramatic, wide-ranging, and usually transformative changes effected under their leadership. Vladimir Lenin created and led a revolutionary party that helped to bring down tsarism, that came to power as a result of growing social and political disintegration during 1917, that initiated the violent restratification of society during the civil war of 1918–20, and that viewed the exigencies of that civil war as the first glimpses of a communist society ('War Communism'). Joseph Stalin launched the so-called 'Second Russian Revolution' that began in 1928–9 and that extended party control over the peasantry (and six million peasant deaths in the name of 'liquidating the *kulaks* [rich peasants] as a class'), a breakneck drive for industrial development, a frenetic pace of recruiting cadres into the Party-State apparatus, and a so-called 'cultural revolution' in social policy. In 1935–6, he initiated the 'Great Terror,' which resulted in a massive turnover of state and party elites. Nikita Khrushchev sponsored a process of 'de-Stalinization' that sought to dismantle the extremes of Stalinism, to recruit a new ruling class committed to making peace with a newly reconstructed Soviet society, and to greatly diminish status differentials between officialdom and 'all the people.' Little more than two decades after Khrushchev's overthrow, Mikhail Gorbachev initiated a non-violent 'revolution from above' against an entrenched and corrupted Party-State elite, liberalizing and then democratizing the political order to the point that the entire system collapsed around him. Boris Yeltsin hastened that collapse with his public challenges to Gorbachev and his encouragement of maximal autonomy from Kremlin dictates in both Russia and the other republics of the USSR. Yeltsin became President of the Russian Federation and, after he conspired in the formal dissolution of the USSR, launched his own revolution from above with 'shock therapy' economic policies of 1992–3, his forcible dissolution of parliament in October 1993, and his introduction of a new, 'super-presidentialist' constitution in December 1993.

[1] The author is grateful to Alex Pravda, Peter Reddaway, and Yuri Slezkine for trenchant comments on an earlier version of this chapter.

All these leaders viewed themselves as system-builders: Lenin was bringing down tsarism and allegedly bringing to power the 'dictatorship of the proletariat'; Stalin claimed to be 'building socialism'; Khrushchev was 'building communism'; Gorbachev was 'building socialist democracy'; and Yeltsin was 'building capitalism.'

Clearly, Vladimir Putin's leadership has not been of these sorts. Few observers would characterize it as transformative. But Putin's leadership is not *sui generis* either, for Soviet and post-Soviet history have also been marked by regular periods of *political consolidation*, of which Putin's presidency is one example. If we wish to understand the kind of regime Putin presided over during 2000–4, it is useful to explore the nature of consolidative regimes in general and the specific forms they have taken in Soviet and post-Soviet history.

On Regimes of Political Consolidation in Soviet and Post-Soviet History

Consolidation, as I use the term, means to make solid, strong, and stable. *Regimes of political consolidation are those that define their main task to be strengthening the instruments of state power.* Beyond this core task, such regimes typically also seek stability by adopting social policies that attempt to appease groups that had been most alienated by the preceding, transformative policies.

The concept, 'consolidation,' has been used in diverse ways in the literature on Soviet and post-Soviet history. In the kremlinological literature, it was common-place to refer to newly selected leaders as having to consolidate—that is, strengthen and solidify—their hold on power. But, in macropolitical conceptual-ization, the term has been used variously to characterize the general trajectory of policy at different stages of Soviet history. J. P. Nettl, for example, referred to the period of the New Economic Policy (1921–8) as one of 'consolidation' that followed the period of Revolution (1917–20) and that preceded the years of 'Industrialization' (1929–40) and 'Rigidification' (1940–52).[2] Raymond Bauer, by contrast, refers to the years 1934–7 as a period of 'consolidation' of the new social order, following the collectivization and industrialization drives of 1928–33.[3] Kenneth Jowitt treats the period from the mid-1930s through the death of Stalin as a stage in which the regime defined its main task as consolida-tion, following the transformative thrust of earlier years and preceding the post-Stalinist shift to a posture of 'inclusion'.[4] Huntington, by contrast, treats all of

---

[2] These are the titles of chapters 2–5, respectively, in J. P. Nettl, *The Soviet Achievement* (New York: Harcourt, Brace & World, 1967).

[3] Raymond Bauer, *The New Man in Soviet Psychology* (Cambridge, MA: Harvard University Press, 1952), 45–4 and 122–3.

[4] Jowitt also generalizes this posture to all Leninist regimes during their analogous phases and elaborates at unprecedented length and originality on the defining characteristics of Stalinist

Stalinism as a stage of 'transformation' and characterizes the post-Stalin era as one of 'consolidation'.[5]

Let me clarify my use of the term. I treat political consolidation, not as a discrete, single phase in Soviet political history, but rather as a recurring phenomenon throughout Soviet and post-Soviet history. Leaders came to define political consolidation as the main task at given points in time. This typically occurred after a period of transformative leadership, when a new leader (Brezhnev, Putin), or a previously transformative leader (Lenin, Stalin, Yeltsin), sought to consolidate gains and to enhance political stability and control. What all periods of political consolidation had in common was a concern to strengthen the central leadership's control over, and autonomy from, concentrations of societal political or economic power. Hence, what all periods also had in common was an emphasis on *strengthening the state*. It is in this sense that Putin's declared emphasis on 'strengthening the state' represents a familiar pattern of political consolidation following a transformative period, albeit this time in post-Soviet history.[6]

Of course, the specific policies chosen to advance that cause varied greatly over time, as did the social policies of appeasement that accompanied them. Political consolidations of the 1920s, 1930s, 1960s, 1990s, and 2000s were based on greatly differing policies, just as the transformative phases that preceded consolidation differed markedly from each other. The approach to strengthening the state was a function of the content of the transformative policies that preceded the consolidative thrust. The forms of consolidation have varied according to whether the teleology of the authorities led them, during the preceding transformation, to define themselves historically as being in a stage of building socialism in a hostile society, building communism (or socialist democracy) in a reconstructed Soviet society, or building capitalism in a post-Soviet society. Hence, political consolidation as a task or challenge may be defined generically as the effort to stabilize and strengthen the state by one means or another. But consolidative policies in any given period can only be specified in their historical context. This is the type of leadership that Vladimir Putin has tried to provide, but it is of a very different content from consolidative strategies pursued in earlier historical periods.

---

consolidation regimes (Kenneth T. Jowitt, *New World Disorder: The Leninist Extinction* (Berkeley: University of California Press, 1992), 57, 62–3, 89, 96, 102, 171–3). He defines consolidation as 'the attempt to create the nucleus of a new political community in a setting that ideally prevents existing social forces from exercising any uncontrolled and undesired influence over the development and definition of the new community ... Consolidation yields a structure of domination, as the politically defeated but "hostile" society must be prevented from "contaminating" the nuclei of the new socialist society', ibid. 57.

[5] Samuel Huntington, 'Social and Institutional Dynamics of One-Party Systems' in Samuel Huntington and Clement Moore (eds.), *Authoritarian Politics in Modern Society* (New York: Basic Books, 1970), 25–40.

[6] I use 'the state' as a broad term that refers to the governing apparatus of a political order. Concerning Soviet times, my use of 'the state' refers to the 'Party-State'.

The New Economic Policy (NEP), 1921–7

The period 1921–7 was one of political consolidation. After the turbulence of 1917–20, Lenin argued in 1921 that the country needed a breathing spell (*peredyshka*) to consolidate Bolshevik rule. Peasant revolts and the devastation caused by the First World War and the civil war led Lenin to fear that Bolshevik rule could be imperiled. The New Economic Policy, announced in 1921, entailed liberalization on the socio-economic and foreign-policy fronts. But it also entailed changes in policy geared toward strengthening the Bolshevik Party's capacity to dominate politics and to protect the regime against concentrations of autonomous social and economic power that the NEP would spawn.

Lenin conceived the NEP as a necessity following a period of intense conflict between the regime and the numerically predominant class in society, the peasantry. NEP permitted citizens to own small-sized enterprises, to lease larger ones, and to engage in privatized trade, as a result of which a new social stratum of so-called NEP-men appeared, bearing resemblance to a new bourgeoisie. Foreigners were permitted to lease enterprises, foreign aid was sought to alleviate the effects of famine, trade talks began with Britain, France, and Germany, and diplomatic recognition was sought from the leading capitalist powers.

At the same time, Lenin initiated a series of policy changes in 1921–2 that sought to prevent these socio-economic changes from undermining the 'leading role' of the 'organizational weapon' he had created in the Bolshevik Party.[7] State control of the 'commanding heights' of the economy remained in force; there would be no privatization or foreign ownership in this crucial realm. Within the Bolshevik Party, factions were banned, several oppositions were defeated, and a large-scale purge of the Party's membership was launched. The GPU's (secret police's) right to engage in extra-judicial repressions was enlarged in 1922.[8] Mass executions of clergy took place in 1922–3. Large numbers of professionals were deported from the country. Leaders of the Socialist Revolutionary and Menshevik parties were put on trial. The political rights of NEP-men were severely restricted.

The fact that this mixture of policies included the NEP, which moved toward limited remarketization of some sectors of the economy, as well as a renaissance in literary and visual culture, has led some specialists to treat this as a 'reformist' stage of Soviet history. In fact, generations of Soviet 'reform communists' have referred back to the NEP to legitimize their urge to liberalize the Soviet economy and society by pointing to Lenin's sponsorship of the shift. But when we treat the NEP years as a period of social and economic liberalization that was accompanied by a determined tightening of political discipline among party cadres, the period

---

[7] Philip Selznick, *The Organizational Weapon: A Study of Bolshevik Strategy and Tactics* (New York: McGraw-Hill, 1952).

[8] Mikhail Heller and Aleksandr Nekrich, *Utopia in Power: History of the Soviet Union from 1917 to the Present* (London: Overseas Publishing, 1986), 220.

looks more like one of political consolidation. In this case, consolidation was marked by selective appeasement of classes that might threaten regime stability and by a determined strengthening of the capacity of the Party-State to control politics and to set limits on independent societal initiative. Reformist policies, in this case, were part of a larger programme for consolidating a regime that was seeking to regain its balance after a highly disruptive transformative phase.

High Stalinism

The next phase of consolidation was the period of 'high Stalinism' that, again, followed a highly disruptive, transformative program—the collectivization, industrialization, 'cultural revolution', and state-building drives that replaced NEP in 1928–9. This is the period that provides the empirical basis for Bauer's and Jowitt's use of the term 'consolidation'. Some observers trace the initiation of this phase to the early 1930s, when policies in many realms became more conservative and anti-egalitarian following the widespread social and economic disruptions of 1929–33. Timasheff dubbed this shift 'The Great Retreat' and traced changes in many realms of policy to 1934.[9] But whether we date the shift from 1931 or 1934 (the so-called 'Congress of the Victors', at which the leadership claimed that the 'foundations of socialism' had been successfully built), the important point is that, after a 'revolution from above' had been prosecuted for several years, Stalin and his henchmen turned their attention to consolidating the Party-State's domination of society, while Stalin turned his attention to consolidating his personal dictatorship over both the Party-State and society.

In most social, cultural, and political policy realms during 1931–6 consolidation entailed a widespread effort to strengthen the state's domination, and to stabilize society, through anti-egalitarian measures, combined with a diminution of the pace of forced collectivization, somewhat greater tolerance of private plots in rural areas, and a more balanced allocation of resources in the second five-year plan. Heller and Nekrich, when discussing this period, refer explicitly to 'the struggle for the creation of a strong state'.[10] Measures were taken to impose hierarchy, organization, and discipline in all spheres of life. Meritocratic criteria (e.g. piece-rate work) became ascendant once again in social and wage policy, while extensive privileges were awarded to the newly recruited elite of Party-State cadres in order to ensure their loyalty. From 1935 onward, new ranks and titles, reminiscent of tsarist symbolism, were introduced in civilian organizations. Russian nationalism and Soviet patriotism were embraced by the regime to help

---

[9] Nicholas Timasheff, *The Great Retreat: The Growth and Decline of Communism in Russia* (New York: E. P. Dutton, 1946), *passim* and 332–43.

[10] Heller and Nekrich (n. 8), 269.

legitimize the rigid and comprehensive domination. In the name of 'strengthening state discipline' draconian laws were passed for theft of state property and internal passports were imposed to control population movements. The individual, no longer society, was declared personally responsible for criminal behaviour. Egalitarian experiments in education were brought to an end and strict hierarchy, based on the authority of the teachers, was imposed. Family law was changed to make families collectively responsible for the criminal deeds of any family member. From 1935 onward, children aged twelve or older would be treated as adults in criminal law, even eligible for capital punishment. To strengthen the family as a unit of both reproduction and control, divorce was made more difficult and abortion was banned in 1936. To prevent parents from using their authority in 'anti-socialist' ways, children were required, under threat of severe punishment, to denounce any observed 'treason' by their parents. The cultural, professional, and scientific intelligentsia were forced into national organizations, amidst a purge of the Old Guard in these professions and recruitment of new cadres to control them. 'Socialist realism' became the enforced dogma in culture. One million party members were purged between 1931 and 1933. The new Constitution of 1936, superficially bursting with guaranteed freedoms, negated the appearance of liberalism by demanding that all freedoms be exercised 'for the purpose of strengthening the socialist system'.[11]

Some of the tightening of discipline and law was a response to the society-wide disruptions unleashed by the 'Second Russian Revolution' of 1929–31. The sheer masses of humanity fleeing from the countryside to cities, and the rising crime rates that resulted, needed, by some means, to be kept within bounds. We do not have to determine whether each of these policy shifts was driven by such pragmatic considerations, by a collective ideological vision of a fully disciplined, organized, and insulated Party-State, by a collective belief that the international environment was becoming increasingly threatening, requiring total mobilization to fend off challenges, or by Stalin's lust for totally unchallenged personal power. What is striking is that this period, like NEP, was one of political consolidation that followed a highly disruptive period of transformation. And it, too, was devoted to 'strengthening the state,' albeit by different means and to a greater extent, in order to enhance the state's control over autonomous social and economic forces.

A leadership posture of regime consolidation extended from the early 1930s until the death of Stalin in 1953. Political control remained a top priority throughout, as did most elements of the Great Retreat: institutional entrenchment, cultural conservatism, ethnic primordialism, and Russian patriotism. From the standpoint of conceptualizing Stalin's justification for a regime of political consolidation, Jowitt argues that the intended purpose was to insulate newly recruited cadres from corrupting social influences, and to prevent any

---

[11] Heller and Nekrich (n. 8), 287.

'backsliding' in the face of 'contamination' by unreconstructed elements within the USSR and by 'imperialist' and fascist forces abroad.[12] The purpose was to consolidate gains won during the earlier struggle for transformation of the social order, in order to make those gains irreversible and thereby to prevent 'capitalist restoration'.

But while a leadership posture of political consolidation, along with social policies geared toward heightening political control, marked the last two decades of Stalin's rule, this continuity was interrupted several times during these years: by the Great Terror, by the Second World War, and by the Zhdanovshchina. The Great Terror of 1936–8 was transformative, but not systemic, for it attacked people but did not overhaul institutions. It affected disproportionately the critical intelligentsia and the cadres of the Party-State itself. In order to ensure his unquestioned status as *Vozhd'*, or supreme leader, Stalin used the Great Terror to wipe out much of the generation of Party-State cadres that had been recruited during the civil war and the collectivization drives. He replaced them with hastily recruited cadres who had little experience of independent initiative and who were prepared to serve loyally in the new, patrimonial system of rule. He also used the Great Terror to imprison, eliminate, or intimidate a generation of critical intelligentsia who had been inherited from tsarist society and to replace them with more docile experts, products of Soviet-era educational institutions. In all, the Great Terror proved to be an instrument for consolidation of Stalin's patrimonial rule over both state and society.

The Second World War, by contrast, was thrust upon the Soviet Union by the Nazi war machine. Its impact on Soviet politics and society was, in certain senses, analogous to the impact of the Second Russian Revolution of 1928–32: a loosening of central control over heroic local cadres whose initiative and ingenuity were needed to win the struggle against a powerful enemy. And just as that struggle of the early 1930s led, at the 'Congress of the Victors' (1934), to questions about how to relate to a reconstructed society, so, after a period of reconstruction following the devastation caused by the Second World War, the question again arose as to whether maintenance of a posture of political consolidation was still necessary. Had the new socialist society become solid, strong, and stable? Had it been effectively reconstructed such that it no longer needed to be held in such terror and austerity by a privileged and insulated elite of Party-State cadres? Stalin's response was unequivocal. Many Soviet soldiers who had been prisoners of war in Europe were deported to camps in Siberia. Many military officers who had become used to exercising independent initiative on the war front were similarly exiled. Younger members of the cultural intelligentsia who had been permitted to think independently during the nationalist mobilization of the Second World War were subjected to a murderous campaign against 'cosmopolitanism' after the war (the aforementioned 'Zhdanovshchina'). A stratum of officials who had come

---

[12] Jowitt (n. 4).

to see victory in the war as a sign that their loyalty had been demonstrated, and that they could now look forward to living lives of comparative luxury and less pressure, were rebuffed by Stalin, who insisted on continuation of an austere, high-pressure existence.[13] Some theorists within the ideological establishment asked again whether a successfully reconstructed socialist society merited less austere and less draconian policies. Stalin's response was to launch more purges against free-thinkers and scapegoats, as he attempted to maintain and reconsolidate the regime following the turbulence and independent initiative engendered by the Second World War. All these were among the issues debated by Soviet leaders as they fought for political position in the months and years following Stalin's death. Khrushchev's victory in that struggle led to the introduction of a new set of transformative policies.

Brezhnev's Consolidative Regime

The social, economic, and political disruptions caused by Khrushchev's efforts at transformative leadership during 1956–64 led both to his overthrow and to a conservative reaction against his policies.[14] The Brezhnev era can therefore be seen as another stage of political consolidation that followed a period of transformation. For in contrast to Khrushchev's efforts to transform the Party-State elite into a less privileged, less socially-distant ruling class that would be more directly politically accountable to the populace, Brezhnev and his associates abandoned Khrushchev's plans for rotating party and state officials out of office every few years and instead announced a new policy of 'trust in cadres' and 'stability of cadres.' In contrast to Khrushchev's proclamations that the goal of his administration was the 'full-scale construction of communism,' both materially and culturally, Brezhnev's regime announced that the social order was now— and for long would be—in a stage of 'developed socialism,' in which the main task was to 'combine the advantages of socialism with the fruits of the scientific-technological revolution', and in which the regime's main claim to legitimacy would lie in its ability to ensure that the masses of the population could 'breathe easily, work well, and live tranquilly'. In contrast to Khrushchev's allegedly 'voluntarist' and 'subjectivist' approach to decision-making, the Brezhnev regime promised greater 'realism' in the setting of targets, and a sober, more 'scientific'

---

[13] For a vivid depiction of these new yearnings, see Vera Dunham, *In Stalin's Time: Middle-Class Values in Soviet Fiction* (New York: Cambridge University Press, 1976).

[14] Two issues I will not address in this chapter are the distinction between 'transformative' and 'transformational' change—I treat them as synonymous for present purposes—and the question of whether Khrushchev's policies should be dubbed 'transformative' as opposed to 'reformist'. These nominalist concerns do not alter the argument I am presenting about the alternation of transformative and consolidative periods in Soviet and post-Soviet history.

approach to the 'management of society' in a period when so many social problems required 'complex' analysis. In contrast to Khrushchev's pitting of the interests of the public against the interests of officialdom, the Brezhnev regime reasserted a 'solidary', non-antagonistic image of state–society relations but conceded that the party had a responsibility to explore the 'interests' of social groups and to 'take them into account' when making its 'scientific' and 'realistic' decisions.[15] In contrast to Khrushchev's claims that the state would wither away on the road to communism, the Brezhnev regime reasserted the doctrine that 'the state withers away by strengthening itself'.[16]

This is the language of consolidation in a post-Stalinist but still Leninist regime. It is very different from the language and posture of consolidation employed by Stalin in the 1930s and 1940s. Stalin's consolidation phase merged a solidary image of state–society relations with the language of class struggle against unreconstructed elements that were in the minority numerically but that were said to have retained the potential to regain their ascendance, given the political immaturity of the majority of the population. The alleged purpose of maintaining a terroristic, despotic regime and a war economy after the foundations of socialism allegedly had already been constructed was to insulate and protect the embryonic socialist society against enemies at home and abroad. In the post-Stalin era, by contrast, consolidation took a new form, dictated by the fact that a new, 'socialist' society had been successfully constructed and that the threat of capitalist restoration no longer was claimed to loom large. Thus, Brezhnev's consolidationist posture did not reject Khrushchev's proclamation that the class struggle within Soviet society had ended or his claim that the majority of the population was now 'politically mature.' But it rested on the argument that the period of great transformations was over and that the Party-State could now consolidate its grip without mass terror and could concentrate on delivering to the mass of the population steady improvements in their material, social, and physical security, in return for their not challenging the political status of Party-State officialdom. In this respect, Khrushchev's de-Stalinization campaign had some lasting effects, even though the public anti-Stalin campaign came to an abrupt end in 1965–6. The Brezhnev regime adopted the language and policies of consolidation within what Lowenthal called an 'established communist party regime'.[17] It would strengthen the political autonomy and collective identity of the Party-State while searching for ways to improve the standard of living of

---

[15] The idea of Soviet ideology being governed by variants of a 'solidary' image of state–society relations comes from Gregory Grossman, 'The Solidary Society: A Philosophical Issue in Communist Economic Reforms' in Gregory Grossman (ed.), *Essays in Socialism and Planning in Honor of Carl Landauer* (Englewood Cliffs, NJ: Prentice Hall, 1970).

[16] This paragraph is based on the evidence in George Breslauer, *Khrushchev and Brezhnev as Leaders: Building Authority in Soviet Politics* (London: Allen & Unwin, 1982), chs. 8–11.

[17] Richard Lowenthal, 'On "Established" Communist Party Regimes', *Studies in Comparative Communism*, 7/4 (Winter 1974).

the population within traditional political institutions. Brezhnev's was the language and posture of system-management, not system-building.[18]

The Brezhnev era lasted eighteen years and went through distinct phases that I have delineated elsewhere.[19] Most notable for our purposes, however, is that this general stage of political consolidation, like 'high Stalinism', became increasingly stagnant and controversial in its last years. Pressure was building from within segments of the Party-State and the intelligentsia for 'getting the country moving again', as also had been the case in 1950–2 and in 1927–8. These were the very pressures that led eventually to Gorbachev's ability to justify launching a transformative revolution of his own. Boris Yeltsin laboured vigorously to accelerate the pace of Gorbachev's revolution in both the USSR as a whole and the RSFSR. After the collapse of the USSR, which Yeltsin helped to bring about, he continued transformative policies in the newly independent Russian Federation, forcing through radical economic reforms (macroeconomic stabilization policies accompanied by liberalization and privatization of the economy) in 1992–3 and violently breaking through the parliamentary opposition to his rule and sponsoring the adoption of a new constitution. But at the beginning of 1994, Yeltsin put an end to further transformative thrusts and another phase of political consolidation set in. In our survey, this is the first consolidative phase of the post-Soviet and post-Communist era.

Yeltsin's Consolidative Phase[20]

The shift to a posture of political consolidation found expression in Yeltsin's rhetoric, in his private behaviour, in his patterns of political alliance, and in the pattern of policy followed during 1994–9. Yeltsin's rhetoric began to sound like that of Brezhnev in 1965–71. He started to emphasize 'normalization', stability, order, and social peace. In a memoir that he signed to press in early 1994, he concluded with a promise to provide Russians with 'stability and consistency in politics and the economy.' The concept of 'reform' still appeared in his speeches, but it now referred, not to radical restratification and structural breakthroughs, but rather to the slow development of the infrastructure for a market economy: better tax collection, stabilization of the ruble's exchange rate, improved functioning of the courts, diminished corruption, and the like. This was the rhetoric of a system-manager, no longer the rhetoric of a system-builder. To complement this

---

[18] See Alfred G. Meyer, 'Authority in Communist Political Systems' in Lewis J. Edinger (ed.), *Political Leadership in Industrialized Societies* (New York: Wiley, 1967).

[19] Breslauer (n. 16), chs. 8–15.

[20] This section is based on the evidence compiled in George Breslauer, *Gorbachev and Yeltsin as Leaders* (New York and Cambridge: Cambridge University Press, 2002), chs. 8–10.

rhetoric, Yeltsin built alliances with 'centrist' politicians at the expense of the more radical-transformative forces with whom he had allied in 1991–3.[21]

I have argued that the mark of a political consolidator is an effort to enhance the political autonomy of the governing apparatus (the state) from autonomous social and economic forces. Stated this broadly, the definition allows us to place Communist and post-Communist consolidators in analogous categories—just as we can speak of 'building socialism' and 'building capitalism' as analogous transformative postures when they rely on analogous strategies of revolutionary breakthrough. Indeed, reminiscent of Soviet-era rhetoric of consolidation, Yeltsin's 'State of the Federation' address on 24 February 1994 was entitled 'Strengthening the Russian State'. Even the most dramatic policies of this period were consolidative in intent, geared toward preventing the Communist Party from regaining power. Just as Lenin hoped through NEP to stave off threats to the nascent Bolshevik regime; just as Stalin touted his consolidative posture as necessary to prevent 'capitalist restoration'; just as Brezhnev claimed that his policies would prevent 'voluntarism', 'subjectivism', assaults on the Party-State apparatus, and, implicitly, 'anti-Stalinism' from again rearing their heads; so Yeltsin defined his main task from 1994 onward as preventing threats to the survival of the new regime from the 'Red–Brown' alliance of Communists and ultra-nationalists. This is why he demanded a 'super-presidentialist' constitution in December 1993. This is why he sought 'asymmetrical' treaties and agreements with local governors as a means of stabilizing centre–periphery relations within Russia. This is why his 'loans for shares' policy of 1995 gave away entire lucrative companies in the natural resources sector to a few, favoured plutocrats: '[H]is advisors convinced him that rapid transfer of large assets into the hands of monopoly capitalists would create a stratum of wealthy property owners who would be potent allies in the continuing struggle to prevent communist restoration'.[22] Indeed they were, and their assistance helped him, perhaps decisively so, to win the 1996 presidential election despite his widespread unpopularity among voters. Consolidating and defending the regime against Communist restoration was an accomplishment that Yeltsin, correctly or not, would later tout as his major achievement as president.[23]

To be sure, there were important differences between the policies and postures of consolidation during Yeltsin's last years compared to the Brezhnev consolidation. The volatility of economic performance, and Yeltsin's political unpredictability during the second half of the 1990s, distinguish this consolidation from the growing institutional degeneration and performance stagnation during the second half of Brezhnev's years in power. The difference can be traced largely to the fact that Brezhnev's consolidation took place in an established Communist Party regime, whereas Yeltsin's consolidation took place in the early stages of 'building

---

[21] Yegor Gaidar sensed the shift and resigned from his position in the Cabinet in January 1994.
[22] Breslauer (n. 20), 186   [23] Ibid. 218.

capitalism'. Hence, the political and economic institutions that Yeltsin was seeking to consolidate were far from entrenched, such that 'strengthening' involved reworking and makeshift reshuffling of lines of authority. This remained a brittle regime, as events would reveal.

Vladimir Putin and Consolidation

Yeltsin's last six years in office are analogous in other respects to Brezhnev's last six or more years in power. In both cases, the emphasis on consolidation had led to a period of crisis: the so-called 'stagnation' of late Brezhnevism and the crash of the Russian financial system in August 1998. Just as Brezhnev's last years set the stage for re-evaluations under Andropov and, ultimately, Gorbachev, so the erratic economic performance of Yeltsin's last years, and the fickle personnel policies of the Russian president, set the stage for Vladimir Putin to try to set things right.

But Putin was no Gorbachev, nor did he promise to be. If Gorbachev launched a transformative revolution, Putin sought to improve and strengthen the fragile system he had inherited from Yeltsin. He sought to strengthen the state by increasing its autonomy from social forces to which Yeltsin had deferred. And his rhetoric echoed that of earlier consolidators. Throughout his first term as president, Putin defined 'strengthening the state' and, relatedly, the creation of a 'dictatorship of law' as the main tasks facing him as president. As Putin put it in his April 2001 State of the Federation address:

The strategic objective of the past year was to strengthen the state, the state as represented by all institutions and all levels of power. It was obvious that without resolving this key problem we would be unable to achieve any success either in the economy or in the social sphere . . . A really strong state is also a strong federation. One can say today that the period of disintegration of statehood is behind us.[24]

The 'disintegration of statehood'—this was Putin's verdict on the Yeltsin era in post-Soviet Russian politics, an era that Yeltsin had touted, to the contrary, as having strengthened the state. In kicking off his re-election campaign in 2004, Putin went even further than this in disparaging the legacy Yeltsin had bequeathed to him. As summarized by two political observers, Denisov and Ryzhkova[25]:

---

[24] Vladimir Putin, 'Text of Russian President's Annual Address to Federal Assembly', BBC Monitoring, 3 April 2001, in *Johnson's Russia List*, No. 5185 (4 April 2001).

[25] Andrei Denisov and Natalia Ryzhkova, 'The Price of Freedom: Putin Calculates the Cost of the Yeltsin Era', *Vremya novostei*, 13 February 2004, in *Johnson's Russia List*, No. 8065 (13 February 2004).

After showing due appreciation for the citizens who chose freedom in the early 1990s ('it was a real and great achievement for the people, perhaps even the most momentous achievement made by our country in the 20th century'), Putin asked: 'But what price were we forced to pay for this?' The list was long: 'Political speculation on the people's natural longing for democracy', 'serious errors in economic and social reforms', 'one-third of the population living below the poverty line', 'widespread wage arrears', 'Russians frightened by the default and the loss of their savings overnight', 'wave of strikes sweeping the nation', 'taxes rising while all of fiscal policy was centered around survival', 'the nation relying on international financial organizations and foreign profiteers', 'Russia losing its independence in international affairs', 'the Constitution and federal laws ignored in many parts of the country', 'certain regions essentially withdrawing from the common legislative and financial-fiscal system', 'separatist processes fomenting in Russia unattended'.

All these miseries were to be overcome, however, without the revolutionary breakthroughs that had characterized transformative periods in Soviet and Russian history. In his 'State of the Federation' speech of spring 2001,[26] Putin had declared as much:

Esteemed members of the Federation Council and deputies of the State Duma, the last decade has been a turbulent and, one can say without any exaggeration, a revolutionary one for Russia. Against that background, the year 2000 and the start of 2001 seem relatively calm. For many people accustomed to constant crises, the absence of political shocks has provided the basis for predicting structural and personnel changes. I would like to say categorically—we are not afraid and should not be afraid of changes. But any changes, be they political or administrative, must be justified by circumstances. Of course, public expectations and apprehensions do not arise out of nowhere. They are based on the well-known logic that revolution is usually followed by counter-revolution, reforms by counter-reforms and then by the search for those guilty of revolutionary misdeeds and by punishment, all the more so since Russia's own historical experience is rich in such examples. But I think it is time to say firmly that this cycle has ended. There will be no revolution or counter-revolution. *Firm and economically supported state stability* is a good thing for Russia and its people and it is long since time we learnt to live according to this normal human logic (emphasis added).

Indeed, a prominent Western scholar interprets the field of expectations within which Putin has governed as highly conducive to consolidative leadership: 'The elite as a whole craved stability and consolidation of the status quo, after the constant upheavals and confrontations of the Yeltsin years. It wanted its near-monopoly on political and economic power to be secured and guaranteed. At the same time, conveniently, ordinary people longed for their wages and pensions to be paid on time. Thus both elite and people felt that the floundering institutions of a weakening state needed reinforcement, and an infusion of *siloviki* was required'.[27]

[26] Putin (n. 24).
[27] Peter Reddaway, 'The Advance of the *Siloviki*: Notable But Still Limited', *Post-Soviet Affairs*, 20/1 (January–March, 2004), 5–6.

Putin's policies and results have responded to these yearnings. The economy and the federal budget have benefited from windfall oil profits and from the beneficial impact on Russian manufacturing of the sharp devaluation of the ruble in 1998. Putin has used these benefits to see that back-wages and back-pensions were paid and that new arrears did not accumulate. He has pushed through the Duma a number of bills on taxation and land ownership that promise to improve both economic performance and the investment climate, and has skillfully sought opportunities abroad for Russian companies and the Russian state to benefit materially from foreign economic relations. In other policy realms, Putin introduced determined measures to reduce centrifugal regionalism within the Russian Federation and to bring local laws and constitutions into conformity with federal law and the federal constitution. He created new plenipotentiary positions to partially offset the authority of regional governors, and staffed those positions largely with officials drawn from the military and security agencies. He redefined the national powers of regional governors by diminishing their role in the upper house of parliament in Moscow. In politics, Putin has squeezed much (not all) of the pluralism, liberalism, and democratic proceduralism out of the political order, gaining thereby a highly compliant parliament, a more homogeneous and less critical print and broadcast media, a more predictable electorate, and a less autonomous, more cowed civil society, a pattern that Balzer refers to as 'managed pluralism'.[28] He has recruited into the state economic administration large numbers of officials from the military and security services.[29] As regards the tycoons who became billionaires during the Yeltsin era, Putin has cut three of the biggest of them down to size (two are in exile abroad and one is in jail), sending a strong signal to the others that, should they defy the president or seek too much autonomy from the priorities dictated by the state, they too could fall. He relaunched the war against Chechen secession and has prosecuted it at great human and material cost, as an affirmation that Russia will not be allowed to go the route of the USSR. All of which has been accompanied by a steady determination to integrate into global multilateral economic and political institutions, as a guarantor of Russia's national security and economic health.

Is this a consolidative phase of post-Soviet history? I think it is, but of a different sort. The late Brezhnev and late Yeltsin years were a form of consolidation that was characterized by relative stagnation in policy and deferral to certain concentrations of power: regional party officials under Brezhnev, economic tycoons and regional governors under Yeltsin. Putin, by contrast, seeks, with varying levels of success and failure, simultaneously to liberalize much of the economy and to integrate it into global capitalism, while pushing the political system back toward greater authoritarianism, gaining greater central control over

---

28 Harley Balzer, 'Managed Pluralism', *Post-Soviet Affairs*, 19/3 (July–September 2003, 189–227).
29 Olga Kryshtanovskaya and Stephen White, 'Putin's Militocracy', *Post-Soviet Affairs*, 19/4 (October–December 2003, 289–306).

the regions, breaking the power of selected economic tycoons, and ensuring that Moscow retains dominant influence over one of the commanding heights of the economy—the energy and resources sector. In most of these respects, the parallel may be with the 1920s rather than the late 1970s or late 1990s. Or another parallel could be with the Andropov years following Brezhnev's death, when the General Secretary sought through purges to resuscitate a political instrument for breaking through constraints on change by recruiting the 'uncorrupted' into key positions within the Party and State apparatus. And there is a parallel with the early Brezhnev era, when stability was touted as the alternative to Khrushchev's 'voluntarism' and 'subjectivism', just as Putin has promised to overcome the erraticism of Yeltsin's behaviour.

Explaining Consolidative Stages

Tranformative policy captures the imagination, with its large-scale challenges to the existing order of things and its typically heroic leadership posture. Consolidative policy enjoys none of these attention-grabbing features. Hence, less has been written about it as a phenomenon. Yet consolidation has appeared as often and as regularly as transformation and has lasted for many more years. What brings about such consolidative stages?

There is a predictable, cyclical quality to the emergence of consolidative phases in Soviet and post-Soviet history. They typically followed the disruptions of a transformative phase. As the costs of transformative efforts mounted, a reaction set in. The motives and sources of this reaction varied. When the leader remained in power who had presided over transformation, it was he who defined the terms of consolidation and his perceptions and perspectives that determined when and whether a consolidative phase would ensue. Thus, Lenin defined the terms and purposes of consolidation in 1921 (he personally sponsored both the NEP and the ban on factions within the Party), Stalin defined them in the 1930s, and Yeltsin defined them in 1994. When consolidation was embraced by a successor regime (Brezhnev, Putin) after the discrediting of a transformative leader (Khrushchev, Yeltsin), the terms and purposes of consolidation were the product of a broader political backlash against what went before. But whether the driving force was personal or broader, what was common to consolidative phases is that they were usually reactions to the disruptions attendant upon transformation.[30] Put differently, transformational policies do not typically last for very many years, either because of a flagging of the energy and staying power required to sustain them or

---

[30] Thus, what Reddaway (n. 27) wrote about the field of expectations surrounding Putin in 2000 was broadly true also of the field of expectations surrounding the Brezhnev–Kosygin leadership after the overthrow of Khrushchev in 1964.

because of reconsiderations in the face of mounting political, economic, and other costs.

But why do consolidations take the form of efforts to strengthen the state? Here the answer may lie in the centrifugal impacts of many transformative policies. Consolidative phases have tended to reconcentrate political and administrative power as a check against centrifugal forces unleashed during the preceding transformative phase. During the civil war and 'War Communism' of 1918–20, the Bolshevik Party experienced a huge influx of new members, the purging of whom began in 1921. During the same period, 'the heroes of the civil war wanted their reward; each behaved like a prince in his own domain. Former front-line comrades formed cliques and challenged the authority of the Central Committee'.[31] Peasant uprisings (such as the one in Tambov), and the Kronstadt rebellion among sailors in 1921, threatened to turn social rebellion against the Bolsheviks after the defeat of the 'Whites' in the civil war. Lenin's response was to ban factions within the Party and to reassert the authority of the Central Committee.

Similarly, the 'Second Russian Revolution' that began in 1928–9 required the exercise of independent initiative by many thousands of party cadres who were charged with finding ways to collectivize agriculture, build new cities, and 'liquidate enemies'. Many members of this generation would become beneficiaries of the Great Terror and the Great Retreat before expiring quietly during Brezhnev's consolidation. But many others were targeted for purge during 1931–3 and, in many cases, for elimination during the Great Terror. Moreover, many of the draconian legal measures enacted from 1934 onward were responses to the vast social disruptions and unregulated social activity (such as crime and population movements) unleashed by the collectivization and industrialization drives of 1928–33.

Khrushchev's de-Stalinization campaign unleashed forces among the critical intelligentsia that threatened to challenge the leading role of the party apparatus. His division of local party organs into separate 'industrial' and 'agricultural' hierarchies undermined the ability of those organs to perform essential coordinative functions at the local and regional levels. His regionalization of economic administration (the *sovnarkhozy*) increased both regionalist and nationalist centrifugal forces. All these policies were quickly reversed during the first years of the Brezhnev administration.

The Gorbachev revolution unleashed forces that brought down the Soviet Union and that threatened the disintegration of the Russian Federation thereafter. Yeltsin's phase of consolidation was geared toward strengthening the ability of the state to prevent further disintegration. He did so through a futile and furtive military effort in Chechnya during 1994–6 and through ad hoc, asymmetrical treaties between Moscow and the regions. Putin, in effect, declared Yeltsin's efforts in each regard to have been a failure, though he continued to embrace

---

31 See Heller and Nekrich (n. 8), 129.

his goals. Putin sought military victory in Chechnya and strived to construct a new political apparatus that could rein in the regions, the parliament, the press, and the economic tycoons.

Periods of political consolidation have also typically been marked by an easing of pressure on those social classes that were most deprived during the preceding transformative drives. The NEP, of course, went farthest in this regard. But the slowdown in the pace of collectivization after 1932, and the priorities of the second five-year plan, reflected decisions to ease somewhat the socio-economic deprivations, as the authorities concentrated on strengthening the state.[32] Much the same was true of the Brezhnev and Putin eras, while Yeltsin's consolidative phase was marked by increasingly desperate efforts, ultimately unsuccessful, to gain Western aid to meet basic economic needs of the citizenry and hopefully thereby to reinforce social stability. All of which reflected a causal dynamic within consolidative regimes. The reigning idea within consolidative leaderships was consistently that efforts to strengthen the state after a transformative thrust must be accompanied by efforts also to appease social forces whose alienation was high as a result of the transformative policies, but whose political access was now being restricted by efforts to augment the autonomy of the state.

Evaluating Consolidative Stages

Consolidation may be predictable, but is it, in some sense, useful from a developmental standpoint? This depends on what one considers to be the alternative. If consolidation is conceptualized merely as the slowing or halting of transformative policies that have resulted in widespread disruption, then a period of consolidation may be, depending on circumstances, both predictable and useful ('two steps forward, one step back'; a 'breathing spell' to consolidate gains). Indeed, alternation of periods of reform with periods of consolidation or backlash is probably characteristic of many polities, including the United States, during much of the nineteenth and twentieth centuries.[33] What is distinctive about Russia have been the scope, intensity, and social costs of transformative efforts and the extent to which the subsequent consolidative phases have sought to insulate the state from formal and regular accountability to civil society, which has in turn led to a kind of stagnation that makes the next transformative thrust more easily justified. But such an observation does not address whether anything positive and functional for the longer-term maintenance of the system is thereby accomplished.

[32] To be sure, a major exception was the state-induced famine in Ukraine during 1932–3.
[33] Ruth Berins Collier and David Collier, *Shaping the Political Arena: Critical Junctures, the Labor Movement, and Regime Dynamics in Latin America* (Princeton, NJ: Princeton University Press, 1991). See also Arthur M. Schlesinger, *The Cycles of American History* (Boston: Houghton Mifflin, 1986).

Consolidation can lead to stagnation, or it can be viewed as a 'necessary' respite after a period of disruption. The former outcome is presumably a negative one; the latter is, at minimum, developmentally neutral. Much depends on the policy follow-up to the necessary respite.

Practitioners of consolidation have often justified their policies as necessary to offset, mitigate, or roll back the side effects of transformative policies. This is how Lenin justified the policies of 1921, how Stalin justified the policies of the 1930s, and how Brezhnev justified the consolidative posture of his regime in the years immediately following the overthrow of Khrushchev. Putin too embraces this justification for consolidation in the aftermath of the turbulent 1990s. Nor are these justifications necessarily always devoid of theoretical justification. Jowitt, for example, argues that large-scale organizations typically engage in consolidation following a transformative stage, and that this is useful for infusing the organization with character.[34] Military commanders, in turn, extol the functionality of consolidating gains before launching new offensives. In early evaluations of the policies introduced under Brezhnev in the mid-1960s, some Western observers recorded their belief that a period of bureaucratic rationalization under a 'post-revolutionary oligarchy' might be necessary following the administrative and political dysfunctions of Khrushchev's last years.[35] Over time, as Brezhnev's consolidation allowed political controls to stymie both bureaucratic rationalization and economic performance, 'degeneration' proved to be the more accurate prediction.[36] What this may suggest is that, when consolidation is treated as a long-term strategy, rather than as a short-term tactic to solidify gains, there is an ever-present danger that active consolidation will give way to degeneration and stagnation. The costs of such stagnation will typically multiply, leaving the social order increasingly out of touch with environmental challenges to which it ought, ideally, to be adapting.

The parallels with evaluation of Putin's presidency are suggestive. Vyacheslav Nikonov, an admirer of Putin, extols his strengthening of the state as his main accomplishment:

State management has been re-established, which is President Putin's major achievement. When Mr. Putin took office, Russia resembled a sinking ship abandoned by the captain and seized with panic and chaos. Thankfully, the man who stepped onto the bridge knew what had to be done to overcome the grave economic crisis, restore legal order and the central government's authority. President Putin understood that the unlimited power of regional governors and their defiance of the central government threatened the country's territorial integrity and the smooth functioning of the state. By dividing the country into

[34] Jowitt (n. 4).

[35] Richard Lowenthal, 'The Soviet Union in the post-revolutionary era: An overview' in Alexander Dallin and Thomas B. Larson (eds.), *Soviet Politics Since Khrushchev* (Englewood Cliffs, NJ: Prentice Hall, 1968).

[36] Zbigniew Brzezinski, 'The Soviet System: Transformation or Degeneration?', *Problems of Communism*, 15/1 (January–February, 1966). Jowitt referred to this, in retrospect, as neo-traditionalization. See Jowitt (n. 34).

seven federal districts, the President ensured improved co-ordination between the Russian Federation's constituent members and enhanced the centre's efficiency and authority. Vladimir Putin restored the vertical of power by forcing the governors, who enjoyed unlimited power under his predecessor Boris Yeltsin, to comply with Russian legislation. He settled all contradictions between the Russian Constitution and local laws.[37]

Nikonov goes on to praise the economic and foreign-policy improvements that have taken place under Putin's stewardship. But he concludes with observations that raise questions about the sustainability of economic progress:

Many crucial reforms, for example in the judicial and administrative spheres, are being implemented too slowly. The efforts against corruption, Russia's age-old problem, are not being conducted quickly or effectively enough. The development of the structure of civil society must be accelerated. These and many other issues will dominate the agenda of President Putin's next term of office, which will hopefully begin with the March 14 elections.

Another Russian political pundit, Mark Urnov, is persuaded that the pessimistic scenario is very likely to be realized: 'I'm under the impression that over the next four years we will see a widening gap between what we want, what Putin said in this speech, and what we will really observe. The existing political system will breed corruption, pressure from the state on business, inefficient behavior by business owners. At the same time, it will not save the state from incorrect legislative initiatives.'[38]

What Urnov's observations suggest is that the strengthening of the state under Putin may have been a precondition for maintaining Russia's territorial integrity and improving her economic performance, but that the very strength of that state could prove to be an obstacle to further progress. Judicial reform, civil service reform, the tempering of systemic corruption, and the development of civil society are realms in which little progress has been made or absolute regression has taken place since 1999. The implication is that the state may now be muscle-bound, not just strong, and that excessive strength could stymie the judicial, administrative, and political development required to prevent stagnation or another economic crash.

Whither Russia?

Putin's statement (2001), quoted earlier, that the historical 'cycle has ended. There will be no revolution or counter-revolution. Firm and economically

---

[37] See Vyacheslav Nikonov, 'Vladimir Putin's Successful First Term', *RIA Novosti*, 10 February 2004, in *Johnson's Russia List*, No. 8058 (10 February 2004).
[38] Mark Urnov in *Vremya novostei*, 13 February 2004, in *Johnson's Russia List*, No. 8065 (13 February 2004).

supported state stability is a good thing for Russia and its people and it is long since time we learnt to live according to this normal human logic' is a statement of relevance to this discussion. It amounts to a claim that the scope and intensity of policy changes (and, by implication, of consolidative backlashes) will be less than has been the case throughout modern Russian history. Putin claims, in effect, that Russia will become a 'normal' country, one in which there will be serious, state-led efforts to effect changes, but no more great transformations. The amplitudes of waves of change, followed by waves of consolidation, will be much smaller—more in line with what happens elsewhere. The pattern of convulsive transform-ations, followed by repressive/Sybaritic consolidations, followed by stagnation and threats of instability that help to justify new convulsions, will give way to a normal pattern of rationalized reform followed by measured consolidation of gains. Indeed, in his May 2004 'State of the Nation' address, Putin treated strengthening of the state as an accomplished fact and instead devoted the address to discussions of ways in which the now-strengthened state could be further modernized to support rapid economic growth and social improvement.[39]

Time will tell. Much will depend on Putin's perceptions of the situation, on his power and ability to implement changes (if so inclined), and on whether a corrupted bureaucracy and lack of liberal democracy will actually prove to be decisive constraints on economic growth, territorial integrity, and national secur-ity. These are all matters of uncertainty and dispute at the moment. If the perspectives that Putin had enunciated in his 2003 State of the Federation address were not momentary political speech acts but reflections of his true beliefs,[40] then the Russian president would appear to be hoping to build a strong developmental state with a national security emphasis that will have little use for political pluralism and dissent. That would be a logical extension of the consolidative trajectory of policy during his first term. The key question is: will Putin's political consolidation lead to stagnation in policy and performance, as has befallen every other consolidative phase in Soviet and post-Soviet history? Or will it break the mould by breaking through constraints on further rationalization?

The most prominent recent cyclical theories of Russian history lead one logically toward pessimism about the future. According to Reddaway and Glinski, 'Russia's perennial problem has been that the modernizing activity of the state and the self-organization of society have as a rule proceeded in inverse proportion to each other'. [41] From the standpoint of this theory, only reform that emerges from, and is sustained by, an alliance between moderates within the state and within civil society can break the historical cycle of revolutions from above followed by

---

[39] Vladimir Putin, 'Full text of Putin's state of the nation address to Russian parliament', BBC Monitoring, 26 May 2004, in *Johnson's Russia List*, No. 8225 (27 May 2004).

[40] Vladimir Putin, 'Transcript of Putin's State of the Nation Address', BBC Monitoring, 16 May 2003, in *Johnson's Russia List*, No. 7186 (19 May 2003).

[41] Peter Reddaway and Dmitri Glinski, *The Tragedy of Russia's Reforms: Market Bolshevism Against Democracy* (Washington, DC: United States Institute of Peace, 2001), 23.

instability or breakdown. Yanov's theory is similar in claiming that a break-through toward some form of elitist liberalism or a parliamentary 'bourgeois democracy' is required for Russia to break out of its historical pattern. Minus that breakthrough, an extended 'time of troubles' will ensue and will build pressure for a convulsive resolution of growing tensions.[42] Neither theory would treat the Putin era as a breakthrough, because of Putin's continuing emphasis on state-led political initiative, his suffocation of civil society, and his diminution of parliamentary power. In these theories, then, the absence of some form of institutionalized democracy opens the door to chronic instability, fol-lowed eventually by renewed convulsions. When exactly these convulsions will occur is unpredictable, for chronic instability can last a long time—as it has during many phases of Russian history.

But what exactly are the constraints on such a breakthrough toward institu-tionalized accountability? Are they primarily to be found in the realm of elite and mass political culture: a widespread deference to state-led initiative and a wide-spread assumption that the only alternative to such imposed 'order' is social 'anarchy'? Perhaps such a viewpoint has been reinforced by the frenetic experi-ence of 'democracy' under Yeltsin, but there is plenty of evidence to suggest that the younger generations of Russian citizens no longer buy into such beliefs.[43] Or perhaps there is a politico-cultural tendency to embrace a messianic mentality that makes the population susceptible to the appeals of salvationist leaders who promise to resolve problems through additional transformative convulsions? Surely there are people who think this way in Russia today, but the widespread popularity of Putin for delivering order and stable expectations, the loss of popularity of such salvationist leaders as Zhirinovsky, and mass surveys of popular opinion suggest that such extremist propensities are in the small minority within the population.

If the main constraint is not politico-cultural, is it perhaps institutional: the self-interest of corrupted elites that now dominate public administration at all levels and that have the power and incentive to sabotage policies, programmes, and initiatives that threaten their power and privilege? This strikes me as a more plausible argument than the politico-cultural, for elites are capable of manipulat-ing conditions, rallying followers, and targeting ethnic scapegoats to justify convulsive policies geared toward protecting their own power and perquisites. The question, however, is whether Russian elites have been through enough convulsions that have subsequently devoured their initiators to leave them col-lectively shy of such 'solutions.' Moreover, the economic and international costs of such a reaction in this era of globalization would be enormous. It is notable that Gorbachev, Yeltsin, and Putin, whatever the differences among them, all came to

[42] Alexander Yanov, *The Origins of Autocracy: Ivan the Terrible in Russian History* (Berkeley: University of California Press, 1981).
[43] Timothy J. Colton and Michael McFaul, 'Are Russians Undemocratic?', *Post-Soviet Affairs*, 18/2 (April–June 2002, 91–121).

embrace, often unexpectedly, an attitude that the Soviet Union or Russia had no choice but to integrate into multilateral, capitalist global institutions.

None of this is meant to suggest that, minus the historically convulsive pattern, Russia's future will be a smooth path toward rationalization of either an authoritarian-developmental or a liberal-integrationist regime. The end of convulsions would not mean the end of cycles. As I have noted, cycles marked by smaller amplitudes of both reform and consolidation mark most industrialized countries' contemporary histories. And instability of one or another type, degree, and frequency is also prevalent in much of the world. It is notable that Shleifer and Treisman debunk notions that Russia has experienced catastrophic setbacks in the past decade. They argue that Russia's patterns of economic, social, and political change are analogous to those experienced in the second half of the twentieth century by most 'middle-income countries' such as Argentina, Brazil, Mexico, Venezuela, the Philippines, Turkey, Malaysia, South Korea, and others.[44] This may be good news or bad news, depending on one's perspective. The swings that most of these middle-income countries have experienced between populist-authoritarian rule and democratic development, the ups and downs of their economic development, the problems induced by entrenched corruption and periodic efforts to fight it suggest that, even if Russia has broken out of its cycle of historical convulsions, it may yet fall into a pattern of chronic but contained instability and high political uncertainty. Hence, even if Russia breaks out of its convulsive historical pattern, the question remains: what would a leader such as Putin have to do to institutionalize an alternative that also avoids falling into the 'more-normal' pattern of chronic but contained instability found in other middle-income countries?

[44] Andrei Shleifer and Daniel Treisman, 'Normal Country', *Foreign Affairs*, 83/2 (March–April 2004).

4

Soviet Political Leadership and 'Sovietological' Modelling

Robert Service

Studies of the USSR have traditionally interwoven questions about leadership with questions about periodization as well as about the nature and nomenclature of the Soviet order. Indeed most writers have started, empirically and in theoretical analysis, from the leadership question and moved outwards to the others. It is easy to understand why. Communist Party leaders from Lenin onwards had immense personal power. Their activities and ideas had much impact on the history of their times, an impact that in all cases—except for the ineffectual Chernenko's—lasted years after their retirements or deaths. Lenin was the prime mover in the foundation of a novel type of state, and his successors in their various ways sought to conserve this state against its rivals in the rest of the world. Highly centralist and oligarchic (when it was not monocratic, as it became under Stalin in the late 1930s and Khrushchev in the early 1960s), the system of leadership in the USSR was regarded as having enabled and promoted the consolidation of the political, economic, and social characteristics of the Soviet order over many decades. It is hardly surprising that 'leaderology' from 1917 to 1991 was a cardinal preoccupation of 'Sovietologists' as long as the USSR existed.[1]

In the years immediately after the October 1917 Revolution, the most penetrating studies of the USSR were carried out either by émigrés or by persons who had been associated with the political conflicts in that country. In the first category were Yuly Martov, Nikolay Trubetskoy, Nikolay Ustryalov, Leon Trotsky, Nikolay Berdyaev, and Fedor Dan;[2] in the second were Karl Kautsky and Boris

---

[1] I put this name in quotes since many practitioners declined to accept the designation until, in the late 1980s, it ceased to be used pejoratively by Soviet spokesmen and became instead a term of respect. It is also somewhat doubtful whether the study of Soviet affairs should attract a designation putting it on a scholarly par with biology or zoology.

[2] Yuly Martov, *Mirovoi bol'shevizm* (Berlin: Iskra, 1923); Nikolay Trubetskoy, *K probleme russkogo samosoznaniya: sobranie statei* (Paris: Evraziiskoe knigoizdatel'stvo, 1927); Nikolay Ustryalov, *Pod znakom revolyutsii* (Harbin: Poligraf, 2nd rev. edn., 1927); Leon Trotsky, *The Revolution Betrayed: What is the Soviet Union and Where is it Going?* (London: Faber and Faber, 1937); Nikolay Berdyaev, *The Russian Idea* (London: G. Bles, 1947); Theodore Dan, *The Origins of Bolshevism* (London: Secker and Warburg, 1964).

Souvarine.[3] W.H. Chamberlin's magisterial narrative history from the fall of the Romanovs to the rise of Stalin was the product of a visiting journalist's direct observation.[4]

Initially it was the Soviet leadership and its policies which held attention; but with the inception of the New Economic Policy in 1921, writers began to discuss whether the nature of the Soviet order had already undergone basic change. There was speculation that Bolshevism's ideological commitment had vanished. Not only Mensheviks but also, from 1923, Trotsky suggested that the October Revolution had undergone degeneration.[5] Just as the French Revolution had turned away from its early radicalism, so the Bolsheviks were said to have deviated from the Party's revolutionary principles. Nikolay Ustryalov, the leading member of the 'Change of Landmarks' group in the Chinese city of Harbin, agreed. But unlike Trotsky, he welcomed the perceived transformation as a symptom of a desirable consolidation of the regime on the basis of traditional Russian imperial ambitions and economic modernizing objectives.[6] Thus two periods of the Soviet order were claimed to have occurred, carrying with them two different kinds of political orientation. Interrelated questions of leadership, periodization, and definition had come to the fore.

Stalin's campaign for industrialization and collectivization from 1928–9 gave a further stimulus to discussion. For some writers, the alteration of policies was so drastic that it made sense to characterize the process as having inaugurated a wholly new period in the history of the USSR. Stalin's personal dominance was recognized and his powers were categorized as despotic. The features of vertical command in Soviet public life had long been discerned. In the 1930s, though, the state underwent radical internal organization in the direction of intensifying obedience to the 'centre'; and the state itself was equipped with the resources to penetrate and manage society to a much higher degree than ever before.

All this led to much debate, especially among the outstanding émigré writers. For Eurasianist thinkers such as Nikolay Trubetskoy, Stalinist despotism was essentially a manifestation of the immutable geopolitical requirements for governance across a country stretching from eastern Europe to the Pacific Ocean.[7] The Christian philosopher Nikolay Berdyaev, himself a former Marxist, stressed instead that political and cultural traditions—rather than objective geopolitical conditions—had become deposited inside communism and resulted in a regime which bore fundamental traces of the imperial order.[8] Both Trubetskoy and Berdyaev proposed that behind a façade of novelty the USSR was really a restored

    [3] Karl Kautsky, *The Dictatorship of the Proletariat* (Ann Arbor: University of Michigan Press, 1964); Boris Souvarine, *Stalin: A Critical Survey of Bolshevism* (London: Secker and Warburg, 1940).
    [4] William H. Chamberlin, *The Russian Revolution, 1917–1921* (London: Macmillan, 1935).
    [5] Leon Trotsky (n.2). The neatest summary of the Menshevik position was Dan's *The Origins of Bolshevism* (n. 2). Both works were written after Stalin's rise to political supremacy.
    [6] Nikolay Ustryalov (n. 2).   [7] Nikolay Trubetskoy (n. 2).
    [8] Nikolay Berdyaev (n. 2).

version of Old Russia. Mensheviks, Socialist-Revolutionaries, and Trotsky dis-
agreed, refusing to accept the primacy of continuity: for them it had always been
obvious that elements of a socialist state had been constructed in the Soviet Union
even though this had been accomplished in an undesirable manner. While accepting that the tsarist legacy was important for an understanding of recent developments, they insisted that the Bolshevik distortion of principles of socialism
constituted the key to accurate analysis.

The Mensheviks, Socialist-Revolutionaries, and Trotsky were also at variance
among themselves. Mensheviks and Socialist-Revolutionaries as primordial opponents of Bolshevism proposed that the 'degeneration' of the October Revolution was inscribed in the genes of Bolshevik ideas before 1917. Dictatorship and
terror were essential to Leninist doctrine and precluded the possibility of introducing democracy which the Mensheviks and Socialist-Revolutionaries claimed
to be indispensable for the development of socialism. Trotsky, who joined the
Bolsheviks only in summer 1917, at first suggested that the degeneration had
commenced with the New Economic Policy (NEP), but increasingly over the
years he conceded that the prospects for socialist development in Russia had
always been too slight to countervail against the weight of the country's socio-
economic backwardness and its centuries of political autocracy. The Mensheviks
and Socialist-Revolutionaries believed that the October Revolution had never
succeeded in installing a 'workers' state', whereas Trotsky maintained that the
foundations for such a state had been laid only to be dissolved by bureaucratic
petrifaction and the emergence of a privileged Communist Party elite.

In the late 1930s, however, a fresh analysis started to be made. Its nucleus was
the idea that Stalin's USSR should be analysed not in terms of Russian historical
continuity or socialist development (or degeneration) but through a comparison
with other existing ultra-authoritarian states. The description applied to such
states was 'totalitarian'. It was used, somewhat vaguely, by Mussolini about the
kind of Italy he aimed to build. Gradually the theoretical framework was elaborated with reference to Hitler's Third Reich and Stalin's USSR. Advocates of the
totalitarian 'model', who existed on both the political left and the political right,
argued that the similarities between contemporary Communist and fascist states
were much greater than the dissimilarities.

They contended that in Berlin and Moscow alike there ruled a supreme leader
who had the automatic obedience of his party, government, and state. Governance, moreover, took place without consultation of popular opinion. Society was
treated as a mere resource for political mobilization and economic exploitation.
Lines of command stretched unbroken from the centre to the outmost corners of
state and society. Upward pressure on the leadership had become impossible. The
effects of violent purges and sustained indoctrination was said to have produced a
situation impervious to change from within each of the countries that acquired
such systems of rule. By implication, totalitarianism could be eliminated only be
external intervention; and this in turn would require the waging of a successful

war or the maintenance of a severe economic blockade by foreign states. The emphasis of the 'model' was tilted towards the axiom that totalitarian states were effective in achieving the goals of their policies. Individuals and social groups were regarded as incapable of resistance to orders sent down to them; supposedly they were unable to think outside the bounds of ideas relayed to them by the official media.[9]

The totalitarian model was intensively refined only after 1945. Although the Third Reich had been destroyed, its history was incorporated in the discussion. The cold war erupted in full fury in 1947. Stalin remained in power in the USSR; the structures of state control were reinforced during years when the Soviet–US rivalry was at its height. Certain scholarly and political interests converged in the same historical phase. Nazism was a vivid, alarming memory and the current menace of the Soviet military nuclear power—as well as the possibility of the expansion of Communist power beyond eastern Europe and China—grew. It was in this global environment that a theoretical model stressing the systemic horrors of the Soviet Union acquired much appeal for many scholars of history and social science.

The attractiveness of the totalitarian model was enhanced by state support for the academic study of the USSR. The most lavish finance was supplied in the United States; institutes were also established in Britain, West Germany, France, and elsewhere. The result in the United States was the near-universal dissemination of the model in scholarly books and articles. Writers who raised intellectual objections to it were shuffled to the margins of their institutions, and for two or three decades there was a distinct preference on appointment committees to give the new jobs to young academics who accepted the model.[10] The situation was more complex in the United Kingdom (which in those years was second only to the United States in the quantity of Sovietological output) and a quasi-official orthodoxy was not consistently imposed. Decisions on academic employment were nevertheless affected. At the School of Slavonic and East European Studies in London University, the British communist activist and opponent of the totalitarian model Andrew Rothstein was pushed out of his job.[11] The British government, while not starting a witch-hunt of the kind induced by Senator Joe McCarthy in the United States, did not stand idly by when key jobs in Soviet studies were under discussion.

---

[9] See, in particular, Franz Neumann, *Behemoth: The Structure and Practice of National Socialism* (London: Gollancz, 1942); Carl Friedrich and Zbigniew Brzezinski, *Totalitarian Dictatorship and Autocracy* (Cambridge, MA: Harvard University Press, 1956). On the early development of the totalitarian model, see Ian Kershaw and Moshe Lewin (eds.), *Stalinism and Nazism. Dictatorships in Comparison* (Cambridge: Cambridge University Press, 1997).

[10] See Stephen F. Cohen, *Rethinking the Soviet Experience* (Oxford: Oxford University Press, 1985).

[11] See Jonathan Haslam, *The Vices of Integrity: E.H. Carr, 1892–1982* (London: Verso, 1999).

Totalitarianist writers were producing outstanding books. In the United States, Merle Fainsod published *How Russia is Ruled*, which quickly became a textbook used in hundreds of universities.[12] Leonard Schapiro wrote an equally influential history of the Soviet Communist Party.[13] Also important were Robert Conquest's study of de-Stalinization and Richard Pipes's study of the formation of the USSR.[14] Zbigniew Brzezinski had an impact with his work on recent Soviet politics.[15] Such books contributed to the empirical and analytical base for the totalitarian model as it was developed in the 1960s.

Yet the model failed to win universal acceptance. France had a large communist party, the PCF, whose historians attacked their own country's critics of the USSR—and among such critics, of course, were French advocates of the model. Italy too had a large communist party, the PCI, whose writers replied in kind to Western denunciations of the Soviet order. Both the PCF and the PCI, however, were inhibited from encouraging serious scholarship on the USSR; their allegiance to the world communist movement involved the need to avoid being seen to contradict the current and ever-changing analysis by Soviet politicians and propagandists. Non-communist French and Italian scholarship, meanwhile, tended mainly to reproduce the approaches and insights developed by 'Anglo-Saxon' writers, especially the totalitarianists. German scholarship on the USSR was confined to West Germany at a time when East Germany lay under direct Soviet control. Consequently German writers in the early years of the cold war innovated little in the interpretation of the Soviet historical or contemporary experience. The majority of West German scholars accepted the totalitarian model without much scrutiny; all East German scholars rejected the model without arguing a full case against it. Sovietology in other European countries incorporated 'Anglo-Saxon' works without developing indigenous analyses.

There was a notable exception to this pattern. Scholarship in the United Kingdom, while supplying some cardinal texts for the totalitarian model, was characterized by much interpretative variety. The Glasgow-based journal *Soviet Studies* gave space to several British scholars who repudiated the model with closely argued studies. In the wider public arena, moreover, E. H. Carr and Isaac Deutscher achieved a deep impact upon debate. They criticized totalitarianism as an anti-historicist theory that ascribed permanent static features to the USSR and Soviet-type regimes. Carr and Deutscher also denied that the main negative aspects of the Soviet order derived either from a malignant original ideology or from deliberately brutal leading politicians.

[12] Merle Fainsod, *How Russia is Ruled* (Cambridge, MA: Harvard University Press, 1953).

[13] Leonard Schapiro, *The Communist Party of the Soviet Union* (London: Eyre & Spottiswoode, 1963).

[14] Robert Conquest, *Power and Policy in the USSR* (London: Macmillan, 1961); Richard Pipes, *The Formation of the Soviet Union: Communism and Nationalism, 1917–1923* (Cambridge, MA: Harvard University Press, 1954).

[15] Zbigniew Brzezinski, *Ideology and Power in Soviet Politics* (Westport, CT: Greenwood, 1976).

Carr was a left-liberal thinker who had served in the Foreign Office before becoming deputy editor of *The Times* in the Second World War; Deutscher was a Polish-Jewish refugee and Trotskyist who had made his home in the United Kingdom. Neither had an easy time with the British academic establishment (although Carr, as a fellow of Trinity College, Cambridge, could hardly claim to have suffered severe persecution). Both wrote popular textbooks which were widely reviewed and purchased. Carr and Deutscher appeared frequently on radio discussion programmes. Their erudition as well as their ability to write lively, clear English ensured too that American publishing houses picked up their books. Carr's *History of Soviet Russia* was among the most prominent works available in the US libraries and bookshops.[16] Deutscher's biography of Trotsky had a similar profile.[17] Even in North America, where most leading scholars adhered to the totalitarian model, there were ripples of dissent across the Sovietological pond.

It ought to be mentioned that not all American scholars subscribed to the model. For example, Joseph Berliner's study of Soviet industrial managers had broken ground by showing how fundamental to the operation of the Soviet economy were the often illegal deals done in the factories by staff charged with meeting the current five-year plan's quotas. Berliner and his sympathizers did much to undermine the picture of the USSR as a well-ordered police state.[18]

Yet the totalitarians and their critics were not in conflict with each other on every front; the polemics were in fact waged over only limited sectors of Sovietology—Berliner's preoccupation with micro-level economic relations was more the exception than the norm. Indeed Fainsod and Schapiro shared an unvoiced consensus with Carr and Deutscher about much that went on in the USSR. They concurred that developments at the 'centre' predetermined everything else. They were preoccupied by the policies and personnel of the leadership. They therefore prioritized the study of politics—and high politics at that. They accorded little importance to the middle and lower levels of the Soviet public order. They omitted to investigate large organizations except for the Party; and when they subjected the Party to scrutiny they used central data. They attempted no examination of the working mass of people and their dependants and relatives. And so behind the lines of their many fundamental disputes the most influential scholars of their time started from several common premises. The ferocity of their exchanges as well as the implications of their analyses for 'domestic' politics camouflaged this situation.

[16] Edward Hallett Carr, *The Bolshevik Revolution, 1917–1923* (London: Macmillan, 1950). This is volume 1 of Carr's multi-volume *History of Soviet Russia*, of which later volumes were written with R. W. Davies.

[17] Isaac Deutscher, *The Prophet Armed: Trotsky, 1879–1921* (London: Oxford University Press, 1954); *The Prophet Unarmed: Trotsky, 1921–1929* (London: Oxford University Press, 1959); *The Prophet Outcast: Trotsky, 1929–1940* (London: Oxford University Press, 1963).

[18] Joseph Berliner, *Factory and Manager in the USSR* (Cambridge, MA: Harvard University Press, 1957).

Consequently many critics of the totalitarian model offered a description of the operation of the Soviet state and society which to a large extent overlapped the description given by the totalitarianists: there was little discrepancy in the two sides' pictures of how the USSR was constructed and ruled. Furthermore, terminological controversy held little appeal for Carr and Deutscher. Neither invented a word or phrase to counterpose totalitarianism. The result was that totalitarianism as a term dominated public debate to a greater degree than would otherwise have been the case; and when writers started in the mid-1970s to rethink questions of Sovietology, the tendency was for them to pick out the totalitarian model for special challenge.

Among the most incisive critics of totalitarianism in those years were T. H. Rigby, Moshe Lewin, and Jerry Hough. Rigby pioneered the investigation of clientelism and local political groupings.[19] Lewin, benefiting from Khrushchev's campaign to drive an interpretative wedge between the policies of Lenin and Stalin, resuscitated the discussion about the possibility of alternatives to the course taken by Soviet politics after Lenin's death.[20] The post-war fields of academic debate were at last being reploughed. Jerry Hough looked at the powers exercised by provincial party committee secretaries. Like Rigby, Hough contended that political affairs in the 'localities' had some autonomy from the wishes of the central leadership.[21] Also growing in scholarly popularity was the idea that Soviet Communism had not been predestined to adopt a severely authoritarian shape. Following up Lewin's insistence that Lenin's last writings broke with the dictatorial propensity of Bolshevism, Stephen Cohen's biography of Bukharin suggested that a more humane and democratic form of socialism would have been feasible if only Bukharin rather than Stalin had won the struggle to succeed Lenin.[22] These writers rejected the totalitarian model while at the same time repudiating or declining to adopt the positions developed by Carr and Deutscher.

Carr responded to this with a dismissive review of Cohen's arguments. Increasingly, however, the most recent generation of scholars gave priority to the offensive against the totalitarianists and treated Carr and Deutscher gently. Politics played a part in this. Deutscher and Carr had sympathy with the aspirations of the Bolsheviks in the October Revolution of 1917. Many younger scholars accepted that the Bolsheviks may have acted desirably or at least understandably in overthrowing the provisional government and introducing socialist policies through a revolutionary government led by themselves. Along with this

[19] See Thomas H. Rigby, *Political Elites in the USSR: Central Leaders and Local Cadres from Lenin to Gorbachev* (Aldershot: Elgar, 1990) and *The Changing Soviet System* (Aldershot: Elgar, 1990).

[20] Moshe Lewin, *Lenin's Last Struggle* (London: Faber, 1969).

[21] Jerry Hough, *The Soviet Prefects: The Local Party Organs in Industrial Decision-Making* (Cambridge, MA: Harvard University Press, 1969).

[22] Stephen F. Cohen, *Bukharin and the Bolshevik Revolution: A Political Biography, 1888–1938* (New York: A.A. Knopf, 1973).

was a widespread dislike for the current foreign policies of the leading Western powers, and opposition to the US military in Vietnam was extensive. Scepticism about the West's self-image, furthermore, inclined a growing number of writers to suggest that not every aspect of the Soviet self-image should be repudiated as false.

The eagerness also arose to enquire how much the history and politics of the USSR might be studied in a comparativist framework. Totalitarianism had been elaborated specifically as a theory demarcating the USSR and Nazi Germany entirely from other modern types of state and society. By contending that the USSR should be examined as much for its similarities as for its dissimilarities to its US rival superpower, the newer authors detonated an explosion of intellectual and political discussion. Comparativism was hardly a new phenomenon. Carr had always insisted that the USSR was subject to the universal pressures of societies undergoing industrialization. Even Carr's position was far from being a novel one. The Russian émigré 'Change of Landmarks' group in the 1920s had long ago proposed that the USSR, albeit in an idiosyncratic fashion, was following a general path of economic and social modernization. Non-Sovietologists from the 1960s gave a further impetus to this analysis. Barrington Moore wrote about the social roots of differing routes to the same economic modernity[23]; and Daniel Bell claimed to be able to discern a 'convergence' in the orders of politics and economy in the USSR and the United States.[24]

Thus there arose a polarity between the totalitarianists, original and current, and a younger generation which claimed that the long-overlooked aspects of the Soviet past and present should be incorporated in Sovietology. These aspects included non-central political and economic affairs and general sociology. In historical studies the new trend was frequently referred to as 'social history' or 'history from below'; its exponents were sometimes designated as 'revisionists'. There was no equivalent nomenclature in contemporary studies, but a sense of common purpose existed between the historians and social scientists involved.

A response was not long in coming. Schapiro regarded the onrush of publications as a sign of political and moral degeneration.[25] He was not alone. Richard Pipes too was aghast at recent developments in historical and political debate and attacked them in several works.[26] Robert Conquest, whose *The Great Terror* had appeared in 1968, exhibited similar disquiet.[27] Schapiro treated Lenin's ideas

[23] Barrington Moore, *The Social Origins of Dictatorship and Democracy: Lord and Peasant in the Making of the Modern World* (London: Allen Lane, 1967).
[24] Daniel Bell, *The End of Ideology: On The Exhaustion of Political Ideas in the Fifties* (New York: Free Press, 1962).
[25] Leonard Schapiro, *1917: The Russian Revolution and the Origins of Present-Day Communism* (Hounslow: Maurice Temple Smith, 1984).
[26] Richard Pipes, *Russia under the Bolshevik Regime: A Concise History of the Russian Revolution* (London: Fontana, 1995).
[27] Robert Conquest, *The Great Terror* (London: Macmillan, 1968).

as having been intrinsically important (as well as wrongheaded) whereas Pipes preferred to trace the connections between Bolshevik practices and the practices of the tsars; and Schapiro found a successor in Martin Malia, who stressed the importance of communist ideology to the course of Soviet history.[28] Conquest's work avoided the details of this internal totalitarianist controversy—and with his eclectic approach he secured readership unrivalled in size by any Sovietologist since Carr. Schapiro, Pipes, Malia, and Conquest defended the analytical validity of the totalitarian model with vigour.

The 'revisionists' produced a sparkling profusion of interesting studies. Certain aspects of the Soviet experience acquired extraordinary attention. The workers and, to a lesser extent, the peasants and non-Russian groups in 1917 were scrutinized.[29] Bolshevik local party committees in revolution and civil war were investigated.[30] Such studies sought to show that the lower social orders were active—and not just passive recipients of the ideas of Bolshevik politicians— in the months when Bolshevism was establishing itself in power. The rationality of 'ordinary' people was insisted upon; and the argument was put that the pressure of workers and peasants itself contributed to the changing content of Bolshevik policies. There was also work on the social basis of the Soviet order in the 1930s. From this issued the contention that Stalin, far from simply instigating a 'revolution from above' against the aspirations of most working people, was relieving those deep pressures in society which had not yet been tackled by the Bolsheviks since the October Revolution.[31] Thus the Soviet order before the Second World War was represented as having done much to achieve the primordial purposes of Bolshevism, especially through the promotion of newly trained administrators to high office.

Even the personal role of Stalin underwent reconsideration. J. Arch Getty made the case that Stalin had been more a power broker in the Politburo than a domineering leader. The conventional interpretation of the Great Terror had ascribed the greatest responsibility to him. Getty instead suggested that Stalin had had to decide between two strong factions in the Communist Party leadership which were in dispute about the pace of industrial growth, the efficiency of Party administration, and the desirability of reinforcing repression.[32]

[28] See Martin Malia, *Russia Under Western Eyes: From the Bronze Horseman to the Lenin Mauso- leum* (Cambridge, MA: Harvard University Press, 1999).

[29] Ronald Suny, *The Baku Commune: Class and Nationality in the Russian Revolution* (Princeton, NJ: Princeton University Press, 1972); Stephen.A. Smith, *Red Petrograd: Revolution in the Factories, 1917–1918* (Cambridge: Cambridge University Press, 1983); Diane Koenker, *Moscow Workers and the 1917 Revolution* (Princeton, NJ: Princeton University Press, 1981); Orlando Figes, *Peasant Russia, Civil War* (Oxford: Clarendon Press, 1989).

[30] Robert Service, *The Bolshevik Party in Revolution: A Study in Organisational Change* (London: Macmillan, 1979).

[31] Sheila Fitzpatrick, *The Russian Revolution* (Oxford: Oxford University Press, 1982).

[32] J. Arch Getty, *Origins of the Great Purges: The Soviet Communist Party Reconsidered, 1933–1939* (Cambridge: Cambridge University Press, 1985).

There were also influential works on contemporary politics and society. The Party's provincial committee secretaries continued to be one of the most densely studied features of the Soviet order. Another prominent topic was Soviet political culture and its pre-revolutionary antecedents in the USSR.[33] Investigations were undertaken of whole social and national groups; their result was to indicate that customs and attitudes endured despite successive attempts by the authorities to change them.[34] The unamenability of the economy to deep political control was demonstrated, at least at the point of industrial and agricultural production.[35] Accounts of clientelism, regionalism, and corruption became commonplace.[36] There was growing recognition of the pressures on supreme leadership to meet popular demand for material goods.[37] The general effect was to suggest that the Kremlin ruled a people which had found innumerable ways to elude official directives. Not everyone went so far as to claim that the USSR and the United States had converging social systems; indeed few writers were convinced of this. But many felt that there was sufficient evidence that the 'totalitarian' model misdescribed the Soviet order. And several revisionist writers were Americans: the appearance of an academic monolith in the United States was shattered.

Revisionism was paralleled and reinforced by work done especially in West Germany and Italy. The Italian scene was particularly interesting. Giuliano Procacci, a leading Communist Party member, founded a school who sought to prove that the October Revolution had not predestined Russia to severe authoritarian rule.[38] Associated with the Eurocommunist tendency in west European Marxism, some of these scholars were intent on proving that the course of Soviet history would have been better if only Bukharin had won the struggle for the political succession in the 1920s. The school associated itself too with the dense type of empirical research pioneered by E. H. Carr (who, as it happened, repudiated the constructive potential of Bukharinism[39]).

This interest in the 'alternatives' to the actual course of Soviet historical development was warm in the rest of western Europe and North America. It was suppressed by the authorities in Communist states despite the fact that Stalin

---

[33] Stephen White, *Political Culture and Soviet Politics* (London: Macmillan, 1979).

[34] Basile Kerblay, *Modern Soviet Society* (London: Methuen, 1983).

[35] Among the most interesting contemporaneous analyses was Archie Brown and Michael Kaser (eds.), *Soviet Policy for the 1980s* (London: Macmillan, 1982).

[36] Thomas H. Rigby, *The Changing Soviet System* (n. 19); Michael Voslensky, *Nomenklatura: The Anatomy of the Soviet Ruling Class* (London: Bodley Head, 1984).

[37] George Breslauer, *Khrushchev and Brezhnev as Leaders. Building Authority in Soviet Politics* (London: Allen & Unwin, 1982).

[38] See for example Francesco Benvenuti, *The Bolsheviks and the Red Army* (Cambridge: Cambridge University Press, 1988); Fabio Bettanin, *La Fabbrica del Mito. Storia e Politica nell' URSS Staliniana* (Naples: Edizioni Scientifiche Italiane, 1996); Anna di Biagio, *Le Origini dell' Isolazionismo Sovietico. L'Unione Sovietica dal 1918 al 1928* (Milan: F. Angeli, 1990); Alberto Ponsi, *Partito Unico e Democrazia in URSS. La Costituzione del '36* (Rome: Laterza, 1977).

[39] See n. 23.

had been denounced in the USSR since Khrushchev's closed-session speech to the Twentieth Party Congress in 1956. The official line was that the course of socialist development had been unbroken and positive despite all the damage done to the country by Stalin. An exception to this were the pieces by Roy Medvedev which inclined, not without vacillation, to the idea that Bukharin rather than Stalin should be regarded as Lenin's most appropriate successor.[40] Medvedev's work, however, was banned from publication under Brezhnev; he remained a dissident until his rehabilitation by Gorbachev's *perestroika* in the late 1980s. Yet his books reached the West and were translated into foreign languages, and he became an inspiration to the Eurocommunists in Italy, Spain, and France. The Bukharin biography by Stephen Cohen, himself no communist, also entered the literature of Eurocommunism.

As the ossification of the Soviet political system proceeded in the 1970s, several Western social scientists turned to enquiring whether there genuinely existed a prospect of reform in the USSR once Brezhnev left office. Attention was turned on the leading candidates for the succession. Two writers, Archie Brown and Jerry Hough, were confident that if the Politburo chose the appropriate person, fundamental changes could quickly be made to the Soviet order. Brown at an early stage identified Mikhail Gorbachev as the potential reformer-in-chief. Both Hough and Brown drew attention to the pile of difficulties needing rapid resolution in the USSR and to the frustrations felt by middle ranking Party officials while Brezhnev and his fellow gerontocrats held on to life and power; and Brown stressed that the mechanisms of highly centralized rule would give Gorbachev an unrivalled opportunity to act decisively if he were indeed to become Party General Secretary.[41]

Such works challenged any notion that the Soviet order was static and incapable of self-development, and traditional expositions of the totalitarian model came under renewed attack. But if the model as customarily understood was open to criticism, what was to take its place? Here there was significantly less work. The revisionists had a greater eagerness to demolish the model using newly discovered empirical material than to delineate a theoretical alternative. To that significant extent, books and articles were written in a self-limiting spirit. For example, historians and social scientists noted that institutional conflicts were inherent in the entire Soviet order and that policies were framed by leading politicians in line with the interests of the institutions they headed. This was the line taken by Sheila Fitzpatrick in history and Jerry Hough in contemporary political analysis. Occasionally the term 'bureaucratic pluralism' was given an airing. Only T. H. Rigby

[40] Roy Medvedev, *Let History Judge: The Origins and Consequences of Stalinism* (London: Macmillan, 1972).

[41] See J. Hough's revised edition of Fainsod's *How Russia is Ruled*, published as Jerry Hough and Merle Fainsod, *How the Soviet Union is Governed* (Cambridge, MA: Harvard University Press, 1979); Archie Brown, *The Gorbachev Factor* (Oxford: Oxford University Press, 1996), where the importance of Gorbachev was retrospectively summarized.

made a comprehensive attempt at reconceptualization with his suggestion that the USSR was a 'mono-organizational society' with elements of extreme centralization of rule, clientelism, cultural traditionalism, and eradication of most institutions of 'civil society'.[42]

Rigby's was the most ambitious attempt to articulate a replacement for the totalitarian model. It merited scrutiny not least because it sought to blend diverse aspects of the Soviet order which recent academic works, including his own, had identified as basic and constant since the October Revolution. Its weakness was in its blandness. 'Mono-organizational society' gave little impression of the USSR red in tooth and claw, of the KGB, the Gulag, and the enduring impact of the Great Terror of 1937–8. Furthermore, 'mono-organizational society' listed features without ranking them in order of importance. And lastly it implied— without expressly saying so—that several features of the 'mono-organizational society', especially clientelism, was what prevented the USSR from becoming a totalitarian one. I shall return to this last point in particular in due course. For the moment my aim is to indicate that even this most sophisticated of endeavours to reconceptualize the Soviet order made it appear rather inoffensive. That order requires an appellation which more strikingly encapsulates the sufferings of millions of people under a state intent on penetrating the most rudimentary aspects of daily life.

One of the problems of most revisionist writings, in any case, was their misreading of the use of the model by its exponents. Several innovative studies in the totalitarianist tradition, such as the early monographs of Robert Conquest and Merle Fainsod, had in fact stressed that cracks existed in the USSR's monolith.[43] This was also true of their general works (such as Fainsod's *How Russia is Ruled* and Schapiro's *The Communist Party of the Soviet Union*). They had drawn attention to the ceaseless dissension about policy and hierarchical position among the Kremlin leaders. In practice, then, the totalitarianists had treated the model as a Weberian-style ideal type which was useful for analytical purposes while being only partially realized in any known country.

Some supporters of the model went still further than this. Among them were Geoffrey Hosking and Archie Brown. Hosking in his history of the USSR contended that pre-revolutionary attitudes of faith, nationhood, and intellect survived in the Soviet decades and functioned as an impediment to the Politburo's commands.[44] His argument was that the degree of totalitarianism changed under successive rulers, having been at its most intense under Stalin. Brown found the model applicable only to the decades immediately before Stalin's death. He maintained that Khrushchev's loosening of the political system and his reduction

[42] Thomas H. Rigby, *The Changing Soviet System* (n. 19).
[43] See in particular Robert Conquest (n. 14) and Merle Fainsod, *Smolensk under Soviet Rule* (Cambridge, MA: Harvard University Press, 1958).
[44] Geoffrey A. Hosking, *A History of the Soviet Union* (London: Fontana, 1985).

of the security police's arbitrary powers meant that the Soviet order ceased to be totalitarian and became better described as extremely authoritarian.[45] By this means he introduced a dynamism to the periodization of the Soviet decades. The diverse approaches of Hosking and Brown succeeded in incorporating the empirical data and analytical insights of the revisionist school while accepting the validity of theoretical legacy of the totalitarianists.

The blending of these two post-war scholarly traditions is an appropriate route towards an understanding of the Soviet order between 1917 and 1991—and the time is overdue for each tradition to recognize the useful contribution made by the other. Blending alone, however, is insufficient without an assessment of the actual operation of totalitarian systems of rule. Here the task is to evaluate the schizoid nature of the USSR. It may be summarized as follows: (a) The Soviet order was regulated to an exceptional degree in some sectors while eluding central political control in others. (b) Behind the façade of Party congresses and Red Square parades there was greater disobedience to official authority than in most liberal-democratic countries—and the Kremlin's panoply of dictatorial instruments was incapable of altering this situation. (c) Informal and mainly illegal practices pervaded the Soviet Union. (d) Clientelist politics and fraudulent economic management were ubiquitous and local agendas were pursued to the detriment of central policies. (e) Misinformation was systematically supplied to superior bodies in each institution. (f) Lack of conscientiousness at factory, farm, and office was customary. (g) Deep popular scepticism was widespread.[46] Such features had lasted in the Russian Empire for centuries. But far from fading, they were strengthened under Communism and characterized the Soviet order for its entire existence.

What, I think, is required is a drastic reworking of the totalitarian model. The problem is that the model as customarily deployed takes it for granted that the many forms of opposition and non-compliance in the USSR constitute evidence of the incomplete condition of totalitarianism. This judgement is of course shared by the revisionist school of thought. But there is another way of interpreting the evidence. Undoubtedly opposition and non-compliance were the object of disapproval by the central political leadership throughout the Soviet decades— and often the leadership launched campaigns of discipline and repression to eliminate them.

This sometimes led to purges from the Party under Lenin, mostly involving mere expulsion from the ranks; but in the 1930s and the 1940s the 'cleansing' was accompanied by terror. Throughout the years after the October Revolution, furthermore, institutions were established to inspect and control other institutions. A central determination existed to set quantitative objectives to be attained

---

[45] Archie Brown (n. 41).
[46] See Moshe Lewin, *The Making of the Soviet System* (London: Methuen, 1985) and Thomas H. Rigby, *The Changing Soviet System* (n. 19).

by local government and Party bodies in economic and political affairs. Stalin followed Lenin by resorting to exhortations, instructions, and outright threats and gave preferential promotion in public life to those showing implicit obedience to them. Lenin killed many fewer people in the process even though he continued to use immense violence after the civil war. But repression and compulsory mobilization were standard features of the Soviet order throughout the years before the Second World War; intrusive political campaigns were recurrent and exaggerated rhetoric was employed as the regime, centrally and locally, tried to impose its wishes within the structure of the order created since the October Revolution. Being determined to maintain and develop that order, Lenin and Stalin used such methods of authoritarian control as were available to them.

These measures were the product of the leadership's perceptions of the opportunities and risks facing them at the time. They were not entirely successful. The measures themselves induced individuals, institutions, and nations to strive after a quiet life. Evasiveness and downright disruption were locally fostered. This in turn impelled the central leadership to strengthen the intrusiveness of official campaigns—and the trend did not disappear with Stalin's death. Khrushchev and even Brezhnev tried to insert dynamism into public life through campaigns for higher economic quotas and for renewed ideological commitment. There was an ineluctable logic to the process so long as the leadership aimed to preserve the compound of the Soviet order intact. Soviet leaders lacked the aura of legitimacy conferred by multi-party elections; they were also bereft of the useful channels of information embodied in pluralist politics and free media. The leadership had little option, short of transforming the system of power (as Gorbachev did from the late 1980s), but to use peremptory methods to achieve its objectives.

Even as dominant a ruler as Stalin, however, eventually had to have an eye for the internal necessities of the system. In ending the Great Terror in late 1938, he was motivated to a considerable extent by the recognition that the bloody purges of the previous couple of years had come close to undermining the foundations of state power. The chaotic carnage had become politically and economically counterproductive for him.

The Soviet order was anyway continuously imperilled, to a greater or less degree, by both popular dissatisfaction and dissatisfaction among the ruling elites. Stabilizing ingredients had to be introduced, and rewards were provided to be used as well as punishments. The attempt at stabilization started soon after 1917 with the introduction of a tariff of privileges for the officials of Party and government. Before the October Revolution there had been a tension in Leninist thought between hierarchical methods and egalitarian goals; but as soon as the communists actually held power, the choice was persistently made in favour of hierarchy. Officialdom did not have entirely its own way. Far from it: in the late 1930s the life of a politician or an administrator became a cheap commodity. But the general tendency to give high remuneration to this stratum of the population was strengthened. The young promotees who stepped into dead men's shoes were also occupying their homes and using their special shops and special hospitals. Social equality had become the goal of an ever-receding future, and Marxist professions of egalitarianism sounded ever more hollow: from Stalin to Gorbachev they were little more than ritual incantations.

Once Stalin had died, the ruling elites endeavoured to protect their power and material privileges from erosion by the central leadership. Khrushchev's boisterous campaigns of sackings as well as his drastic institutional reorganizations were among the reasons why his fellow leaders were acclaimed for sacking him in 1964. Brezhnev introduced a policy of 'stability of cadres'. Over his long period of dominance the informal and illegal patterns of administrative practice became ever more overt. Andropov made a brief attempt to reassert full central control against corruption and disobedience at lower levels of the Party and government. Gorbachev resumed this campaign in 1985 but, unlike Andropov, he chose to rely on an expansion of open discussion and elective procedures. Predictably the ruling elites were annoyed by Gorbachev's initiatives; his fall from power in 1991 was regretted by few of their members. Even though the USSR was dismantled, the old Soviet elites proved able to protect their interests in 'the transition to the market economy' accelerated by Yeltsin and Putin. Yeltsin recognized the pragmatic necessity to avoid direct conflict with the former *nomenklatura*; and although Putin has picked off individual super-wealthy businessmen, he has held back from any consistent campaign against the corrupt beneficiaries of marketization.

Thus the sinews of the Soviet order had the robustness to withstand assault not only by successive Communist Party leaders but also, to a considerable extent, by post-Communist presidents. That order combined the formal with the informal, the official and constitutional with the unofficial and indeed the unplanned and illicit. Such dualism was fundamental in the entire course of the Soviet history. And the unofficial, unplanned, and illicit features of existence in the USSR were not 'lapses' or 'aberrations' from the essence of totalitarianist state and society: they were integral elements of totalitarianism. Perfect—or even semi-perfect—formal totalitarianism is a chimerical practical goal.

Caution is also required about periodizing the decades between 1917 and 1991. Totalitarianism was not immediately installed. The Soviet state and its people were enveloped in civil war and administrative disorder after the October Revolution. It took until early 1919 before most of the basic features of the governing order were put in place; and some took further years to be added. For example, the comprehensive preventive censorship authority—*Glavlit*—was not created before 1922. It is equally true that most of the lingering aspects of totalitarianism had been undermined by 1989 and that the Soviet state and its people were subsumed in an immense process of transformation a couple of years before the USSR's irreversible collapse. Gorbachev's political and cultural policies undid the cement of the traditional order. In the intervening seven decades, however, there was a cardinal continuity in political dictatorship,

economic regulation, social mobilization, and cultural control. And if this radically reworked version of the totalitarian model is used, it is hard to resist the
conclusion that greater continuity than discontinuity characterized the Soviet
order across its history.

This was a judgement to which, eventually, Gorbachev subscribed. Having
come to power with a commitment to reform, he decided that only radical
transformation would be adequate; and although he retained a subjective fondness
for Lenin and Leninism, in practice he acted to destroy the Leninist legacy. In
doing this, he behaved as if something basically rotten entered the body politic of
Russia much earlier than Stalin's assumption of personal power in the 1930s.
Russia's troubles, of course, predated 1917. But a drastically defective way of
dealing with that heritage was introduced by Lenin and his party in the October
Revolution and the civil war. Leadership initially played a crucial part in
spreading the flaws to the operation of public administration, the economy, and
society. Individual leaders through their decisions had an impact in preserving
and consolidating the state. Sometimes their decisions harshened or lightened
conditions for administrators, workers, and indeed the leaders themselves. But the
leaders generally accepted that the Soviet order's survival required them to desist
from fundamental attacks of its basic features.

This was an insight which caused little controversy among those astute
early émigré observers of the Soviet order. They agreed—Yuly Martov, Nikolay
Trubetskoy, Nikolay Ustryalov, Leon Trotsky, and Fedor Dan—that the ascendant leadership was highly centralist and authoritarian in Russia. Their disputes
revolved around questions about the connections of this leadership to the country's past and about the likely future developments. All concurred, though, that
the underbelly of the body politic in the USSR was filled with corruption,
cynicism, and unreliability. Further disputes occurred after the Second World
War as Merle Fainsod, Leonard Schapiro, E. H. Carr, and Isaac Deutscher
adjusted their arguments in the light of the Soviet victory over Nazism and its
resumed economic developments. It was the merit of the revisionists to show that
these post-war debates had played down the difficulties of the central political
leadership in increasing its control over its people throughout the Soviet decades;
and the newer work examined the Soviet order's underbelly more assiduously
than had been done by the pre-war émigrés. But for too long the polemics between
the totalitarianists and the revisionists have dominated theoretical work on history
and social science in Sovietology. Both sides have contributed much; both also
have shortcomings. For an understanding of the basic nature of the Soviet
order—and of the role of leadership within it—it is essential to use, blend, and
develop their best insights.

5

Russian Corruption and State Weakness in Comparative Post-Communist Perspective

Leslie Holmes

In his first media briefing following his re-election as Russian president, Vladimir Putin claimed that one of the major achievements of his first term of office was that there had been 'without any doubt' a strengthening of the state. He also claimed that he would continue to fight corruption.[1] In a real sense, the two points are linked. Corruption can be both symptomatic of, and a contributory factor to, a weak state. These two phenomena—corruption and state weakness—and their interaction will be a key theme in this chapter. Putin's own statements and actions will be analysed in the context of Vladimir Shlapentokh's contentions that 'Putin's position on corruption is an enigma for the whole world'; that Putin had essentially done nothing after two years in office to combat corruption; and that the Russian state has actually been *weakened* under the current president.[2] Given the widespread agreement that the Russian state was very weak in the later Yeltsin era, such a claim is controversial.

A second, related theme is that Putin's approach to corruption reflects the ambiguity of his leadership style, and helps to explain why analysts *still*—in Putin's second term of office—find it difficult to agree on the nature and direction of his leadership. While some, such as Shlapentokh and Lilia Shevtsova, see Putin as weak and indecisive, others see him as authoritarian.[3] Perhaps he is neither, but forced by the Russian situation to act in ways that can appear enigmatic, ambiguous, even contradictory. Russia is a society in which there is too little faith in

---

[1] 'Vstrecha s zhurnalistami v izbiratel'nom shtabe po okonchanii vyborov Prezidenta Rossii', 15 March 2004, online at http://president.kremlin.ru/text/appears/2004/03/61835.shtml, accessed March 2004. Much of the data and information cited in this paper are the result of research into 'Corruption and the Crisis of the State', funded by the Australian Research Council (Large Grant No. A79930728).

[2] Vladimir Shlapentokh, 'Russia's acquiescence to corruption makes the state machine inept', *Communist and Post-Communist Studies*, 36/2 (2003), 159, 160.

[3] Ibid.; Lilia Shevtsova, *Putin's Russia* (Washington, DC: Carnegie Endowment for International Peace, 2003), *passim* and esp. 141–3 and 172–3. Reflecting Putin's own ambiguity, Shevtsova *also* sees him as authoritarian (ibid. 4, 221). The concepts of democracy and authoritarianism are considered later in the chapter.

democracy, too little centrist politics, too little culture of compromise, too much faith in strong leaders, too much lawlessness, and an underdeveloped civil society. Attempting to bring order *and* democracy to such a society, at the same time as one is trying to enhance the state's economic performance, legitimacy, and sense of self, would be a major challenge for anyone. Attempting to do that while also being sensitive to the fact that one's efforts are being described as either inadequate or authoritarian is extraordinarily difficult, and should be recognized as such.

Many Russians were relieved and optimistic when Putin was officially elected president in March 2000, believing that at last they had a strong leader who would steer their country away from almost a decade of confusion, humiliation, and false starts. Indeed, many hoped Russia would once again become a strong state; for them, Putin was to be a saviour, and they identified with a comment he made at his inaugural speech in May 2000—'We want our Russia to be a free, prosperous, rich, strong and civilized country, a country of which its citizens are proud and which is respected in the world'.[4] But other Russians, as well as a number of external observers, feared that the type of leadership Putin appeared to represent, and too much emphasis on a strong state, could return Russia to authoritarianism, possibly even dictatorship.[5] This chapter locates recent developments in Russian leadership politics within the context of post-Communist leadership and state-building more broadly. It is maintained that those who hoped Putin would turn Russia into a strong state underestimated the scale of the task, while those who believe Putin is inherently authoritarian have underestimated the need for strong leadership in contemporary Russia. The scale and nature of the tasks Putin still has before him help to explain apparent ambiguities in his leadership.

The argument is structured in four principal parts, most of which include a comparative post-Communist dimension. The first provides a brief comparison with other post-Communist states of two policy areas that have concerned those who fear Russia is deviating from the democratization path, namely Putin's treatment of the mass media and his approach to political parties. Are Russian developments in these areas so different from what is happening in countries now considered to be consolidating democracy?

Second, the reasons for the weakness of the Russian state since the collapse of Communism are examined, and compared with the situation in other post-

---

[4] The full speech is available in English at http://news.bbc.co.uk/1/hi/world/monitoring/media_reports/739432.stm (reaccessed March 2004).

[5] For an example of a previous optimist about Russia's democratization prospects changing his position in light of developments under Putin, see Michael McFaul, 'Vladimir Putin's Grand Strategy . . . for Anti-Democratic Regime Change in Russia', *Weekly Standard*, 9/10 (17 November 2003). On the need for a strong state in Russia, but also the possible dangers under certain circumstances, see e.g. Stephen Holmes, 'What Russia Teaches Us Now: How Weak States Threaten Freedom', *American Prospect*, 8/33 (1997), 30–9; Leslie Holmes, 'The Democratic State or State Democracy? Problems of Post-Communist Transition', *Jean Monnet Chair Papers*, 48 (Florence: European University Institute, 1998); Thomas Remington, 'Russia and the "Strong State" Ideal', *East European Constitutional Review* (hereafter *EECR*), 9/1–2 (2000), 65–9.

Communist states. While some aspects of Russia's weakness are unique, others are not unlike the position of other transition countries. For example, all faced severe difficulties in attempting to privatize and marketize economies in the near-absence of indigenous bourgeoisies.

The third main topic is corruption. While others in this volume, notably William Tompson, analyse the oligarchs, the focus here is on corruption in the various state organs, and the extent to which this has contributed to, or is reflective of, the weak state. Putin's declared emphasis on the rule of law is interrogated in the context of the actions he has taken to combat corruption. Once again, his approach and policies are compared with those in other post-Communist states.

Fourth, and building on the previous three sections, a theoretical section examines the connections between coercion, legitimacy and the strength of the state. It is argued that the balance between coercion and legitimacy is not always a zero-sum game. This is followed by the conclusions, in which Shlapentokh's arguments are evaluated, and the difficulties facing Putin emphasized. Putin has been attempting to reconcile differences that are deeper in Russia than in any other post-Communist state, and this should be more widely recognized. The conclusions also advocate a customized, relativistic, and dynamic approach to Russia's transition, rather than one based on Western ideals, expectations, and conditions.

Two Key Policy Areas

Before considering two areas of Putin's leadership that have led to suggestions that he is becoming (or already is) authoritarian, it is necessary to specify how the terms democratic and authoritarian are used in this chapter. Entire books have been written about each concept; here, only brief guidelines can be provided for the purposes of the argument. The minimalist (or Schumpeterian) approach on the distinction is attractively simple—democracy requires competitive elections and universal suffrage, authoritarianism does not, and is undemocratic.[6] This is a useful starting point, but is insufficient. Another approach focuses on the balance between coercion and legitimacy. A democratic system will employ *some* coercion, but will focus on the need to maximize the legitimacy of the political arrangements. It does this through testing its own right to rule—not only through elections, but also independent political surveys, free mass media, and granting citizens the right to protest openly. Authoritarianism will typically employ a higher level of coercion and be less concerned with genuine testing of its own legitimacy. Arguably just as important as either of these criteria is the notion of

[6] See, for instance, Samuel P. Huntington, *The Third Wave: Democratization in the Late Twentieth Century* (Norman: University of Oklahoma Press, 1991), 7–13.

the rule of law. In a democracy, laws provide predictability, as well as a form of citizen equality, since even strong leaders are bound by the rules.[7] Authoritarian systems override or ignore such rules in an essentially *arbitrary* manner when it suits them; while parliaments might formally ratify changes to rules, they rarely do so independently of the authoritarian leader. Nor do they seriously challenge the leader.

In the real world, many systems do not fit neatly into either of these categories—which are ideal types—and are located somewhere along an axis between them. Hence, a level of subjectivity is involved in categorizing a particular system, in terms both of where to locate it on the axis, and determining the point at which being closer to the democratic end of the spectrum is crossed into being closer to the authoritarian. While some states (consolidated democracies; dictatorships) are clearly located near or at one end of the spectrum or the other, many are in a contested position.

The Mass Media

While minimalist theorists believe that democracy is basically about competitive elections, most analysts maintain that it involves much more. One of the many additional features of a genuine democracy is independent mass media able to conduct their own investigative journalism. During the Yeltsin era, the process of opening up the Russian media that had already commenced under Gorbachev in the final days of Soviet power developed substantially, so that most observers considered the Russian media to be relatively free. But Putin has clamped down on the media, so that they are now under much greater centralized state control than they were in the 1990s.[8] One way in which this can be demonstrated, and compared with the situation in other post-Communist states, is to consider the Freedom House rankings of media freedom in the post-Communist states in 1994 and 2003; this is done in Figure 5.1.

In Figure 5.1, countries are scored according to three variables—legal environment, political influences, and economic pressures. Individual countries are assessed by Freedom House on each variable to form a composite score out of 100; the higher the score, the less freedom of the press there is perceived to be. Russia slipped from the 'partly free' to the 'not free' category in the space of a decade. This was in contrast to most post-Communist states, which either improved their ranking, or else did not descend into a lower overall category (i.e., free, partly free, or not free); of the twenty-seven states listed by Freedom House, only Armenia, Kazakhstan, Kyrgyzstan, and Ukraine were in a similar position to Russia. Thus,

---

[7] For a controversial analysis of the links between democracy and the rule of law, see Joseph Maravall and Adam Przeworski (eds.), *Democracy and the Rule of Law* (Cambridge: Cambridge University Press, 2003).

[8] For an early claim that Putin was tightening his grip on the media, see Oleg Panfilov, 'Glasnost under Siege: Putin and the Media—No Love Lost', *EECR*, 9/1–2 (2000), 60–4.

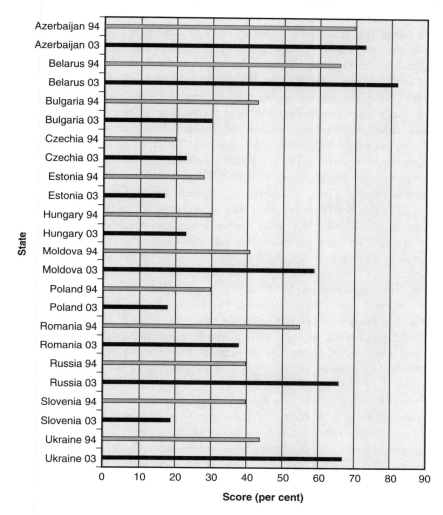

Figure 5.1. Freedom House Press Freedom Rankings of Selected Post-Communist States, 1994 and 2003.
Sources: Based on Freedom House Annual Survey of Press Freedom Rankings 1994–2002 (online at www.freedomhouse.org/research/pressurvey.htm) and Karin Karlekar, *Freedom of the Press 2003* (Lanham, MD: Rowman & Littlefield, 2003), 10–11.

only CIS states have deteriorated over the past decade; no CEE state has been relegated to a worse overall classification.

In fairness, the Freedom House scores for Russia began to slip already in the mid-1990s; but they remained in the lowest category of 'partly free' until 2003, when the score slipped substantially (10 per cent) from 60 (2002) to 66. Freedom

House justifies this reclassification primarily in terms of three factors.[9] The first was a formal (i.e. sanctioned by both houses of parliament) tightening of censorship in November 2002, following some critical reporting of the Moscow theatre hostage crisis in October; this was the main reason for the deterioration of the 'legal environment' score.[10] In terms of 'political influence', the forced closure in January 2002 of the only remaining independent television broadcasting company, TV-6, was a major factor contributing to the worsening image of media freedom. Finally, although the print media are still primarily in private ownership, most are in the hands of a small number of oligarchs. Yet those oligarchs who have in recent years been perceived by the Russian authorities to have challenged Putin—notably Gusinsky and Berezovsky in 2000, Khodorkovsky in 2003—have suffered the consequences. Thus, the remaining oligarchs know that they should not be overly critical of the Putin regime if they are to retain control of their newspapers and magazines. In what in a sense is a version of a *matrioshka* doll, the oligarchs exert pressure on their journalists through the formers' ownership of the print media, but the oligarchs are in turn subject to political pressure from the Putin regime.

The Putin government has been subjected to international criticism for its tighter control over the mass media, but has sought to justify its position by reference to the special and new situation in Russia. Thus Russian media minister Mikhail Lesin argued in April 2002 at the National Press Club in Washington, DC, that it was inappropriate to expect the Russian media to meet US standards of journalism, and that they were experiencing understandable 'growing pains'.[11]

There is no question that several other post-Communist countries have experienced serious problems of state interference in the mass media. Even relatively liberal Hungary has been subject to censorship and interference of a type and scale that is of concern in countries allegedly democratizing.[12] But such examples have for the most part been temporary or less blatant than in

---

[9] Karin Karlekar, *Freedom of the Press 2003* (Lanham, MD: Rowman and Littlefield, 2003), 129.

[10] The legislation basically forbade the media from questioning actions taken by the Russian state against terrorism. Under pressure from several newspaper editors, Putin eventually vetoed the legislation; but this occurred too late to impact upon the Freedom House ranking. Additional legislation restricting the media—this time, in connection with election campaigns—was passed in June 2003; but it was subsequently vetoed by the Russian Constitutional Court (S. Glasser, 'Russian Court Throws Out Election Coverage Restrictions', *Washington Post*, 30 October 2003).

[11] *RFE/RL Newsline*, 10 April 2002.

[12] However, it should be noted that the Hungarian Constitutional Court has passed down various rulings that have limited the government's capacity to control the media—see e.g. *EECR*, 4/3 (1995), 11; 4/4 (1995), 14; 8/4 (1999), 22–3; 9/1–2 (2000), 18–19; and Laszlo Sólyom and Georg Brunner, *Constitutional Judiciary in a New Democracy: The Hungarian Constitutional Court* (Ann Arbor: University of Michigan Press, 2000), esp. 239–45. The 1996 Law on Radio and Television sought to reduce political interference; but subsequent developments revealed several loopholes in the legislation.

Russia.[13] The countries in which state interference in the media has been significant and sustained are mostly autocracies, in some cases even dictatorships, such
as Turkmenistan, Belarus, or Slovakia during the second Mečiar era (1994–8). If
Russia is to avoid being widely perceived as authoritarian, the current state control
of the media will have to prove to be more akin to the Hungarian 'blip' than the
ongoing Belarusian situation.

The Law on Political Parties[14]

When a new law on political parties was passed in Russia in July 2001, a number of
commentators interpreted it as another sign of the increasing moves towards
authoritarianism or even dictatorship under Putin.[15] After all, the law was overtly
intended to reduce the number of political parties in Russia. However, the
assumption that this was yet another indication of Putin's desire to return to the
days of Russian autocrats or dictators, be they tsars or Communist Party General
Secretaries, must be questioned. Putin spent much of his early career in Germany,
and speaks fluent German. He is aware of the significance of the Weimar
Republic. A major cause of the collapse of that republic was the existence of
many small parties in parliament, which rendered it ineffective, as the various tiny
groupings squabbled among themselves. Putin has been determined to avoid this,
and believed that the Duma was relatively weak in part because of the large
number of parties and independent deputies.

The new law has certainly reduced the number of officially registered political
parties in Russia. But any suggestion that the new legislation would reduce their
numbers to a tiny fraction of their former number is contradicted by the facts. As
of August 2003, there had been fifty registrations[16]; this compares with almost
190 parties and political organizations before the introduction of the law.[17] In fact,

[13] In 2002, there were charges that proposed amendments to the media law in Poland were
designed to strengthen government control over broadcast media; but the government's claim that
the amendments were intended to avoid excessive concentration of media ownership was at least
plausible—see *EECR*, 11–12/4 and 1 (2002–3), 39–40. For evidence of concern that Bulgarian
journalists were being excessively muzzled when attempting to investigate and publish claims of
corruption, see *Sofia Echo*, 27 June 2003.

[14] The section on parties has benefited from research into 'Political Party Financing Scandals: An
East-West Comparison', funded by the Australian Research Council (Large Grant No. A00103841).

[15] See S. Lunev in *NewsMax.com*, 6 June 2001—online at http://www.newsmax.com/archives/
articles/2001/6/6/182452.shtml (reaccessed March 2004). The new law is available in English
online at http://www.democracy.ru/english/library/laws/parties_fz95_eng.

[16] *Novosti* online—17 August 2003; accessed August 2003. This figure had already been reached
by January 2003—see the article by Alexander Sadchikov in *Izvestiya*, 31 January 2003; also *Pravda*,
29 January 2003.

[17] A. Ivanchenko, 'New Legislation on Parties' in Yuri Senokosov and John Lloyd (eds.), *Russia
on Russia Issue 5: Administrative and State Reforms in Russia* (Moscow and London: Moscow School
of Political Studies and the Social Market Foundation, 2001), 33. For an analysis of Russia's parties
in the late 1990s, see I. N. Barygin (ed.), *Politicheskie partii, dvizheniya i organizatsii sovremennoi
Rossii na rubezhe vekov* (St Petersburg: Izd. Mikhailova V. A., 1999).

Putin now needs to take the reform one step further if he is serious about enhancing the power of the Duma by reducing its fragmentation. Given the nature of the Russian electoral system, many deputies are formally independents. While the December 2003 elections (the first held under the new party law) resulted in domination by only four parties or blocs—United Russia; the Communist Party of the Russian Federation; the Liberal Democratic Party; and the Motherland Bloc—a number of small parties (The People's Party, Yabloko, and the Union of Right Forces) also secured seats. On their own, these parties have too few seats to play any disruptive role. But a *relatively* large number of independents (76 out of a total of 450 deputies) were also elected. Although their numbers were well down on the 1999 figure of 106 seats, and even though most subsequently aligned themselves with one or other of the major groupings, the fact that they are not subject to party discipline can exert a fragmenting and negative influence on the work of the Russian lower house. It would make sense—and probably be a good thing for democracy—for the Russians to move to a system that encourages tighter party allegiance and discipline. Democracy should never be confused with anarchy.

Several other post-Communist states have either introduced new laws on political parties in recent years (e.g. Romania, 1996; Poland, 1997; Moldova was considering the draft of a new law in early 2004), or else introduced substantial amendments to existing party laws (e.g. Poland 1998; Bulgaria 1998; Moldova 1998 and 2000).[18] While few of these changes were as radical as the Russian, merely comparing party laws is in any case insufficient for assessing the extent to which particular post-Communist governments have sought to consolidate party systems. Electoral laws should also be examined, since changes to these have in many cases been oriented towards a reduction in the number of parties represented in the legislature.[19] Thus, most CEE states have in recent years introduced threshold requirements for representation in parliament; parties that do not reach this threshold are excluded, even though some citizens have voted for them.[20]

[18] Useful starting points for details on parties and party configurations in CEE are Paul Lewis, *Political Parties in Post-Communist Eastern Europe* (London: Routledge, 2000); Paul Lewis (ed.), *Party Development and Democratic Change in Post-Communist Europe: The First Decade* (London: Cass, 2001); and Janusz Bugajski, *Political Parties of Eastern Europe: a Guide to Politics in the Post-Communist Era* (Armonk, NY: M. E. Sharpe, 2002).

[19] The Russian electoral law of 20 November 2002 (175-F3) raised the threshold for representation for parties elected on a proportional representation basis to the 50% of Duma seats in the nationwide multi-member constituency from its current 5% to 7%. Once again, however, various aspects of the change warn against drawing the overly hasty conclusion that it constituted further evidence of a move towards authoritarianism. First, even the liberal Yabloko deputies voted in favour of the change. Second, some deputies had called for a much higher threshold of 12.5%. Third, the law also stipulates that at least four parties must be represented in parliament, even if one or more do(es) not reach the 7% 'cut-off' point. Finally, the 7% requirement in the law was not to become effective until 2007, to allow small parties time to negotiate with others about possible mergers. See *EECR*, 11–12/4 and 1 (2002–3), 44–5.

[20] Thresholds are mostly between 3% and 5%, but can be much higher for coalitions in some countries (up to 20% in the Czech Republic), depending on the number of parties in them.

The recent Russian developments are therefore subject to very differing interpretations, but in themselves do *not* necessarily indicate moves towards authoritarianism. Rather, they can be seen as symptomatic of the problems *many*
post-Communist states have faced in attempting to crystallize party systems.[21]

Russia as a Weak State

The Russian state certainly was weak during the Yeltsin era. This manifested
itself in numerous ways, but, most fundamentally, in that it was incapable of
raising sufficient taxes to function efficiently. This had numerous implications,
including that officers of the state were often not paid in full, or sometimes at all,
for long periods. This undermined their loyalty to their employer, the state, which
in turn resulted both in legitimation problems for the post-Communist Russian
state and corruption (see the next section).[22]

In the introduction, it was mentioned that some aspects of the weakness of the
Russian state under Yeltsin—which Shlapentokh argues has increased under
Putin—were essentially unique. One was the increasing fragmentation and regionalization of such a huge country, which is considered elsewhere in this
volume. Another was the impact of the identity crisis the country experienced
from the early 1990s. This was largely a function of the identity ramifications of
the 'quintuple loss'. In the space of approximately two years, Russia lost its outer
empire (e.g. Comecon and the Warsaw Pact); its inner empire (the rest of the
former USSR); the cold war; its status as a 'superpower'; and its role as the home
of socialism and thus as the premier socialist model. Such a series of losses in so
short a time is without precedent; even empires that collapsed rapidly, such as the
Ottoman and Habsburg, were not recognized as superpowers, which is a relatively

---

[21] See Leslie Holmes, 'Towards a Stabilisation of Party Systems in the Post-Communist Countries?', *European Review*, 6/2 (1998), 239–54. For an argument that Russia had a 'pseudo multi-party
system' and a 'feckless and destructive parliament' under Yeltsin, see Vladimir Ryzhkov, 'Lessons of
the Nineteen-Nineties' in Edward Skidelsky and Yuri Senokosov (eds.), *Russia on Russia Issue 3:
Russia under Putin* (London: Social Market Foundation, 2000), 14. That other countries, even
parliamentary and mixed ones, are still experiencing severe problems in consolidating party systems
can be seen in the Polish and Bulgarian cases. In the former, the party that won the 1997 election did
not gain a single seat in the October 2001 election. In the latter, the 2001 election was won by a 'party'
(*formally*, it was not even a party, but a movement!) that was only months old and headed by
Bulgaria's former king.
[22] For a fascinating analysis of why so relatively few Russians protested against the fact they were
not being properly paid in the 1990s, see Debra Javeline, *Protest and the Politics of Blame: The Russian
Response to Unpaid Wages* (Ann Arbor: University of Michigan Press, 2003). A major reason appears
to have been that many unpaid or underpaid Russians did not know whom to blame for their sorry
condition. While this might be seen as advantageous to political elites, the surveys which form the
core of Javeline's study reveal a widespread mistrust of the state, and cynicism that it could do
anything much to improve the situation. In short, it constitutes further evidence of the low level of
popular legitimacy experienced by the Russian state in the 1990s, as well as its perceived weakness.

new concept that relates *inter alia* to weapons of mass destruction of a type unknown until the middle of the twentieth century.

Given the sheer scope and rapidity of Russia's losses, it is not surprising that so many Russians experienced a form of identity crisis in the 1990s. Many had not even thought of themselves primarily as Russians until the collapse of the USSR (December 1991), identifying at least as much with the much larger unit, the Soviet Union.[23] Part of the explanation for the strong electoral performance of more extreme parties in recent years relates precisely to this identity crisis; whereas some—particularly older—voters have sought refuge in the one party they believe they know from the past (i.e. the Communist), others have rejected the Communist past, but have supported a leader and party (Zhirinovsky and the Liberal Democratic Party) that claims to be able to make Russia great again.

The problems of state-building and nation-building have not been peculiar to Russia. Indeed, many post-Communist states have from some perspectives had more severe problems, in that those that were previously part of a federal state have had to establish (or re-establish) new state loyalties and identities, as well as major new institutions, including ministries of foreign affairs and defence, armies, and diplomatic corps. Moreover, all of the post-Communist states faced similar problems in terms of marketizing and privatizing their economies in the near absence of an indigenous capital-owning class (bourgeoisie); while the '*nomenkla-tura* privatization' appears to have been more widespread and debilitating to the state in Russia than in other countries, it was a common enough problem.

On the other hand, only Serbia lost its de facto dominance of a much larger political unit in a way at all comparable to Russia's situation. But even Serbia did not lose an external empire, an international competition (i.e. the cold war), its role as a superpower, or its role as a model emulated by others. Thus, there were significant ways in which Russia lost far more than any other post-Communist state, and experienced unique state- and nation-building problems. These difficulties were compounded in the mid-to-late 1990s by the poor leadership given by a sick and often inebriated president!

Corruption and Putin's Record

In May 2000, shortly after being officially elected president, Putin publicly repeated the commitment he had made months earlier to the creation of a

---

[23] John Dunlop, 'Russia: In Search of an Identity' in Ian Bremmer and Ray Taras (eds.), *New States, New Politics: Building the Post-Soviet Nations* (Cambridge: Cambridge University Press, 1997), 29. More generally on Russians' post-Soviet identity problems, see Vera Tolz, *Russia* (London: Arnold, 2001), esp. 235–73.

'dictatorship of laws' in Russia.[24] While some saw this as a thinly-veiled reference to the need for a dictatorship plain and simple, such an assumption should not be made too readily. It is equally feasible that this was part of his model of the strong but democratic Russian state. Putin himself had already indicated, in an article published in December 1999 (when he was still prime minister), that he was committed to a strong 'democratic, law-governed, effective federal state', and that he had learnt from history that 'all dictatorships and authoritarian systems of government are transient.'[25] Moreover, given the evidence on the behaviour of the oligarchs (see Chapter 10 of this volume), and on organized crime from the early 1990s,[26] it was appropriate for the incoming leader to commit his government to bringing Russia's lawlessness under control. In this section, we consider one important aspect of this lawlessness, official corruption.

According to the most widely-cited comparative assessment of corruption levels, Transparency International's (TI) annual Corruption Perceptions Index (CPI), Russia is among the most corrupt of the post-Communist states. The 2003 CPI assessed twenty-six CEE and CIS states, out of a total of 133 states of all types; Russia's position among this subgroup was fifteenth (where first position is perceived to be the least corrupt), while it ranked eighty-sixth among all states. Although Russia was considered to be less corrupt than any of the Central Asian CIS states, most of the Transcaucasian ones (apart from Armenia), and Ukraine, it fared worse than all CEE states apart from Serbia and Montenegro, the Republic of Macedonia, and Albania.

Transparency International has been producing the CPI since 1995, but first ranked Russia in 1996 (see Table 5.1).[27] Although there are problems of cross-polity comparability of CPI data from one year to the next, a *general* over-time picture of any given state can legitimately be drawn. Since the mid-1990s, Russia has not only fared poorly in comparison with many other post-Communist states, especially CEE ones, but has failed to make *significant* progress in its own corruption score.

Thus it has moved around in a narrow band; its lowest score (2.1) was in 2000, while its best were in 2002 and 2003, when it scored 2.7.[28] Being charitable, it

---

[24] Putin had already used the term in a speech to officials from the Ministry of Justice at the end of January—*EECR*, 9/1–2 (2000), 37. Putin is aware that the term is unpopular in many quarters (see his 'state of the nation' speech to the Federal Assembly, 8 July 2000), but believes that it is an appropriate term for what he advocates.

[25] Cited in Remington (n. 5), 65.

[26] On Russian organized crime, see e.g. Phil Williams (ed.), *Russian Organized Crime: The New Threat?* (London: Cass, 1997); Federico Varese, *The Russian Mafia: Private Protection in a New Market Economy* (Oxford: Oxford University Press, 2001); and Vadim Volkov, *Violent Entrepreneurs: The Use of Force in the Making of Russian Capitalism* (Ithaca, NY: Cornell University Press, 2002).

[27] Only one post-Communist state—Hungary—was ranked in 1995, and that year has been omitted from Table 5.1.

[28] The CPI is scaled 1–10, in which 1 represents the highest level of corruption, and 10 the lowest. Russia's score thus places it clearly among the highly corrupt countries.

Table 5.1. TI Corruption Scores of Selected Post-Communist States 1995–2003*

	1996	1997	1998	1999	2000	2001	2002	2003
Azerbaijan	n.a.	n.a.	n.a.	1.7	1.5	2.0	2.0	1.8
Belarus	n.a.	n.a.	3.9	3.4	4.1	n.a.	4.8	4.2
Bulgaria	n.a.	n.a.	2.9	3.3	3.5	3.9	4.0	3.9
Czech Rep.	5.37	5.20	4.8	4.6	4.3	3.9	3.7	3.9
Estonia	n.a.	n.a.	5.7	5.7	5.7	5.6	5.6	5.5
Hungary	4.86	5.18	5.0	5.2	5.2	5.3	4.9	4.8
Moldova	n.a.	n.a.	n.a.	2.6	2.6	3.1	2.1	2.4
Poland	5.57	5.08	4.6	4.2	4.1	4.1	4.0	3.6
Romania	n.a.	3.44	3.0	3.3	2.9	2.8	2.6	2.8
Russia	2.58	2.27	2.4	2.4	2.1	2.3	2.7	2.7
Slovenia	n.a.	n.a.	n.a.	6.0	5.5	5.2	6.0	5.9
Ukraine	n.a.	n.a.	2.8	2.5	1.5	2.1	2.4	2.3

*This selection of states is based principally on the availability of over time data (scores).

could thus be argued that, according to these scores, Putin has made a little progress in reducing corruption in Russia. Moreover, while Russia has been improving in the early twenty-first century, countries such as the Czech Republic, Poland, and to a lesser extent Hungary, have been deteriorating. Russia also performs better than several CIS states (although only marginally in many cases, and markedly worse than Belarus). On the other hand, the Russian improvement is modest, and there was no apparent change between 2002 and 2003. In addition, Russia had scored 2.6 in 1996, which makes the improvement look less impressive. Even allowing for the slight progress under Putin and the worsening situation in several Central European states, the latter still emerge as less corrupt than Russia. Finally, given that there are currently only three scores since Putin's first full year in office, it is also too early to be confident of a sustained improving trend.

The TI Index has been criticized on various grounds, including that it is based on perceptions rather than actual experience. In an endeavour to address this issue, researchers from the World Bank have conducted two surveys—in 1999 and 2002—in which owners and managers of enterprises were asked to indicate *inter alia* the percentage of their enterprise's sales or income devoted to bribes (unofficial payments or gifts) to public officials.[29] The interviewers used various methods to reassure respondents that they could not be identified. Nevertheless, it is

[29] These are the Business Environment and Enterprise Performance Surveys, or BEEPS. The 1999–2000 results can be found online at http://info.worldbank.org/governance/beeps/, while the 2002 results (BEEPS II) are at http://info.worldbank.org/governance/beeps2002/. In March 2004, a full-length analysis of the two sets of results was published—see Cheryl Gray, Joel Hellman, and Randi Ryterman, *Anticorruption in Transition 2: Corruption in Enterprise-State Interactions in Europe and Central Asia 1999–2002* (Washington, DC: World Bank, 2004).

reasonable to infer that some respondents *were* apprehensive about providing answers that might result in prosecution. Given this, the somewhat disturbing data provided should be seen as *minimum* figures. Using this methodology, Russia and the CIS states emerged as more corrupt, on average, than CEE states in both 1999 and 2002. In the earlier year, the mean average payment for CIS states was 3.7 per cent, and for CEE states 2.2 per cent. Russia was below the CIS average, at 2.8 per cent, but still well above the CEE average. The averages in both CIS and CEE states were lower in the 2002 Business Environment and Enterprise Performance Surveys (BEEPS), at 1.97 per cent and 1.27 per cent respectively. Russia once again emerged as less corrupt than the CIS average, though still more corrupt than the CEE average, at 1.37 per cent. But, using this completely different methodology, the trend line in Russia—namely, some improvement in the early twenty-first century—is the same as in TI's CPIs. It must be emphasized once again, however, that the timeframe is too short to be reasonably confident that the apparent trend will continue.

Critics of these and other cross-polity surveys sometimes argue that a problem with many of them is that they are not directed by domestic agencies. It is therefore worth considering the results of two of the best known surveys of Russian corruption conducted by Russians; while it must be acknowledged that the first was largely funded by an outside agency (the World Bank), the survey is well regarded by many Russian specialists. The report was published by INDEM in May 2002, although it was based on two large-scale surveys—one of citizens, the other of entrepreneurs—conducted in late-1999 and 2001.[30] The surveys sought *inter alia* the views of citizens and entrepreneurs on the 'corruptibility' of twenty-nine agencies and groups. Some of these were not state bodies (e.g. the Church and environmentalist organizations), and in this sense would be excluded from consideration by most analysts of corruption; but most were.[31] In general, the INDEM surveys revealed a high level of agreement in the rankings of various agencies by the two groups. Unsurprisingly, however, entrepreneurs considered themselves much less corrupt than citizens perceived them to be, whereas they considered trade unions far more prone to corruption than citizens did. The other group or agency over which there was some disagreement was the mass media; entrepreneurs considered the media more corruptible than did citizens. But let us consider the large number of areas in which entrepreneurs and citizens were very much in agreement.

---

[30] Georgy Satarov (ed.), *Diagnostika Rossiiskoi korruptsii: sotsiologicheskii analiz* (Moscow: INDEM Foundation, 2002) (available online at http://64.49.225.236/rc_survey.htm#Russia; accessed January 2003).

[31] I have deliberately omitted consideration here of the meaning of the term corruption, since it is contested and highly problematic. It would thus have detracted too much from the principal focus of this section. Suffice it to say that, for all its problems, the conventional definition—private abuse of public office—is used here. It can be noted that TI used a very similar definition until 2000, but then broadened their approach to include improper behaviour within the private sector (except in CPIs).

According to the INDEM surveys, the most corruptible groups in Russia at the turn of the millennium were the traffic police and political parties.[32] These were followed by parliamentarians (members of the Duma), and then police and customs officers. At the other end of the spectrum, the state agencies perceived to be least corruptible were welfare-related offices, organs of national security, and higher courts. These results are rather similar to those produced by another series of Russian mass surveys, those by the Public Opinion Foundation (POF). These were made available on the Web in January 2002, and are particularly useful since they are longitudinal. So far, the results for three surveys on corruption in Russia—July 1998, March 1999, and January 2002—have been made publicly available. One of the most interesting features is that the relative assessment of different groups remained remarkably stable over the three surveys. As with the INDEM findings, 'police, customs and law enforcement agencies' emerge as the most corrupt agencies, closely followed by 'the courts, prosecutors' and 'the traffic police'.[33] Thus, it appears that most Russians consider the law-enforcement and law-adjudicating agencies the most corrupt branches of the state. Perhaps Putin should have called for a dictatorship *over* the law!

There is a serious legitimacy problem for a state in which most citizens do not have confidence in the agencies that are supposed to uphold the law. These findings also have major implications for the notion of the strong or weak state. For instance, it appears from a survey commissioned by the author and conducted by the leading Russian survey organization VTsIOM in mid-2000 that an over-whelming majority of Russian citizens believed at the time that there was a close connection between organized crime and corrupt officials. When asked how close they believed the connections were between organized crime and official corrup-tion, 43.5 per cent of respondents answered 'very close', while an almost identical percentage, 43.2 per cent, answered 'close'. Thus, according to this survey, almost 87 per cent of Russians perceived there to be a close or very close connection

---

[32] It is worth noting here that when TI introduced a new cross-polity (that is also intended to become longitudinal) analysis of corruption in 2003—the TI Global Corruption Barometer—there was a remarkably consistent pattern across most of the forty-seven countries (of all types, and in all continents) surveyed. Thus, in almost three-quarters of them (33 out of a total of 44; the question was apparently not posed in three others), the agency in which the highest percentage of citizens most wanted to eliminate corruption was political parties. On this issue, Russia was in line with the majority of states. In four of the other post-Communist states surveyed (Bosnia and Hercegovina, Republic of Macedonia, Poland, and Romania), citizens likewise ranked political parties top of their wish-list for eliminating corruption; in Croatia, parties were ranked third behind medical services and courts, while in Georgia they were ranked fourth behind medical services, courts, and the police. The second and third choices on the Russian respondents' wish-list were the police and medical services. The full results are available online at www.transparency.org/surveys/barometer/dnld/barometer2003_release.en.pdf.

[33] The POF results can be found at http://english.fom.ru/virtual/frames and were accessed by the author in January 2003. Unfortunately, political parties were not included in the POF surveys as a discrete category.

between organized crime and corruption.[34] Whether or not such a perception bore much relationship to reality—and this cannot be determined—is not ultimately important; the significant point is that any state in which the citizens hold such beliefs has a serious legitimacy problem.

So does the evidence suggest that Putin has been serious about reducing corruption in Russia—and therefore, by implication, increasing the state's legitimacy? Shlapentokh is quite correct that the Russian authorities under Putin have on occasions turned a blind eye to corruption. Moreover, from some perspectives, the new (acting) president made a bad start, since his very first official act in December 1999 was to issue decree 1763 granting an amnesty to Yeltsin.[35] But while this could be seen as having condoned corruption, it could also be interpreted as indicative of Putin's desire for closure—to look forward, rather than to the past. Such a sympathetic interpretation could only be justified if Putin's subsequent actions suggest he has been actively attempting to deal with corruption.

In comparison with Yeltsin, Putin has engaged little in anti-corruption campaigns.[36] But this is sensible. Most analysts of corruption agree that anti-corruption campaigns are often not merely ineffective, but counterproductive. Such campaigns have to be short, infrequent, and be able to demonstrate tangible results; otherwise, citizens treat them as not merely irrelevant, but indicative of weakness, incompetence, or—arguably worse—mere rhetoric from leaders anxious to deflect attention from their *own* corruption. In short, unless they are clearly exercising a positive effect, anti-corruption campaigns lead to popular cynicism and delegitimation. Putin's approach has been to focus more on improving existing laws or introducing new ones, structural changes, firmer application of the law, and incentives.

New legislation has been introduced under Putin, sometimes rapidly, to close loopholes conducive to corruption; after all, corruption is often in part a function of inadequate or ambiguous legislation. Following criticism from the OECD's Financial Action Task Force (FATF) in June 2001 that Russia still had no

[34] The omnibus survey was conducted by VTsIOM in July 2000; N was 1000, of a nationally-representative sample. Given the comparative nature of this chapter, readers may be interested to know that the aggregate Russian figure of nearly 87% compared poorly with Bulgarian, Hungarian and Polish results for surveys conducted at about the same time; respectively, these were c. 56% (*N* = 1870, conducted by Vitosha), c. 60% (*N* = 1526, conducted by Tárki), and c. 54% (*N* = 1066, conducted by CBOS). All results here are based on inclusion of the 'don't know' category.

[35] Many have linked the timing of Yeltsin's resignation and Putin's first decree to the Mabetex corruption scandal surrounding Yeltsin and his daughters. See e.g. *Economist*, 8 January 2000, 17.

[36] Although Luc Duhamel maintains that the last anti-corruption campaign in Russia was launched in 1982 ('The Last Campaign Against Corruption in Soviet Moscow', *Europe-Asia Studies*, 56/2 (2004), 187), Ariel Cohen has noted that Yeltsin launched no fewer than seven anti-crime campaigns, targeting both corruption and organized crime, between 1991 and mid-1994 alone—see his 'Crime Without Punishment', *Journal of Democracy*, 6/2 (1995), 40. The POF surveys referenced in n. 33 indicate that Russian citizens also see campaigns as being of little use in fighting corruption.

anti-money-laundering laws, legislation was rushed through the Russian parliament in July 2001; this became effective in February 2002. Once the FATF had been persuaded that the new laws were really being implemented, Russia was removed from its 'List of Non-Cooperative Countries and Territories' in October 2002.[37] Indeed, Russia's progress in this area was considered sufficient for it to be granted observer status in February 2003, and full membership of the FATF in June 2003.[38] Another piece of legislation designed to combat corruption was an August 2002 decree on increasing transparency in the state bureaucracy by providing new and clearer guidelines on integrity and conflict of interest.

Putin has introduced a number of structural changes designed to address the issues of corruption (and its frequent bedmate, organized crime), casting further doubts on Shlapentokh's claim of the do-nothing president. According to the United States' Drug Enforcement Administration, 'Low- and mid-level regional corruption is one of the primary reasons President Putin created Russia's Federal District system in 2000'.[39] Another change was to bolster the work of the National Anti-Corruption Committee (NAK), which was first established in 1999, and is a committee of the Duma.[40] And in November 2003, Putin decreed the formation of a new council to fight corruption. The council comprises the prime minister, the leaders of both houses of parliament, and the heads of the Constitutional, Supreme, and Arbitration courts. Once a year, the general prosecutor is to provide a report to the council, which has then to brief the president. Various commissions for combating corruption (including resolving conflicts of interest) are to work with the council.

Fighting corruption is difficult in all countries. Corruption often has no obvious victims to report it; the unfortunate citizens who are required to pay bribes to obtain goods or services to which they should have free and ready access, for instance, are typically nervous about reporting the corrupt official for fear of being punished themselves for breaking the rules. Where citizens do not fear punishment, they may fear revenge from corrupt officials (or other criminals) if they testify in court. Hence, the introduction of a witness protection scheme—Russia's first—in Moscow in February 2002 was a welcome step in the fight against crime, including corruption.[41]

Several post-Communist states with serious corruption problems have considered and in some cases introduced various kinds of amnesty; they include Albania,

[37] Russia was in fact not far behind several other post-Communist states in terms of legislation targeting money-laundering. For instance, Poland and Slovakia only passed such legislation in October 2000 (*TI Newsletter*, March 2001, 9).

[38] Bureau for International Narcotics and Law Enforcement Affairs, *International Narcotics Control Strategy Report 2003* (Washington, DC: US Department of State, 2004), online at http://www.state.gov/g/inl/rls/nrcrpt/2003/vol2/html/29931.htm.

[39] Drug Enforcement Administration, 'Heroin Trafficking in Russia's Troubled East', *Drug Intelligence Brief*, October 2003, 7.

[40] *Izvestiya*, 6 October 2000.

[41] Russian television, cited in *RFE/RL CCW*, 28 February 2002.

Kazakhstan, Poland, Romania, and Ukraine. In addition to that granted to his predecessor, Putin offered a form of amnesty to the oligarchs at a July 2000 meeting. Since this does not relate directly to corrupt officials, it will not be explored in detail here.[42] However, it suggests that Putin is flexible and radical enough to 'think outside the circle' on occasions in attempting to deal with serious problems. The meeting was also of symbolic importance in terms of corruption. Just as the Chinese leadership reached the conclusion by the 1990s that they could not seriously reduce corruption among 'flies' (lower-ranking officials) unless they made examples of some leading corrupt 'tigers' (senior officials), so Putin's move could be seen on one level as designed to set an example. It is a reasonable assumption that lower-level corrupt officials will think twice about continuing with their antisocial behaviour if they see a new leadership clamping down on more powerful people further up the chain; proposing an amnesty for past actions, but tougher action in the future, could be seen to have sent such a message.

China's determination to make an example of corrupt 'tigers' has resulted in some *very* severe punishments, including the death penalty. The treatment of senior Russian officials found guilty of corruption during the Putin era has sometimes been harsh in comparison with the Yeltsin era, but not as extreme as in China. In April 2000, for example, Rear Admiral Vladimir Morev was sentenced to eight years' imprisonment for attempting to sell radar equipment for the rather modest sum of approximately $3,000.[43]

According to the 'grandfather' of comparative corruption studies, Arnold Heidenheimer, one of the most effective ways of reducing corruption is to increase state officials' salaries to a level where they are much less tempted to be corrupt; he often cites Singapore as an exemplar in this regard.[44] Putin has recognized the value of this approach, and in April 2004 decreed substantial increases for some 10,000 of Russia's federal state officials, linking this explicitly to his fight against corruption.

Finally, Putin has claimed that some of the major personnel changes he has introduced relate to his fight against corruption. When he named Mikhail Fradkov as his new prime minister in March 2004, for example, the president mentioned that Fradkov's experience in the Security Council and as head of the tax police (2001–3) meant that his new premier had 'thorough experience in fighting corruption'.[45]

[42] See the chapter in this volume by Tompson. For conflicting views on the July 2000 meeting, see E. Dikun, 'The Kremlin changes the Oligarchs' Diapers.... For which they thank the President', *Prism* (online), 6/8 (31 August 2000); D. Jensen, 'Russia: Analysis of Putin's Meeting with Tycoons', *RFE/RL*, 28 July 2000; S. Lambroschini, 'Russia: Oligarch Meeting Offers Few Results', *RFE/RL*, 28 July 2000; and Alexander Tsipko, 'Will Putin Confiscate the Oligarchs' Property?', *Prism* (online), 6/8 (31 August 2000).

[43] *Vladivostok News*, 19 May 2000.

[44] A. Heidenheimer, 'Introduction' in Duc Trang (ed.), *Corruption and Democracy* (Budapest: Institute for Constitutional and Legislative Policy, 1994), 18.

[45] *Interfax*, 1 March 2004.

Unfortunately, many of the positive steps just outlined have a downside. For example, the August 2002 decree was only advisory, and tougher, follow-up legislation is needed.[46] The body established in November 2003 was only a consultative organ and first met in January 2004, so it is too early to assess its impact. And the April 2004 increase in salaries was only for approximately 3 per cent of federal officials, mostly senior ones; hence, while it might succeed in reducing corruption in the upper echelons of the state bureaucracy, it could exacerbate the problem at the lower levels if it increases a sense of 'them' and 'us'.[47]

There are other disappointing aspects of Putin's approach to corruption. One is that the 'Public Reception Centres' established by the National Anti-Corruption Committee in 1999, and intended *inter alia* to encourage public whistleblowing against corrupt officials, were shut down by late 2000, allegedly because of inadequate funding.[48] Another is that the number of officials investigated, prosecuted, and convicted for corruption almost certainly remains very low.[49] While comprehensive up-to-date Russian statistics on this did not appear to be publicly available at the time of writing, recent data from the Russian Far East may be indicative. In 2003, Russian Interior Minister Boris Gryzlov revealed that 151 cases of bribery were registered in the region in 2001 and 2002, of which twenty resulted in prosecutions, and even fewer in convictions. In fact, only one person was sent to prison as a result of the investigations and court cases![50]

At first sight, one of the most disappointing aspects of Putin's putative commitment to reducing corruption is that he allegedly resisted a draft bill successfully passed through its first reading in the Duma in early October 2003. The draft was introduced by deputy Nikolay Gonchar, with the approval of the National Anti-Corruption Committee, and was designed to permit legislators to investigate alleged wrongdoings, including corruption, by senior state officials.[51]

[46] However, knowledge of what happens elsewhere is relevant in assessing this decree. Thus, what has been seen as the first set of international recommendations on fighting corruption, those produced by the OECD in 1994 to combat bribery, was only advisory too. It took several years to progress this to a stage where its successor document became binding (February 1999), and even longer before the legislatures of a majority of signatory states ratified it. Hence, Putin is not alone in finding it difficult to push through effective anti-corruption legislation quickly.

[47] This is not the *only* possible effect. A 'cleaner' senior bureaucracy could set a positive example to those working at lower levels. Only time will tell which of the two scenarios eventuates.

[48] *Izvestiya*, 6 October 2000. It is possible that there were other reasons, however. One is that the centres were less effective than had been hoped for; international experience suggests that many citizens fear the repercussions of open whistleblowing, preferring the 'safety' of anonymous actions.

[49] For evidence to this effect from the Yeltsin era, see V. Luneev, *Prestupnost' XX Veka: Mirovie, regional'nye i rossiiskie tendentsii* (Moscow: Norma, 1997), 277–8.

[50] Cited in B. Lintner, 'Spreading Tentacles', *Far Eastern Economic Review*, 166/39 (2 October 2003), 56. Once again, however, Putin's lack of success here needs to be contextualized; most Western states also find it very difficult to prosecute officials for corruption, largely because of the problems involved in obtaining hard evidence of wrongdoing.

[51] See Yelena Rudneva's article in *gazeta.ru*, 8 October 2003 (online at http://www.eng.yabloko.ru/Publ/2003/I-NET/031008_gazeta_ru.html).

But once again, this development can be interpreted in quite different ways. Admittedly, many deputies from the pro-Kremlin parties did not vote, since they were absent from parliament that day. It must also be acknowledged that the chances of the bill proceeding to a second reading were greatly reduced by both the October result (i.e. deputies opposed to the bill would likely turn up for a second reading) and then the changed composition of the Duma from the end of 2003. Nevertheless, the fact that it was accepted, against Putin's wishes, by a parliament that, even as it was constituted prior to the December 2003 parliamentary elections, was claimed by some to be too deferential towards Putin, is hardly evidence of an authoritarian regime.

Endorsing the last point is the fact that, although Putin is said to want this bill adopted, the long-awaited and long-debated anti-corruption bill has still to be passed by the Duma. The draft law took eight years to reach its first reading, partly because Yeltsin had publicly criticized an earlier version, produced by a working committee of the Duma's Security Committee, for being too harsh and wide-ranging.[52] Such criticism sends the wrong message if a leadership is serious about wanting to reduce corruption. Putin did not make such criticisms. The fact that the draft bill passed its first reading in November 2002, but then floundered once again, constitutes another example of the type of delay in adopting important legislation that indicates deep divisions within parliament and frustrates the president. The delay also sends a wrong message about the commitment to fighting corruption. But such frustration for the president hardly testifies to authoritarianism.

How does Putin's record compare with other post-Communist leaders' attempts to combat corruption? As noted, the perceived levels of corruption have been increasing recently in countries such as the Czech Republic and Poland. Several other post-Communist leaders have made the fight against corruption a top priority; but nearly all have sooner or later been judged to have either failed, or to have been less successful than citizens had hoped. Three prominent examples are former Presidents Stoyanov (Bulgaria), Shevardnadze (Georgia), and Constantinescu (Romania).[53] Thus in comparative terms, and despite his mixed record—no really senior corrupt officials are in prison—the fact that Putin may have made modest headway in the fight against corruption in Russia puts him ahead of many of his peers. Given that the problem is in various ways more difficult to control in Russia, *inter alia* because of the sheer scale of the country, this is an achievement of sorts.

---

[52] Vitaly Nomokonov, 'On Strategies for Combating Corruption in Russia', *Demokratizatsiya*, 8/1 (2000), 126–8.

[53] The public disappointment may have been particularly inappropriate in the Bulgarian case. As suggested by the Bulgarian scores in Table 5.1, the country has been making steady progress in recent years. This has been recognized by the World Bank, which has praised Bulgaria (as well as Latvia and, perhaps more surprisingly, Romania) for its anti-corruption measures.

Coercion, Legitimacy, and the Strength of the State

The relevance of legitimacy to the issue of the strong state, mentioned earlier, can now be considered. Our initial premise is that power in *any* state is exercised through a mixture of coercion and legitimacy. Quite what a strong state means will vary, according to the relative mix of legitimacy and coercion. In a state in which power is exercised primarily through coercion, a strong state is a repressive one. Conversely, in a relatively legitimate state, strength refers more to effectiveness. Thus a strong state can be either authoritarian or democratic. But it would appear to follow from the point made above about the legitimacy levels in Russia in mid-2000 that, if a strong state exists there, it must be a repressive one.

However, it is crucial to note the caveat 'if a strong state exists'. Yeltsin's Russia was a *weak* state that neglected many of its responsibilities. Its leader was a metaphor for the system he headed; during the 1990s, the president became weaker (and possibly corrupt), in both literal and figurative senses. If this generalized picture is accepted, the important point can be made that the rela-tionship between legitimacy and coercion is *not* necessarily a zero-sum one. It is both theoretically possible and empirically demonstrable that a state can simul-taneously enjoy low levels of legitimacy and exercise relatively little coercion.

Once this point about a non zero-sum situation is accepted, the obverse should also be seen as a possibility, albeit as an atypical situation. Thus the legitimacy of a state can in some situations be enhanced by a regime that increases coercion levels. From this perspective, Putin's various measures designed to make the state stronger—whether through administrative centralization,[54] tighter control of what could be seen as insufficiently responsible media, dealing with the oligarchs, or clamping down on corruption—do not *necessarily* represent authoritarianism. If most citizens want such developments, and have shown in democratic ways that they do, then power is being exercised in a way that can enhance legitimacy.

However, although a state can in certain circumstances simultaneously increase both coercion and its own legitimacy, there are conditions attached if an increase in coercive power is not to be indicative of growing authoritarianism. First, and as suggested at the end of the previous paragraph, there must be some form of genuine popular control of the more coercive regime. At the very least, and in line with minimalist theories of democracy, there must be regular, genuinely competitive elections. In the case of Putin's Russia, parliamentary elections were held on schedule in December 2003. The fact that the party most closely associated with the president won those can be seen as indicative of the popularity of Putin and his approach. The presidential elections held in March 2004 resulted in a landslide win for Putin (more than 70 per cent for him in the first—and hence

---

[54] See the chapter in this volume by Melvin; also Cameron Ross, 'Putin's Federal Reforms and the Consolidation of Federalism in Russia: One Step Forward, Two Steps Back!', *Communist and Post-Communist Studies*, 36/1 (2003), 29–47.

only—round), but *were* contested.[55] Hence, using the minimalist approach, the Russian electoral situation does not indicate authoritarianism. But what of our other criteria, arbitrariness and the rule of law? In briefly addressing this issue, it is worth considering developments in other post-Communist CIS states that suggest a concrete indicator for assessing whether or not future Russian developments are likely to result in authoritarianism or a legitimate strong democratic state.

One clear indication that Putin really was becoming more authoritarian and moving away from the rule of law would be if he were to emulate many of the Central Asian leaders in holding a referendum designed to prolong his term of office beyond the second four-year one (i.e. beyond 2008). According to the currently valid (1993) Russian Constitution, a president may only serve a maximum of two full terms of office (akin to US regulations). Any suggestion that Putin is attempting to circumvent this temporal limitation on his presidency should be taken as evidence of an attempt to move Russia to authoritarianism, possibly even dictatorship.[56] Equally, moves to delay parliamentary elections would, unless justified by a real crisis situation such as war, constitute concrete evidence that Russia was moving away from its current imperfect and incomplete democracy. Attempts to change the constitution so as to further upgrade the position of the presidency would be a third clear indicator.

Let us now consider the *effectiveness* of the Russian state, which can also be an important indicator of 'strength'. It appears that Russian officials are now being paid in full and on time. As noted above, some groups have also received substantial pay increases under Putin.[57] Thus, to the extent that corruption is sometimes a genuine coping mechanism, this change under Putin is likely to be part of the reason for the apparent improvement in Russia's corruption situation in the early 2000s. However, the *culture* of post-Communist corruption—to borrow a term popularized by Miller, Grødeland, and Koshechkina[58]—had by the early 2000s become well-entrenched in Russia, which helps to explain why the

---

[55] Admittedly, none of the other candidates running for the presidency had a particularly high political profile. In this sense, Putin faced little real competition. But there is a cause and effect issue here. It appears that most potential higher profile candidates decided that they stood little chance of defeating the popular Putin, so opted not to run against him. Putin surely cannot be blamed for this, especially as he did not in any meaningful sense campaign for himself.

[56] In early February 2004, a number of Russian deputies openly suggested that the term of the Russian presidency be extended to seven years (see *Russia Journal* online, 6 February 2004); this proposal had apparently first been mooted in late 2003. Putin's initial reaction was to reject it, claiming that such a move would be controversial and thus destabilizing to Russia. It remains to be seen whether or not the president's reaction was a cleverly staged ploy—i.e. that he was hoping that pressure would mount for such a constitutional change, so that he could benefit from such an extension of his powers without appearing to have promoted it himself.

[57] In November 2001, the Deputy Minister of Internal Affairs announced a pay rise for traffic police officers. However, there was a sting in the tail; the rise was to be funded largely by reducing the number of officers by 15–20% (*RFE/RL*, 28 November 2001). Perhaps Lenin's notion of 'better fewer, but better' was considered apposite here!

[58] William Miller, Åse Grødeland, and Tatyana Koshechkina, *A Culture of Corruption: Coping with Government in Post-Communist Europe* (Budapest: Central European University Press, 2001).

improvement has apparently been modest, and may even have stalled.[59] Given this, it becomes clearer why Putin has become more draconian in dealing with both the oligarchs and corrupt officials. If an amnesty (suggestive of an initially soft approach) does not work, it may be appropriate to use tougher measures. Several oligarchs appear not to have adhered to the agreement made between them and the president in July 2000. As for corrupt officials—Putin could well become tougher in his treatment of them if Russia's reputation for corruption does not continue to improve. The president understands that both the domestic and international legitimacy of the Russian state and his regime are affected by perceptions of corruption levels. He also knows that foreign investment can be discouraged—with negative implications for economic growth and eudaemonic legitimation—if a country is widely perceived to be highly corrupt. A responsible leader *should* attempt to reduce corruption.

Conclusions

It should by now be clear that Putin's position on corruption is less enigmatic than Shlapentokh claims; that the president has taken some measures to address the problem; that the Russian state has in many ways been strengthened in the early 2000s; and that there are some encouraging—though not outstanding—results in Russia's fight against corruption. More could and should be done. But given the resistance from powerful vested interests in Russia, Putin has to steer a difficult path between a tougher anti-corruption policy and charges of becoming increasingly authoritarian. This said, clamping down on corrupt officials, or on multi-millionaires who have made their fortunes in questionable ways and at the expense of ordinary Russians, should not in itself be perceived as moving towards authoritarianism.

But are there other ways in which Russia is becoming authoritarian? In a recent article, Levitsky and Way argue that there can be *competitive* authoritarianism, and that Putin's Russia constitutes an example of this—while Webster and de Borchgrave liken Russia to the early years of the Fifth French Republic, which they describe as 'democratic authoritarianism'.[60] Carothers characterizes Russia as close to being in a category he calls 'dominant power politics', in which there

---

[59] Both Shlapentokh (n. 2), esp. 152–3, and Shevtsova (n. 3), 8, argue that Russians now consider corruption 'normal'. But this term needs to be problematized. There is an important normative distinction between being genuinely indifferent to something on the one hand, and, on the other, learning to live with it because of a feeling of helplessness to do anything about it.

[60] S. Levitsky and L. Way, 'The Rise of Competitive Authoritarianism', *Journal of Democracy*, 13/2 (2002), 52; William Webster and Arnand de Borchgrave, 'Foreword' in W. Webster (ed.), *Russian Organized Crime and Corruption: Putin's Challenge* (Washington, DC: Center for Strategic and International Studies, 2000), xiv–xv. For another comparison between Putin and De Gaulle, but that also emphasizes the limitations of this, see Shevtsova (n. 3), 172.

are 'most of the basic institutional forms of democracy', but also domination by one political grouping.[61] Such concepts testify to the confusion that exists in interpreting contemporary Russia. They are also incompatible with the minimalist approach to authoritarianism; while this does not in itself disqualify them, given the broader approach adopted here, they are problematical when applied to contemporary Russia. This can be demonstrated by reference to the three criteria spelled out at the beginning of the section on the media and political parties.

The evidence suggests that, while Russia is clearly further from the democratic end of the spectrum than Western states, it has not yet crossed the point at which it is closer to the authoritarian. It still conducts competitive elections at regular and timely intervals, and suffrage is near-universal. Putin is concerned about legitimacy; and while the level of coercion is much higher than in most Western systems, and the media unquestionably less free (for which Putin deserves to be censured), the latter can and do still criticize the president on occasions, and have been supported by the Constitutional Court as recently as October 2003.[62] Putin has not yet clearly overridden the constitution on significant issues; and it has been shown in this chapter that, in the fight against corruption, he does not invariably get his own way.

Nor has the president clearly sought to put himself above the rule of law. In fact, Putin currently compares favourably in this regard not only with the clearly dictatorial Lukashenko in Belarus, the Ukrainian leadership in recent times, or even Yeltsin (especially during late 1993), but also some Western leaders, notably Italy's Berlusconi. He is also more concerned than any of these other leaders with both his own and his country's image and acceptance by the rest of the world.

This is not to claim that Russia has a consolidated democracy; that would be not merely naive, but wrong. Rather, it is to argue two points. First, Russia currently remains marginally closer to the democratic end of the spectrum than to the authoritarian. Second, it would be less confusing if we were to use a simple axis between democratic and authoritarian ideal types, along which individual countries can be located (and shifted, as changes occur), rather than continue to attempt to devise new labels—some of which are oxymoronic—to describe putative groupings of changing and different individual countries.

What further elements of Putin's rule encourage commentators to argue that Russia is moving towards authoritarianism, or is already there? In a December 2003 issue, the *Economist* analysed the results of the recent Russian parliamentary elections in terms of 'the slow death of democracy'.[63] Such language is punchy and sells, but is not necessarily accurate. The article maintained that some of the 2003 parliamentary election results were manipulated in various ways, and may have been fraudulent. But the main point was that 'the centre' was in decline in Russian parliamentary politics, which it considered ominous.

[61] Thomas Carothers, 'The End of the Transition Paradigm', *Journal of Democracy*, 13/1 (2002), 11–13.

[62] While the practical significance of this should not be exaggerated, its *symbolism* was important.

[63] 'Putin's Way', *Economist*, 13 December 2003, 22–4.

In an oft-cited observation, Barrington Moore argued in the 1960s that democracy would not take root in societies lacking a bourgeoisie.[64] Putin realizes that
if democracy and the rule of law are to establish firm and deep roots in Russia, the
country needs to develop a solid and respectable middle class (bourgeoisie). At
present, this class is still far too small, leading Richard Rose to describe Russia as
an 'hourglass' society, and possibly explaining in part the decline of the centre that
so concerned the *Economist*. There remains too much of a 'them-and-us' attitude,
in which there exist plenty of horizontal linkages and networks, but all too few
vertical ones.[65] The poor electoral performance of parties that would normally be
expected to represent democracy-oriented middle-class groups is one indication
of Russia's unusual social structure.

Thus, there is little doubt that, from the perspective of democratization, the
poor showing of parties such as Yabloko and SPS in the 2003 elections was a
concern. However, it should be noted that research conducted by John Dryzek,
Tatyana Rogovskaya, and this author in 1996–7—to cite just one source—suggested that democracy in Russia was *already* in trouble, long before Putin became
leader.[66] There were already too many losers in the new order, who resented the
small elite of significant winners, and associated 'democracy' with injustice.[67] The
winners were seen as having essentially bought up the state—or, to use the term
preferred by the World Bank, engaged in 'state capture'.[68] This point casts
Putin's leadership and approach in a different light, and leads us away from
overly-deterministic analyses that see authoritarianism or even dictatorship as
the most likely outcome of recent developments under Putin.

If a population is cynical, and civil society underdeveloped,[69] a strong leader
backed by an effective state can help to increase a new system's institutionalization

[64] Barrington Moore, *Social Origins of Dictatorship and Democracy* (Harmondsworth: Penguin,
1967), 418.

[65] Richard Rose, 'Russia as an Hour-Glass Society: A Constitution without Citizens', *EECR*, 4/3
(1995), 34–42.

[66] John Dryzek and Leslie Holmes, *Post-Communist Democratization: Political Discourses across
Thirteen Countries* (Cambridge: Cambridge University Press, 2002), esp. 92–113.

[67] Whilst this was also true of many other countries analysed for the book detailed in the previous
footnote, there was one important difference between them and Russia. This was that there was at
least one group of respondents—one discourse—in most countries who still believed in and were
committed to the *concept* of democracy; their disappointment was with their politicians' poor
implementation of the concept, rather than with the idea itself. But Russians did not, in general,
appear to recognize this distinction.

[68] On this see Joel Hellman, Geraint Jones, and Daniel Kaufmann, 'Seize the State, Seize the Day:
State Capture, Corruption, and Influence in Transition', *World Bank Policy Research Working Papers*,
2444 (2000); see also V. Ganev, 'The Dorian Gray effect: winners as state breakers in postcommu-
nism', *Communist and Post-Communist Studies*, 34/1 (2001), 1–25. Weber's notion of a respectable
business class acting as a check on states has little resonance in contemporary Russia.

[69] On the sorry state of civil society in most post-Communist states, including Russia, see
Marc Howard, *The Weakness of Civil Society in Post-Communist Europe* (Cambridge: Cambridge
University Press, 2003). In his May 2004 inauguration speech, Putin made the development of civil
society a key objective of his second term; the full speech is available in English in *Johnson's Russia
List*, No.8199, 7 May 2004.

and legitimacy, which can have positive knock-on effects for civil society, and hence democracy in its more meaningful (non-minimalist) sense. Although it should be fairly obvious, two basic points about post-Communist civil society are often overlooked. One is that it takes time for civil society to emerge following decades of authoritarian Communist rule. The other is that the pace of this emergence will depend partly on how well the particular post-Communist society is functioning, in terms both of introducing new institutions and of facilitating legislation, and the economy. If either of these—let alone both of them—falters, the development of civil society is likely to be much slower and more troubled. In the 1990s, under Yeltsin, both *did* falter, and Russian civil society's development *was* troubled. This was the legacy with which Putin has had to deal. In order to overcome it, Putin needed to strengthen the state and grow the economy; the former requires the latter. But the stronger state also needs to ensure that it and society—not oligarchs, corrupt officials, or criminals—benefit from that growth.

Whilst this is not the place to examine the details, it is worth noting that Putin has taken significant steps to stimulate the economy. These include the introduction of a land reform (clearer laws on land ownership are likely to stimulate investment), and both reducing and simplifying personal and corporate taxation. His simplification of the tax laws may be criticized from various perspectives, including the socially regressive effects of a flat rate personal income tax system.[70] On the other hand, their introduction has three likely ramifications that are potentially beneficial for strengthening the state and increasing its legitimacy. One is that tax collection becomes easier, so that state revenues should increase.[71] Second, the simplified system substantially narrows the scope for officials to exercise individual discretion, which in turn reduces opportunities for corruption; assuming this results in lower perceived levels of corruption, state legitimacy should be enhanced. Finally, the prosperity of 'middle Russia' should increase, thus contributing to the rise of a bourgeoisie that could help to consolidate democracy. The Russian economy has been growing under Putin;[72] while much of this can be attributed to luck, given Russia's huge oil reserves and the high price of oil on international markets in recent years, reforms like those just mentioned

[70] Flat income tax rates—which Russia introduced with effect from January 2001—can increase Gini coefficients, or the gap between rich and poor, unless compensatory measures are taken by the state. For evidence that the Russian coefficient *has* increased since 2001, see *RIA Novosti*, 30 April 2004, cited in *Johnson's Russia List*, No.8191, 1 May 2004.

[71] The 2002 figure on tax returns suggested that some progress had been made—but also just how far the Russian tax authorities still needed to go (even allowing for those on low incomes); only some 3 million personal tax declarations were lodged, out of an adult population of more than 120 million—see http://www.newsru.com/finance/20feb2003/declare.html (I am grateful to Donald Bowser for having alerted me to this source.)

[72] GDP growth rate was 10.0% in 2000 (following what many saw as an impressive rate of 6.4% in Yeltsin's last year in office, 1999), 5.0% in 2001, 4.3% in 2002, and 7.1% in 2003. The dips in 2001 and 2002 look less concerning when it is recalled that the global economy generally suffered in the aftermath of 9/11.

should stand Russia in better stead once oil prices drop. This should contribute to the strengthening of the state in a positive sense (i.e. making it more effective and legitimate).

In a recent comparative study of democratization and the consolidation of democracy, Przeworski and Limongi subjected classical modernization theory to empirical, cross-polity longitudinal testing. In a nutshell, they were able to demonstrate persuasively that, while attempts at establishing democracy can occur at very different levels of economic development, the likelihood that such attempts will succeed in the long term is highly correlated with the per capita GDP.[73] If, despite its unique features, Russia more or less accords with the pattern identified by Przeworski and Limongi, then Putin's goal of doubling Russia's 2000 GNP by 2010 might be more important to the future of Russian democracy than the treatment of the media. But if there is to be any hope of reaching that goal, the state will have to be more effective—stronger—and less corrupt.

Along with focusing on the strong state and economy, Putin needed to develop a greater sense of identity and pride among Russians, given the trauma of the unique quintuple loss. The *Economist* article cited above expressed concern that the percentage of deputies who are members of parties that 'usually or always' support the Kremlin (i.e. the president) was much higher in the newly elected Duma than in previous post-Communist Russian elections. But the results can be interpreted from a very different perspective. The overwhelming victories of the United Russia party and Putin respectively in the December 2003 and March 2004 elections may give cause for optimism that Russians are beginning to cohere better, and politics is becoming less polarized, than at any time since the collapse of the USSR. *Other things being equal*, a less fragmented society will make Russia more conducive to the consolidation of democracy.

It should by now be clear that the weak state and corruption are in a dialectical, symbiotic relationship. Dealing with either should impact upon the other. Policies designed to strengthen the state and/or reduce corruption will be seen by some as symptomatic of nascent authoritarianism. But it should be acknowledged that systems that are led by strong leaders are not necessarily authoritarian, even if the leader him- or herself displays authoritarian personality traits (the United Kingdom under Thatcher exemplifies this point). Moreover, the Russian situation is so different from that in other countries that it is inappropriate to expect the sudden emergence of a system akin to that in the United States, the United Kingdom, or France. As long as basic democratic controls are in place and Putin continues to operate more or less within constitutional rules, Russia should be accepted as a

---

[73] Adam Przeworski and Fernando Limongi, 'Modernization: Theories and Facts', *World Politics*, 49/2 (1997), 155–83. See too Adam Przeworski, Michael Alvarez, Jose Cheibub, and Fernando Limongi, *Democracy and Development: Political Institutions and Material Well-Being in the World* (Cambridge: Cambridge University Press, 2000).

nascent and imperfect democracy with an overly powerful but not yet dictatorial president.[74]

Although it has been argued here that Putin's Russia is still—just—closer to the democratic end of the axis than to the authoritarian end, it is worth considering Russia's position from a radically different perspective. Let us suppose either that those who claim that it is already authoritarian are correct, or that the current disturbing tendencies continue, so that Russia *does* cross the midpoint between the democratic and authoritarian ideal-types. Would that ultimately matter?

From many perspectives, of course, it would—especially if it involved a resurrection of gulags and apparently arbitrary state coercion against its citizens, and/or the creation of a state that threatens other states. But if it were to become more like Lee Kwan Yew's Singapore—or indeed the political regime of any of the East Asian 'little tigers'—then the longer-term prognosis for Russia might look quite different from the dire picture currently being painted by many analysts. If that does happen, the concept of 'Eurasianism' might assume a new, more positive connotation.

But what is already clear is that it is as valid to interpret current Russian developments from a Rortian (i.e. relativistic) and dynamic perspective as from a deterministic one that necessarily assumes authoritarianism. Russian democracy was already in trouble when Putin came to power, and his rule might in hindsight prove to be a necessary corrective to place the consolidation process back on track. This said, a move in the direction of any of the three indicators identified in our fourth section *would* signify an unambiguous crossing of the median point between democracy and authoritarianism.

---

[74] The Russian political system is often described as 'super-presidential'. But it was Yeltsin, not Putin, who established this system.

6

Putin and the Attenuation of Russian Democracy

Timothy J. Colton

Real-world approximations of democracy, as Robert A. Dahl has incisively argued, are defined essentially by the presence of two things: inclusion of a majority of the adult population in political life and contestation among differing points of view in the public sphere.[1] Neither is sufficient to bring forth a democratic outcome in the absence of the other. Without the simultaneous involvement of ordinary people, openness of the governing elite to competition will produce a regime with some internal diversity yet no orderly feedback from popular preferences.[2] Without vigorous intra-elite competition, high rates of grassroots participation breed merely the mute mobilization of compliant subjects in support of officialdom. The latter pattern reached its twentieth-century apogee in the single-candidate elections and other political rituals pioneered in Lenin's and Stalin's USSR and then exported to other Communist countries.[3] 'The USSR', Dahl noted (writing in the 1970s), 'still has almost no system of public contestation, though it does have universal suffrage'.[4] The great reforms of the Gorbachev and Yeltsin years took aim primarily at this second side of political organization. By eliminating the ruling Communist Party's monopoly on representation and allowing a multiplicity of parties, associations, and freelance politicians to take the stage, their authors seemed to have put Russia and its fellow post-Soviet states squarely on the democratizing path.

It is hence especially painful to realize today, two decades after Mikhail Gorbachev so boldly inaugurated the transformation process, that Russia—not to mention its post-Soviet neighbours in Eurasia—has significantly regressed and is by standard measures further removed from being governed democratically

---

[1] Robert A. Dahl, *Polyarchy: Democratization and Public Opposition* (New Haven: Yale University Press, 1971).

[2] One scholar calls this solution 'feckless pluralism'. Thomas Carothers, 'The End of the Transition Paradigm', *Journal of Democracy*, 13 (January 2002), 5–21.

[3] And not only to Communist countries. The right-wing dictatorships of inter-war Europe also emulated Soviet praxis in this field. See Richard Pipes, *Russia under the Bolshevik Regime, 1919–1924* (New York: Alfred A. Knopf, 1994); and Abbott Gleason, *Totalitarianism: The Inner History of the Cold War* (New York: Oxford University Press, 1995).

[4] Dahl (n. 1), 5.

than it was at the beginning of the 1990s. Consider the widely cited scores generated by Freedom House, the human rights watchdog group based in New York. It rates countries for political rights and civil liberties on a scale of 1 to 7, with 1 being the most favourable score and 7 the least. In 1991, the year the USSR was disbanded and an independent Russian state was born, it assigned Russia 3 points on political rights and 3 on civil liberties; by 1999, the final year of Boris Yeltsin's presidency in Moscow, those indicators had worsened to 4 and 5; in 2003, several years into the tenure of Vladimir Putin, they stood at 5 and 5. In Freedom House's tripartite master classification, the new Russia in 1991 was 'partly free' but on the verge of being reckoned a 'free' polity; in 2003 Russia was still 'partly free' but now on the verge of dropping into the 'not free' category, where it would sit in the company of the central Asian nations and Alexander Lukashenko's dictatorship in Belarus.[5]

The Freedom House dimensions of political rights and civil liberties match up only imperfectly with Dahl's dimensions of inclusion and contestation.[6] Possibly for that reason, and possibly for others, its monitors attribute a greater part of the decline of Russian democracy to the Yeltsin years, and a lesser part to Putin's incomplete reign, than I am inclined to do. Any assessment of the timing and substance of the shift would hinge on contestation, since, at least until recently, deterioration has been much more palpable by this touchstone than with respect to inclusion. In the electoral realm—the decisive one in most theories of democracy—few measures were taken until 2004, under either Yeltsin or Putin, to exclude the public from participation. Indeed, splashy Kremlin-sponsored drives to maximize voter turnout have accompanied every national election campaign.[7] De-democratization in Russia has so far been principally a matter of encroachments on competition.

The Dwindling of Electoral Competition in Russia

Encroachments of what kind, exactly? Theorists of democracy tend to be pre-occupied with formal political rights. On this plane, it would be inaccurate to say

[5] Freedom House, *Freedom in the World*, various editions; compilation kindly made available to the author by Lucan A. Way of Temple University. In the Freedom House scheme, countries are considered free if their average ratings for political freedoms and civil liberties are less than 3, partly free if the average is 3 to 5.5, and not free if it is higher than 5.5. For discussion of Freedom House scores, see the chapter in this volume by Leslie Holmes.

[6] Freedom House (www.freedomhouse.org/research/freeworld) defines political rights as rights that 'enable people to participate freely in the political process'. Civil liberties 'include the freedom to develop opinions, institutions, and personal autonomy without interference from the state'.

[7] Putin's plan to put an end to the popular election of provincial governors, introduced after the carnage of the Beslan terror incident in September 2004, may herald the onset of a radically more restrictive policy on inclusion.

that political contestation has been systematically curtailed in post-Soviet Russia. Legal and institutional curbs on the rights to organize and compete have been rare, even on the austere Putin's watch, and have mostly been limited to the rules covering the formation and accreditation of parties.[8] Informal infringements on the pursuit of political points of view are more troubling. The most damaging have, of course, applied to the mass media, national television above all, and to the funding of opposition parties and non-governmental organizations by members of Russia's emerging business elite.[9] I am concerned in this chapter with *behavioural* manifestations of the attenuation of competition, manifestations we can reliably observe at the mass level but that ultimately are tied up with formal and informal changes at the elite level as well.

I confine myself here to electoral politics, and within it to presidential elections. Russia's autocratic heritage and presidentialist constitution make the election of a chief executive an incomparably more consequential event than the election of deputies to the relatively toothless State Duma, the lower house of parliament.[10] Three presidential elections have been staged since the post-Soviet constitution was ratified by referendum in 1993. Boris Yeltsin, who had initially been elected president in June 1991, when Russia (as the Russian Soviet Federative Socialist Republic) was still a subordinate unit of the Soviet Union, won re-election in a two-round contest on 16 June and 3 July 1996. On 26 March 2000, his anointed successor, Vladimir Putin, already running as a quasi-incumbent (in his last act as president on 31 December 1999, Yeltsin had appointed him prime minister and acting president), achieved a first four-year term. On 14 March 2004, Putin won a second mandate.

The most straightforward indicator of the decline of competition in Russian politics is the proportion of the total vote secured by the winners in consecutive presidential races. In the qualifying round of the 1996 election, Yeltsin took 35.8 per cent of the votes tendered; in the run-off, confronting the communist nominee, Gennady Zyuganov, he took 54.4 per cent. In 2000, Putin was to have a much easier time of it than Yeltsin had in 1996, garnering 52.9 per cent of the votes and prevailing in the first round. In 2004, Putin did better still, as his share of the vote swelled to 71.3 per cent.

The general trend, from more to less competition, is obvious. What needs to be underlined is the strength of the second phase of the trend, that is, the one

---

[8] Most noteworthy is the federal law on parties passed with President Putin's backing in 2001. It stiffened the requirements for registration, stipulating that to qualify for the party-list, half of the election of the State Duma, a party must have a minimum of 10,000 members and branches of no fewer than 100 members in forty-five provinces of Russia. It also required electoral blocs, which are common in Russian legislative elections, to contain at least one registered political party. The statute did not have much effect on the parliamentary election of 2003, in which twenty-three parties and blocs ran slates of candidates, only three fewer than in 1999.

[9] See Dale R. Herspring (ed.), *Putin's Russia: Past Imperfect, Future Uncertain*, 2nd edn. (Lanham, MD: Rowman & Littlefield, 2005).

[10] Only in 1993–5 was the Federation Council, the upper house, popularly elected.

bridging Putin's election in 2000 with his re-election in 2004. When all is said and done, the presidential election of March 2000 was a respectably competitive one, albeit not nearly as competitive as the hard-fought election of 1996. Putin faced a line-up of ten opponents, the same number as his predecessor had faced in 1996, and three of them (Zyuganov, Grigory Yavlinsky, and Vladimir Zhirinovsky) were seasoned leaders of national parties who had been on the presidential ballot in 1996.[11] Putin was hard pressed in 2000 to make it over the 50 per cent line and escape an expensive run-off battle.[12] The election of 2004 had a qualitatively different flavour. Facing only five opponents, none of whom was remotely a figure of major stature, Putin harvested almost three-quarters of the votes cast. The 1996 election had been *more* competitive than the election of 1991, still under Soviet auspices, which Yeltsin had swept in a landslide. Yeltsin in the first round in 1996 attracted fewer votes (22.1 percentage points fewer, to be precise) than he had in 1991.[13] The 2000 campaign was *less* competitive than the 1996 campaign, as Putin exceeded Yeltsin's percentage of the popular vote by a healthy 17.1 points. And by 2004 the degree of contestation was *much less* than at the outset. Putin succeeded in lifting his share at the ballot box by 18.4 percentage points, a bit of a wider gap than the one separating his 2000 performance from Yeltsin's in 1996.

Personality and Performance Explanations

What might lie behind this two-step decrease of electoral competition in Russia? Post-election surveys of eligible voters in 1996, 2000, and 2004 permit us to test some individual-level explanations. I selectively target the discussion here on three of them.[14]

[11] Zhirinovsky had also been a candidate for president in 1991.

[12] For a description of the campaign and of the Putin camp's determination to avoid a run-off, see Timothy J. Colton and Michael McFaul, *Popular Choice and Managed Democracy: The Russian Elections of 1999 and 2000* (Washington, DC: Brookings Institution, 2003), ch. 7.

[13] Candidate vote totals here are reckoned as a percentage of all ballots cast. Three per cent of all ballots submitted in 1991 were spoiled by the participating voters; in all subsequent presidential elections, this quotient was below 1 per cent. If spoiled ballots are omitted and the Yeltsin vote is calculated in relation to valid votes cast, his share in 1991 increases to 59.7 per cent, and the shift from 1991 to 1996 increases to 23.4 per cent.

[14] Comprehensive statistical models of voting choice in Russia, as in any country, tend to be very complex and quite static. For models of how Russians vote based on snapshot surveys of citizen opinion, see Stephen White, Richard Rose, and Ian McAllister, *How Russia Votes* (Chatham, NJ: Chatham House, 1997); Timothy J. Colton, *Transitional Citizens: Voters and What Influences Them in the New Russia* (Cambridge, MA: Harvard University Press, 2000); Timothy J. Colton and Michael McFaul, *Popular Choice and Managed Democracy* (n. 12); and Timothy J. Colton and Henry E. Hale, 'Voting Behavior in the 2003 Duma Elections', paper presented at the annual meeting of the American Political Science Association, Chicago (3 September 2004). None of these efforts pre-empts the present analysis. My objective here is to address trends over time, not the minutiae of the formation of electoral preferences at any one moment.

One superficially appealing interpretation would be to peg electoral results to the personal qualities of Yeltsin and Putin. Perhaps presidential elections have become more lopsided because Russian voters simply like Putin better than they liked Yeltsin and find him more palatable as a head of state. Anecdotally, there is much to recommend this approach. Yeltsin, already in his sixties when sworn in, could be a capricious decision-maker, sometimes appeared out of his depth in shaping policy and representing Russia in international affairs, showed an inordinate fondness for vodka, and was often ill or indisposed, spending much of his second term shuttling in and out of hospital and rehabilitation facilities. Twenty-one years younger than Yeltsin, Putin is steady at the helm, a teetotaler, and a physical fitness buff and workaholic. Putin, Russians will volunteer in conversation, is somehow more presentable, more 'cultured', and more 'presidential' than Yeltsin and arouses greater confidence in his ability to lead wisely.

Survey data provide harder evidence of the relevance of the personality factor. Table 6.1 summarizes how Russian citizens rated and ranked incumbents in the 1996, 2000, and 2004 elections. They were asked to assess the incumbents and several of their campaign rivals on four generic character traits often screened for in such surveys. The queries were couched in affirmatory language about intelligence (was the candidate 'an intelligent and knowledgeable person'?); strength ('a strong leader'?); integrity ('an honest and trustworthy person'?); and empathy ('really cares about the interests of people like you'?). Respondents answered whether the candidate definitely had, probably had, probably lacked, or definitely lacked the specified quality.[15]

As can be seen, Boris Yeltsin as a person was not treated tenderly by his compatriots in the 1996 poll. Only on the intelligence scale did positive answers outnumber negative answers; on integrity and more forcefully on empathy, negatives outnumbered positives; on strength, positive and negative responses came out equal. Yeltsin fared miserably in relation to his opposition, ranking fourth of the five candidates inquired about on intelligence, integrity, and empathy, and third on strength. General Alexander Lebed, the flamboyant paratroop commander and hero of the Russian intervention in the republic of Moldova, who finished third in the vote count in round one, was ranked first on all four facets of personality save none. On an average, the runner-up, Gennady Zyuganov, ranked second on the personality assessments, while Grigory Yavlinsky, who came in fourth in the election, ranked third. Only the fifth-finishing Vladimir Zhirinovsky was afforded a worse character reference than Yeltsin by our survey respondents.[16]

---

[15] In the 1996 survey we also asked about the candidates' vision (did the person 'have his own vision of the country's future'?), but that question was not repeated in the 2000 and 2004 polls.

[16] Yeltsin, in other words, won the 1996 election in spite of his personality and not because of it. For discussion, see Timothy J. Colton, 'The Leadership Factor in the Russian Election of 1996' in Anthony King (ed.), *Leaders' Personalities and the Outcomes of Democratic Elections* (Oxford: Oxford University Press, 2002), 184–209.

Timothy J. Colton

Table 6.1. Evaluations of Incumbent's Character Traits

| Trait | Rating (per cent)[a] | | | |
	Yes/ Probably yes	No/ Probably no	Yes/Probably yes; minus: No/Probably no	Ranking of net rating among candidates
YELTSIN 1996[b]				
Intelligent and knowledgeable person	64	27	37	4
Strong leader	45	45	0.1	3
Honest and trustworthy person	39	42	−3	4
Really cares about people like you	28	58	−30	4
PUTIN 2000[c]				
Intelligent and knowledgeable person	92	3	90	1
Strong leader	83	6	77	1
Honest and trustworthy person	70	7	63	1
Really cares about people like you	64	14	50	1
PUTIN 2004[d]				
Intelligent and knowledgeable person	94	2	92	1
Strong leader	88	6	83	1
Honest and trustworthy person	83	5	78	1
Really cares about people like you	74	13	60	1

[a] Columns 1–3 plus 'Don't know' responses, not shown here, sum to 100 per cent.

[b] Panel survey of the electorate organized by Colton and Zimmerman, as described in Timothy J. Colton, *Transitional Citizens: Voters and What Influences Them in the New Russia* (Cambridge, MA: Harvard University Press, 2000). Wave 3, July–September 1996 ($N = 2{,}472$ weighted cases). Questions asked about five candidates: Boris Yeltsin, Gennady Zyuganov, Alexander Lebed, Grigory Yavlinsky, and Vladimir Zhirinovsky.

[c] Panel survey organized by Colton and McFaul, as described in Timothy J. Colton and Michael McFaul, *Social Choice and Managed Democracy: The Russian Elections of 1999 and 2000* (Washington, DC: Brookings Institution, 2003). Wave 3, April–June 2000 ($N = 1{,}755$ weighted cases). Questions asked about four candidates: Vladimir Putin, Gennady Zyuganov, Grigorii Yavlinsky, and Aman Tuleyev.

[d] Panel survey organized by Colton, Hale, and McFaul. Wave 2, April–May 2004 ($N = 1{,}494$ weighted cases). Questions asked about three candidates: Vladimir Putin, Nikolay Kharitonov, and Irina Khakamada.

In 2000, though, Vladimir Putin was to receive rave reviews from the citizenry. Positive responses outweighed negative responses on all four character traits, by margins ranging from 50 percentage points (for empathy) to a massive 90 points (for intelligence). Moreover, Putin was placed a resounding first on all criteria, easily outstripping the three other candidates about whom we posed the questions. In 2004, the picture had become even rosier for Putin. On every score, the percentage of positive evaluations rose and the percentage of negative evaluations fell.

Putin dominated the field of candidates in still more decisive fashion than in 2000. For both 2000 and 2004, the contrast with Yeltsin in 1996 could hardly be starker.

The Russian public's appreciation of Putin, when juxtaposed to its censorious view of Yeltsin, may well have helped drive the jump in the incumbent's vote share between 1996 and 2000, and along with that the diminution in electoral competition over the four-year span. But the personality factor provides little if any analytical purchase over the no less salient swing in the electorate's mood in the next four-year span, from 2000 to 2004. Only in a minor way were assessments of Putin's character more flattering in 2004 than they had been in 2000. The raw numbers imply that those assessments were already starting from such an elevated plateau that there was precious little room for upward movement. Those assessments cannot be the chief reason for the exaggerated shift toward Putin, and away from robust political competition, witnessed in the 2004 election.

A second promising line of inquiry fastens on incumbents' performance in office, as distinct from their characteristics as human beings. Yeltsin in 1996 had been president of Russia for five years. Putin in 2000 had been head of government for seven and half months and acting head of state for three months, and as of the 2004 election he had occupied the office of president for a full four-year term. Quite separate from what they knew about the two men's personal attributes and styles, citizens accordingly had plenty of retrospective information about the two men's actions in government, information which one would presume would have had an impact on people's voting choices. Yeltsin had a crucial part in the breakup of the Soviet Union, had weathered a constitutional confrontation in 1993, and had launched radical market reform of the planned economy. Putin in 2000 had tinkered with social policy and taken command of the second Chechen war; by 2004, he had made a multitude of decisions extending and rejecting aspects of the Yeltsin legacy. Voters were free to reward incumbents for decisions they favoured and punish them for decisions they opposed.

Popular assessments of the work of Yeltsin and Putin are laid out in Table 6.2. The overall Gestalt is not so different from the character assessments encapsulated in Table 6.1. The survey question reported on here asked respondents to evaluate the incumbent's 'activity' (*deyatel'nost*) in his high office, that office being president for Yeltsin in 1996 and Putin in 2004 and prime minister and acting president for Putin in 2000. The evaluation was on a five-point scale stretching from strong disapproval to strong approval, with a neutral category in the middle. The modal response for Russia's first president in 1996, furnished by half the respondents, was the non-committal middle category; outside that range, negative evaluations of his activity overshadowed positive evaluations by about three to one. For Putin in 2000, the modal response to his record as interim leader of the country is qualified approval, and positive assessments are about ten times as plentiful as negative assessments. His profile in 2004 is similar, with a barely detectable loss of lustre. The modal response (by a tiny, statistically insignificant amount) is the neutral one; as in 2000, positive evaluations of Putin's

Table 6.2. Approval of Incumbent's Record in Office (per cent)[a]

Evaluation	Yeltsin 1996	Putin 2000	Putin 2004
Fully disapprove	12	1	2
Disapprove	21	4	4
Approve some, disapprove some	50	32	38
Approve	11	41	37
Fully approve	2	15	17
Don't know	3	6	2

[a] Survey details same as in Table 6.1.

record are about ten times as frequent as negative evaluations, reserved or unreserved.

As with the personality factor, retrospective evaluations of incumbents' records aid us some in understanding the trend toward presidential dominance of the electoral arena, and yet are by no means the whole answer. Again, the pronounced pro-Kremlin shift in citizen sentiment from 1996 to 2000 is entirely consistent with Putin's electoral success in 2000. Russian voters were as likely to see Putin as an improvement on Yeltsin in policy and performance terms as in personality terms. But this same variable is of no utility in ferreting out why Putin was so much more proficient a vote-getter in 2004 than he had been in his maiden election in 2000. If anything, grassroots perceptions of Putin's record were a tad less enthusiastic in 2004 than they had been four years before. They had more room to grow in a positive direction than the extremely favourable take on Putin's personal traits, and that growth did not take place. Logically, then, mass evaluations of Putin's past presidential performance are not the key to comprehending the leap in his electoral support—and the thinning out of democratic competition—between 2000 and 2004.

Filling the President's Shoes

If personality and past performance do not satisfactorily account for the recent decline in electoral contestation in Russia, then what else might? I believe there is leverage to be gained by focusing on a third candidate-centred variable, namely, the public's anticipation of the *future* activity of the candidates. My guiding assumption is that Russians, like many citizens in consolidated democracies, are sensitive to what they feel potential officeholders will do with power after the ballots have been tallied. Students of presidential elections in the United States have learned much from survey questions that refer implicitly, and sometimes very explicitly, to campaign promises with emphases that have varied from domain to domain as candidates try to match their own credibility against the opponent's weaknesses.[17] The citizen's willingness to identify one candidate or another as best prepared to cope with a certain issue is often predictive of a tendency to vote for that candidate. Russian elections are unlike American elections in numerous regards, but the tendency to link voting choice with expected behaviour in office is universal enough that it should in principle be operative.

Beginning in 1996, my research collaborators and I have put to our survey respondents a series of expected-performance questions. Shown a list of presidential nominees, the individual respondent was invited to volunteer which candidate 'could handle better than the others' (*smog by luchshe drugikh spravit'sya s*) a set of policy problems, described one by one. The grab bag of problems probed for altered slightly from election to election. Identically or similarly worded question items about economic policy, crime and corruption, human rights and democracy, and foreign policy appeared on all the questionnaires; the 1996 item about unemployment was broadened out to social security in 2000 and 2004; a query about Chechnya in 1996 and 2000 was rephrased to aim at terrorism in 2004; and an item on social stability was administered in 1996 only and not repeated. The body of each question item expressly gave the respondent the option of replying that there was 'no special difference' (*net osoboi raznitsy*) among the candidates as to capacity for dealing with the problem.

In the 1996 election, as is nicely brought out in Table 6.3, President Yeltsin had as much difficulty distinguishing himself in the electorate's eyes as a future problem solver as he had selling his unique personality and his demonstrated record in power. Across all seven policy areas, the size of the group willing to say Yeltsin was the candidate best prepared to handle the issue averaged just 13 per cent among all those polled, and 24 per cent among those able to finger a candidate. In but two issue areas (democracy and foreign policy) did the incumbent lead the field; he limped in fourth on a pair of issues, third on two, and second on one. The formidable General Lebed was ranked top in three areas (crime and corruption, Chechnya, and social stability), with truly spectacular evaluations for the war in Chechnya (74 per cent of all who named a candidate) and crime and corruption (77 per cent). The Communist Gennady Zyuganov was judged most proficient in two areas (the economy and unemployment).[18]

By 2000, there had been a sea change. Pluralities of Russians felt acting president Putin to be best qualified to handle three of six problems on the issue, and majorities gauged him best on the remaining three, for an average of 46 per cent across the issue areas, and 61 per cent among persons able to identify a candidate as competent. Unlike personality and retrospective evaluations, which

---

[17] Warren E. Miller and J. Merrill Shanks, *The New American Voter* (Cambridge, MA: Harvard University Press, 1996), 392.

[18] On the economy, Yeltsin was judged less competent than Grigory Yavlinsky in addition to Zyuganov. On crime and corruption and Chechnya, he was outshone by Lebed, Zyuganov, and the demagogic populist Zhirinovsky.

Table 6.3. Prospective Evaluations of Incumbent's Issue Competence[a]

Year and issue	Per cent	Say incumbent is best prepared	
		Per cent of those who named a candidate	Ranking
1996			
Economy	16	25	3
Unemployment	10	17	2
Crime and corruption	3	4	4
Chechnya	3	5	4
Foreign policy	21	41	1
Democracy	25	53	1
Stability and social tranquility	12	21	3
Average	13	24	3
2000			
Economy	38	50	1
Social security	38	51	1
Crime and corruption	52	66	1
Chechnya	62	77	1
Foreign policy	50	69	1
Human rights and democracy	37	52	1
Average	46	61	1
2004			
Economy	57	81	1
Social security	55	77	1
Crime and corruption	58	84	1
Terrorism	63	87	1
Foreign policy	66	88	1
Human rights and democracy	54	79	1
Average	59	83	1

[a] Survey details same as in Table 6.1.

were basically static after 2000, prospective evaluations of Vladimir Putin as leader of the nation *continued to improve* from the 2000 election to the 2004 election. In 2004 majorities of over 50 per cent ascribed Putin superior capability in all the half dozen issue areas, for a mean of 59 per cent, averaging an incredible 83 per cent among respondents who named a competent candidate.

Table 6.4 fills in important details on the electorate's perceptions of issue competence. Column 1 repeats the first column in Table 6.3, reciting the percentages considering the incumbent, be it Yeltsin or Putin, the best able to handle the given issue. Columns 2–4 set down the alternatives to siding with the man in the Kremlin: giving the nod to an opposition candidate, detecting no difference to speak of between the candidates, and not being able to express an opinion about who would acquit himself best.

The story Table 6.4 tells is a fascinating and depressing one. In the first presidential election of the post-Soviet era, in 1996, fewer than 15 per cent of Russian electors on average discerned the incumbent president, Yeltsin, as having the answers to the country's most pressing problems; almost one in two, from problem to problem, found an opposition candidate to be best qualified; and about 40 per cent had an indifference response (seeing no special difference or not knowing what to answer). In 2000, pro-incumbent responses have come to eclipse pro-opposition candidate responses by more than 20 percentage points, and the number of indifference responses is down to one quarter of the electorate. In 2004, there are two striking departures in the array of responses. One is that, as never before, an absolute majority of Russians (59 per cent of our sample) held the

Table 6.4. Prospective Evaluations of Incumbent's Issue Competence as Compared to the Alternatives[a]

Year and issue	Assessment of who is best prepared (per cent)			
	Incumbent	An opposition candidate	No particular difference	Don't know
1996				
Economy	16	48	18	18
Unemployment	10	49	23	18
Crime and corruption	3	73	10	13
Chechnya	3	67	13	18
Foreign policy	21	30	24	25
Democracy	25	23	24	28
Stability and social tranquillity	12	47	19	22
Average	13	48	19	20
2000				
Economy	38	38	11	13
Social security	38	36	15	11
Crime and corruption	52	27	10	11
Chechnya	62	18	9	11
Foreign policy	50	22	14	14
Human rights and democracy	37	33	15	14
Average	46	29	12	12
2004				
Economy	57	13	17	12
Social security	55	16	18	12
Crime and corruption	58	11	18	13
Terrorism	63	9	15	12
Foreign policy	66	9	15	10
Human rights and democracy	54	15	18	14
Average	59	12	17	12

[a] Survey details same as in Table 6.1.

incumbent, Putin, to be master of the typical policy realm. Unprecedented, too, is that indifference responses (seeing no one candidate as fit and not knowing what to say) have come to predominate over responses favouring one of the non-incumbent candidates, by a ratio of 29 per cent to 12 per cent. Contrary to notions of electoral democracy, Russians who did not actively judge the sitting president to be the safest bet for doing the job were more than twice as likely to shrug their shoulders in bemusement and boredom than to visualize an adversary of Putin's in the campaign as being the one equipped to cope.

We are confronted here, as much as anything, by Russians' progressive loss of the ability to *imagine* anyone other than the incumbent as up to the task of filling the president's shoes. This diminution has been accompanied by a gradual decline in the quality—visibility, prior high-level experience, standing in the political elite—of the challengers to the status quo. Putin won re-election in March 2004 against the Russian equivalent of five Ralph Naders. The Communist Party of the Russian Federation nominated the chairman of the Party's agrarian wing (Nikolay Kharitonov), whose stodgy persona was guaranteed to turn off urban voters. Two candidates (Sergey Glazyev and Irina Khakamada) were independents who headed factions within opposition parties, and another (Sergey Mironov) led a boutique party and actually endorsed President Putin. The final candidate (Oleg Malyshkin) was nominated by Zhirinovsky's Liberal-Democratic Party of Russia but had made his reputation within the party as its chief bodyguard. In the run-up to election day, I did not hear a single pundit, Russian or foreign, express doubt that Putin would roll to victory. The only question beforehand was the size of his majority. One reason for Putin's having to contend with so lightweight a slate of rivals was that more mainstream and more credible political personalities refused to let their names stand, certain that they would be humiliated at the polls and fearful in some cases that they might face non-electoral consequences to boot.[19] The result is a vicious circle. Russians are deeply skeptical of opposition candi-dates; this keeps non-Naderesque politicians out of the electoral arena; and the paucity of serious candidates in turn deepens public apathy.

Surprisingly, most Russians were not able to imagine alternatives to President Putin in the 2004 election even when they were critical of elements of his government's performance. Table 6.5 helps tease out this association. It breaks down prospective evaluations on two of our six issue clusters, crime and corrup-tion and terrorism, by assessment of trends in the interval since the 2000 election. The trends were elicited in four discrete areas: crime, corruption, terrorism, and the Chechen war. In each area, the telling point is made in the first row, the one giving evaluations of issue competence for individuals who thought the national trend since 2004 was negative. Compared to citizens who felt that crime was

---

[19] Examples would be Zyuganov, the leader of the CPRF, Zhirinovsky of the LDPR, Dmitry Rogozin of the Motherland bloc, Grigory Yavlinsky of the Yabloko party, and Yury Luzhkov, the mayor of Moscow.

Table 6 Prospective Evaluations of Issue Competence on Crime and Corruption and Terrorism, by Assessments of Trends since 2000 [a]

Issue and trend	Assessment of who is best prepared (per cent)			
	Incumbent	An opposition candidate	No particular difference	Don't know
Crime[b]				
Increased	53	14	21	13
Decreased	72	7	12	10
No change	65	9	14	12
Corruption[c]				
Increased	51	15	21	12
Decreased	76	9	12	4
No change	63	8	17	12
Fear of terrorists[d]				
More	64	10	17	9
Less	83	2	7	8
No change	61	11	14	13
Situation in Chechnya[e]				
Worsened	52	12	23	12
Improved	73	7	13	7
No change	57	12	17	15

[a] Survey details same as in Table 6.1.

[b] Question: 'What do you think, has crime in Russia increased over the past four years, has it decreased, or has there been no change?' Assessment is for candidates' preparation to handle crime and corruption.

[c] Question: 'What do you think, is there more corruption in Russia than four years ago, less, or has there been no change?' Assessment is for candidates' preparation to handle crime and corruption.

[d] Question: 'Compared to four years ago, do you fear terrorists more, do you fear them less, or has there been no change?' Assessment is for candidates' preparation to handle terrorism.

[e] Question: 'What do you think, has the situation in Chechnya improved over the past four years, has it worsened, or has there been no change?' Assessment is for candidates' preparation to handle terrorism. First and second responses are reversed in the table.

becoming less worrisome in Russia, those who thought is was becoming more worrisome were rather less likely to identify Putin as the best able to handle crime and corruption. But a mere 14 per cent of these people, one in seven, could bring themselves to identify an opposition candidate as best qualified to deal with crime and corruption versus the indifference responses given by 34 per cent, one in three, of this group. The pattern repeats itself with uncanny regularity on the other issues. Among persons who thought corruption was flourishing, 15 per cent could envision an alternative to Putin and 33 per cent gave an indifference assessment. Among respondents who gave a gloomy assessment of terrorism, it was 10 per cent and 26 per cent. For Chechnya, Putin's signature issue in his rise to power in 1999–2000, it was 12 per cent and 35 per cent.

Prospects

It is enticing to impute the attenuation of political contestation to some timeless strand in Russian political culture. But drawing such a connection would be unpersuasive. Culture is supposed to be more or less invariant, and the climate of politics in Russia, however determined, was permissive and in fact encouraging of electoral and political controversy from the late 1980s to the late 1990s.

The most plausible culprits in the attenuation of Russian democracy, as evinced in the withering of competition in the electoral sphere, are twofold. The first is the failure of parties with some meaningful autonomy from government to ensconce themselves as the definitive structuring forces in mass politics. Yeltsin's staunch refusal to found a pro-reform, pro-presidential party when Russian politics was at its most open and idea-infused is as responsible as anything for this omission, and the error limited his options in choosing an heir in 1999. His pick, Putin, was plucked from the most ingrown and secretive segment of the Russian bureaucracy, the national security establishment. Once confirmed by the electorate, Putin sponsored United Russia, a top-down 'party of power' bereft of any vision of the future other than glorifying the current leader and buttressing the prerogatives of officials in the central executive agencies, a notion marketed under the slogan of 'strengthening the state'. He wedded this innovation to a second move—the abridgment of public discourse. In swift and ruthless strokes, Putin and his allies rescinded the editorial freedoms of state-owned media outlets and employed financial and administrative clout to hedge in and cow most of the privately-owned media. When the president sought a public mandate for his second term, there thus were neither effective non-state-dependent parties to put forward a credible alternative to him nor communication channels able and willing to carry a dissenting message. His victory in March 2004 was as close to preordained as any election could be, short of reversion to the single-candidate charades of Soviet days.

In light of these origins, the prospects for the attenuation of democratic contestation being reversed any time soon are dim. Symbiosis of the upper echelons of the governing elite with United Russia will continue to grow throughout Putin's tenure, as will the effort to continue the Naderization of the opposition. It is hard to believe that the leash on the mass media will be loosened, either. The impetus for changing the status quo, therefore, will have to come from elsewhere, if anywhere. A catastrophic failure—in foreign policy (the 'loss' of Ukraine to NATO and the European Union, for instance), in the economy (maybe due to a slide in world oil prices), in the shaky security environment of the North Caucasus, in some spectacular act of terrorism in Moscow or St Petersburg—might encourage Russians to imagine some other kind of person leading them in future. At the same time, disaster would also tempt those in charge to try abrogating both mass inclusion in politics and all semblance of contestation in the name of saving the nation. A less fanciful source of disruption would be the arrival of a new supreme leader, should Putin and his inner circle consent to a passing of the baton later in the decade. All three incoming leaders of Russia since 1985— Gorbachev, Yeltsin, and Putin—have to varying extent repudiated and refashioned the works of their predecessors. It says something about the blunting of political reform that the brightest hope for resuming its forward progress may lie in the urge of one man in a high and lonely place, as yet unknown, to make history by doing the right thing for his society.

7

Majority Control and Executive Dominance: Parliament–President Relations in Putin's Russia

Paul Chaisty

Since the collapse of Communism, Russia's presidents have enjoyed varying degrees of success when governing through parliament. Although the 1993 constitution laid the foundations for executive dominance, the political control required by the president to realize these powers has oscillated depending on the strength of presidential support within the Federal Assembly. Boris Yeltsin's inability to build a stable and disciplined presidential majority post-October 1993 produced a weak form of what Arend Lijphart might term 'consensual' as opposed to 'majoritarian' parliament–president relations.[1] Although legislative politics endured periods of adversarial conflict, such as the impeachment vote of 1999 or numerous votes of confidence, the executive was forced to bargain and compromise with the assembly. Institutional innovations during this period served to mitigate intra- and inter-branch conflict: arrangements for sharing power between parties within the lower house of the Federal Assembly, the State Duma, and the creation of consensus-seeking bodies like the 'Council of Four'.[2] These developments assuaged fears that the paralysing inter-branch conflict of the early post-Communist period would reappear. However, the transaction costs of building majority support for policy initiatives from many different constituencies of interests—partisan, corporate, administrative, and regional—weakened the executive's capacity to impose its agenda, particularly during Yeltsin's second term.

The Putin presidency has changed the dynamic of parliament–president relations in Russia. The relationship between the parliament and the president has become more majoritarian, which has in turn advanced executive dominance in the policy sphere. The Kremlin's strategy is majoritarian in that it seeks the creation of narrow decision-making majorities—ideally confined to one discip-

---

[1] Arend Lijphart, *Patterns of Democracy: Government Forms and Performance in Thirty-six Countries* (New Haven: Yale University Press, 1999).

[2] A forum created during Yeltsin's second term, which provided an opportunity for the chairmen of both houses of the Federal Assembly to meet with the president and prime minister on a regular basis.

lined party—as opposed to broad majorities composed of different interests. The formation of a dominant and disciplined government party has therefore been central to the Kremlin's desire to assert greater executive control over the parliamentary agenda. From the early months of Putin's presidency, the preference for party was demonstrated by the introduction of a law 'On Political Parties', which was intended to consolidate Russia's emerging party system.[3] However, executive control over Russia's legislators has not just taken a partisan form. The reform of the composition of the upper house of the Federal Assembly, the Federation Council, has produced what one writer calls a *nomenklatura* method of composing majorities.[4] Although Putin's reform gave regional executive and legislative branches of government the power to appoint 'senators', in practice, presidential officials at both the federal and regional level have strongly influenced the process of appointment.[5]

The result of both the majority-building approaches is that Putin has established a basis of political support not enjoyed by his predecessor. In this chapter, the partisan, institutional, and policy effects of this move toward majoritarianism will be assessed. First, the problems faced by the executive during Yeltsin's presidency are examined. Second, the measures taken by the Kremlin to address these problems are explored, and finally the impact of the new arrangements on political behaviour in the assembly and policy outputs is considered. Although it is important to note that some of the developments observed predate Putin, the evidence presented shows a marked change in the nature of inter-branch relations. The executive's dominance in the legislative sphere is not absolute, however. Putin is still constrained by particularistic interests that encumbered Yeltsin's presidency. But the conflicts on legislation that previously spilled out on to the floor of the assembly are now largely confined to the government's party, United Russia. This development is indicative of the Kremlin's more effective management of parliamentary politics under Putin.

Parliamentary Resilience in Russia's Early Transition

President Yeltsin struggled to impose his will on the Russian parliament in the aftermath of the Soviet collapse. Lacking the institutional power over, and

---

[3] See the chapter by Leslie Holmes in this volume; and Edwin Bacon, 'Russia's Law on Political Parties: Democracy by Decree?', in Cameron Ross (ed.), *Russian Politics Under Putin* (Manchester: Manchester University Press, 2004).

[4] Thomas Remington, 'Majorities without Mandates: The Russian Federation Council since 2000', *Europe–Asia Studies*, 55 (2003), 675.

[5] According to Aleksey Makarkin, presidential staff either recommended or approved the appointment of up to 80 per cent of the Federation Council's new composition. Aleksey Makarkin, 'Sovet Federatsii: novyi sostav i perspektivy deyatel'nosti', at http://www.politcom.ru/aaa_c_v12.php (accessed 15 May 2002).

political support within, Russia's first post-Communist parliament, the Supreme Soviet (1990–3), Yeltsin was unable to bring Russian legislators to heel. A constitution that placed significant powers in the hands of the parliament, such as control over the composition and survival of the government, and limited executive influence over the parliamentary agenda, constrained the presidency in the early post-Communist period. These constitutional obstacles were further augmented by half-hearted presidential efforts to build a political basis of support in the legislature. President Yeltsin's reluctance to give parliamentary democrats a say on executive appointments and policy matters undermined attempts by pro-Yeltsin deputies to create a parliamentary 'Coalition for Reforms'.[6]

The introduction of new constitutional arrangements after the crisis of October 1993 moved legislative power into the president's orbit. The new constitution conferred on the executive significant legislative powers of initiation, veto, scrutiny, and decree, and gave the president key powers in relation to the composition and survival of the government and parliament, such as the conditional power to dissolve the lower house, the State Duma. In addition, the introduction of a mixed electoral system devised to strengthen political parties was intended to enhance executive support in the lower house. However, whilst these arrangements produced more constructive executive–legislative relations in the post-October 1993 period, Yeltsin never acquired the political control needed to subordinate the two houses of the new parliament. In the first two Dumas, Russia's new electoral system failed to deliver a cohesive parliamentary majority for pro-Yeltsin parties, and the method for selecting members of the upper house, the Federation Council, produced a 'governors' club', which proved itself capable of acting independently of the president's wishes. Without a powerful presidential party to control the parliamentary agenda, deputies enjoyed a significant degree of legislative autonomy.

During Yeltsin's rule, power was dispersed between a number of institutional actors and interests within the legislative branch. In the Supreme Soviet, leadership officials, notably the chairman of the Supreme Soviet, and the heads of the assembly's standing committees competed for influence over the legislative agenda. Although parliamentary chairman, Ruslan Khasbulatov, used his considerable powers and institutional resources to steer the direction of policy in the assembly, the system of law-making was too fragmented to allow the chair undivided control. Committees and their chairs exerted a high degree of influence over the Supreme Soviet's legislative work,[7] and became the main focus of ministerial lobbying within the assembly. In the post-1993 Federal Assembly, agenda control was divided between different forces in each house. The Duma's

[6] See Jeffrey Gleisner, Leonti Byzov, Nikolai Biryukov, and Victor Sergeyev, 'The Parliament and the Cabinet: Parties, Factions and Parliamentary Control in Russia (1990–93)', *Journal of Contemporary History*, 31 (1996), 427–61.

[7] See Joel Ostrow, *Comparing Post-Soviet Legislatures* (Columbus: Ohio State University Press, 2000).

internal arrangements gave political parties formal power over the legislative agenda. However, in the absence of a cohesive parliamentary majority, parties shared control over the assembly's chief presiding organ, the Duma Council, and its main leadership posts: the chair and his deputies, committee chairs, and their deputies. In practice, such power dispersal weakened the rule of both party leaders and the executive over the assembly's legislative priorities. The Duma Council was relatively ineffective in preventing the assembly's committees and its deputies in plenary sessions from diluting its legislative plan;[8] the parliamentary chairman enjoyed a significant degree of autonomy from his party's leadership; and the Duma's committees and its deputies were susceptible to extra-parliamentary lobbies. The particularistic character of legislative behaviour was even more marked in the upper house, the Federation Council. In contrast to the Duma, political parties were not part of the Council's organizational structure. Regional interests predominated in the upper house under Yeltsin, and the work of the assembly was steered by its leading officials: the chair and his deputies, the heads of the legislature's committees and commissions, and the chamber's *apparat*, its standing bureaucracy.

Parliamentary institutions therefore posed obstacles to executive dominance in the early years of Russia's post-Communist transition. Although Yeltsin stacked the rules in the executive's favour after his victory in October 1993, the absence of coherent and stable parliamentary presidential majorities weakened his ability to govern through parliament. Unlike De Gaulle's Fifth Republic, Yeltsin's constitution did not give the Russian executive the power to determine the parliamentary agenda, and the option of rule by decree had its limitations.[9] As a consequence, Yeltsin struggled to impose his will on the direction of reform. The passage of legislation necessitated extensive bargaining with partisan and regional forces, as well as with departmental and corporate interests that exploited the opportunities provided by the parliament's dispersed structure of decision-making; the corollary was a comparatively low proportion of laws initiated by the executive. As Yeltsin explained in his 1997 annual presidential address to the Federal Assembly:

Out of nearly 750 bills introduced into the State Duma in 1996 the government initiated only 188. Of these, 53 were bills concerning the ratification of international agreements and treaties. At the same time, lobbying of this or that bill by departments flourished behind the scenes. Several of these bills contradicted the policy direction defined by the president, and even the position of the government.[10]

   [8] Paul Chaisty and Petra Schleiter, 'Productive but Not Valued: The Russian State Duma, 1994–2001', *Europe-Asia Studies*, 54 (2002), 712.

   [9] See Thomas Remington, Steven Smith, and Moshe Haspel, 'Decrees, Laws and Inter-Branch Relations in the Russian Federation', *Post-Soviet Affairs*, 14 (1998), 287–322.

   [10] *Rossiiskaya gazeta* (7 March 1997).

Throughout the Yeltsin presidency, politicians within both branches recognized that weak agenda control hampered effective policy-making and initiated measures aimed at rationalizing legislative activity. Khasbulatov criticized Supreme Soviet committees for having 'converted themselves into branches of ministries',[11] and his deputy, Nikolay Ryabov, headed a working group charged with the task of prioritizing the parliament's agenda. This initiative had some success in streamlining the assembly's legislative plan, but the agenda continued to be a source of conflict. Under the new constitution, a more deliberate effort was made to increase the executive's influence over the parliament's legislative direction with the formation of the United Commission for the Coordination of Legislative Activities in November 1994. This Commission, formed as part of the process of 'Social Accord' in the aftermath of the October 1993 crisis, involved the executive more directly in drafting the parliament's legislative plan, but the parliament's effectiveness in realizing its priorities continued to be hampered by countervailing pressures. Weak political control was at the heart of the problem. Without the party political levers to discipline legislators, the existing institutional arrangements lacked force. Under Putin, the executive finally acquired those partisan controls.

The Move Toward Majoritarian Control

The recognition of parliament's importance in achieving executive dominance has been a notable feature of Putin's presidency. Political strategies aimed at building a parliamentary basis of support, and institutional changes centred on curtailing the dispersed system of parliamentary agenda-setting, have been employed to considerable effect. The Kremlin's determination to play a more central role in parliamentary affairs was evident from the start of Putin's rule. In contrast to Yeltsin, Putin paid greater attention to building alliances with parties in the Duma, and used flexible tactics in doing so. During his first term, Putin was not averse to making deals with the Communist opposition on procedural and substantive issues. At the start of the Third Duma (2000–3), the Kremlin-backed party, Unity, cooperated with the Communist Party to undo the power-sharing 'package' method for dividing up key leadership and committee assignments in the assembly. The exclusion of smaller parties from the assignment process revealed a desire by the larger parties to assert their dominance, which had been present in previous Dumas but was never fully realized.[12]

---

[11] 'Itogi Shestoi Sessii', *Parlamentskaya nedelya :informatsionnyi byulleten'*, 23–4 (1993), 10.
[12] See Paul Chaisty, 'Defending the Institutional Status Quo: Communist Leadership of the Second Russian State Duma, 1996–99', *Legislative Studies Quarterly*, XXVIII (2003).

The Kremlin was also more effective in uniting centrist forces in the lower house. In the spring of 2001, a majority coalition consisting of Unity, People's Deputy, Fatherland-All Russia (OVR), and Russia's Regions was formed in the Duma. Although the 'coalition of four' was far from united on many issues, and the Kremlin continued to engineer cross-party alliances on many key votes,[13] it produced a further shift toward majoritarian control. In the spring of 2002, the pro-government bloc achieved a procedural majority with the support of several parties outside the coalition, and finally managed to break the package regime by successfully forcing the expulsion of seven Communist committee chairs. Alexander Mitrofanov, a leading member of the Liberal Democratic Party of Russia (LDPR), captured the essence of majoritarian governance when he warmly welcomed Unity's assault on the Duma's power-sharing arrangements in the corresponding parliamentary debate:

You know, it's possible to talk a lot about professionalism, but this [the assignment process] is a political thing. Those people who currently wish to make these changes in the Duma are simply larger in number, do you understand? In America, with just a majority of one the whole apparatus becomes theirs, all the committee chairs become theirs, and the speaker theirs, without discussion, do you understand? With just one additional person! Therefore, every vote is fought for. But we have got used to the idea that the minority is entitled to equal treatment. Why is this the case? . . . I'll tell you what's needed: the victors should get everything, that's politics. We absolutely agree that professionalism is preferable. But democracy is that kind of game.[14]

The landslide election victory of the Kremlin's United Russia party in December 2003 consolidated majority rule in the lower house. With seats in excess of 300, United Russia comfortably enjoyed the simple majority needed to institutionalize the executive's control over the Duma's internal arrangements, and acted decisively to translate its electoral success into institutional power. The ability of independent deputies to form 'groups' in the assembly, thereby profiting from internal rules that gave groups the same rights as 'factions',[15] was restricted. By raising the number of deputies required to form a deputy group from 35 to 55, United Russia precluded the creation of deputy groups at the start of the Fourth Duma. This measure cajoled office-seeking independents into joining United Russia, and prevented the leftist opposition from forming 'satellite' groups to increase their representation in the Duma Council—a tactic used effectively by the Communist Party in previous Dumas.

United Russia also gained almost total control over the key leadership posts in the assembly. Previous arrangements that gave each party leader one vote of equal

---

[13] Thomas Remington, 'Putin, the Duma, and Political Parties', in Dale Herspring (ed.), *Putin's Russia: Past Imperfect, Future Uncertain* (Lanham, MD: Rowman & Littlefield, 2003), 47.

[14] *Stenogramma zasedanii Gosdumy*, 157 (3 April 2002), 9. Author's words in parentheses.

[15] Partisan organization in the Duma takes two forms: 'factions'—parties that gain 5 per cent or more of the national ballot in parliamentary elections; 'groups'—political associations formed by deputies on their election to parliament.

Table 7.1. Duma Posts Assigned to the Largest Party or Coalition (1994–2004)

	First Duma: (1994–5)	Second Duma: (1996–9)	Third Duma (2000–March 2002)	Third Duma (April 2002– December 2003)*	Fourth Duma (2004–)
Party/Coalition (Seats %)†	RC (17)	CPRF-APG -PP (49)	CPRF- AIDG (29)	Unity-OVR- RR-PD (52)	UR (68)
Leadership: Duma chair and deputy chairs (%)	17	43	30	40	73
Duma Council (%)	10	50	30	44	73
Committee chairs (%)	17	50	39	68	100
Committee deputy chairs (%)	17	31	25	61	66

Key: RC (Russia's Choice); CPRF (Communist Party of the Russian Federation); APG (Agrarian Party Group); PP (Popular Power); AIDG (Agro-Industrial Deputy Group); OVR (Fatherland–All Russia); RR (Russia's Regions); PD (People's Deputy); UR (United Russia).
* The package agreement was changed during the spring of 2002. An anti-CPRF majority successfully unseated several leftist committee chairs and removed the casting vote of the Communist Duma chairman, Gennadi Seleznev.
† There are 450 seats in the State Duma. At the time of the package agreement, the number of seats held by each party or coalition was as follows: RC (76), CPRF-APG-PP (222), CPRF-AIDG (131), Unity-OVR-RR-PD (236), UR (306).

weight within the Duma Council were replaced by a new composition, consisting of the chair of the Duma and his deputies. United Russia gained the majority of these posts, and also acquired control of the overwhelming number of senior committee positions. In contrast to previous Dumas, the assignment process was heavily loaded in favour of the largest party, with the minority confined to nominal representation on the Duma Council and a share of deputy committee chairs (see Table 7.1). The Duma's rules were also changed to allow party leaders to hold leadership positions in the assembly. This rule change enabled the leader of United Russia, Boris Gryzlov, to become Duma chair. Moreover, the leaders of the various subgroups within United Russia each gained a deputy chairmanship. Consequently, the relative autonomy that parliamentary leaders had enjoyed from their parties in previous Dumas was reversed; the leadership of the Duma was now the leadership of the dominant party: United Russia.

The parliamentary minority was, with the exception of LDPR, left extolling the virtues of consensual democracy. Motherland leader, Sergey Baburin, argued 'democracy is not the power of the majority, democracy is respect for the rights of the minority, it is about finding a balance of forces and interests'.[16] Ironically, Communist presidential candidate Nikolay Kharitonov warned of a return to one-party rule:

[16] *Stenogramma zasedanii Gosdumy*, 1 (29 December 2003), 18.

Yes, there were 202 patriotic voices [Communist supporters] in the Second Duma, but it was never permitted to shut up the minority in such a way! . . . I appeal to all colleagues and to the praesidium: after we have seen the business of democratic centralism—which today the constitutional majority has permitted—we should introduce into the constitution Article 6 of the constitution on the leading and guiding role of the party.[17]

However, the new majoritarian arrangements belie United Russia as a homogeneous and ideologically cohesive party. United Russia is a presidential coalition comprising different partisan, regional, corporate, and administrative interests. The existence of four intra-party subgroups, each coordinated by a Duma deputy chair, illustrates the party's different constituencies: former Unity members (*medvedy*) comprise the Vladimir Pekhtin group; former members of OVR (*luzhkovtsy*) are represented by the group of Vyacheslav Volodin; deputies representing regional administrative interests (*shaimievtsy*) are led by the Oleg Morozov group; and corporate interests compose a group led by former head of the Duma's Energy Committee, Vladimir Katrenko.[18] In practice, the procedural advantages and benefits that the party's leadership derive from the Duma's new rules provide a means for reconciling the interests of these different constituencies. In the same way that earlier power-sharing rules provided a mechanism for building consensus between the Duma's different parties, the new majoritarian rules are sufficiently flexible to accommodate key figures within United Russia. The assignment of committee posts, for example, is a useful carrot at the disposal of the party leadership. To resolve intense intra-party conflicts over committee positions, the number of committees increased by one on the previous Duma, despite a pledge by the party's leadership to streamline the committee structure.

Nonetheless, the decision not to divide United Russia into several parliamentary groups following its election victory, which was anticipated by some commentators, reduces the transaction costs the Russian government faces when governing through the lower house. The Kremlin is not required, as in previous Dumas, to consult separately the leaders of different parties, but just one party: United Russia. Although the party's leader, Boris Gryzlov, does not enjoy the undivided loyalty of party members, as evidenced by disagreement within United Russia on substantive policy issues,[19] the establishment of one-party rule has empowered the government to tighten its control over the parliamentary agenda. In ways reminiscent of other states in transition, party dominance has provided a vehicle for executive control over the internal activities of the legislature.[20] This is highlighted by a number of procedural innovations.

---

[17] *Stenogramma zasedanii Gosdumy*, 2 (16 January 2004), 19. Author's words in parentheses.

[18] Andrey Stepanov, 'Izbiratel'. Gosduma 'Edinoi Rossii', *Moskovskie novosti*, 30 December 2003.

[19] See 'Differences emerge within Unified Russia Faction over Nationalization', *RFE/RL Newsline*, 8/105, Part I, June 2004.

[20] On the institutionalization of executive dominance in the British House of Commons, for example, see Gary Cox, *The Efficient Secret* (Cambridge: Cambridge University Press, 1987).

Under the Duma's new arrangements, the parliamentary leadership is more directly involved in the coordination of legislative activity with the executive branch. An additional first deputy post was created to strengthen the leadership's capacity to coordinate work on legislation between the various branches of government.[21] Most significantly, first deputies are charged with regularizing the informal practice of 'zero readings' in the legislative process.[22] In effect, 'zero readings' reconcile conflicts between the executive and parliamentary leaders on legislation before its official 'readings' (first, second and third) in the assembly, thereby increasing the likelihood that legislation will be passed without the serious delay or amendment that hampered government bills in the past. Such 'readings' were originally introduced in the Third Duma to iron out disagreements on government budget bills, but following the expulsion of Communist committee chairs in the spring of 2002, they were extended to other legislation. Since 2003, the executive has sought to integrate 'zero readings' into the legislative process.[23] According to Chairman Gryzlov, this development will enable the parliament to realize the 'strategic aims of the president.'[24] By building a political majority on legislation before it reaches the assembly, the executive is seeking to limit the capacity of partisan and particularistic interests to alter the content of legislation during its passage through the Federal Assembly; to prevent the situation where bills '... do not fulfil their stated aims because they are passed under pressure from narrow groups or departmental interests'[25] as Putin averred in his 2001 presidential address. In theory, such 'readings' are open to all parties, but in reality the main purpose of this innovation appears to centre on the resolution of conflicts on legislation within United Russia.[26]

A further measure aimed at controlling the law-making process concerns the gate-keeping powers of committees. In earlier Dumas, the Duma Council struggled to impose the assembly's legislative plan. In addition to laws assigned 'priority' status, deputies initiated large numbers of bills that inhibited efforts to streamline the Duma's work. At the Second Duma, the volume of bills in the legislative system was on average nearly double the number originally planned.[27]

---

[21] Following the appointment of Alexander Zhukov to the Russian government, Vladislav Reznik, chairman of the Banking Committee, assumed this role.

[22] *Stenogramma zasedanii Gosdumy*, 1 (29 December 2003), 24.

[23] Kseniya Veretennikova, 'Edinaya Duma Rossii. Nakanune novogo goda partiya vlasti vsekh rasstavit po mestam', *Vremya novostei*, 29 December 2003.

[24] 'M. Kas'yanov: 'Protseduru "nulevogo chteniya" budut prokhodit' vse znachimye zakonoproekty, podgotovlennye pravitel'stvom RF', *RosBiznesKonsalting*, 13 January 2004, at http://www.rbc.ru (accessed 19 May 2004).

[25] *Rossiiskaya gazeta*, 4 April 2001.

[26] Ivan Rodin, 'Nulevoe zakonotvorchestvo: Aleksandr Zhukov otvechaet za to, chtoby na Okhotnom Ryadu bol'she ne bylo diskussii', *Nezavisimaya gazeta*, 30 January 2004.

[27] Gosudarstvennaya Duma: Analiticheskoe upravlenie, *Gosudarstvennaya Duma vtorogo sozyva (1996–1999): Informatsionno-analiticheskii byulleten'* (Gosudarstvennaya Duma, Moscow, 1999), 84.

Although the assembly considered most of this legislation, it was rarely enacted, and as a consequence it clogged up the legislative timetable of committees. In the Third Duma, for example, the assembly enacted just 10 per cent of such bills, but scrutinized over 50 per cent.[28] Responding to this problem, United Russia introduced a rule change in March 2004 that gives committees the power to propose the rejection of any bill already approved in its first reading that is considered to have 'no prospect' of passage.[29] Aimed principally at clearing up a backlog of bills (in excess of 1,000) under consideration from the previous parliament, this measure seeks to restrict lobbying activity within the assembly. In practice, it may also limit the capacity of minority parties to introduce legislation. The combination of greater executive control over the parliament's agenda, plus United Russia's dominance over the Duma Council and the chamber's legislative committees, imposes significant constraints on the legislative influence of minority parties. According to one commentator, key ministers now meet only with the leaders of United Russia on a regular basis: 'Members of the government now consider it superfluous to build relations with the leaders of other factions.'[30]

Such innovations were aided by earlier developments within the Federation Council. Putin's reform of the assembly's composition in 2000, and the election of a parliamentary chair closely connected to the Kremlin, Sergey Mironov, gave a new impetus to executive-backed initiatives to rationalize the legislative process.[31] Indeed, Mironov reportedly first developed the use of 'zero reading' during his chairmanship of the St Petersburg Legislative Assembly.[32] Several measures aimed at 'systematizing' the legislative process were introduced: weekly planning meetings to coordinate the activities of an expanded committee system; the formation of 'three-sided' working groups to mediate inter-branch and inter-cameral conflicts; and the creation of a steering body, the Council Chamber, to coordinate the policy positions of legislative leaders in the chamber.[33] However, executive control in the upper house has not been exercised through party control. The decision by the reformed house to prohibit the creation of partisan factions and parliamentary associations suggests that the indirect method of electing members has given the Kremlin sufficient leverage over the composition of the

[28] *Informatsionno-analiticheskii byulleten'*, *2000–2003. Gosudarstvennaya Duma tret'ego sozyva (itogovoi)*, at http://www.duma.gov.ru (accessed 12 June 2004).

[29] See *Stenogramma zasedanii Gosdumy*, No. 14 (24 March 2004), 54–5

[30] Aleksandr Kolesnichenko, 'Printsip konveiera', *Novye izvestiya*, 25 March 2004.

[31] See I. Lavrinenko, 'O parlamentskikh slushaniyakh po voprosu 'Razvitie parlamentskogo prava Rossiiskoi Federatsii v svete sovershenstvovaniya zakonodatel'noi deyatel'nosti Federal'nogo Sobraniya Rossiiskoi Federatsii'', *Sovet Federatsii i konstitutsionnye protsessy v sovremennoi Rossii: ezhekvartal'nyi byulleten'*, 2 (2002), 10–12.

[32] Aleksey Zudin, 'Ot rezhima—k sisteme: posledstviya dumskogo perevorota', at http://www.mfit.ru/power/pub_2_73.html (accessed 19 May 2004).

[33] This body predates the reform of the Federation Council's composition. The chamber, which consists of the chair, his deputies, and the heads of the assembly's committees and commissions, was created in January 1999.

assembly. The role of the presidential administration in filtering the appointment of senators and the centralization of the assignment of leadership and committee posts has reduced the autonomy of the upper house.[34] This was illustrated by the appointment of Mikhail Margelov and Dmitry Mezentsev to head the foreign affairs and Media committees. Both senators enjoyed close ties to the Kremlin.

The Effects of Executive Dominance

Although the view is frequently expressed that legislative politics under Putin has become more executive-centred,[35] it is too early to examine systematically the impact that majority control has had on the Federal Assembly. It is also problematic to attribute all of the changes that have occurred under Putin to the measures introduced since he came to power. Nonetheless, there is evidence of an exponential tightening of executive control over the parliament's internal activities, in particular since the spring of 2002 when the Kremlin majority asserted its majority power over the internal organization of the assembly. This can be illustrated with reference to both the partisan and the policy effects of majoritarianism.

Partisan Effects

One indicator of the impact of the Kremlin's influence over Duma parties is the extent to which its coalition-building initiatives have produced more cohesive government parties. The consolidation of parties within the assembly and the growth of party discipline is a development that predates Putin.[36] However, the creation of the 'coalition of four' and the assertion of its institutional power in the spring of 2002 appears to have contributed to higher levels of discipline among government-supporting parties, albeit with some interesting variation. By securing a stable basis of support within the assembly, the presidency's effectiveness in building winning coalitions has been enhanced. Consequently, parliament–presidential relations have been less confrontational under Putin.

Two measures of the voting discipline of government parties are considered: voting cohesion and the level of absenteeism on key and contested votes.[37] The

---

[34] See Anna Kozyreva, 'Novaya zhizn' tret'ei modeli. SF: khoroshie lyudi poluchili khoroshie dolzhnosti', *Vek*, 1 February 2002.

[35] Kseniya Veretennikova (n. 23); Andrew Jack, 'Critics See No Room for Dissent in New Duma,' *Financial Times*, 5 February 2004; Tat'yana Stanovaya, 'Duma monopolizirovana tsentristami', 12 January 2004, at http://www.politcom.ru/search.php (accessed 19 May 2004).

[36] See Paul Chaisty, 'Party Cohesion and Policy-Making in Russia', *Party Politics*, 11 (2005, forthcoming).

[37] Contested votes are votes where at least 10 per cent of Duma deputies dissented from the majority position. Key votes are those deemed to be salient by commentators and politicians at the

Paul Chaisty

Rice Index is used to indicate voting cohesion on a scale from 0 to 100.[38] The cohesion score moves towards 0 as the difference between aye and nay votes within a party increases; a score of 100 indicates unanimous voting by party members. The data for deputies who were absent on individual votes was treated as a separate indicator of the capacity of government parties to mobilize their members on key issues. Although non-voting is used strategically by some parties in the Duma, notably LDPR, the motivation for not voting is often unclear, and few examples of unanimous non-voting by government parties were found. Hence, non-votes were not recoded as 'nay' votes.[39]

The results of this analysis for all government parties since 1994 are summarized in Figure 7.1. The findings show that the voting cohesion of the main government parties—Russia's Choice (First Duma, 1994–5), Our Home is Russia (Second Duma, 1996–9), and Unity (Third Duma, 2000–3)—has steadily

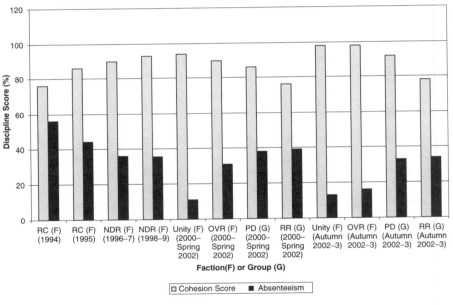

Figure 7.1. Rice Cohesion Scores and Absenteeism Rates for Government Parties (1994–2003).

time. The number of votes selected for each period observed varied between 126 and 242, and only the votes of those deputies who remained members of a party for the entire period observed were calculated.

[38] This index measures the absolute difference between the percentage of aye and nay votes within each party. Deputies who abstained on votes were recoded as nays.

[39] On the problems of analysing non-voting in Russia, see Steven Smith and Thomas Remington, *The Politics of Institutional Choice: The Formation of the Russian State Duma* (Princeton, NJ: Princeton University Press, 2001), 165.

increased. In the latter half of the Third Duma, Unity came close to achieving unanimous voting on the key votes selected. However, the general trend toward more cohesive government parties since 1994 is mirrored by most opposition parties and therefore cannot be attributed solely to the leadership of Putin. In addition to the presidential administration's role in engineering more cohesive government parties, factors such as the mode of election, institutional benefits, and intra-party arrangements have all played an important role in raising discipline. More striking is the decline in the percentage of Unity members absenting on key votes since 2000. Unity had higher voting participation rates than both of its predecessors—Russia's Choice (RC) and Our Home is Russia (NDR)—according to this set of data. Moreover, absenteeism for Unity members was lower than for all other parties. While on average 34 and 27 per cent of party members in both periods of the Third Duma were absent for the votes analysed, Unity had an absenteeism rate of just 11 and 13 per cent.

The formation of the 'coalition of four' had a notable impact on voting discipline within Fatherland–All Russia (OVR). Although relations between OVR and Unity were strained at first, the consolidation of the coalition's institutional power in the spring of 2002 contributed to far higher levels of discipline. Both the Rice cohesion score and the level of absenteeism illustrate this development. However, for the other parties in this coalition, People's Deputy (PD) and Russia's Regions (RR), the results were mixed. As in previous Dumas, Russia's Regions continued to register low levels of cohesion. Composed of single-mandate deputies representing the interests of regional authorities, members of this group were more susceptible to parochial pressures on certain issues. By contrast, People's Deputy, which was more closely aligned with the Kremlin, achieved far higher levels of voting cohesion after the formation of the Kremlin coalition. Yet both groups continued to show high levels of absenteeism, which hampered efforts to convert the 'coalition of four' into a disciplined voting bloc. With a majority in single digits, the Kremlin alliance was vulnerable to defections. None the less, the 'coalition of four' established a solid basis on which to construct winning majorities. Data on voting affinity between Unity and its coalition partners found Unity's allies to be more reliable toward the end of the Third Duma (see Figure 7.2).[40] Moreover, the Kremlin received important support from other parties on key votes, notably LDPR and SPS, and as a consequence became less reliant on dealing with its principal opponent: the Communist Party. This is a luxury that Putin's predecessor did not enjoy.

Policy Effects

Following the collapse of Communism, the Russian executive struggled to impose its legislative priorities on the parliament. Corporate, regional, and departmental

---

[40] Voting affinity is registered when the majority of one faction or group votes with the majority from another faction or group. The data set used to calculate party discipline was also used to construct these affinity scores.

Paul Chaisty

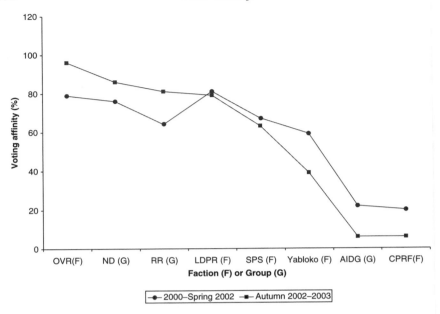

Figure 7.2. **Variation in the Voting Affinity of Duma Parties to Unity, 2000–3**

lobbying all contributed to a bloated legislative agenda, and the law-making organs empowered to steer the assembly's legislative activities, such as the Duma Council, proved to be relatively ineffective. Reflecting on the difficulties facing the Duma Council in the Second Duma, Russia's Regions head, Oleg Morozov, revealed the scale of the problem:

... we must reject the principle of mechanically combining all the proposals of parties. This principle exists today and produces a gigantic calendar, often making it difficult to determine which [bill] should receive primary attention, and which secondary. A lot depends on how smart those who propose legislation are.[41]

The steps taken to tighten executive control over the Duma's legislative activities do appear, however, to have had an impact on the size and content of the Duma's plan, and the effectiveness of legislators in realizing their legislative priorities. Aggregate data on the volume of 'priority' laws introduced since 1996 shows a marked decrease during the Third Duma.[42] In the first five sessions of this Duma,

[41] RTR (All-Russian Television), *Parlamentskaya nedelya*, 5 October 1996, time 10.15 a.m. (printed transcript). Parentheses added by the author.

[42] The Duma's plan (*primernaya programma*) comprises two sets of legislation: (1) 'priority' laws, which before autumn 2001 were included in section I of the Duma's plan; (2) all other legislation under consideration by committees. Since the autumn session of 1996, priority bills have been organized into six thematic categories: 'state building and the constitutional rights of citizens', 'economic policy', 'social policy', 'budget, tax, financial legislation', 'defence and security', and the 'ratification of international treaties'.

an average 150 bills were scheduled for priority consideration in each session, and following the assertion of the 'coalition of four's' majority power in the spring of 2002, this figure fell to an average of around 130 bills.[43] These figures contrast favourably with the Second Duma, when on average more than 250 bills were considered to be of priority importance in each session.[44] Such streamlining of the assembly's legislative priorities suggests that the Duma Council was more successful in curtailing the ability of committees and individual deputies to acquire priority status for their legislative projects. This development cannot however be attributed directly to the establishment of a pro-government majority. Initiatives to raise the effectiveness of the Federal Assembly's law-making process, and the concomitant decline in the number of priority laws, predate the formation of the 'coalition of four'.

Yet the Duma's capacity to scrutinize and pass priority laws was enhanced by the institutional control gained by the government majority in the spring of 2002. Data on the percentage of priority bills scrutinized and passed by the Duma following the rout of Communist committee chairs shows a notable increase on both the Second Duma and the earlier sessions of the Third Duma (see Figure 7.3).

More striking are the data on the authorship of priority legislation. The number of priority bills initiated by the executive dramatically increased in the latter half

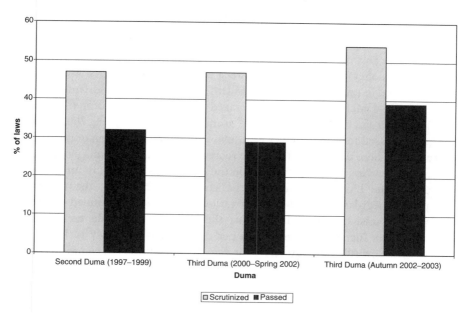

Figure 7.3. **Percentage of Priority Bills Scrutinized and Passed (1997–2003).**

[43] *Informatsionno-analiticheskii byulleten', 2000–2003* (n. 28)
[44] *Gosudarstvennaya Duma vtorogo sozyva (1996–1999)* (n. 27), 86.

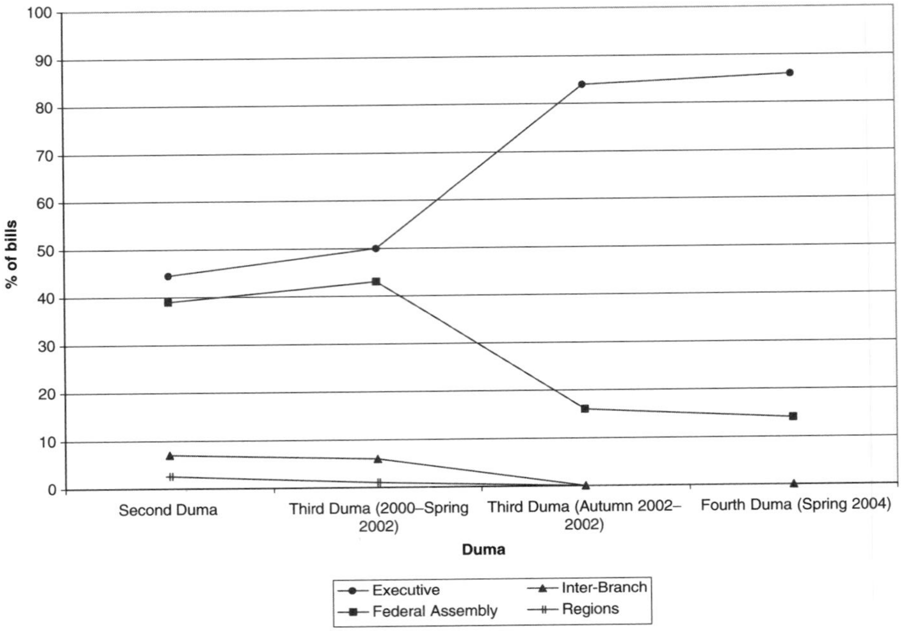

Figure 7.4. Authors of Priority Economic Legislation, 1997–2004

of the Third Duma, and this trend has continued into the Fourth Duma. Figure 7.4 illustrates this development with reference to priority legislation in the area of economic policy. While the gap between the number of priority laws initiated by the executive (government and president) and the Federal Assembly (Duma deputies and Federation Council) averaged less than 10 per cent in both the Second Duma and the Third Duma (up to and including the spring 2002 session), the gap increased to around 70 per cent following the renegotiation of the package agreement. These data suggest that the reorganization of the Duma along majoritarian lines had an immediate impact on the executive's capacity to influence the content of the Duma's agenda. At the same time, however, the volume of non-priority legislation in the Duma's various committees continued to rise. In the last three sessions of the Third Duma, the volume of bills under consideration by committees increased by over 100 per cent.[45] It is too early to know how effective the new rules strengthening the gate-keeping powers of committees have been in curtailing this outlet for legislative autonomy, but government critics revealed that much of the Fourth Duma's early work was concerned with clearing this backlog of laws from the legislative process.[46] By constraining the legislative

45 *Informatsionno-analiticheskii byulleten', 2000–2003* (n. 28).

46 ' "Edinaya Rossiya" ustanavlivaet svoi poryadok v Dume. Derzhat' i ne pushchat', *Sovetskaya Rossiya* (3 April 2004).

activity of deputies in this respect, the executive appears to be acquiring further control over the Duma's timetable.

Another indicator of the policy effects of majoritarianism is the impact that executive control has had on the parliament's capacity to veto legislation. For the Federation Council, the power to veto bills is a key source of legislative influence. Although the Council can initiate legislation, in practice this power has been used to a limited extent. Vetoes provide members of the upper house with a more fruitful opportunity to shape the content of legislation. The 'conciliation commissions' formed to resolve conflicts on vetoed bills between both houses, and the 'special commissions' that are created to reconcile disputes between both houses and the executive, give regional lobbies a say on the content of legislation. Conciliation commissions dealing with financial matters, in particular budgetary and taxation legislation, were most common during Yeltsin's tenure.

Under Putin, inter-cameral and inter-branch relations have certainly become less confrontational. The number of Duma bills vetoed by the upper house has fallen significantly since 2000. In the First Duma, one third of all Duma bills were initially rejected by the Federation Council; this figure fell to around a quarter in the Second Duma, and in the Third Duma to less than 10 per cent. Early evidence from the Fourth Duma shows a further decline in the use of Federation Council vetoes. Thus, 'senators' appear less willing to hold out for concessions during the process of legislative amendment. The use of conciliation and special commissions, for example, has declined. In the Second Duma, 188 laws were passed in an agreed form on the recommendation of conciliation and special commissions;[47] in the Third Duma, this figure fell to sixty-four.[48] The relative timidity of the upper house under Putin is further illustrated by cases when 'senators' followed the Kremlin on legislation that clearly undermined the powers of regional authorities, such as new laws on regional elections, and the rejection of legislation empowering regional legislators to determine the level of the minimum wage at the local level.[49]

The Duma's willingness to confront both the upper house and the executive has also been tempered. Data show that the number of Duma bills that remained vetoed by both the upper house and president has declined: from 102 bills in the Second Duma to just ten bills in the Third Duma. Interestingly, no Duma bills were vetoed by both the Federation Council and President Putin after the institutional consolidation of the executive's Duma majority in spring 2002. However, the executive's overall contribution to legislation enacted continues to remain comparatively low. The proportion of enacted laws initiated by the government and president was 58 per cent in the Third Duma, just a 3 per cent increase on what the executive branch achieved during the Second Duma. The Russian government

[47] Gosudarstvennaya Duma: Analiticheskoe upravlenie, 'Statisticheskie kharakteristiki zakonoda-tel'noi deyatel'nosti Gosudarstvennoi Dumy vtorogo sozyva (1996–1999)', *Analiticheskii vestnik. Vypusk 3* (Moscow, 2000), 12.

[48] *Informatsionno-analiticheskii byulleten'*, *2000–2003* (n. 28).

[49] *RFE/RL Newsline*, 7/144, Part I, July 2003.

does, nevertheless, appear determined to improve this statistic. Speaking at the opening session of the Fourth Duma, the then Prime Minister, Mikhail Kasyanov, told deputies that the executive's output would increase to a minimum of 60 per cent over the life of the Fourth Duma.[50]

Conclusion

Parliament–president relations have become more majoritarian under Putin. The Kremlin has acquired majority backing in both houses of the Federal Assembly, and this political support has been used to strengthen the executive's influence over the internal legislative arrangements of both houses. New techniques for resolving conflict on legislation, such as the use of 'zero readings', have shifted the centre of law-making from the legislative branch to the executive, and the policy effects of this development appear to be supported by data on legislative decisions in the latter half of the Third Duma.

It would be inaccurate to attribute all these achievements to Putin. Proposals to rationalize and streamline law-making in Russia have been present since the early years of transition. In Khasbulatov's Supreme Soviet, and in earlier State Dumas, a number of initiatives were proposed to address the problems caused by particularistic lobbying and legislative overload.[51] The difference under Putin is that more effective political control has enabled this desire to be transformed into reality. However, it is premature to talk about total executive dominance in Russian legislative politics. Although the proportion of priority bills initiated by the executive has increased under Putin, the executive continues to be responsible for a comparatively low proportion of all enacted legislation, and the new majoritarian arrangements belie United Russia as a homogeneous and ideologically cohesive party. In the first session of the Fourth Duma, tensions emerged within United Russia on nationalization and welfare legislation, and deputies representing regional interests proposed ways to increase internal party discussion on legislation as a way of mitigating the effects of 'zero readings'.

So long as Putin remains the dominant force in Russian politics, these tensions are unlikely to jeopardize the Kremlin's majority. However, Putin is still required to appease a range of views within what is a very broad presidential coalition. The division of United Russia into subgroups, each with their own leader and seats in the Duma Council, and the use of the Duma's assignment process to distribute patronage, provide a means of managing the heterogeneous preferences within this party. Further measures are being prepared to enhance executive dominance.

[50] *Stenogramma zasedanii Gosdumy*, No. 2 (16 January 2004), 12.
[51] See Alexander Shokhin, *Vzaimodeistvie vlastei v zakonodatel'nom protsesse* (Moscow: Nash dom-L'Age d'Homme, 1997).

At the time of writing, proposals to create a fully proportional system for elections to the State Duma appeared aimed at strengthening party control. By removing deputies elected in single-mandate districts from the lower house, the voice of regional representatives within United Russia could be further weakened. Yet, the heightening of executive power carries risks. Future governments will struggle to blame policy failures on an obstructive parliament, and United Russia may be held to account for potentially unpopular measures, such as housing and welfare reform. Splitting United Russia into its constituent parts is always an option if a new party in power is required, but this could undermine efforts to consolidate executive control in Russia.

8

Putin's Popularity and Its Implications for Democracy in Russia

Stephen Whitefield

Introduction

Understanding the often ambiguous and contradictory character of Vladimir Putin's political leadership is central to making sense of many of the most problematic questions concerning Russia's democratic present and future. Russia's first ever elected leader, Boris Yeltsin, presided over a deep economic decline and political conflict. He was also, for much of his time in office, a highly unpopular president. By contrast, Vladimir Putin's tenure has coincided with economic growth and greater stability of power in the country. Moreover, as the evidence below shows, Putin has been a highly popular leader. He is also accused by many commentators of pursuing illiberal and anti-democratic policies, and of carrying on political vendettas against opponents who criticize him for it. In one particularly trenchant intervention, five ideologically disparate Russians (Boris Berezovsky, Elena Bonner, Vladimir Bukovsky, Ruslan Khasbulatov, and Ivan Rybkin) took out a full page article in the *New York Times* to summarize their views under the title: 'Seven Questions to President George Bush about his friend President Vladimir Putin', among which were:

Mr President [Bush], are you aware ... [t]hat the Russian Parliament, courts and media have been brought under the virtual control of the Kremlin, and elections have turned into a farce? That the Constitution of 1993 that established the democratic foundations of Russia has been effectively destroyed? ... That Russian society is gripped by fear ...?[1]

The concerns of the observers quoted above might be written off simply as politically motivated opposition. But their highly negative picture of the character

[1] *New York Times*, 23 September, 2003, p. A21. It is particularly ironic, given his role in the events that preceded its adoption, that Khasbulatov should name the 1993 constitution as the point at which the democratic foundations of the country were established.

and development of Russian democracy is supported by other more 'objective' indicators. For example, the World Bank's Governance Indicators for Russia show a decline between 1996 and 2002 in the public's capacity for democratic voice and in its ability to hold government accountable, from what was in any case a relatively low initial position.[2] Another influential index comes to a similar conclusion about Russian democracy. Freedom House uses a range of indicators—shown in Table 8.1—all of which suggest that the country has become less democratic since 1997, and that this negative trend has not been reversed since Putin took office in 2000.[3] Russia, which Freedom House classified as only 'partly free' in 1997, appears to have become even less so.

If these characterizations are correct, the very fact of Putin's popularity might be redolent of even deeper problems in the functioning of Russia's political system. How can Putin be popular, if Russia's democracy is as limited as these commentators and indicators suggest? Are Russians ignorant of the true state of affairs in their country or too frightened to speak out against it? But while weakness in the democratic system might explain why ordinary Russians would be unable effectively to use political institutions to constrain him, it would be more disturbing for the democratic prospects of the country if Russians were actually supportive of Putin *because* of the undemocratic policies alleged by his opponents. It is a commonplace to suggest that Russians have a strong desire for order and stability. This preference may be the result of long-standing cultural commitments or may be a consequence of the enormous turmoil in national and personal circumstances that Russians have faced since the collapse of the Soviet Union. But whatever the explanation, in conditions of disorder and instability typical of the Yeltsin years, such a preference might well engender public support for strong leaders like Putin untrammelled by democratic or liberal constraints. Do Russians like Putin because they value the stability that his leadership may provide more than they value democracy? Or are Russians able to support Putin because they are, or have become, uncommitted to democratic values?

This chapter addresses these questions by investigating how and why ordinary Russians evaluate their presidents and their political system, and support Putin

Table 8.1. Freedom House Scores 1997–2003 (1 = Most liberal and democratic; 7 = least)

	1997	1998	1999	2001	2002	2003
Electoral process	3.5	3.5	4.0	4.25	4.5	4.75
Civil society	3.75	4.0	3.75	4.0	4.0	4.25
Independent media	3.75	4.25	4.75	5.25	5.5	5.5
Governance	4.0	4.5	4.5	5.0	5.25	5.0
Constitutional, legislative, and judicial framework	4.0	4.25	4.25	4.5	4.75	4.5

[2] http://info.worldbank.org/governance/kkz2002/country_report.asp?countryid=187.
[3] http://www.freedomhouse.org.

and others electorally. It also considers how the bases of presidential approval and support may have changed over time. In particular, it questions whether Putin's support, by comparison with Yeltsin's and that for other potential candidates for president, is drawn from illiberal and anti-democratic forces, or from sections of the public that may value strong leadership as a way of resolving the country's problems even at the expense of democracy. Moreover, it questions whether there is a relationship between support for political leaders in Russia and the way Russians evaluate the political system in their country.

The logic of the presentation, therefore, is to test the following broad argument and specific hypotheses related to it:

1. Putin's popularity and support is drawn from growing illiberal and anti-democratic public sentiments, and from greater public desire for 'delegative' forms of political leadership, even if this is seen as detrimental to the country's democracy;
2. Putin's leadership has changed the ways in which Russians evaluate their political system, so that it is highly regarded by Putin's supporters *because* it increasingly delivers anti-democratic and illiberal outcomes, but more negatively appraised by opponents of Putin, particularly members of the public who are more democratically inclined;
3. As a consequence, views of the political system increasingly divide support for Putin and other candidates for office in Russia.

Against this negative 'growing illiberalism' scenario, however, alternative logics and hypotheses about the development of Russia and Putin's role in it must be examined. The comparative literature on presidential approval and electoral choice in consolidated democracies points to a number of factors that might also explain Putin's popularity and support, for example, trends in national economic performance and household living standards.[4] In this regard, the positive economic developments since 1998 in Russia are highly suggestive.[5] Additionally, institutional performance and responsiveness measures have been shown to have a significant impact on the ways in which the public make political judgements in Western and post-Communist democracies.[6] While the very negative evaluations of critics of Putin and Russian democracy make this a less obvious alternative explanation, it is unclear whether Russians themselves see institutional performance in such a negative light, particularly when it is compared with the many great

---

[4] Cf. Michael Lewis-Beck, *Economics and Elections* (Ann Arbor: University of Michigan Press, 1988).

[5] GDP. growth between 1999 and projected figures for 2003 was 5.4% per annum on average. Source: *Transition Report* (London: European Bank for Reconstruction and Development, 2003), 79.

[6] Robert Rohrschneider, 'The Democracy Deficit and Mass Support for a EU-wide Government', *American Journal of Political Science*, 46 (2002), 463–75; Geoffrey Evans and Stephen Whitefield, 'The Politics and Economics of Democratic Commitment: Support for Democracy in Transition Societies', *British Journal of Political Science*, 25 (1995), 485–514.

institutional weaknesses of the Yeltsin period, not least in the performance capacity of the president and in the level of conflict between the president and other national and federal institutions. Nor is it clear that positive views of institutional performance should necessarily be connected with growing illiberalism in policies. The effect of improved performance, particularly by the president, moreover, may well have had a positive effect on evaluations of Russian democracy, at least in the eyes of the Russian public, so that the issue of the political system per se no longer divides the electorate. We will therefore also seek to test the competing 'system performance' argument, and its associated hypotheses:

4. Putin's popularity and support is based on perceived improved economic and political performance;
5. Because institutional performance has improved and 'normalized', paradoxically Russians are now less likely to see the democratic system in practice as a basis for judgements about candidates for presidential office.

The data on which the analysis is based are drawn from national probability samples of Russians conducted by the author and colleagues in Oxford University between 1995 and 2003.[7] These data comprise measures of attitudes, declared voting intentions, and numerous social background indicators for respondents and their families. (Details of precise question wording for all measures used in the analysis are provided in the Appendix.) Considerable care was taken in constructing the questionnaire to create valid measures and in sampling to ensure an adequate basis for making valid inferences about the Russian population. While the reliability of the data and the validity of measures used to connect them with the underlying concepts at issue can always be improved upon in surveys, this point is all too often presented as powerful criticism of the survey method per se rather than as part of the normal process of scientific investigation. As always, social scientists see social reality through a glass darkly, but there is nothing in the now large literature on surveys in Russia to suggest that they constitute a particularly problematic measurement instrument in that country. Indeed, for questions such as the ones addressed here, surveys are clearly better than the anecdotal or introspective methods used by many who claim to know how things stand with the attitudes and behaviour of ordinary Russians.

The rest of the chapter is divided as follows. The second section shows how Russians view political leadership in their country, specifically in terms of their evaluation of presidents Yeltsin and Putin, and more generally in their willingness to support 'strong' leadership as a way of solving the country's problems. It also investigates trends in the distribution of liberal and authoritarian attitudes on a

---

[7] A survey was also conducted in 1993, but to ensure comparability of all questions over time, this was omitted from this study. However, more limited analysis that includes 1993 (available from the author) points to the same pattern of results as that found here. For detailed information on the surveys, see Stephen Whitefield, 'Russian Mass Attitudes Toward the Environment, 1993–2001', *Post-Soviet Affairs*, 19 (2003), 95–113.

number of issue dimensions. It then analyses the relationship between presidential approval, on the one hand, and respondents' views of leadership and their broader ideological commitments, on the other. The third section considers evidence about the changing state of Russian democracy as evaluated by Russians themselves, and how well changes in these evaluations may be explained by the outlined factors. The fourth section then investigates the relationship between views of overall system performance, presidential approval, ideological commitments, and support for Putin, Yeltsin, and other presidential contenders since 1995. The conclusion discusses the implications of the analysis for our understanding of the relationship between Putin's popularity and Russian democracy.

Trends in Presidential Evaluation, Views of Political Leadership, and Political Norms, 1995–2003

The aim of this section is to develop a picture of the changing ways in which Russians evaluate their leaders, view leadership more generally, and how they are differentiated on democratic and economic values and some of the central issues facing the country. The purpose in building this picture is to consider some of the claims made in the arguments and hypotheses above, and to prepare for analysis that looks at the relationship between presidential popularity and the other factors mentioned.

How have Russians evaluated their political leaders, in particular their president, since 1995? Table 8.2 presents responses to a question asking Russians to rate the performance of their president, and in particular their views of Yeltsin in 1995, 1996, and 1998, and Putin in 2001 and 2003. The results show a dramatic transformation in public regard for the incumbent. Yeltsin's scores are highly

Table 8.2. Russians evaluate their president (percentages)

	1995	1996	1998	2001	2003
Thinking about the performance of the president of Russia, how highly would you regard his activity?					
Very highly	0.9	2.7	0.6	6.2	10.6
Highly	5.8	12.0	3.2	28.8	43.7
Neither high nor low	33.0	42.4	22.9	49.3	33.5
Low	34.4	27.2	34.6	7.4	5.3
Very low	20.9	10.5	30.6	1.9	2.0
Don't know	5.1	5.2	8.1	6.5	5.0
N=	1993	2009	2008	2000	2000
Overall approval: positive minus negative	−48.6	−23.0	−61.4	+25.7	+47.0

negative. Even in 1996, the year in which he was re-elected, Yeltsin's overall approval rating is −23, a substantial improvement on the previous year when he was at −48.6, but presaging a stunning fall to −61.4 in 1998, when only 4 per cent of respondents had a positive view of his performance. Compare this situation with Putin's ratings, who perhaps not surprisingly after Yeltsin enjoyed a +25.7 rating early in his period in office in 2001, but who has gone on to improve further his standing among the public to +47 more than three years after coming to power.

In the next section we will ask whether Putin's popularity is connected in the public mind with a desire for strong leadership to resolve the country's problems, even if that leadership should be anti-democratic in practice. We next consider, therefore, the attitudes of Russians towards these leadership issues and how these may have changed over time.

Table 8.3 shows responses to two questions that relate to views of strong and delegative leadership. The first asks simply whether Russians would support government with a 'strong hand' if this helped solve the country's economic problems. We see a clear majority in each year expressing support for this proposition and, moreover, there is a significant increase in this support in 2001 and 2003 by comparison with the earlier years, in other words under Putin by comparison with Yeltsin. The second question raises the stakes (rhetorically at least) for respondents to support delegative leadership, since it asks whether it would be worth supporting a leader who would solve the country's problems even if this leader overthrew democracy itself. In this case, we do not find a majority in

Table 8.3. Russians' views on political leadership

	1995	1996	1998	2001	2003
Does Russia need government with a 'strong hand' to resolve its economic problems?					
Strongly agree	25.5	22.8	26.3	30.2	29.3
Agree	33.7	39.4	36.3	34.7	33.6
In between	18.2	16.2	16.0	18.1	17.2
Disagree	12.7	11.7	10.3	7.9	8.5
Strongly disagree	3.7	3.8	3.5	2.3	3.8
Don't know	6.2	6.1	7.6	7.0	7.7
Would it be worthwhile to support a leader who could solve the main problems facing Russia today even if he overthrew democracy?					
Strongly agree	12.0	14.8	15.0	17.3	18.0
Agree	32.1	31.2	29.6	29.7	28.4
In between	18.0	18.4	19.6	21.4	21.0
Disagree	23.6	20.2	15.6	13.6	13.0
Strongly disagree	3.3	5.2	5.1	4.8	6.0
Don't know	10.9	10.1	15.0	13.3	13.7
N=	2001	2010	2008	2000	2000

favour, but even so the largest group of respondents is willing to support the proposition, and notably only a small and clearly declining minority of Russians is opposed. There has also been a significant increase over time in the numbers of those willing to support a potentially undemocratic leader, though this trend is less pronounced than was the case with the first question. We can see in many Russians, therefore, a clear willingness to support strong and delegative leadership and a conditionality to their support for the democratic system as it now operates.

The next issue to be addressed concerns the distribution of attitudes on some central political values and issues that are of particular relevance to the claim that Russians have become more generally illiberal and that Putin's support is particularly related to this growing constituency. Among the values and issues shown in Table 8.4 are democratic norms, commitments to markets or state intervention, support for the rights of individuals against the authorities, or the authorities or majorities against individuals, views of the justification of the dissolution of the USSR, support for the necessity of using armed force to keep the country together (a particularly important item for both Yeltsin and Putin's ratings given their involvement in the two Chechen wars), attitudes towards Russia's Jews, and the right of republics within Russia to secede from the country. These items have been chosen because of what is known about their centrality to divisive questions in post-Communist Russian politics[8] and because of the role that critics of Putin (as with, for example, Berezovsky et al.) claimed some play in Putin's anti-democratic and illiberal policies.

The pattern that emerges from the responses in Table 8.4 does not appear to offer much support to the growing illiberalism contention. While there are significant differences in the distribution of norms and attitudes across years, these are generally relatively small. Russians appear more committed to democracy if 2001 or 2003 is compared to 1995 or 1998, but there is no difference if they are

Table 8.4. Trends in mean scores on central political and economic values and policies (scale of 1 to 5, with 1 = anti-democratic, anti-market, authoritarian, pro-Soviet Union, pro-armed force, anti-Semitic, anti-secessionist; 5 = the opposite)

	1995	1996	1998	2001	2003
Democratic norms	3.09	3.34	2.96	3.35	3.21
Market norms	2.57	2.48	2.39	2.39	2.41
Freedom of speech	4.07	4.15	4.15	4.01	4.14
Freedom of authorities	2.81	2.71	2.53	2.69	2.89
Dissolution of USSR	2.08	2.30	2.05	2.13	2.30
Armed force to keep country together	2.79	2.76	2.77	2.42	2.48
Anti-Semitism	3.05	3.08	2.77	2.77	2.67
Right of republics to secede	2.73	2.89	2.75	2.57	2.75

[8] Stephen Whitefield, 'Partisan and Party Divisions in Post-Communist Russia' in Archie Brown (ed.), *Contemporary Russian Politics: A Reader* (Oxford: Oxford University Press, 2001), 235–46.

compared to 1996. Similarly, Russians have become less willing to support their authorities or a political majority against the rights of the individual if 2003 is compared to 1998, but hardly at all when it is compared to 1995. Russians have become more pro-state interventionist over time, but this shift appears to have occurred in 1998 and has remained stable subsequently. There are, however, two areas in which the trend in distribution of values and attitudes does appear to support the growing illiberalism argument. First, there has been a clear increase in the numbers of Russians who support the use of armed force to keep the country together, with the big jump occurring in 2001. A similar increase, though of a somewhat lesser magnitude, can be seen in opposition to the right of republics to secede from Russia; in this case, however, the jump in opposition in 2001 seems to have reversed by 2003. Second, there has been a clear and consistent increase in the willingness of Russians to support anti-Semitic statements and policies, and 2003 in this respect was the most negative point of all.

Overall, therefore, there appears to be prima facie evidence at least that the observed increase in support for the president may be connected to his pursuit of illiberal and anti-democratic policies using a delegative leadership style that is supported by a great many Russians. At the same time, it is important to consider alternative hypotheses that might explain presidential approval ratings. As pointed out in the introduction, much of the literature on this subject in Western presidential systems, for example, points to the importance of political and economic benefits that presidents may deliver and to the issue of overall institutional performance. Rather than being the result of a delegative leadership style or illiberalism, therefore, Putin's relative popularity may be a consequence of a sense that living standards have improved, as indeed objective measures indicate and as Russians themselves report in these surveys.[9] Alternatively, Russians may believe that Putin has presided over a general improvement in the responsiveness and quality of governing institutions by comparison with the Yeltsin years, as indeed also appears to be the case in these surveys. Mean evaluations of institutional performance, using indicators including whether officials care about what ordinary people think, whether people feel represented by governments, and whether government can make a difference, show an increase from 2.09 in 1995 to 2.23 in 2003. (Details of question wording for these items are found in the Appendix).

The next task, therefore, is to test the relationship between public evaluations of Yeltsin and Putin and, on the one hand, the factors associated with the 'growing illiberalism' hypothesis and, on the other, factors generating presidential approval that are relevant in democratic presidential systems. We undertake this analysis using a multivariate regression analysis that has presidential approval as the dependent variable and includes as explanatory factors, first, views of delegative leadership, normative commitments, and policy preferences, and second, estimates

---

[9] Mean evaluations on a scale from 1 (negative) to 5 (positive) of household living standards over the last five years increased from 1.97 in 1995 to 2.87 in 2003.

Table 8.5. Regression of presidential approval on to views of leadership, ideological values, economic assessments, and institutional evaluation (standardized coefficients)

	1995	1996	1998	2001	2003
Strong hand	−.02	−.07†	−.03	−.05	−.01
Anti-democratic leader	.02	.03	.09†	.02	.03
Democratic norms	.16†	.15†	.13†	.12†	.10**
Economic norms	.05*	.03	.05*	−.02	.03
Freedom of speech	.02	−.03	−.05*	.02	.05*
Freedom of authorities	−.01	−.02	.02	.00	.00
Dissolution of USSR	.16†	.18†	.10†	.02	.03
Armed force to keep country together	−.02	−.06†	.07†	−.03	−.03
Anti-Semitism	.03	.04	.05	.00	.03
Right of republics to secede	.00	.08†	.00	−.02	−.06*
Household past living standards	.03	.05*	.05*	−.01	.09†
Household future living standards	.05*	.12†	.01	.09†	−.00
Government responsiveness	.20†	.29**	.23†	.17†	.13†
Parties offer different programmes	−.03	−.04*	.01	−.01	.03
Corruption	.07†	.03	.02	−.00	.01
Gender	−.05*	−.06**	−.03	−.06†	−.07†
Education	−.08†	−.05	−.09†	−.05*	−.03
Age	.02	−.00	−.04	−.08†	.02
Adjusted r²	.17	.30	.17	.06	.06

*p < .05; † p < .01

of household living standards and views of government performance. There are also controls included for age, gender, and education. These analyses are shown in Table 8.5 and they reveal somewhat surprising and complex results.

First, there appears to be little support for the 'growing illiberalism' account. Presidential approval is only weakly and inconsistently related to Russians' views of political leadership. In 2001 and 2003 in particular, there is no association either way between approval of Putin as president and a desire for government with a 'strong hand' or for a leader to deal with the country's problems even if this meant overthrowing democracy. Nor is there much evidence that Putin is supported by people who have anti-democratic norms—quite the opposite. In this respect, approval of Putin resembles that for Yeltsin. Any signs to the contrary are again weak and inconsistent. Putin is somewhat more likely to be supported in 2003 by opponents of the right of republics to secede—certainly by comparison with the factor as a basis for approval of Yeltsin in 1998. But strikingly, there appears to be no connection between the cases where there has been an overall increase in illiberal attitudes—anti-Semitism and in support for the use of armed force to keep Russia together—and support for Putin. Anti-Semitism appears never to have been a basis for presidential approval, and views of the use of armed force are statistically insignificant in 2001 and 2003.

Second, there appears to be much more support for the alternative hypotheses that presidential approval stems from economic and political performance assessments by the public. Experience or expectations regarding household living standards are consistently and positively related to approval. The largest coefficients across all years relates to estimates of how responsive governments are to the public.

Third, it is notable that the amount of variance in presidential approval explained by these factors has tended to decline over the years. Dissolution of the USSR, for example, goes from one of the largest predictors of whether Yeltsin is approved—with opponents of the dissolution, naturally, disapproving—to statistical insignificance in the Putin period. Similarly, the two major factors, democratic norms and views of responsiveness, also decline significantly as predictors.

These results are puzzling, particularly from the perspective of the 'growing illiberalism' hypothesis. They suggest that Russians do not appear to approve of Putin because he delivers to them desired delegative leadership or anti-democratic and illiberal policies. But equally, they raise interesting questions about the relationship of Russians to their political system and to the issues that this system has to deal with. First, whereas under Yeltsin, the great issues of political and economic transformation were central to his approval, especially as this was manifest in responses to the collapse of the USSR, the analysis suggests that these matters may have become less central to the views of Putin presidency, as might be expected given both the passage of time and, if not more importantly, the way in which Putin has overtly presented himself as a figure who moves on from system transformation to its consolidation. Second, it is striking to note the importance of estimates of government responsiveness as a factor explaining approval, and as a factor therefore that helps to explain the increase in presidential approval. If this is the case, then it suggests that ordinary Russians may view their political system in practice as it has developed under Putin in a quite different way to that presented by the critical voices and indices discussed in the introduction. We turn to evaluations of the political system and its relationship to the divisions that underpin choices of presidential candidates in the next two sections.

Evaluating Russia's Democracy

How then do ordinary Russians evaluate the political system in their country? Table 8.6 presents responses to a number of questions regarding the political system that parallel as closely as possible the evidence available on the items covered by Freedom House in Table 8.1. The results show divergence in some cases in estimates of the absolute (and very negative) state of affairs, but also with respect to some of the perceived trends. Russians are generally negative about the practice of democracy in their country, but no more negative in 2003 than they were in 1996. Most Russians in all years believe that it is possible to speak out

Table 8.6. Russians evaluate Russian democracy

	1995	1996	1998	2001	2003
How would you evaluate the actual practice of democracy in Russia?					
Strongly positive	1.4	2.5	1.3	1.5	2.3
Positive	12.8	25.0	11.7	20.3	22.9
In between	20.3	22.9	20.2	28.1	24.0
Negative	43.9	33.1	39.0	29.2	29.0
Strongly negative	16.2	9.8	19.3	12.7	11.9
Don't know	5.5	6.8	8.5	8.3	10.0
Can people in Russia speak out freely without fear of the consequences?					
Strongly agree	11.9	15.6	14.9	17.5	22.3
Agree	40.0	49.6	42.0	33.8	37.6
Disagree	27.9	19.4	23.5	26.2	20.8
Strongly disagree	10.0	6.6	8.4	10.9	11.5
Don't know	10.2	8.8	11.2	11.8	7.9
Is there freedom of speech and organisation in Russia?					
Strongly agree	9.7	14.3	12.7	11.3	14.4
Agree	42.0	52.5	43.9	36.2	39.4
Disagree	25.3	16.8	21.5	26.1	23.1
Strongly disagree	12.9	7.3	10.5	14.1	14.5
Don't know	10.0	9.0	11.5	12.4	8.7
The government acts for the benefit of the majority of the society?					
Strongly agree	2.5	4.6	3.4	3.7	6.7
Agree	11.3	17.7	8.5	14.4	18.0
Disagree	40.2	38.7	31.9	35.1	36.8
Strongly disagree	41.0	33.4	51.9	38.2	34.1
Don't know	5.2	5.6	4.2	8.7	4.5
All people are equal before the law.					
Strongly agree	31.1	33.8	33.9	34.6	34.8
Agree	22.2	31.6	30.3	23.7	26.0
Disagree	24.6	16.7	17.0	18.8	18.1
Strongly disagree	19.7	15.1	15.7	20.3	18.5
Don't know	2.5	2.7	3.1	2.8	2.7
Average for all indicators combined:					
1 = negative about democratic system	2.76	3.10	2.85	2.88	2.99
5 = positive about democratic system					
N=	1999	2012	2008	2000	2000

freely without fear, and these estimates are not significantly different in 2003 from 1996, though these years show improvements over 1995 and 2001. Most Russians also believe that there is freedom of speech and organization in Russia, though in this case there is a significant decline between 1996 and 2001 and only a slight recovery in 2003. Similarly, a majority considers that there is equality before the law and in this case responses to this question have been essentially stable since 1995. Russians are highly critical of their governments in practice, however, with a clear preponderance of respondents in all years believing that governments do not act for the benefit of the majority in society. Here, however, the trend is markedly towards improvement since 1995 and especially when the late-Yeltsin period is compared with the Putin period.

The overall trend is not straightforward, as the average scores (shown in the second to bottom row) for all the indicators in Table 8.6 combined indicate. While Freedom House and the World Bank measures point to a steady trend to the worse, these data show that estimates of the functioning of the political system worsened between 1996 and 1998, but have improved somewhat since then and are now significantly better than they were in 1995. Clearly, however, many Russians remain highly dissatisfied with the functioning of the 'democratic' system in practice. Indeed, it is worth pointing out that so many are prepared to be negative even in 2003 that it seems unlikely—at least in the context of a survey—that fear of the consequences of criticism, as Berezovsky and others claimed, is what explains the relative improvement.

As was the case when looking at the bases of approval of Putin, these results are somewhat surprising and puzzling. Given all of the criticism of the state of Russian democracy under Putin, why do Russians seem to judge that it has improved overall even while many of them remain highly critical about most of its features? We saw in the previous section that, contrary to the 'growing illiberalism' perspective, Putin's approval does not seem to be founded on delegative leadership or anti-democratic normative commitments. But perhaps this is because evaluations of democracy themselves are associated with illiberal and delegative attitudes. Democracy, after all, is a form of majority rule and perhaps it is better regarded and seen as more responsive by Russians *precisely because* they have found in Putin a president who operates political institutions to deliver illiberal outcomes. Alternately, perhaps Russians' estimate of their political system is strongly influenced by the very fact that it has come to work less well, and therefore people are increasingly unable to obtain sufficient information from parties or the media to arrive at negative judgements.[10] We investigate these possibilities in another regression analysis that takes evaluations of the political system in Russia as the dependent variable and looks at its association with a range of predictive factors (see Table 8.7).

Again, there is little consistent support for the 'growing illiberalism' perspective. Views of delegative leadership are significant for political system evaluation

---

[10] There is evidence that party mobilization on issues is in some democratic contexts crucial to mobilizing public opinion on issues. Cf. Leonard Ray, 'When Parties Matter: The Conditional Influence of Party Positions on Voter Opinions about European Integration', *Journal of Politics*, 65 (2003), 978–94; Robert Rohrschneider and Stephen Whitefield, 'Support for Foreign Ownership and Integration in Eastern Europe: Economic Interests, Ideological Commitments and Democratic Context', *Comparative Political Studies*, 37 (2004), 313–39.

Table 8.7. Regression of views of political system on views of leadership, ideological values, and economic assessments (standardized coefficients)

	1995	1996	1998	2001	2003
Strong hand	.01	−.01	.00	.01	−.02
Anti-democratic leader	.03	.08†	.01	.02	.04
Democratic norms	.24†	.26†	.28†	.19†	.19†
Economic norms	.04	.07†	.05*	.01	.04
Freedom of speech	.17†	.18†	.11†	.13†	.18†
Freedom of authorities	.03	.01	.01	.03	.06†
Dissolution of USSR	.01	.09†	.04	.08†	.02
Armed force to keep country together	−.07†	−.10†	−.11†	−.03	−.08†
Anti-Semitism	.06†	−.01	.06†	.02	.05*
Right of republics to secede	.00	−.03	.10†	.02	.04
Household past living standards	.03	.08†	−.02	−.01	.09†
Household future living standards	.02	.12†	.08†	.11†	.05*
Parties offer different programmes	.02	−.03	−.02	.02	.05*
Corruption	.10†	.10†	.07†	.14†	.13†
Gender	.02	−.06†	−.00	−.02	−.00
Education	−.07†	−.07†	−.09†	−.12†	−.12†
Age	.17†	.12†	.07	.10†	.07
Adjusted r^2	.14	.25	.15	.11	.14

* $p < .05$; † $p < .01$

only once, in 1996. Interestingly, Russians who favour the use of armed force to keep the country together again are more likely to have a positive evaluation of the political system in practice, but this is no more the case under Putin than it was under Yeltsin. Views of Jews do irregularly and weakly predict attitudes toward political practices, but not because anti-Semites are being rewarded by government policies—rather the opposite is the case; anti-Semites find the political system less satisfactory, as much under Putin as under Yeltsin. Finally, there is absolutely no evidence that democracy in Russia is more positively evaluated because of a growing association with anti-democratic outlooks. Support for democratic norms and for the rights of individuals to free speech has remained consistently most predictive of respect for the political system in Russia. This point is highly significant to the points made by many of Putin's critics, who might be expected to find greatest support for their claims that Russia has become less democratic under Putin from those segments of society that are *most* committed to democracy and free speech in principle. However, this perspective does not appear to have found significant support among democratically committed Russians, at least by the summer of 2003.

One possibly highly important caveat to the last point must be noted. Controlling for other differences—since higher levels of education are also associated with greater commitment to democratic and liberal ideals—there is a strongly significant and growing negative relationship between educational levels and views of the political system. More educated Russians are clearly more likely to think that the 'democratic' system works badly—and have become more likely to think this way over time. Given that educated people are likely to have greater access to information, there may therefore be a case to be made that the general rise in estimates of democratic functioning is a consequence of the decline in availability of negative information to most people because of anti-democratic trends in the Russian press and party system under Putin. We return to this possibility in the conclusion.

Presidential Approval, Ideological Commitments, Political System Evaluation, and Electoral Choice in Russia

The analysis in previous sections suggests the following: illiberalism in Russia does not seem to be increasing; Putin's popularity does not seem to be distinctively based on a demand for illiberal policies or from parts of the population who prefer delegative leadership; in the public eye, estimates of the democratic system in practice appear to have improved significantly; economic performance, but even more so, estimates of institutional performance, appear to best explain Putin's popularity; moreover, the improvement in estimates of the political system does not appear to be related to approval by illiberal or pro-delegative sections of society. In the main, therefore, the evidence points away from the 'growing illiberalism' account of Putin's popularity and toward the importance of economic and, especially, institutional performance.

One further important test of the two accounts needs now to be undertaken. From the 'growing illiberalism' perspective, Putin's anti-democratic practices and delegative leadership style might make the issue of the political system more important to how Russians make choices about presidential candidates. From the 'institutional performance' perspective, by contrast, the fact that many Russians see democracy working better in practice might mean that the issue of the political system per se becomes less important to judgements about the best candidate to support. What, then, are the consequences of perceived improved institutional performance and Putin's popularity for the ways in which Russians make choices about presidential candidates?

To address this question, we consider the results of a multinomial logit analysis that compares the relationship of some of the most significant explanatory factors outlined in previous sections with voters' declared first preference for presidents in the hypothetical circumstance put to them that a presidential election were to be held tomorrow. The analysis compares support for Yeltsin and then Putin—who are used as the reference categories—with alternative candidates for various

Table 8.8. Multinomial logit regressions of presidential candidates on political system and presidential evaluations, and democratic norms. Yeltsin (1995, 1996, and 1998) and Putin (2001 and 2003) are the reference categories.

	1995 B (S.E)	1996 B (S.E.)	1998 B (S.E.)	2001 B (S.E)	2003 B (S.E.)
National-authoritarian					
Democratic norms	−.32 (.11)†	−.22 (.08)†	−.36 (.12)†	−.21 (.10)*	−.03 (.12)
Political system	−.47 (.16)†	−.59 (.11)†	−.69 (.19)†	−.17 (.14)	−.58 (.17)†
Strong hand	.06 (.11)	−.17 (.07)*	−.08 (.12)	−.12 (.11)	−.18 (.13)
Anti-democratic leader	−.52 (.11)†	−.24 (.07)†	−.35 (.11)†	−.31 (.11)†	−.35 (.13)†
Right					
Democratic norms	.04 (.09)	−.19 (.10)	−.15 (.12)	.09 (.13)	.23 (.17)
Political system	−.46 (.12)†	−.47 (.14)†	−.53 (.19)†	−.43 (.16)†	.08 (.21)
Strong hand	.30 (.08)†	.16 (.09)	.02 (.11)	.32 (.11)†	−.05 (.15)
Anti-democratic leader	−.04 (.08)	−.02 (.09)	.11 (.11)	.34 (.11)†	−.06 (.14)
Left					
Democratic norms	−.58 (.12)†	−.75 (.08)†	−.71 (.12)†	−.61 (.08)†	−.59 (.09)†
Democratic system	−.61 (.18)†	−.79 (.11)†	−.96 (.19)†	−.26 (.13)*	−.11 (.13)
Strong hand	.08 (.12)	−.20 (.08)†	−.01 (.12)	.02 (.09)	−.04 (.10)
Anti-democratic leader	−.42 (.12)†	−.46 (.07)†	−.50 (.12)†	−.21 (.09)*	−.43 (.10)†
Pseudo-r^2 (Cox and Snell)	.19	.25	.23	.09	.08

*significant at p < .05; †p < .01

years on the authoritarian-nationalist political field (Zhirinovsky and Lebed), on the supposed pro-market and democratic right (variously, Gaidar, Yavlinsky, and other such political figures), and finally with the Communist left represented by Zyuganov. The output from this type of analysis shows the ways in which factors such as views of the democratic system, evaluations of the president, commitment to democratic or market norms, desire for strong and delegative leadership are associated with the choice of presidential candidates, and of course how these relationships may have changed over time. The results are presented in Table 8.8. Once again, there appears to be weak support for the 'growing illiberalism' account.

First, Russians who reject democratic norms do not distinctively support Putin. In this respect, his supporters are indistinguishable from those who said they would vote for Yeltsin or for candidates of the supposedly pro-market and democratic right in all years. On the other hand, those nominating Putin, as with those for Yeltsin and the right, are clearly distinguished from anti-democratic supporters of Zyuganov. Moreover, those for Zhirinovsky (and Lebed in the years for which he was a relevant choice for respondents) appear to have become more like supporters of the presidents and the right as time has passed.

Second, Russians who say they will vote for Putin, unlike both Zhirinovsky and Zyuganov supporters, are not systematically more likely to support delegative leadership. For both left and national-authoritarian respondents, the appeal of government with a strong hand and, especially, a leader who might overthrow democracy to solve the country's problems, is consistently evident when they are compared to supporters of Putin and Yeltsin before him. On the other hand, in both 1995 and, most strongly, in 2001, there is also evidence that supporters of the market-democratic right candidates were more likely to oppose delegative leadership than those backing Yeltsin and Putin. However, this relatively greater opposition to strong leadership disappeared by 2003, and again Putin and market-democratic right supporters are indistinguishable on this question.

Third, and most important, the question of the political system per se no longer distinguishes support for presidential candidates in 2003 in nearly the same way that it did earlier. In fact, the change in the importance of this issue amounts to a transformation of the basis of electoral choice in Russia. Whereas in 1995, 1996, and 1998, supporters of all candidates were much more likely to be negative than supporters of Yeltsin about the democratic system in practice—even in the case of supporters of the right who were also more democratic in their normative orientations—by 2001 the issue had seriously declined as a division for both Zyuganov and Zhirinovsky camps. And in 2003, while again being a source of distinction for Zhirinovsky supporters, it had become insignificant as an issue for people who said they would vote for right or left candidates. Not surprisingly, with this decline in the significance of divisions over the political system, we also see in the pseudo-r^2 statistics a large reduction in the amount of vote choice that is explained.

The decline in political division over the political system does not mean that there is nothing to divide supporters of these candidates. For example, other analysis (not shown here but available) shows that those nominating Zyuganov remain clearly more committed to state economic intervention than Putin supporters or those for candidates of the right. But in theoretical terms there is no question that division over policies of this sort is compatible with lack of division over the 'democratic' system in practice. For opponents of Putin in each of these camps, therefore, policy differences remain but the issue of the political system per se appears largely to have been taken out of the equation as a source of electoral choice. Putin in power, therefore, does not appear to be associated with a growing division within the electorate about a democratic system that appears to be failing those opposed to Putin as a candidate, even among those who are most committed to democracy as a normative order. Rather, it appears that the broader improvement in Russian democracy that is perceived by the electorate, and in particular in the performance of the president even among those who do not support him, is most likely to account for the declining saliency of political system evaluations.

Conclusions: President Putin and Russia's Democracy

These analyses do not show that Russians are satisfied with the state of democracy in their country, because negative views abound. But the broad picture that emerges from them runs quite counter to that presented by critics of Putin's leadership and the development of Russian democracy since he assumed power. In the main, Russians do not seem to live in fear; they perceive that their democratic system has improved, albeit from a very parlous state; this improvement appears to be in large measure the result of hugely increased positive assessments of the performance of Putin as president by comparison with Yeltsin, and with perceptions of improved institutional responsiveness more generally; these positive assessments are not associated with the fact that the system matches growing illiberal, anti-democratic, and delegative preferences; supporters of Putin, moreover, are less not more likely to support delegative leadership by comparison with those for left and national-authoritarian candidates and are no less committed to democratic norms than supporters of pro-market and democracy candidates. Finally, the Russian electorate appear to be less divided overall on the major issues from the early phases of the country's transition from Communist power, and with the improvement in perceived democratic system performance, the issue of the political system in practice also seems to be much less of a factor dividing the electorate in their choice of presidential candidates. The results therefore speak against the 'growing illiberalism' hypotheses put in the introduction, and in favour of the 'system performance' account, and with respect to the latter, interestingly, it appears that improved institutional performance is much more explanatory than what has happened to the economy. While a growing number of Russians express a desire for government with a 'strong hand', there is no necessary connection of this to anti-democratic sentiment. And though the level of criticism of this process and the conditionality of commitment to democracy remains disturbingly high in public opinion, on the face of it the analyses suggest that considerable steps have been taken toward system consolidation under Putin's leadership, at least so far as the relationship of the Russian public to the political process is concerned.

The results shown, therefore, are challenging in a number of respects and need careful interpretation. They run counter to much of the strong negative criticism of trends in Russian democracy, not only from political opponents of Putin but also from more 'objective' indicators. Which raises the question: who is right?

This question is extraordinarily difficult to answer. It is a commonplace to attack the findings of surveys, particularly when they produce results that people dislike, on grounds that they are based on faulty measures of key concepts or because of the unreliability of survey responses in Russia (or elsewhere). Less attention is paid, however, to the weaknesses in measurement and the biases that are found in more 'objective' indicators. The World Bank governance indicators presented reflect the responses on the quality of governance given by a large number of enterprise, citizen, and expert survey respondents, as reported by a number of survey institutes, think tanks, non-governmental organizations, and international organizations.[11] In reaching its judgements, Freedom House employs 'a broad range of international sources of information, including both foreign and domestic news reports, NGO publications, think tank and academic analyses, and individual professional contacts'.[12] The fact that political and economic elites, including Westerners, are often central sources of information for 'objective' indicators on Russia may make it more likely that the anti-Putin perspectives of these elites are reflected in them.

One possibility, therefore, is simply to suggest that Russian critics of Putin and Russian democracy are politically motivated by Putin's efforts to improve institutional performance in a variety of ways, notably by attacking corrupt and overpowerful 'oligarchs' and regional figures and strengthening vertical power structures and the rule of law. In part because of their financial power, those negatively affected by Putin's efforts have been able to create a sense, particularly in the West, that Putin has undermined and manipulated Russian democracy. This political agenda, moreover, may have been aided by Western commentators whose narrative of Russia is often filled with expectations of authoritarian leadership and weak democratic popular commitments.

It is also quite possible, however, that the results shown above paint an accurate picture of how Russians evaluated their two presidents and their country's political system in these years, but that the public fails to understand the extent to which Putin's policies threaten democracy. As was pointed out in the discussion in the section on evaluations of the political system, more educated Russians are increasingly likely to have negative views of Russian democracy in practice. The lack of criticism among many respondents, therefore, may be the result of lack of information that results from the very anti-democratic practices that Putin has promoted, his manner of managing the party system and political opponents, and particularly the way he has restricted press freedom and criticism.

If this is the case, however, then the analysis points to the magnitude of difficulty facing Putin's democratic opponents. There is little to suggest that more democratic Russians have come to negative conclusions about trends in the political system. The political system per se is less of an issue than it was and, as we know from many contexts, institutional questions are not easily mobilized in the electorate as a central political priority. When we consider that the case against Putin's 'attack on democracy' would need to be made in the context of declining democratic opportunities, with weak parties and a more controlled media, the scale of the problem seems great. On the other hand, until political elites—of right or left for that matter—are able successfully to mobilize

---

[11] http://info.worldbank.org/governance/kkz2002/index.htm.
[12] http://www.freedomhouse.org/research/freeworld/2000/methodology.htm.

public opinion, there is little likelihood that the state of democracy in Russia will become a divisive issue or that currently positive trends in its evaluation will be reversed.

The discussion above, therefore, tends to highlight rather than resolve many of the ambiguities about Vladimir Putin and democracy in Russia. Putin's own political commitments and style may be only weakly democratic—or even undemocratic—but this is not the basis for his popularity. Rather, those who support him tend to be more committed to democratic norms than other Russians. There are many Russians who favour leadership with a 'strong hand' but they are not drawn distinctively to Putin, indeed quite the opposite. Putin's popularity does not appear to rest on an 'authoritarian' mass political culture, although there are clearly many Russians who hold authoritarian views. Indeed, Putin's popular base may be quite at odds with his political agenda. He may, therefore, be faced with a difficult and, ultimately, revealing political choice, between his own supporters and his tendency to pursue anti-democratic policies.

Appendix: Survey Questions

All variables use a five-point agree–disagree scales.

Presidential Approval

Thinking about the performance of the president of Russia, how highly would you regard his activity?

Delegative Leadership

1. Does Russia need government with a 'strong hand' to resolve its economic problems?
2. Would it be worthwhile to support a leader who could solve the main problems facing Russia today even if he overthrew democracy?

Norms and Issues

1. How do you feel about the *aim* of introducing democracy in the country, in which political parties compete for government?
2. Thinking next about the economic system, how do you feel about the *aim* of creating a market economy with private ownership and economic freedom to entrepreneurs?

(a) A good society would have... Freedom to create social, economic, political, and other organizations.
(b) A good society would have... Freedom of speech and the right to publicly express different opinions.
(c) A good society would have... Limits put on the public expression of opinions that are opposed to the views of the authorities.
(d) A good society would have... Limits put on the public expression of opinions that are opposed to the feelings and opinions of the majority of people.
(e) The dissolution of the Soviet Union was a good thing.
(f) Russia is justified to use armed force in order to keep the Russian Federation together.
(g) Jews in Russia today have too much power and influence.
(h) Republics within the Russian Federation should be allowed to succeed if the people in the republics wish to do so.

Government Responsiveness

1. Elected officials don't care much what people like me think.
2. On the whole, what governments do in this country reflects the wishes of ordinary people.
3. Elected officials don't care much what people like me think.
4. There is no point in voting because the government can't make any difference.
5. The government acts for the benefit of the majority of the society.

Party Differences

The main political parties in this country all offer the same sorts of programs.

Corruption

Bribery, corruption, and 'knowing the right people' are not important phenomena.

Democracy Evaluation

1. How would you evaluate the actual practice of democracy in Russia?
2. Can people in Russia speak out freely without fear of the consequences?
3. All people are equal before the law.
4. Is there freedom of speech and organization in Russia?
5. The government acts for the benefit of the majority of the society.

Economic Estimations

1. Compared with *five years ago* do you think the standard of living of... has fallen a lot, fallen a little, stayed about the same, risen a little, or has it risen a lot?
2. And *in five years time*, do you think the standard of living of... will be a lot lower than it is now, a little lower than now, about the same as now, a little higher than now, or a lot higher than now?

Presidential Choices

If there were a *presidential election* tomorrow, which of these candidates would you be most likely to vote for?

9

Putin as Patron: Cadres Policy in the Russian Transition

Eugene Huskey

Patronage is a key instrument of political leadership. When regimes collapse, the new leadership has a dual task: to replace individual elites and to create a new system of political recruitment. While the first task must be tackled immediately, the formation of a new patronage system may be postponed. Such was the case in Russia, where the presidency turned its attention to the establishment of a cadres policy only at the end of the 1990s.

Under the Putin presidency, a new approach to patronage is emerging, although neither its philosophical underpinnings nor the mechanisms for its implementation are fully developed. At the core of this policy is the revival of important elements of the Soviet-era *nomenklatura* system, which seeks to replace the unpredictability of political recruitment in a democracy with something that might be termed patronage management. Depending on the interpretive lens one uses to view Russian politics, this revivalist trend under Putin is either ensuring the efficiency and cohesion attendant to all modern states or it is laying the foundations for a neo-authoritarian order.

In Putin's Russia, patronage politics is not limited to the political appointees who serve at the pleasure of the elected leadership, usually as senior staff members or management cadres in the core executive. Elected officials, permanent civil servants, and the leaders of business and non-governmental organizations are at times subject to a spoils system that allows federal and regional leaders to influence personnel decisions in ways that endanger political pluralism. Where others have examined the results of recruitment decisions, primarily through studies of the changing backgrounds of officials,[1] our task is to analyse recruitment practices and their implications for presidential power in Russia.

Patronage politics at the beginning of Yeltsin's second term of office bore little resemblance to the tightly controlled and highly centralized *nomenklatura* system

---

[1] See, for example, Olga Kryshtanovskaya and Stephen White, 'From Soviet Nomenklatura to Russian Elite', *Europe-Asia Studies*, 5 (1996), 711–33; Kryshtanovskaya and White, 'Putin's Militocracy', *Post-Soviet Affairs*, 19/4 (October–December 2003), 289–306; David Lane and Cameron Ross, *The Transition from Communism to Capitalism: Ruling Elites from Gorbachev to Yeltsin* (New York: St. Martin's Press, 1999).

that shaped personnel decisions in the Soviet Union.[2] In the selection of key personnel in federal institutions, the presidency assumed some of the responsibilities exercised earlier by the Communist Party central committee, but the presidency lacked the central committee's reach in recruitment decisions and its well-developed structures and procedures for making appointments. Attempts to create the equivalent of a cadres ministry in the immediate aftermath of the Soviet collapse were unsuccessful, and although the presidential administration experimented with the creation of its own departments of cadres or cadres policy, none acquired the ability to coordinate personnel selection in the federal government.[3] Because personnel policy lacked a coordinating institution in the core executive, primary responsibility for personnel issues devolved onto federal ministers and the leaders of Russia's eighty-nine regions and republics. By the second half of the 1990s, the decentralization of personnel policy had transformed regional governors and republican presidents into the chief patrons in Russian politics. They were able to recruit clients not only in regional and republican institutions but in local government and federal agencies working in the provinces.

The first indication that the centre was intent on introducing a more systematic and centralized approach to recruitment policy came in 1997, with the issuance of a presidential decree that called for the training—in Russia and overseas—of a new generation of cadres who would be eligible for promotion to key positions in government institutions and leading private enterprises.[4] The creation of cadres reserve lists in selected cities and regions across the country followed shortly after that decree. These lists represented the revival in public administration of an essential ingredient of the *nomenklatura* system. However, it was only with the accession to power of Vladimir Putin in early 2000 that one sees a commitment to universalize the cadres reserve system and to reclaim for the president patronage powers that had been dispersed across the capital and the country in the 1990s.

Elected Officials

In democratic regimes, who governs is determined by a complex interplay of state and social forces. The power of the ballot grants ordinary citizens a role in the recruitment of their leaders, but the choices presented to the electorate are

---

[2] Although in the Soviet period a consensus existed on the basic rules of personnel selection, promotion, and dismissal, there was serious political conflict over turnover rates and specific appointments. Indeed, Soviet politics was at its core a contest over intra-party personnel decisions. For an example of cadres politics from the late Soviet era, see Archie Brown, *The Gorbachev Factor* (Oxford: Oxford University Press, 1996), 177 and *passim*.

[3] Eugene Huskey, 'From Higher Party Schools to Academies of State Service: The Marketization of Bureaucratic Training in Russia', *Slavic Review* 63/2 (Summer 2004), 325–48.

[4] 'O podgotovke upravlencheskikh kadrov dlya organizatsii narodnogo khozyaistva Rossiiskoi Federatsii', *Sobranie zakonodatel'stva*, 30 (1997), 3607.

generally made, either formally or informally, by elites in government or opposition. It is not unusual, for example, for parties in European democracies to maintain something akin to *nomenklatura* lists that serve as hierarchically-ordered reservoirs of candidates for elective office. One of the key functions of political parties, after all, is the orderly recruitment of candidates for office.

It should come as no surprise, therefore, that President Putin approved the formation of a political party, United Russia, that supports his administration and offers a pool of personnel who can be tapped to occupy key posts in government. Why, then, the alarm among many analysts about the rise of United Russia as a force in Russian politics? Put simply, the words and deeds of Putin and his supporters indicate a willingness to experiment with a fusing of party and state institutions. Through democratic elections, parties seek to seize control of governing institutions, but only *pro tempore*, as Adam Przeworski noted, and always with a respect for the mythology which asserts that it is the nation alone, and not a leader or party, whose interests are congruent with those of the state. It is one thing for a party or politician to use the state to advance their interests, which in American politics is associated with tactics as diverse as congressional redistricting and franking privileges, but quite another to employ the state as the de facto campaign headquarters for the incumbent elite.[5]

In Putin's Russia, there is a growing unwillingness to accept the uncertainty implicit in democratic procedures. This perspective leads officials to propose the establishment of state-controlled candidate reserve lists of personnel to be elected to executive and legislative office. President Putin has stated that 'we need to change our attitude to municipal elections, where there's not sufficient monitoring (*kontrol'*) or an existing cadres reserve'.[6] As suggested earlier, the formation and ranking of a pool of eligible candidates for elected office has a venerable history in democratic regimes, but this is always a task for politicians in their roles as party leaders rather than as state officials. In Russia, leaders seem unable to distinguish between their political and administrative personae, and therefore a party of power is viewed by many as a legitimate extension of state administration.

The tendency of state officials to use the power of their office to elect Putin and those favoured by him in federal, regional, and even local elections unites politicians of very different policy orientations. Shortly after assuming the post of presidential plenipotentiary in the Volga region, a major figure on the reformist wing of Russian politics, Sergey Kirienko, noted: 'I came to work for President Putin and I will do everything I can so that he is elected again in the next presidential campaign'.[7] For Kirienko, Putin the candidate is inseparable from Putin the ruling president. Likewise, the presidential plenipotentiary in the

---

[5] See the article of Jeffrey Toobin on the ill effects of the American approach to redistricting, 'The Great Election Grab: When does Gerrymandering Become a Danger to Democracy?', *The New Yorker*, 8 December 2003.

[6] Andrey Makarychev, 'Lebedev protiv Putina?', *Birzha*, 20 May 2002.

[7] Mikhail Kushtapin, 'Polpred Kirienko v kruge pervom', *Rossiiskaya gazeta*, 28 February 2001.

neighbouring federal district of the Urals, Petr Latyshev, who is a person with
more traditional policy views, has committed the resources of his office to the
election of members of United Russia. In a surprisingly frank admission of the
mobilization of the state administration behind a partisan campaign, Latyshev
expressed his support for United Russia, arguing that 'it represents the policies of
vlast' to the population' and 'the population supports it'.[8] Latyshev has even
proposed reviving primary party organizations, though unlike in the Soviet era,
the party would presumably serve the state apparatus and not the reverse.
Examples abound of the integration of United Russia with the state, but the
linkage is perhaps nowhere more visible than in Volgograd, where a new bridge
spanning the Volga has a banner that reads, 'Bridge construction placed under the
supervision of United Russia'.[9]

Latyshev's vetting of candidates for parliamentary seats from his federal district
is further evidence of the role of the offices of governors-general as campaign
outposts for Putin and his political allies. In the view of a local United Russia
official, the intervention of an employee of the presidency in party matters is
appropriate. 'We exchange information [with the federal district office],' he
noted. 'Who becomes a deputy is important to the Governor-General'.[10] State
officials do not simply help to identify and select candidates for elected office;
they also offer their 'administrative resources' to promote them during the
campaign itself. Taken together with the actions of the judiciary and election
commissions, whose rulings have frequently disqualified candidates opposed to
the president or his political allies, the administrative resources proffered by
Putin's subordinates create imposing barriers to entry into politics for the opposition.[11]

The influence of the presidency on cadres policy among elected officials is not
limited to the electoral campaign. Once in office, elected officials are subject to
removal by Putin if they do not meet his expectations. However, rather than
employ the draconian weapon of dismissal against recalcitrant governors, the
president has opted instead for a more subtle, but no less effective, tool: he has
promoted them to sinecures in Moscow. With this tactic Putin has revived one of
the central traditions of the Soviet *nomenklatura*, in which elites were circulated
within, but rarely expelled from, the ruling class.[12] Take the examples of elected

[8] Svetlana Ofitova, 'Petr Latyshev: nasha tsel'–edinoe prostranstvo', *Nezavisimaya gazeta*,
22 April 2003.

[9] Evgeniya Albats, 'Navstrechu vyboram. Pora golosovat' mozgami', *Novaya gazeta*, 17 November 2003.

[10] Svetlana Ofitova, 'Polpredy zhdut ot Kremlya deneg i vlasti', *Nezavisimaya gazeta*, 22 April
2003.

[11] See, for example, the comments of Boris Nemtsov and Sergey Markov in 'Prezidentskaya
polovina', *Moskovskii komsomolets*, 25 March 2002.

[12] Commenting on the replacement of the Defence Minister in early 2001, Putin said that the
outgoing minister, 'Igor Dmitrievich [Sergeev], as it is now fashionable to say, remains a member of
our team. He is moving over to the presidential staff and will work as a presidential aide.' 'Statement

leaders in Vladivostok and St Petersburg. Putin undid the will of the electorate in these two areas by pressing the governors to give up their posts and accept a respectable position in Moscow, thereby freeing up their seats for politicians friendly to the president.[13] Whereas Yevgeny Nazdratenko left the governorship in Vladivostok to head the State Fisheries Commission in February 2001, Vladimir Yakovlev gave up his post in St Petersburg to become Russia's deputy prime minister for construction and transportation in June 2003. When Nazdratenko ran afoul of the prime minister several months into his Moscow tenure, allegedly because of irregularities with fishing quota auctions, Putin brought him into the presidential apparatus as an official on the Security Council. For his part, Yakovlev left his Moscow post in March 2004, when Putin reduced the number of deputy prime ministers from seven to one. The president found a post for him as governor-general of the Southern Federal District, one of the most onerous assignments in Russian administration, due to the war in the Northern Caucasus.

With regard to the recruitment of elected officials, Putin has employed a more systematic and ambitious patronage policy than his predecessor. By offering his personal support for United Russia, by allowing or encouraging his subordinates to mobilize the state's resources behind United Russia candidates, and by using his power of administrative appointment to undo electoral results that are not to his liking, Putin has already concentrated in the presidency enormous potential power over cadres policy in the electoral realm. That the opposition continues to win some elections against 'establishment' candidates is testimony to the continuing divisions within the president's own administration, to the independent-mindedness of certain regional politicians and economic elites, who champion their own candidates, and to the inability of some official candidates to connect with the electorate. In the race for the governorship of Magadan region in March 2003, for example, the Kremlin favourite, Magadan mayor Nikolay Karpenko, was upset by the first deputy governor of the region, Nikolay Dudov.[14]

However, by using the tragedy at Beslan to eliminate direct elections for the posts of governors and presidents, Putin has assured that no such surprises will occur in the future in the selection of provincial chief executives, who now fall within the direct patronage of the Russian president.

by the President of the Russian Federation Vladimir Putin Made at a Conference in the Kremlin', 28 March 2001, Official Kremlin International News Broadcast. See also Vitaly Tseplyaev and Aleksandr Kolesnichenko, 'The Kremlin's Cautious Personnel Policy', *Argumenty i fakty*, 26 June 2003, as translated in What the Papers Say (Russia), Nexis-Lexis Online.

[13] See Viktor Loshak, 'Obratnaya svyaz'. Vechnaya oboima', *Moskovskie novosti*, 17 June 2003. A variant of this practice has become popular in the more authoritarian soil of Central Asia, where presidents appoint their opponents to ambassadorial posts outside the country. In Russia itself, Vladimir Babichev was appointed ambassador to Kazakhstan after losing his post as head of the Government apparatus. Also see Tseplyaev and Kolesnichenko (n. 12).

[14] Yakov Radchenko, 'Magadan Voters Vote Against Federal Center', *Kommersant-Daily*, 17 February 2003, as translated in *Current Digest of the Post-Soviet Press*, 55/7 (19 March 2003).

Political Appointees

The primary subjects of patronage in democratic regimes are the political appointees who serve at the pleasure of the ruler, either in his or her personal office or at the apex of ministries and executive departments. The use of this spoils system varies widely, but the functions of those appointed are similar: to offer advice and expertise to elected officials and to ensure that the policies of the political leadership are faithfully implemented by the permanent state bureaucracy. Whereas a change of administration results in little more than 100 new political appointments in British politics, it brings 3,000 new presidential appointees to office in the federal government of the United States.

In Russia, the scale of patronage authority granted to the president may even exceed that enjoyed by his US counterpart. Approximately 600 Moscow-based officials are subject to formal presidential appointment, a figure that includes the leading personnel in the numerous subdivisions of the presidency, the heads of federal ministries and agencies, and the deputy ministers—often ten to a ministry—who work in the so-called presidential ministries, such as foreign affairs, internal affairs, justice, and the FSB.[15] Whereas these presidential appointments may not be vetted or challenged by other institutions, almost 200 Moscow-based officials who are appointed by the president must be approved by parliament. Among this group are the prime minister, the heads of the Audit Chamber and the Central Bank—all confirmed by the Duma—and the procurator-general, the almost 100 members of the Supreme Court, up to seventy members of the Supreme Commercial Court, and nineteen members of the Constitutional Court, all of whom must be confirmed by the Federation Council. Beyond this sizeable group of officials in the capital is a small army of personnel in the provinces who are selected either formally or informally by the Russian president. These range from the governors-general and their first deputies in the seven federal districts, each of which has a staff of approximately 150 persons, to the more than 18,000 judges in commercial, military, and general jurisdiction courts across the country.

Patronage politics in Russia differs from that in most democratic states because the recruitment of political appointees is more continual than episodic and because the turnover rates are lower after general elections. In countries like the United States, the United Kingdom, and France, the accession to power of a new

---

[15] If one included senior military and diplomatic appointments, which are made by the president, the number would be considerably larger. In a move designed to streamline the bureaucracy, Putin is reducing the number of deputy ministers to no more than two per ministry. This reform would bring the number of deputy ministers to well under 100, whereas there were 250 at the end of Putin's first term. In addition, the number of heads of departments will be cut four- or five-fold. See Andrei Litvinov and Nadezhda Kevorkova, 'The Kozak-Kudrin Defence', *Gazeta*, 2 April 2004, as translated in What the Papers Say, Part B (Russia), 2 April 2004, Lexis-Nexis News.

leader occasions a rapid turnover of virtually all the personnel holding political appointments. Where this influx of new cadres may take only a few hours or days in the case of United Kingdom or France, a US president devotes much of the two and a half months between his election and inauguration to the recruitment of replacement personnel. Thus, in most Western countries, when turnover of political appointees occurs after the installation of a new administration, it is usually associated with natural attrition or the occasional mid-course correction designed to reorient policy and revive a government's popularity; witness the cabinet reshuffle launched by President Chirac in March 2004 in reaction to the defeat of the right in France's regional assembly elections.

In Russia, on the other hand, turnover of political appointees is spread more evenly across the presidential terms. Excluding the formal reappointment of incumbent ministers and deputy ministers immediately after his inauguration in May 2000, Putin made forty-seven personnel appointments in the government and its ministries in his first four years in office, with seven occurring in 2000, twenty in 2001, and ten each in 2002 and 2003.[16] When one considers that almost half of this turnover affected only two ministries, the Ministry of Foreign Affairs and the Ministry of Internal Affairs, it is reasonable to conclude that Putin's first term witnessed a remarkable continuity of cadres in the government. Thus, in replacing members of the central executive, whether in the government or in the presidential apparatus itself, Putin has exhibited a restraint that was not characteristic of the Yeltsin era, with its rapid circulation of elites.[17] This stability of cadres was most evident at the summit of the government—whereas Yeltsin appointed five prime ministers during his second term, Putin had appointed only one until the final days of his first term of office, when he replaced Mikhail Kasyanov with Mikhail Fradkov.

One could argue, of course, that the failure of Russian presidential elections to produce a grand purge of political appointees is due in large part to the continuity in power of a single leadership clique since 1991. However, the lack of a 'democracy-consolidating' election does not explain fully Russia's reliance on a kind of rolling admission to appointed posts. In the period before 2000, three other factors also seemed to be at work: Yeltsin's use of regular cadres rotation in the executive as a means of mollifying parliamentary opposition, a practice Putin has eschewed because of his greater parliamentary and public support; the absence of an effective institution within the presidency for identifying and coordinating the selection of political appointees; and the unusual importance and complexity of intra-ministerial politics, which narrows the range of acceptable candidates for ministers and deputy ministers and retards their appointment.

---

[16] The figures here, based on appointments reported in *Sobranie zakonodatel'stva*, include those ministers and deputy ministers who were hired by the issuance of a formal decree of the president.

[17] For a review of appointments made in Putin's first two years of office, see 'O budushchem. Vlast'. Prostie dvizheniya', *Politbyuro*, 17 March 2003.

The last factor is a reminder that, until recently, appointments to leadership positions in the Russian government and its ministries came disproportionately from persons promoted from within a bureaucratic hierarchy, a tradition that encouraged departmentalism in Russian political and administrative life. If in earlier years promotion to the post of minister was more likely to be made from below rather than laterally, under Putin an increasing percentage of federal ministers come to their posts from outside the ministry. By 2001, only slightly over a third of ministers had spent a decade or more in the same institution, and less than 30 per cent were promoted to minister from the post of deputy minister in the same organization.[18] By placing greater emphasis on personal loyalty rather than technical experience when making appointments, Putin has been able to create a government weighted toward political rather than administrative leaders, who are less lobbyists for their institutions than members of a political team. Writing only a year after Putin assumed the presidency, one Russian observer remarked:

No one can say now that the Government is simply a 'cabinet of technocrats' [*tekhnicheskii kabinet*]. It is a cabinet of politicians, whose positions and views are well known. In this sense, for the first time the cabinet corresponds to rational, democratic criteria.[19]

Perhaps the most telling example of this new patronage orientation was the series of personnel appointments in the power ministries in March 2003, which brought in Sergey Ivanov as Minister of Defence. He was the first defence minister to come from outside the ministry since the mid-1950s. Moreover, Putin has recruited personnel from the armed forces and security services to fill a third of the deputy federal ministerial positions, with some of those hires being made in the Ministry of Economic Development and other non-security related ministries. According to the work of the Russian sociologist, Olga Kryshtanovskaya, 'security men are deliberately "parachuted" into high government posts in a manner that resembles the Stalinist system of assigning commissars, or party watchdogs, to keep tabs on professional managers whose political loyalties may be suspect'.[20]

Such a patronage policy poses considerable risks, not just in the effective management of key state bureaucracies, but in the potential militarization of Russian politics. However, it also signals Putin's desire to break with the longstanding tradition of compartmentalizing political careers into individual

[18] *Rossiiskaya vlast' v tsifrakh* (Moscow: Tsentr "Panorama", 2001). A data set of 14 variables on the federal 37 ministers in office in 2001 was generated using information from this book. Although Putin reduced the number of ministries from 30 to 17 in March 2004, there remain numerous state committees and executive agencies whose leaders are appointed with the approval of the Kremlin.

[19] Artur Akopov, 'Sistema predstavlena v litsakh. Rukovoditel' 'Fonda effektivnoi politiki' Gleb Pavlovsky o novykh naznacheniyakh', *Vek*, 30 March 2001. See also Valery Dzhalagoniya, 'Vlast'. Vremya loyalistov', *Ekho planety*, 6 April 2001.

[20] Fred Weir, 'KGB influence still felt in Russia', *Christian Science Monitor*, 30 December 2003. For a recent academic article on the same topic, see Kryshtanovskaya and White, (n. 1).

ministries or branches, which encouraged a 'silo mentality' among Russian bureaucracies and complicated the coordination of public policy. Throughout the
Yeltsin era, Russia had a de facto coalition government, which owed as much to
the tradition of recruiting ministers from below as political concessions made
to the parliamentary opposition. Putin is now constructing for the first time
something akin to a party government, with personnel drawn from the only
'party' on which he could rely, loyalists from his home city of St Petersburg
and from army and security personnel.

Putin's preference for a continuity of cadres appears to have several causes.
First, the bargain between Putin and Yeltsin that facilitated the transfer of
presidential power appears to have constrained for a time the turnover of personnel associated with the Family. The most celebrated case was that of the president's chief of staff, Alexander Voloshin, whose tenure was reportedly assured for
two years after Yeltsin's resignation. The second reason for the lower turnover of
members of Russia's core executive during the Putin era was the president's
deeper support base in parliament and the country. Unlike Yeltsin, Putin has
worked to form a loyal and stable majority in parliament, which was finally
achieved in the December 2003 election. Thus, where Yeltsin sacrificed his
aides, ministers, and even prime ministers with abandon to curry favour with
the parliamentary opposition and the public, Putin has not felt it necessary to
shore up his authority by replacing officials. Finally, Putin recognized the political
and administrative costs of the frequent ministerial reshuffles of the Yeltsin era,
which were captured well by one Russian commentator.

[r]umors of a minister's possible replacement appear a few months before his resignation
and ... [t]he staff cannot work properly because of this stress. The more important an
official's position, the less secure he feels, which is understandable because all the
important positions will be occupied by people from the new team. After the arrival of a
new minister, the personnel replacements take about six months. Altogether, the time of
troubles lasts almost a year.[21]

To reduce such upheavals in the bureaucracy and to enhance his standing among
state officials, Putin has embraced the Soviet ideal of job security as a perquisite of
political power. As illustrated above in the cases of Nazdratenko and Yakovlev, even
persons removed from office under Putin do not head into the political wilderness,
but to another sinecure that usually assures them a measure of dignity and financial
support.

Final responsibility for the appointment of leading figures in the presidential
administration and the government lies with the president, who, we are told,
consults with officials from other branches of government before making key

---

[21] 'Svoi kadry blizhe' and 'Predel lichnoi korysti. Osobennosti kadrovoi politiki v sovremennoi
Rossii', *Literaturnaya gazeta*, 6–12 February 2002, translated as 'Our Own Personnel', in *Russian
Politics and Law*, 4 (2002), 10.

appointments.[22] As one would expect, presidential advisers play an important role in the vetting and recruitment of leading officials. Putin's chief of staff (Alexander Voloshin until December 2003; Dmitry Medvedev after that date) is deeply involved in patronage politics as the leader of the presidential administration, though the formal portfolio for appointments rests with one of his deputies (Viktor Ivanov until November 2003, and then Dmitry Kozak until his transfer to the government apparatus in March 2004).[23] This deputy chief of staff exercises immediate supervision over the presidential department responsible for personnel matters, the administration of cadres (*Upravlenie kadrov*), which is currently headed by a general with experience in the FSB and FAPSI, Vladimir Osipov. Judging by the presence of the head of the administration of cadres at collegium meetings of the power ministries, this subdivision of the presidency appears to represent a modern-day version of the central committee's department of administrative organs, which oversaw cadres policy and other matters in military and legal institutions in the Soviet era. Among other responsibilities, the administration of cadres provides political and criminal background checks on candidates for appointment or promotion.[24]

In the provinces, Putin has sought to introduce a tightly-organized network of presidential personnel offices that oversee the selection of territorially-based federal officials. Putin has been especially intent on wresting control over the appointment of federal law enforcement officials operating in the provinces from regional political leaders, who had 'captured' many judges and prosecutors in the 1990s.[25] Reorienting federal justice officials toward the centre has been a major element of Putin's drive to re-establish a 'ruling vertical' in Russian politics, whose logic is to minimize authority leakage as the policies of the presidency are transmitted to, and implemented by, subordinate levels of the political and administrative hierarchy. To achieve this goal, Putin created in each of the seven federal districts a cadres commission, which removed many of the federal law enforcement officials who had been coopted by regional political networks. In addition, in 2003, Putin began appointing personally the leaders of the MVD in select regions and republics of Russia. With this assault on localism in the legal

---

[22] Vladimir Rudakov, 'Proshu slova. Viktor Ivanov: Ot chinovnikov, deistvitel'no zapyatnavshikh sebya, gosudarstvo izbavlyaetsya', *Profil'*, 10 November 2003.

[23] Kozak's move to the government represented a further step by Putin in the presidency's domination of the other executive apparatus and in what Putin himself called the transformation of the 1000-person government apparatus into 'an efficient and up-to-date tool of administration' rather than a 'parallel "shadow" government.' 'Remarks by President Vladimir Putin and Prime Minister Mikhail Fradkov at RF Government Meeting' (9 March 2004), Official Kremlin International News Broadcast.

[24] 'Kacheli vlasti', *Moskovskii komsomolets*, 3 March 1999. This responsibility is shared with the Security Council.

[25] See Brian D. Taylor, 'Russia's Regions and Law Enforcement' (paper presented to the AAASS National Convention, Toronto, November 2003).

organs well underway, the commissions have been expanding their scope to loosen the grip of provincial elites on federal personnel in other sectors.[26]

Judicial Appointees

Due to their role in cases involving property and elections, which are the gateways to economic and political power, courts have assumed a prominence in post-Communist politics that would have been unimaginable in the Soviet era. As the outcome of the US presidential election in November 2000 illustrates, control over judicial appointments can have serious political and economic consequences. Because of his own legal education, the rising influence of courts in Russian life, and his dissatisfaction with aspects of judicial behaviour, Putin has sought to reassert central control over the selection of federal judges, a move that has encountered both institutional and practical hurdles. Although the 1993 constitution granted the president sole authority to appoint Russian judges to provincial and local courts, subsequent legislation introduced complex procedures for presenting judicial nominees to the president. Since 2002, Russian law has required the participation of judicial qualification commissions, regional assemblies, and the judiciary's own leadership in the nomination of candidates for judicial office in provincial and local courts.

For example, in the highest provincial courts, which are known as charter courts in regions and supreme courts in the republics, the president appoints new judges, but only after they have been nominated by the provincial judicial qualification commission and then vetted by the police, customs officials, and the FSB, the regional or republic assembly, and the head of the charter or supreme court of the region or republic.[27] Before reaching the president's desk, the nomination passes through the office of the governor-general in the relevant federal district and is then reviewed in the Kremlin by a special judicial appointments commission. This board of seventeen members is dominated by conservative forces in the legal community, with officials from law enforcement and security organs outnumbering representatives from the judiciary and independent

---

[26] Svetlana Ofitova, 'Polpredam razreshili "vzyat" ' kassu. Odnako prioritetnye zadachi namestnikov—eto zemel'naya i sudebnaya reformy', *Nezavisimaya gazeta*, 24 April 2003.

[27] Yuliya Mikhailina, 'Kandidatov v sud'i proveryayut militsiya i FSB', *Gazeta*, 18 July 2003, 1; Anastasiya Kornia, 'Bez protokola', *Vremya MN*, 8 August 2003; and 'Valentin Kuznetsov, predsedatel' Vysshei kvalifikatsionnoi kollegii sudei Rossii: my sudim sudei', *Izvestiya*, 19 July 2003. The chair of the Supreme Commercial Court, Venyamin Yakovlev, has criticized the 'secrecy' of the work by the investigators, who at times refuse to approve judicial candidates without giving an explanation to the court's leadership. Anna Zakatnova, 'Eshche odna reforma', *Rossiiskaya gazeta*, 28 November 2003.

legal scholars.[28] Thus, at two points in the nominating process, during the background check on a nominee and then the review of the file by the Kremlin's judicial appointments commission, the police and security organs can effectively veto a candidate who is offensive to law enforcement. These multiple choke-points in nominating procedures for judges dramatically restrict the ability of the president to shape the composition of the judiciary.

Lengthy judicial terms as well as the difficulty of managing a centralized appointment system over a large and far-flung judicial corps further limit presi-dential patronage power over the judiciary. Unlike most political appointees, judges do not serve at the pleasure of the president. Instead, they enjoy life terms, or rather terms that continue until age sixty-five, except for newly appointed judges, who serve a three-year trial period on the bench. Moreover, judges may only be removed for cause by a judicial qualification commission.[29] After heavy lobbying for changes in the law, Putin acquired the right to appoint one member to each judicial qualification commission. In many regions, however, this position remains vacant almost two years after the adoption of the new legislation, which is an indication of the inability or unwillingness of the presidency to devote sufficient resources and attention to the management of personnel policy in the judicial realm.

The difficulty of managing judicial personnel policy is apparent in the extra-ordinary number of court appointments made during Putin's first term. During his first year as president, Putin appointed 4400 judges to office, with almost 800 in June 2000 alone. The following two years witnessed a significant decrease in the pace of judicial appointments, but the numbers were still staggering, with 2100 judges appointed in 2001 (871 in December alone) and 1500 judges in 2002.[30] During President Clinton's first two years, he set an US record by nominating 129 federal judges, a number that would be equalled in a slow month by the Russian president.[31] With appointment responsibilities on this scale, a Russian president has no choice but to delegate to others the review of candidates to the bench.

If the presidency does exercise influence over the courts in cases where property or parliamentary seats are at stake, it appears to be based less on the president's power to appoint rank-and-file judges to the bench than from his right to select court chairmen, who serve six-year terms. The heads of courts at every level enjoy broad authority in the distribution of cases to judges and in the

[28] 'Valentin Kuznetsov, predsedatel' Vysshei kvalifikatsionnoi kollegii sudei Rossii: my sudim sudei', *Izvestiya*, 19 July 2003. For the membership of the commission and its procedures, see 'O Komissii pri Prezidente Rossiiskoi Federatsii po predvaritel'nomu rassmotreniyu kandidatur na dolzhnosti sudei federal'nykh sudov', *Sobranie zakonodatel'stva*, 41 (2001), 3938.

[29] See Peter H. Solomon, Jr., 'Putin's Judicial Reform', *East European Constitutional Review* 11/1–2 (Winter/Spring 2002), 117–25.

[30] The figures are based on counts of appointments listed in *Sobranie zakonodatel'stva* from January 2000 through December 2002. Most of the appointments were in the courts of general jurisdiction, though a significant minority were to military and commercial courts.

[31] United States Department of Justice press release (12 October 1994), http://www.usdoj.gov/opa/pr/Pre_96/October94/591.txt.html.

evaluation of performance on the bench. These evaluations can affect pay and promotion and, in exceptional cases, lead to sanctions or dismissal. In Bashkortostan, for example, the head of the Supreme Court used his office to influence judicial appointments throughout the republic, a practice that played into the hands of his opponents when he began to resist the dictates of the president of Bashkortostan.[32] The Russian legal reformer, Sergey Pashin, may be overstating the case when he claims that Putin has established a ruling vertical in the judiciary, which extends from the president and governors to court chairmen and then to ordinary judges. The numbers of appointments by themselves suggest that the presidential apparatus, never mind the president himself, cannot vet carefully each nominee for chair or deputy chair of a court. In 2000, for example, Putin appointed just over 1300 chairs or deputy chairs of general jurisdiction, commercial, and military courts. However, even when employed on a selective basis, the ability to appoint and remove judges from leadership positions in the judiciary grants the president a considerable measure of influence over judicial behaviour.[33] Judges who wish to assume or retain a leadership post in the court system cross the president at their peril.

Civil Service

The boundaries between political appointees and permanent civil servants are not always clear, even in the most democratic regimes. In a perfect Weberian world, the former would be selected according to a spoils system while the latter would be hired on the basis of merit alone. But those who wield political power often find ways to influence the hiring and promotion of civil servants, especially those in the higher realms of administration.[34] So it is in Russia, where successive governments have often ignored the formal requirements of the law on the civil service, which designates officials up through the grade of deputy ministers as category 'V' personnel, signifying their membership in the permanent bureaucracy.[35] Russian officials who wish to replace functionaries do so at times without apology or a nod in the direction of the formal rules, behaviour that is especially

---

[32] Sergey Ostapenko, 'Vladimira Putina prosyat rassudit' bashkirskikh sudei', *Kommersant-Daily*, 20 December 2002, 3.

[33] More research is needed to determine the motivations of judges in property and election law cases. There is much talk about the revival of 'telephone law' in Russia, that is, the direct interference of politicians in cases *sub judice*, but little hard evidence exists to link politicians directly to judicial decisions that benefit them.

[34] See, for example, the Israeli case in Eva Etzioni-Halevy, 'Administrative Power in Israel', *Israel Affairs*, 4 (2002), 30–42.

[35] Eugene Huskey, 'Nomenklatura Lite? The Cadres Reserve in Russian Public Administration', *Problems of Post-Communism* (March–April 2004), 30–9. This section of the chapter draws heavily on this study.

widespread in, but not limited to, municipal and local governments. Those concerned about appearances will often dismiss unwanted bureaucrats by re-organizing the agency in which they work, a tactic that allows them to remove personnel from eliminated departments without cause.

The distinguishing feature of patronage practice in the Russian bureaucracy under Putin is not the blurred lines between politics and administration but the revival of a recruitment tool from the Soviet era—the cadres reserve. Introduced on a limited basis in the late Yeltsin era, this institution has become a central element of Putin's reform of the civil service, among whose stated aims are the reduction in the size of the bureaucracy, the simplification of government licensing procedures, the elimination of administrative inspections designed to solicit bribes, and the enhancement of the pay and prestige of officialdom.[36] The framework law on the civil service, adopted in April 2003 as the foundation stone of a multi-year legislative edifice on civil service reform, mandates the formation of cadres reserve lists for all state institutions at all levels of government.[37]

Just as in the Soviet era, the cadres reserve lists contain the names of individuals who have been 'pre-qualified' to assume responsible positions in the bureaucracy. Thus, each position at the level of department head and above—and in some jurisdictions and agencies, even lower-ranking posts—has a reserve list associated with it. The list contains a pool of personnel from which the administrative or political leadership can fill vacancies. Where the elected chief executive at each administrative level approves the appointment of candidates to the reserve lists for the most senior permanent civil service jobs, the senior civil servants themselves select the members of the reserve lists for subordinate posts within their depart-ment or agency. Membership on a reserve list means more than eligibility for promotion; it also brings with it the expectation that *rezervisty* will prepare actively to assume a more challenging assignment, whether through formal retraining courses or periodic seminars and shadowing exercises in the office to which they will be promoted.

How does one explain the revival of cadres reserve lists, which appear to be menacing legacies of the Soviet order? First, Russian leaders remain deeply skeptical about the ability of the labour market to provide the requisite cadres for the bureaucracy. In their view, one must identify, train, and nurture personnel not just advertise for them. This attitude is evident in the numerous initiatives advanced at regional and local levels to develop the human infrastructure for both the public and private sectors. Put simply, something as important as the future generation of political, administrative, and economic elites cannot be left to the vagaries of the market, especially in less developed regions of the country. Thus, the cadres departments in several jurisdictions have begun tracking pro-

[36] For an overview of civil service reform under Putin, see Eugene Huskey and Alexander Obolonsky, 'The Struggle to Reform Russia's Bureaucracy', *Problems of Post-Communism*, 50/4 (July–August 2003), 22–33.
[37] O sisteme gosudarstvennoi sluzhby Rossiiskoi federatsii, *Rossiiskaya gazeta*, 30 May 2003.

spective candidates for reserve lists in the bureaucracy as early as high school and university.[38]

Reviving cadres reserve lists allows politicians and senior administrators to develop a loyal as well as a qualified recruitment pool. But the forming of reserve lists of loyal cadres undermines one of the essential principles of civil service reform: merit-based hiring, which requires open competition for vacant posts. In those instances where reserve lists are in place, the authorities are not obligated to follow the competitive hiring rules set out in legislation. With cadres reserve lists, then, the selection of personnel is done in advance and with less transparency than one would find otherwise. Not only does this recruitment method reduce the applicant pool, it also encourages clientelism by linking the success of *rezervisty* to politicians or higher-level administrators who hire and fire the candidates on reserve lists. Binding the fate of *rezervisty* to their patrons only serves to deepen personalist rule. By approving reserve lists, politicians are often meddling in promotion decisions that should rest with the permanent civil servants rather than elected officials.

At least at the beginning of Putin's second term, however, there was little evidence that the Russian president's call for the adoption of cadres reserve lists had substantially increased his own patronage power. The presidency lacks a linking mechanism that could carefully monitor the nomination and appointment of *rezervisty* to leading political and administrative posts. As a result, proposals for a system of geographical rotation of cadres, which was used to good effect in the Soviet era to discourage the rise of localist political networks, have made only modest headway in Putin's Russia. There is, moreover, no senior executive service that could be deployed by the president to assume strategic positions in the upper reaches of federal and regional administration.

The recruitment coordination that does exist between the political leadership and the heads of subordinate departments and agencies is more likely to occur at the municipal or regional rather than the national level. One could argue, therefore, that to this point the reserve system has functioned as a constraint on presidential authority by solidifying the control of local elites over the administrative personnel in their territories. If Putin intends to use the reserve lists as an instrument of presidential rule, he will need to develop an institutional mechanism that controls the appointment of cadres to reserve lists in Moscow and the provinces. To allow others to pre-qualify candidates for promotion undermines the president's appointments prerogative.

Business Elites

Like elites in the United States, and to a lesser extent in France and other European countries, Russian officials circulate regularly between the public and

---

[38] See, for example, Artem Galin, 'Korporatsiya munitsipal'nykh sluzhashchikh', *Kommercheskie vesti*, 2 July 2003.

private sectors, a pattern that became even more pronounced in the Putin era. According to Kryshtanovskaya and White, 15.7 per cent of the top leadership were drawn from representatives of big business under Putin, whereas the figure for the Yeltsin cohort (1993) was only 2.3 per cent.[39] In Russia, not only does the state include private sector personnel on some of its reserve lists for government posts, it has also begun to claim the right to form reserve lists for certain private organizations, whether in the business or non-profit sectors. In Yakutia, for example, the republic's cadres department asserts its right to form reserve lists for 'all economic enterprises with state capital, federal structures located in the republic, scientific establishments, social organizations, and non-productive collectives'.[40] In parts of the Red Belt, south of Moscow, regional governments are creating a 'unified personnel policy' that maintains cadres reserve lists for leading private as well as public organizations.[41]

Extending the reach of the state-constructed cadres reserve lists to include key positions in the private sector represents the formalizing of a policy of state intervention in personnel decisions in the business community that had its roots in the 1990s. By deciding into which private hands state enterprises would pass, President Yeltsin and his entourage recruited, de facto, the first generation of the Russian business community. But with most former state property now under the control of private industrialists and entrepreneurs, the state must adopt different methods if it wishes to continue to influence the recruitment of the business elite. One approach is to restore the Soviet practice of integrating the leaders of enterprises into a patronage system controlled by the state; the other is to employ the threat, or use, of selective prosecution to remove or intimidate business leaders. Whatever the precise mix of forces behind the arrest of Mikhail Khodorkovsky, the use of the criminal law for political purposes—taken together with the formation of state-controlled cadres reserve lists for private sector jobs—is a high-risk strategy that could discourage foreign investment, encourage capital flight, and further erode the boundaries between the public and private sectors.

Conclusions

The turbulence of Yeltsin's personnel policy betrayed a politics of manoeuvre, a bobbing and weaving to avoid or deflect the blows of the opposition. The Putin

---

[39] Olga Kryshtanovskaya and Stephen White, 'Generations and the Conversion of Power in Postcommunist Russia', *Perspectives on European Politics and Society*, 3 (2002), 236. In France, of course, the institution of *pantouflage* allows a distinguished career in the administrative apparatus to serve as a springboard to leading management positions in the private sector or in government-owned enterprises.

[40] 'Aleksandr Samsonov: 'My poluchili real'nuyu kartinu o kadrovom potentsiale respubliki', *Yakutiya*, 6 June 2002.

[41] V. Kizilov, 'Vypusknikov mnogo—spetsialistov net', *Belgorodskaya pravda*, 19 November 2002; 'Kadry reshayut vse!', *Krasnyi Sever* [Vologda], 2 March 2002.

era, in constrast, has witnessed a less dramatic but more purposeful and ambitious approach to patronage policy. For Putin, patronage is not a political tactic but a system designed to support his broader campaign to construct a 'ruling vertical' in Russian political life. Begun as a reaction against the destructive centrifugal forces in Russian politics in the Yeltsin era, patronage policy under Putin has moved beyond a rebalancing of federal–regional relations to the establishment of a centralized recruitment system that would allow the president to rule through administrative rather than political means.

The initiatives in recruitment policy outlined in this chapter have already weakened the role of opposition in Russian politics, in both theory and practice. The question for the future is whether Putin has the will and ability to pursue this campaign to its logical conclusion, which would move Russia beyond managed pluralism—or whatever word combination one employs to describe the constrained competition of current Russian politics—toward an overt form of authoritarianism.[42] Before assuming power, Putin made it clear that in Russia's new political system, the state would direct society in ways that departed from the experience of countries that had passed through the Atlantic Revolution. But for all the talk of Russian exceptionalism, Putin, like Gorbachev and Yeltsin before him, has also been intent on Russia's integration into the world community. There is perhaps no more insistent theme in Putin's presidency than the desire to be accepted economically, politically, and psychologically by the West. To argue that the expansion of Putin's patronage power will put an end to political competition is to believe that the Russian president values the accumulation of personal power more than his country's standing in the world, or that the consolidation of authoritarian rule in Russia would be greeted with equanimity by the West, and thus would have no bearing on Russia's global role. Neither scenario appears plausible. Archie Brown has made a similar point about Putin's ambitions in foreign affairs: 'While he clearly hankers after Russia's becoming again a great power (as distinct, though, from a superpower), he seems temperamentally averse to adventurism'.[43]

It is not agency alone, however, that stands in the way of the remonopolization of political power by a leader. Over the last fifteen years, the partition of property and the dispersal of political authority across regions and agencies has established a sizeable political class of elected officials, bureaucrats, and citizens who will resist—and are resisting—the reconcentration of patronage power in the centre. In this environment, a purge may be effective against a small number of individuals, such as Khodorkovsky and Nazdratenko, but a broader assault on the

---

[42] See the stimulating essay by Harley Balzer, 'Managed Pluralism: Putin's Emerging Regime', *Post-Soviet Affairs*, 3 (2003), 189–227.

[43] Archie Brown, 'Introduction' in Archie Brown and Lilia Shevtsova (eds.), *Gorbachev, Yeltsin, and Putin: Political Leadership in Russia's Transition* (Washington, DC: Carnegie Endowment for International Peace, 2001), 5.

property and prerogatives of the country's elites will invite a counter-offensive that could constrain or even remove the president.

Furthermore, one should not underestimate the sheer administrative difficulties of concentrating vast patronage powers in the hands of a single leader. Recent reports from the front illustrate that the Russian presidency is far from having organized the institutional mechanisms that would allow Putin to identify and appoint in a timely manner loyal and competent cadres, especially outside of Moscow. For example, although the authorities in Karelia have regularly forwarded to Moscow nominations for vacancies on the republic's courts, the president has at times delayed taking action on these candidacies for more than a year and a half, which has left the republic with a depleted judiciary.[44] According to one report, the chancellery of the Russian president requires a minimum of four months to process judicial nominations.[45] If such administrative difficulties could be overcome, it would be in part by the delegation of appointment authority to subordinate personnel and institutions, which would represent a diffusion of power in its own right. Given the constraints outlined here, it appears likely that Putin is approaching the limits of his ability and desire to concentrate patronage power in the presidency.

At the beginning of his second term, Putin stands at an important crossroads. One path leads to a continued reliance on the presidency as his primary institutional base. The other would shift his instrument of governance from the presidency to a party, United Russia, and in so doing raise the spectre of an integrated Party-State. Such a course would expand his reach but it would subject him to the potential for a party revolt and, as we noted above, to a revolt from the West. It would also require the establishment of a 'ruling vertical' within United Russia itself, which is still a deeply fragmented political institution, with regional subdivisions that are often more loyal to the local governor than to Putin.[46] To choose party over presidency as his primary instrument of rule would bring to an end an almost fifteen-year period of presidential rule, which began when Gorbachev abandoned the party as his institutional base to take his chances with a newly created presidency. The greater uncertainties and complexities associated with ruling through a party make the further integration of party and state problematic. Instead of a fused party and state, an awkward and unstable coalition between presidency and party appears the most likely course for Russian political development in Putin's second term and beyond.

---

[44] 'Podsudimyi, vstan'te v ochered'', *Rossiiskie vesti*, 4 June 2003.

[45] Ekaterina Grigor'eva and Grigory Punanov, 'Myagkoi posadki! Konstitutsionnyi sud zapretil prokuroram arestovyvat' lyudei', *Izvestiya*, 15 March 2003.

[46] For an article on the autonomy of the party in Bashkortostan, see Vitaly Ivanov, 'Bashkirskaya vertikal'', *Vedomosti*, 20 May 2003.

10

Putin and the 'Oligarchs': A Two-sided Commitment Problem

William Tompson[1]

In Russia, in contrast to America, the government machine has always been much stronger than any individual or any company or any set of companies.

—Mikhail Khodorkovsky, 2001[2]

One of Vladimir Putin's primary objectives on assuming power was to re-establish the authority of the Russian state, which had been severely weakened from the late 1980s. Putin sought, in particular, to strengthen the presidency vis-à-vis the other major institutions and actors in the political system.[3] This meant redefining the Kremlin's relations with the Federal Assembly, the regional elite, and, above all, the so-called 'oligarchs', the handful of spectacularly wealthy tycoons who had shot to prominence under Boris Yeltsin and who appeared to dominate Russian politics in the late 1990s.[4] The Federal Assembly was the softest target. The State Duma had always been relatively weak and the 1999 elections had produced a chamber that was ready to follow the president's lead. It proved an eager partner when Putin set out to emasculate the Assembly's upper house, the Federation Council, by replacing the elected regional bosses who sat ex officio in the Council with appointed senators. The new Council was even less likely than the old to act

[1] Senior Economist, Non-Member Economies Division, Organization for Economic Cooperation & Development; william.tompson@oecd.org. The views expressed in this paper are those of the author and do not necessarily reflect those of the OECD or its member states.

[2] *Los Angeles Times*, 26 December 2001.

[3] Archie Brown, 'Vladimir Putin and the Reaffirmation of Central State Power', *Post-Soviet Affairs*, 17/1 (January–March 2001); Thomas F. Remington, 'Russia and the "Strong State" Ideal', *East European Constitutional Review*, 9/1–2 (Winter/Spring 2000); and Martin Nicholson, 'Putin's Russia: Slowing the Pendulum without Stopping the Clock', *International Affairs*, 77/4 (October 2001).

[4] On Putin's relations with the regional elite and the Federal Assembly, see the chapter by Melvin in this volume; see also Thomas F. Remington, 'Putin and the Duma', *Post-Soviet Affairs*, 17/4 (October–December 2001); Matthew Hyde, 'Putin's Federal Reforms and their Implications for Presidential Power in Russia', *Europe-Asia Studies*, 53/5 (July 2001); and Gordon M. Hahn, 'The Impact of Putin's Federative Reforms on Democratization in Russia', *Post-Soviet Affairs*, 19/3 (July–September 2003).

as a serious counterweight to the executive.[5] The restructuring of the Federation
Council, in turn, was part of a wide-ranging drive to bring the regional bosses to
heel, which Neil Melvin discusses in the next chapter. The results of this
campaign were mixed, at best, but there is little doubt that it succeeded in
strengthening central authority at the expense of the subjects of the federation.[6]

Tackling the oligarchs was an altogether more difficult business.[7] Having
promised prior to his election that the oligarchs would 'cease to exist as a class'
and that he (and, by implication, the state) would adopt a position of 'equidistance' from all of them, Putin sought, in the interests of stability, to tame
them rather than to exterminate them, redefining and institutionalizing their
relationship with the state. This chapter seeks to understand how Putin went
about pursuing these ends and to emphasize, in particular, that the redefinition of
business–state relations on which he embarked was an ongoing process, rather
than the once-for-all negotiation of a new modus vivendi, as the oligarchs
themselves, and many other observers, believed.[8]

The central argument of the chapter is that no such stable accommodation
between Putin and the oligarchs was possible, for at least three reasons. First, both
sides had strong incentives to defect from any agreement that was reached.
Second, for reasons set out below, both sides would have found it extremely
difficult to uphold the terms of such a deal even if they had wanted to do so.
Third, neither side could make a credible commitment to abide by any bargain:
even if they had *wished* to adhere to its terms, they would have been unable to
convince each other of their good faith. Of the two, the president faced the more
acute commitment problem, one which actually grew more pronounced as he
consolidated power. Putin's dominance meant that both he and the oligarchs knew
very well that they would find it difficult to enforce the terms of any bargain if the
president should later decide to defect from it; the more powerful Putin became,
the more evident it was that such enforcement would be impossible. This
commitment problem reflects more than just Putin's personal standing. It is
also the product of an underlying institutional problem: the lack of effective
constraints on the coercive capacities of the Russian state. Simply put, Russia
lacks strong institutions capable of ensuring that the state abides by its own rules.
Since agreements between the state and its subjects are not generally subject to
any third-party enforcement, the lack of such institutions means that the state
cannot easily make a credible commitment in any agreement with domestic actors.

[5] For an examination of the reconstituted SF, see Thomas F. Remington, 'Majorities without
Mandates: The Russian Federation Council since 2000', *Europe-Asia Studies*, 55/5 (July 2003).

[6] Hyde, 'Putin's Federal Reforms' (n. 4) and Hahn, 'Impact' (n. 4). See also Daniel Treisman,
'Russia Restored?' *Foreign Affairs*, 81/6 (November–December 2002); and also William Tompson,
'Russia: Putin's Power Plays', *The World Today*, 56/7 (July 2000).

[7] Lee S. Wolosky, 'Putin's Plutocrat Problem', *Foreign Affairs*, 79/2 (March–April 2000).

[8] It should be acknowledged that the author of this chapter was among those who initially—and
mistakenly—believed that Putin had negotiated a lasting settlement with the oligarchs in 2000.

The Oligarchs: Yeltsin's Legacy to Putin

Before proceeding with the argument, it is necessary to consider briefly who the oligarchs were. The term itself, though widely used, is something of a misnomer, in at least two respects. First, it greatly exaggerates the extent to which the tycoons represent power independent of, and dominating, the state. In fact, the oligarchs' fortunes were amassed thanks chiefly to the patronage of state institutions and officials, and they have always needed to remain in the state's good graces. It is for this reason that they have worked so assiduously to colonize state structures. Oligarchs who fall out of favour with the Kremlin can soon find themselves out of business, or at least out of the country, as the careers of men like Vladimir Vinogradov, Alexander Smolensky, Vladimir Gusinsky, and Boris Berezovsky attest. Second, the term 'oligarch' implies something like an 'oligarchy', a small ruling clique. In fact, Russia's tycoons have never been good at cooperating with each other and have tended to unite only when faced with a common, immediate threat, as when they banded together to assist Yeltsin's re-election effort in 1996.[9] This is a critical point, as Putin rapidly demonstrated how easily the state could play on the oligarchs' rivalries and mutual enmities.

Nevertheless, there is no doubt that the oligarchs were a force to be reckoned with. The privatization contests of the 1990s had left Russia with an extraordinarily concentrated structure of ownership, one that, indeed, grew even more concentrated during Putin's first years in office. By the end of 2001, it was estimated that 85 per cent of the value of Russia's sixty-four largest privately owned companies, with aggregate sales of $109 billion in 2000, was controlled by just eight shareholder groups.[10] Another major study found that, in 2002, Russia's ten largest business groupings accounted for 38.7 per cent of industrial output and 31 per cent of exports.[11] This implies a level of ownership concentration in excess of those found in Western Europe, the United States, or even South Korea with its famous *chaebols*. The individuals who controlled these groupings largely corresponded to conventional perceptions of who the 'oligarchs' were: Roman Abramovich, Vladimir Potanin, Mikhail Khodorkovsky, Vagit Alekperov, and others.[12] To them one might add the heads of at least two state-controlled

[9] The oligarchs' contribution to Yeltsin's victory has generally been exaggerated, not least by the oligarchs themselves. The money they committed to his campaign was dwarfed by the state funds that were diverted to this end.

[10] Peter Boone and Denis Rodionov, 'Rent Seeking in Russia and the CIS' (paper presented at the tenth anniversary meeting of the EBRD, London, December 2001). See also World Bank, *From Transition to Development: A Country Economic Memorandum for the Russian Federation* (Washington, DC: World Bank, April 2004).

[11] *Krupnyi rossiiskii biznes – 2003* (Moscow: Fond perspektivnykh issledovanii i initsiativ, 2004); see also *Vedomosti*, 14 January 2004. The groupings included: Menatep, Lukoil, Alfa-Renova, Base Element, Surgutneftegaz, AvtoVAZ, Interros, AFK Sistema, Severstal', and MDM.

[12] The list also corresponds closely to the Russians named in the February 2004 *Forbes* magazine list of the world's billionaires; see *Forbes*, 15 March 2004.

companies: Anatoly Chubais, the CEO of the electricity monopoly RAO EES, and, until his removal in May 2001, Rem Vyakhirev, the long-serving CEO of the gas monopoly OAO Gazprom.[13] During the Yeltsin era, the oligarchs constructed lobbying networks that reached into virtually every state institution, from the Kremlin, the Duma, and the federal ministries down to regional and local bureaucracies. It was this penetration of state structures at all levels that enabled the oligarchs to thwart the adoption—or at least the implementation—of unwelcome policy initiatives and that prompted many observers to speak of their 'privatization of the state'.

Despite the role of certain tycoons in facilitating his rise to power, Putin's distaste for them was soon apparent, not least in his campaign promises concerning equidistance from business groups and the elimination of the oligarchs as a class (the latter with its almost certainly intentional echoes of Stalin). At his first meeting as president with the leading representatives of big business in July 2000, Putin told them, 'I want to draw your attention to the fact that you have yourselves to a significant extent formed this state, through political and quasi-political structures under your control. So perhaps what one should do least of all is blame the mirror.'[14] Nevertheless, though he was clearly determined to curb the power of big business vis-à-vis the state (or, at least, the Kremlin), Putin was constrained in his dealings with them by the need to avoid any threat to political or economic stability.

He was also constrained by the dearth of close, reliable associates to whom he could entrust key posts. For most of his first term he continued to rely on Yeltsin-era holdovers, many of whom had close ties to the oligarchs. Particularly prominent were representatives of the Yeltsin-era political clan known as 'the Family', with which both Prime Minister Mikhail Kasyanov and presidential chief of staff Alexander Voloshin were identified. At the same time, Putin began to advance the careers of his long-standing associates, many of whom shared his KGB background. Over time, a new faction emerged to rival the Family, the so-called 'Petersburg *chekisty*'. This group had its roots in the security services and related structures and was generally believed to be led by Viktor Ivanov and Igor Sechin, two long-time associates of Putin's who were appointed to the presidential administration after Putin took power. Not all of Putin's protégés from St Petersburg could be categorized as *chekisty*, for a third tendency was also identifiable in Putin's administration. Known colloquially as the 'Petersburg liberals', these were the reform-minded lawyers and economists who had worked with Putin in the St Petersburg city administration in the early 1990s—men like

---

[13] Vyakhirev's successor, Aleksey Miller, is a close Putin associate and an outsider to Gazprom. He has thus relied on the Kremlin's support since his appointment and has not really established himself as an independent figure as Vyakhirev did.

[14] Here and elsewhere, quotations from Putin are, unless otherwise indicated, taken from the archive on the presidential web site, http://president.kremlin.ru.

Finance Minister Aleksey Kudrin and Minister of Economic Development and Trade, German Gref.[15]

Most observers focused on the rivalry between the Family and the *chekisty*, seeing the Petersburg liberals as by far the weakest group. They did not control key businesses, like the Family, nor did they share the apparent influence of the *chekisty* in the security organs and the military. However, the Petersburg liberals' success in shaping policy was considerable, suggesting that it would be a mistake to underestimate them.[16] Nevertheless, given the nature of the weak and divided opposition to Putin, the Family–*chekist* rivalry was viewed by many as the main axis of political conflict in Russia. It would be a mistake, however, to see it simply as a contest between the oligarchs and a rising new class of Putinites: many of the oligarchs did not enjoy good relations with the Family and sought to pursue their interests on their own, and the *chekisty* themselves were closely linked to a number of large companies and financial–industrial groups, albeit ones which tended to be largely state-owned (like the oil company Rosneft) or at any rate rather *étatiste* in their orientation (like Sergey Pugachev's Mezhprombank).

These conflicts appear to have served the president well. Like his predecessor, Putin maintained a balance among competing political clans. Initially, this was probably a matter of political survival: the new president could ill afford to risk any attempt to exclude the Family from positions of power and, in any case, he needed their expertise. Yet by 2004, Putin clearly had consolidated his position and his continued balancing of factions appears to have reflected preference rather than necessity. While there was a clear tendency to sideline the Family, Putin never gave free rein to any single grouping and, indeed, he appears to have regarded each as being useful for particular purposes and to have preferred something of a division of labour among them. Thus, as members of the Family were removed from office in the face of a sustained onslaught by the *chekisty* in 2003–4, it was most often the representatives of the Petersburg liberal faction who replaced them.

Such balancing of factions appears to have served at least two ends. First, it impeded the emergence of any serious open opposition to the president. As long as all of the major elite factions enjoyed some access to, and support from, the president, they were more likely to achieve their ends by competing for his favour than by openly challenging him. Cutting off any significant faction entirely would effectively have left a potentially powerful segment of the elite with no choice but

---

[15] One might also add two of Voloshin's most influential deputies to the list: Dmitry Kozak and Dmitry Medvedev.

[16] Political 'factions' and 'clans' at such a level of politics are difficult to define with precision, and it might be objected that these labels are attached to various groups and individuals by external observers. It may well be true that the labels are originally journalistic invention. However, in conversation, senior officials in the government and the presidential administration often describe developments in terms of these factions and the evidence suggests that such insiders also view political conflicts around the president in terms of the sorts of factional conflicts described here.

to move into opposition. Second, Putin was able to hold himself above the fray, playing off the various factions against one another and acting as the final arbiter in their disputes. This meant that very often it was unclear to outsiders just how far the president was really involved in any given initiative. Even his victims often saw him as their best hope of salvation. In 2003, for example, when the legal and political campaign directed against the owners of Yukos was in its early stages, Putin maintained his silence for several months despite calls for him to speak out and take a stand. As a result, even Yukos' strongest supporters remained reluctant to attack Putin directly, preferring to blame the campaign on the out-of-control *siloviki* and to pin their hopes for an early and satisfactory resolution of the conflict on presidential intervention.

There were clear echoes here of pre-revolutionary peasants' appeals to the 'just tsar' who alone could save them from the predations of his boyars. It is not clear to what extent the peasants ever actually *believed* in the just tsar, any more than it is evident that Yukos' supporters really imagined that Putin was not involved in the campaign against the company. In both cases, the regime's victims had strong incentives to *hope* that this was the case—otherwise, they had little prospect of being rescued. They also had every reason to behave as though they believed in the tsar's justice, since open defiance was bound to fail.

First Steps: The Oligarchs under Pressure

Despite his determination to assert his authority over Russia's financial–industrial magnates, the newly elected Putin recognized that he must proceed with caution. A frontal assault on the oligarchs as a group would have led to falling tax revenues and rising capital flight, putting at risk both the economic recovery that was getting under way and Putin's own consolidation of power. Nevertheless, the new president moved rapidly to signal that the terms of the relationship between big business and the Kremlin had changed.[17] This implied, in the first instance, giving the oligarchs a demonstration of the state's power and of their own vulnerability. In the spring and summer of 2000, therefore, the country's most prominent businessmen found themselves, one by one, under official pressure. The first target was media tycoon Vladimir Gusinsky, who had backed Putin's opponents in the elections of 1999/2000. He and his companies were subjected to a series of criminal investigations that were conducted with little regard for due process. Next in line was Boris Berezovsky, who had actively aided Putin's rise and helped engineer the Kremlin's Duma election victory in 1999. Yet, Gusinsky

---

[17] This was evident in both the pre-election promises mentioned above and in Putin's handling of the drive to put the oligarchs under pressure after the election, which culminated in the 28 July meeting discussed later.

and Berezovsky were not alone. Potanin faced a renewed attempt by state prosecutors to overturn the privatization of the metals giant Norilsk Nickel. Four
subsidiaries of the Tyumen Oil Company (TNK), controlled by the Alfa-Renova
consortium, were raided by investigators in conjunction with allegations of illegal
privatization deals. For a time, the state even appeared to withdraw its support
from Chubais, who looked set to lose his position on the EES board.

These developments did not, however, mark the onset of a campaign of
annihilation against the oligarchs. Instead, in case after case, Putin intervened as
their protector. Gusinsky was released from police custody after Putin criticized
his detention. Then Putin met with Potanin to discuss the future of Norilsk
Nickel. Shortly thereafter, federal prosecutors took the Norilsk case over from the
Moscow city prosecutors and settled it without litigation. The president publicly
signalled his support for Chubais, who was duly re-elected to the EES board.
A private meeting with Putin helped Lukoil chief Vagit Alekperov silence ru-
mours that he was about to be arrested. In each case, the lesson for the tycoons
involved was much the same: they were vulnerable, but the president was in a
position to protect them. The corollary, of course, was that his protection might
be withdrawn. On 1 July 2000, even as this 'catch-and-release' campaign was
unfolding, Prime Minister Mikhail Kasyanov declared that there would be no
drive to overturn past privatization deals. This appeared to give the business elite
what it most desired: the assurance that its ownership of assets acquired in the
chaotic and corrupt privatization processes of the 1990s was secure. However,
Kasyanov added an important caveat: some deals, which had involved legal
violations, might yet be overturned.[18]

Kasyanov's statement appeared to reflect Putin's own approach, reassuring the
elite that the new administration could and would respect big business—if the
businessmen behaved themselves. Investors and other observers were quick to
place just such a construction on Putin's remarks at his meeting with twenty-one
of the country's top businessmen on 28 July 2000, which marked the culmination
of the state's offensive against the oligarchs. The meeting took place against the
backdrop of the renewed investigation into Potanin's acquisition of Norilsk
Nickel, an investigation which, because of its focus on privatization abuses, was
far more threatening to the wider elite than the attacks on Gusinsky. Putin
reportedly assured the businessmen that there would be no 'political campaign'
to 'redistribute property' or to overturn the privatizations of the 1990s.[19] The
oligarchs, rattled by the events of the previous weeks, were all too ready to accept
any reassurance Putin might offer and to trade political restraint for confirmation
of their property rights. Thus was born the belief, which soon hardened into a
conviction, that Putin and the oligarchs had struck a deal.

This tacit understanding was never formalized in any way, and it is not clear
from contemporary reports of the meeting exactly what, if anything, either side

[18] *Vremya novostei*, 2 July 2000.   [19] *Washington Post*, 29 July 2000.

really promised the other. On the contrary, the official account of Putin's own remarks was limited to his relatively anodyne opening address; accounts of the meeting were otherwise based on claims made by those present about what the president had said and what he had meant by it. Nevertheless, the bargain supposedly struck at the July meeting soon became something akin to a foundational political myth.[20] It was seen as the cornerstone on which business–state relations were to be constructed under Putin. Journalists believed in it; investors believed in it; and, critically, the oligarchs themselves believed in it.[21]

Not all of the oligarchs, however, were welcome in the new dispensation. The campaigns against Gusinsky and Berezovsky continued. Politically motivated civil and criminal suits were used to deprive them of key assets and, in due course, both went into exile in order to avoid criminal charges in Russia. These attacks aroused concerns about freedom of the press and about the evident politicization of the police, the courts, and the security organs, but they did not provoke any larger confrontation between the Kremlin and the oligarchs. After a half-hearted attempt to intervene on Gusinsky's behalf in the summer of 2000,[22] the other tycoons chose discretion over valour and left the two men to their fate. In any case, the rest of the commercial elite apparently did not feel threatened by the campaigns against Berezovsky and Gusinsky, who were, in important respects, different from the rest. Both had accumulated extensive media holdings, which they had used to advance their own political agendas and which the Kremlin now wished to control. Moreover, their political activities had long been more visible and more extensive than those of their rivals. If most of the oligarchs appeared to engage in high politics in order to protect and advance their business interests, Berezovsky and Gusinsky often gave the impression that their businesses were instruments for advancing their political agendas. Gusinsky's role in opposing the Kremlin during the 1999/2000 electoral cycle also set him apart, as, ironically enough, did Berezovsky's support. Putin had no interest in appearing beholden to the ambitious and unpopular Berezovsky. Thus, Gusinsky was punished for opposing Putin, Berezovsky for having aided him.

For a time, the rest of the business elite appeared to have drawn the 'appropriate' conclusions from the destruction of Gusinsky and Berezovsky. While they did not by any means withdraw from politics, the major tycoons adopted a lower

---

[20] In 2004, one government official insisted to the author that the real understanding between Putin and the tycoons had been reached not at the 28 July meeting but at a series of bilateral meetings with individual businessmen during summer 2000.

[21] On the immediate reaction to the July meeting, see the *Washington Post*, 29 July 2000; and the Jamestown Foundation's *Russia's Week*, 5/30 (2 August 2000). See also later comments by oligarch Petr Aven and Russian Union of Industrialists and Entrepreneurs Vice-President Igor' Jurgens in the *Washington Post*, 14 December 2002. See also *Moscow Times*, 4 July 2003; and Aleksey Makarkin, 'Kreml': Novaya bor'ba klanov', Politcom.ru, 8 September 2003.

[22] For details of the letter addressed to Putin by Gusinsky's fellow oligarchs, see *Moscow Times*, 14 June 2000.

political profile and accepted many of the constraints imposed on them by the new administration. Access to Putin himself was increasingly restricted and was institutionalized via quarterly meetings between the president and the presidium of the Russian Union of Industrialists and Entrepreneurs (RSPP), which consequently came to enjoy a quasi-official status as the 'oligarchs' trade union'.

To be sure, there was more to Putin's strategy for managing relations with big business than merely making examples of Berezovsky and Gusinsky. While throwing his weight behind a range of broadly liberal economic reforms that Russian business welcomed,[23] Putin tightened his hold over key industrial and financial assets such as the gas monopoly Gazprom, the oil transport monopoly Transneft, and the state savings bank, Sberbank. This was aimed at least partly at shoring up his position vis-à-vis big business. State control over the pipeline infrastructure remains the government's best lever when it comes to managing the powerful oil barons, and the authorities have emphatically rejected the idea of allowing private pipelines to be built. Putin's reluctance to restructure the gas monopoly Gazprom also appeared to reflect, at least in part, the requirements of his 'oligarch-management' strategy. Gazprom's managers appear to have persuaded Putin—not without some foundation—that any radical restructuring of the gas industry could leave Russia with a sector which not only resembled the oil industry in structure but which was also dominated by the same players.[24] For Putin, handing control of the gas sector over to the oil barons might have been too high a price to pay for a more efficient industry. Putin's WTO accession ambitions were important here, too. While WTO membership would benefit some oligarchs and threaten others, it would represent an important external constraint on all of them.

The Bargain under Strain

Putin's initial bargain with the oligarchs seemed to be a clear and fairly pragmatic exchange of political restraint for secure property rights. For a time, this appeared to form the basis for a mutually acceptable modus vivendi between the new president and big business. This reflected the fact that much of Putin's early

---

[23] These included some easing of the tax burden, the relaxation of currency controls, and measures to ease licensing requirements and curb bureaucrats' power to interfere in the affairs of private business; see William Tompson, 'Putin's Challenge: The Politics of Structural Reform in Russia', *Europe–Asia Studies*, 54/6 (September 2002); and *idem*, 'The Russian Economy under Vladimir Putin', in Cameron Ross (ed.), *Russian Politics under Putin* (Basingstoke: Palgrave, 2004).

[24] Gazprom management has made this point quite explicitly; see OAO Gazprom, 'Zamechaniya po materialam Minekonomrazvitiya Rossii o restrukturizatsii OAO "Gazprom" ' (Mimeo: Moscow, 19 September 2003). See also Christopher Granville, 'Gas, Electricity and Political Will', *Russia: Strategy & Politics* (Moscow: UFG, 27 January 2003), 4–9.

agenda was reasonably congenial to most of the tycoons. The oligarchs, after all, had an interest in Putin's state-building project. Having acquired vast fortunes under Yeltsin largely as a result of their success in exploiting the state's weakness, they had much to gain from Putin's drive to rebuild the state. Anxious to consolidate their positions, the more forward-thinking tycoons recognized that only an effective state could protect their new property rights and provide an environment in which they could develop their businesses and enjoy their newly acquired wealth. Thus, men like Khodorkovsky and Potanin, who had exploited the weakness of state institutions in the 1990s, soon reinvented themselves as champions of better corporate governance, shareholder rights, and the rule of law. While it would be a mistake to take such 'conversions' at face value, neither should they be dismissed as empty rhetoric: they reflected the oligarchs' reassessment of their interests and the recognition that these would be better served by a stronger, more effective state.[25]

At the same time, the business elite broadly welcomed many of the reform initiatives that Putin adopted under the influence of the 'Petersburg liberals'. A great deal of the new legislation was aimed at 'civilizing' Russia's business environment, largely by improving the protection of property rights in general and raising standards of corporate governance in particular. Moreover, the aim of such efforts in many cases was not so much the protection of property rights per se as the protection of the 'particular conflation of ownership and control' that had emerged in Russian companies in the Yeltsin era.[26] This was entirely consonant with the shift in elite interests and priorities described above: the new reform legislation was being used not only to bring order and stability to Russian business but also to entrench the positions of those who had prevailed in the scramble for assets after 1992. For Russia's new rich, state-building and structural reform were intended to consolidate the victories they had won in the 1990s.

This concern with consolidation was evident in the behaviour of some of the leading oligarchs. As their confidence in the security of their property rights grew, they shifted from asset-stripping and predation towards investing and developing their assets. Although capital flight continued on a large scale, the marginal propensity of wealthy Russians to invest in the country rose markedly, and 2003 witnessed net private capital inflows for the first time in the post-Soviet period.[27] While standards of corporate governance remained generally very low, a number of Russia's 'blue-chips' made tremendous strides in this area. Khodorkovsky's Yukos oil company, notorious for its abuse of minority shareholders in the 1990s,

[25] For comments on Khodorkvosky's transformation, see *Vedomosti*, 30 March 2004; and *Moscow Times*, 2 April 2004.

[26] On the 2002 bankruptcy law, for example, see David M. Woodruff, 'The End of "Primitive Capitalist Accumulation"? The New Bankruptcy Law and the Political Assertiveness of Russian Big Business' (Washington, DC: PONARS Policy Memo, No. 274, October 2002), 1.

[27] See the central bank data at http://www.cbr.ru/statistics/credit_statistics/print.asp?file =bal_of_payments_est.htm.

led the way and soon came to be seen by many observers as Russia's best-governed company.

At the same time, the owners of Yukos, Sibneft, and other major companies began to create more transparent structures of ownership. These structures were still parked safely offshore, suggesting that the oligarchs' growing confidence in Russian institutions still had its limits. Group Menatep, which controlled Yukos, was based in Gibraltar, while Millhouse Capital, established as a vehicle for Abramovich's industrial holdings, was registered in the United Kingdom.[28] Even so, companies like Millhouse represented a much more transparent set of structures than had been seen before. They reflected, *inter alia*, the owners' desire to make their holdings as legally secure as possible—secure not only from the state or rival business clans but also from their own partners and allies, for such structures often formalized shares in previously somewhat informal partnerships.[29] And while legal and political manoeuvring scarcely disappeared, the theatre for contesting control of stakes in major corporations shifted increasingly to the financial sphere.[30] In short, an important part of the commercial elite was becoming more and more 'rule-conscious',[31] if not yet entirely rule-obeying.

Reform, legalization, and consolidation did not by any means constitute the whole story of Putin's first term. In a detailed analysis of the evolution of Russia's major business groupings after 1998, Barnes shows that the struggle for property continued largely unabated into the Putin era.[32] In many cases, the desirability of the assets being contested stemmed not from their current or future profitability but from their political utility or their 'strategic' importance vis-à-vis rival groupings.[33] The few major privatizations that took place still triggered the mobilization of lobby resources on a large scale, and the outcomes still tended to be determined in advance, on political grounds.[34] There were other continuities with the 1990s. While resort to physical force in commercial conflicts was perhaps less common than in the Yeltsin years, it was still employed with disturbing frequency, especially when the stakes were high. Increasingly, this involved the

[28] At the time, Abramovich's assets included, among other things, some 88% of the oil company Sibneft and 50% of Russian Aluminium. See *Vedomosti*, 25 October 2001.

[29] A. Radygin, 'Delo "Yukos": popytka interpretatsii', *Rossiiskaya ekonomika: tendentsii i perspektivy* (July 2003), 36–8.

[30] See Roland Nash, 'Hostile Liquidity', *Renaissance Capital Morning Monitor*, 17 April 2003.

[31] I am grateful to Hodson Thornber of Renaissance Capital for this phrase, which nicely captures the transitional stage between lawlessness and real respect for law in which many Russian businesses operated during the early Putin era.

[32] Andrew Barnes, 'Russia's New Business Groups and State Power', *Post-Soviet Affairs*, 19/2 (2003), 154–86.

[33] Barnes (n. 32), 156–61. See also the discussion of 'chaebolization' in Tompson, 'The Russian Economy under Vladimir Putin' (n.28).

[34] This certainly appears to have been the case with respect to the major oil-sector privatizations (e.g. Onaco, a further stake in TNK, Slavneft, and the Eastern Oil Company).

use of law-enforcement agencies and other state bodies as the servants of private interests—a disturbing reminder of the extent to which private interests continued to penetrate state institutions at all levels.[35] Indeed, for several months in 2002, the then state-owned oil company Slavneft had two rival chief executives, each backed by both armed force and conflicting court orders.[36] In other words, the oligarchs had done more to lower their political profiles than actually to curb their political activities; to some, it appeared that nothing had really changed.[37] In so far as they were successful at all, Barnes argues, Putin's efforts to curb the oligarchs' political involvements led them to concentrate their efforts at regional level.[38]

The oligarchs were not the only party to defect from the informal understanding supposedly reached between Putin and big business in July 2000. The state never really honoured it either. As Barnes observes, the state under Putin did sometimes manage to act independently of big business, but it did not necessarily act differently.[39] The Kremlin used its influence over the prosecutors, the police, and the courts to punish men who crossed it, like Berezovsky, Gusinsky, or Sibur boss Yakov Goldovsky. Like the oligarchs, it was particularly fond of manipulating the defects of the 1998 bankruptcy law, though the authorities frequently decried the abuse of this law by private litigants.[40] Such behaviour encouraged the tycoons to do likewise, not to mention the regional elites, who were often more aggressive in their interventions than the federal centre.

The point is not, as Barnes seems to suggest, that the 'consolidationist' interpretation of the Putin era must be rejected in favour of one emphasizing continuity with the 1990s. Rather, it is that both processes proceeded in parallel. Indeed, the consolidation drive by the dominant tycoons of the 1990s helped to ensure that the struggle for property continued. This is because the process of ownership consolidation described above threatened the interests of two elite

[35] For descriptions of hostile takeovers involving the use of state institutions in the service of private business, see Vadim Volkov, 'The Selective Use of State Capacity in Russia's Economy: Property Disputes and Enterprise Takeovers after 2000' (Washington DC: PONARS Policy Memo, No. 273, October 2002). For an all-too-typical example, see Agros's attempt to secure control over the Smolmyaso meat processing plant and the Tagansk Meat Combine (TAMP); *Vedomosti*, 25 March 2003; *Moscow Times*, 27 March 2003.

[36] 'Oligarchs Battle Openly for Slavneft', *Oxford Analytica East Europe Daily Brief*, 21 June 2002, II.

[37] For Treisman (n. 6), the main difference was that the oligarchs ceased to 'brag about their influence' or 'try to manipulate politics in a public way'; see also Peter Baker, 'Oligarchs' Power Unfettered under Putin', *Washington Post*, 14 December 2002, A18.

[38] Barnes (n. 32), 178–80; Treisman (n. 6) also observes the increasing tendency of the oligarchs to invest in political power at regional level.

[39] Barnes (n. 32), 177.

[40] See William Tompson, 'Reforming Russian Bankruptcy Law', *International Company and Commercial Law Review*, 14/4 (April 2003). See also *Kommersant*, 6 August 2003, on the bankruptcy of the Korshunov Mineral Enrichment Combine.

groups: those who still wished to contest ownership of the assets that the 'consolidationists' were trying to secure and—less obviously, but perhaps more importantly—the bureaucrats, police officials, prosecutors, and others whose cooperation, support, and protection (not to mention turning of blind eyes) were needed by the new owners as long as the legitimacy of their property rights remained in question.[41] If the new owners had really succeeded in securing their property rights—in law and in fact—then some of the most lucrative rents available to the police and security agencies would have dried up, while business groups that had done less well out of the asset contests of previous years would have found it ever harder to reverse past defeats. It is significant that representatives of these two groups were prominent in the campaign launched against Yukos in 2003: while the prosecutors and security organs took the lead, companies like Rosneft, which had previously lost asset-control contests and other commercial conflicts with Yukos and which had close ties to the security services, also appeared to have been involved in the attacks.[42]

By 2003, moreover, there was mounting evidence of renewed tension between the Kremlin and the oligarchs. This was partly driven by splits over policy. The oligarchs' lobbying had stalled a number of pieces of structural reform legislation in the Federal Assembly, while securing substantial revision of other government bills. It soon came to appear that structural reform could progress only when the government and the oligarchs had reached agreement, as in the cases of electricity restructuring and tax reform. Where big business objected (e.g. oil-sector taxation), government initiatives stalled. If the Kremlin objected (e.g. gas-sector reform), nothing happened.

These tensions between business and the Kremlin were aggravated by the escalating factional conflict *within* the Kremlin and the government. Almost four years after Putin's rise to power, both economic policy-making and the most important state and private companies remained overwhelmingly in the hands of the Family.[43] While the *chekisty* and other representatives of the military and security services (the *siloviki*) had increasingly colonized large parts of the state during Putin's first term,[44] their economic influence was extremely limited. Many observers believed that it was only a matter of time before they

[41] Radygin (n. 29), 38.

[42] On the involvement of Rosneft, Mezhprombank, and other companies with close ties to the Kremlin in the early stages of the Yukos campaign, see Yulia Latynina., 'The Chekist "Chelseafication" of the Oligarchy', *Moscow Times*, 9 July 2003; Sergei Markov, 'The Yukos Affair and Putin's Second Term', *Moscow Times*, 29 July 2003; Valeria Korchagina, 'A Whiz at Black PR Stirs up a Storm', *Moscow Times*, 5 August 2003; and Anatoly Medetsky, 'Dissecting the Siloviki's Pyramid of Power', *Moscow Times*, 24 December 2003. See also Gleb Pavlovsky, 'On the Negative Consequences of the "Summer Opposition" of the Minority Opposed to the Course of the President of the RF', *Novaya gazeta*, 11 September 2003; and Makarkin (n. 21).

[43] See Treisman (n. 6).

[44] Olga Kryshtanovskaya and Stephen White, 'Putin's Militocracy', *Post-Soviet Affairs*, 19/4 (October–December 2003). See also the chapter by Huskey in this volume and Medetsky (n. 42).

made a bid to wrest control of the commanding heights of the economy from the oligarchs and the remaining Yeltsinites. The great surprise of 2003 was not the fact of the *chekist* offensive but its timing; it had generally been expected that any assault would have to wait until Putin was safely re-elected.

The 'Yukos Affair'

The 'Yukos affair', which erupted in mid-2003, must be seen in this context. The arrest in early July of one of the oil company's core shareholders marked the beginning of a protracted and wide-ranging legal and political campaign directed against Yukos and its owners by the Kremlin. Many of the charges involved were probably true, but there was no doubt that Yukos was the victim of politically motivated and highly selective law enforcement. Charges pertaining to alleged privatization abuses could have been directed against hundreds of Russian companies, while charges of tax evasion could have been brought not only against most businesses but probably also against most Russian citizens who earned anything more than subsistence wages in the 1990s. Moreover, the simultaneous eruption of so many criminal cases and investigations—many of them eight or nine years old—made it hard to conclude that the attacks were anything but political.

This is not the place for a detailed consideration of the chronology of the Yukos affair, or even for a consideration of the factors that might have accounted for the selection of Yukos's owners as targets of the Kremlin's wrath. There was no shortage of the latter. Khodorkovsky had clashed with both the Kremlin and a number of companies linked to it. Alone among the oligarchs, he had allowed himself publicly to contradict the president, doing so on at least one occasion to Putin's face. He had also publicly hinted at future political ambitions of his own, leading many to suspect that he wished to succeed Putin. Khodorkovsky provided substantial financial support to at least two opposition parties, Yabloko and the Union of Right Forces, while another core Yukos shareholder contributed to the Communists. In short, the Yukos chief seemed no longer to regard himself as bound by any bargain, implicit or explicit, to stay out of politics. The scale of Khodorkovsky's wealth and the openness of his political ambitions set him apart from his fellow oligarchs, while his plans to sell a stake in the newly merged Yukos–Sibneft to a US oil major threatened to create a company too large and too influential in Washington for the Kremlin to manage easily. In all likelihood, each of these factors, and others besides, played a role in the decision to destroy Khodorkovsky. Yet the real significance of the affair far transcended the specific complaints against the tycoon. Initially, perhaps, the aim of the assault on Yukos was to discipline Khodorkovsky or to destroy him as a political force, but as the campaign unfolded, it became clear that Khodorkovsky's destruction was a means to a larger end—the redefinition of the Kremlin's relationship with big business.

As in the summer of 2000, the campaign was directed at a target audience as well as a specific victim, and, once again, the target audience consisted of the remaining oligarchs. The Yukos campaign was largely intended to remind the oligarchs that they remained vulnerable—and also to scare off foreign investors, whose acquisition of large stakes in 'oligarchic' companies would make those companies harder to subject to political pressure or bureaucratic rent-seeking. The other oligarchs were reminded of their own vulnerability by a series of warning shots fired across their bows while the assault on Yukos was unfolding. A number of oil companies were threatened with licence withdrawals by the Ministry of Natural Resources, while a number of state institutions raised questions about Sibneft's tax affairs and about the finances of Chukotka, where Abramovich was governor. Attempts were made to revive investigations into the restructuring of Norilsk Nickel and the privatization of Sibneft.[45] Alfa Group came under pressure from the communications ministry, which became involved in a complex battle with Alfa's Vimpelcom mobile phone company. Vimpelcom's travails demonstrated anew what could happen to a company when facing a federal minister with a commercial interest in one of its rivals.[46] None of these cases developed into anything like the assault on Khodorkovsky, but they served to remind the other tycoons that they could be next.

As in 2000, the president and other leading officials were at pains to stress that there would be no political campaign to reopen past privatizations and that property rights were secure, but, as in 2000, such promises were always qualified enough to keep the issue open. Indeed, at the height of the campaign against Yukos, Putin went further than he had ever gone before, declaring, 'I keep hearing here and there that the laws were complicated and that it was not possible to observe them. Yes, the laws were complex and knotty, but it was quite possible to respect them. If five, seven, or ten people broke the law, that doesn't mean others did the same.' He went on to insist that 'those who were involved in deliberate fraud' should not now enjoy more favourable conditions than those who obeyed the law. 'The latter may not have earned as much money, but for now they sleep soundly.'[47] Less than a week later, the Federal Assembly's Accounts Chamber announced that in 2004 it would 'analyse the results of the privatizations of the last ten years'.[48]

As the conflict escalated, an anxious business community began to appeal to the president for a new 'social contract', implicitly acknowledging that the unwritten

---

[45] See *Kommersant*, 29 October 2003; *Vedomosti*, 4 November 2003, 2 February 2004.

[46] Communications Minister Leonid Reiman was among the founders of Vimpelcom's St Petersburg-based rival, Telekominvest. It was widely rumoured in Moscow that Reiman continued to hold an interest in Telekominvest; some even claimed that Putin himself retained a stake.

[47] *Moscow Times*, 24 December 2003.

[48] *Moscow Times*, 30 December 2003; see also the Audit Chamber's web site at http://www.ach.gov.ru. The report was promised for July 2004.

pact of July 2000 was a dead letter.[49] Putin publicly rejected such proposals, but then outlined the basic elements of a revised business–state contract in a series of public statements in November–December 2003. In particular, he defined a set of 'priority tasks' with which he expected Russian big business to assist the state; these included enhancing the social protection extended to Russian citizens, as well as education and health reform, utilities reform, and even military reform.[50] The government followed his lead, as Kasyanov and other ministers began to outline an increasingly demanding agenda concerning the 'social responsibility' of big business. Kasyanov's successor, Mikhail Fradkov, also took up the theme of business's 'social responsibility'.[51] There was little doubt that those who failed to honour their social responsibilities would suffer the consequences. Before considering the prospects for this new deal, however, it is necessary to see why the old one failed.

The Contract That Never Was

The bargain Putin was supposed to have struck with the oligarchs in 2000 was never likely to last. It was both unwritten and unequal, a combination which made it highly probable that the president would be tempted to extend and reinterpret it to suit his needs. Putin's control over the security organs and his broad public support ensured, from the outset, that he would prevail in any showdown with the business elite. While open conflict with the oligarchs as a class would have been extremely costly and perhaps economically destabilizing, the coercive resources at Putin's disposal would have made it difficult for the oligarchs to resist him, especially as his power was far more legitimate than their wealth. As the Gusinsky and Berezovsky cases soon demonstrated, it was relatively easy to isolate individual tycoons and to discipline, or even destroy, them one at a time. Moreover, Putin had actually promised the oligarchs remarkably little in the summer of 2000: for all the importance attached to the meeting of 28 July, the president did not say or do anything that actually committed himself or the government to refrain from prosecuting fraud, tax evasion, or any other economic crimes—including violations of privatization legislation.[52] The readiness of the business elite to take the president's words at rather more than face value was born at least in part of

[49] On the increasingly urgent, pleading tone of big business's appeals to the president, see Lola Kuchina, 'RSPP v poiske kontrakta', Politcom.ru, 16 October 2003; and *Kommersant*, 23 October 2003.

[50] Vladimir Putin, 'Vystuplenie na zasedanii pravleniya Torgovo-promyshlennoi palaty Rossii', 23 December 2003 (http://president.kremlin.ru/appears/2003/12/23.shtml).

[51] *Moscow Times*, 9 April 2004.

[52] One of the few observers to recognize this at the time was the Jamestown Foundation's Harry Kopp; see *Russia's Week*, 5/30 (2 August 2000).

wishful thinking: they applied the most reassuring interpretation possible to Putin's words because they wished so badly to be reassured.

Inequality of power, coupled with the absence of any third party capable of upholding the deal, meant that Putin could not credibly commit to uphold his side of the bargain even if he genuinely wished to honour it. There was no effective means by which he could bind himself *ex ante* and so assure other actors that he could not later renege on the deal. It was, moreover, clear that as Putin consolidated his position, this inequality of power would increase. This further reduced his ability to make a credible commitment. Understanding this, the business elite could hardly be expected to make a wholehearted commitment to the bargain either.[53] In any case, the tacit nature of the deal meant that no one knew precisely what was permitted and what was not. Violations might well be—and, in due course, were—defined both unilaterally and retrospectively.

In any case, the incentives for Putin to violate the deal were enormous. The overriding motivation to do so was his own determination to concentrate ever-more power in his own hands. Throughout his first term, Putin conducted a protracted campaign to strengthen the 'vertical of power', extending the authority of the presidency at the expense of other state institutions, while simultaneously extending state control over the media and the party system. Sooner or later this drive for supreme power was bound to bring him into conflict with the most important centres of power outside the state—the oligarchs' business empires. Moreover, as noted above, many of the president's closest associates were never very happy with his accommodation with the oligarchs and hoped, indeed, to extend their own control over the economy. Finally, Putin could hardly be expected to ignore the fact that the oligarchs themselves were never very faithful to the terms of the deal. On a number of issues, their lobbying clout in the Federal Assembly, the regions, and even the upper reaches of the federal executive was sufficient to inflict defeats upon the government.

In many ways, the tycoons' position was the mirror image of the president's. Like him, they faced powerful incentives to defect and they, too, would have found it difficult to stick to the terms of the deal even if they had wished to do so. Above all, this was simply because there was no clear-cut line between business and politics for them to observe. Government policies often impinged directly on their business interests, as did decisions taken on a daily basis by lower-level officials. The stakes were simply too great for the oligarchs to give up politics. They might lower their profiles and curb their more blatant interference in the

---

[53] For an assessment of this problem in respect of attempts to negotiate a new 'social contract' between the state and business in late 2003, see Scott Gelbach, 'Business-State Contract Lacks Credibility', *Moscow Times*, 6 August 2003. For an excellent analysis of this type of commitment problem, albeit in an entirely different context, see James Fearon, 'Ethnic War as a Commitment Problem' (paper presented at the Annual Meeting of the American Political Science Association, New York, 1994).

political process, but, as the owners of Russia's biggest companies, they could hardly be expected to adopt a passive political stance.

Furthermore, all the business clans had invested heavily in the resources needed to play the political game by the old rules. Their representatives occupied key posts in the government, the Duma, and even the Kremlin itself, and they had built up close ties to important political figures at federal and regional levels. These investments could not easily be written off, not least because politicians and officials who enjoyed the oligarchs' patronage would be unlikely to welcome their withdrawal. Rent-seeking state officials—many of whom were far less eager than Putin to reverse the Yeltsin-era 'privatization of the state'—made it danger-ous for the major business groupings to cease to play the political game by the old rules. Private 'capture' of state institutions and political-bureaucratic rent-seeking were to some extent two sides of the same coin. In theory, one might distinguish between 'offensive' and 'defensive' corruption—between the aggressive suborning *of* officials and racketeering *by* officials. In reality, the two were closely intertwined.

This merely aggravated Putin's commitment problem: even if he were prepared to respect the tycoons' property rights in return for their non-interference in policy-making, he could not enforce such a commitment on the state's own servants. As president, Putin could destroy any oligarch he chose; he could likewise dismiss or otherwise discipline any official. What he could not do was to root out the corruption and unaccountability that characterized the state apparatus as a whole. Moreover, despite much talk of administrative reform, Putin's first term saw virtually nothing done to make the bureaucracy either less corrupt or more responsive to the president. Despite attempts to institution-alize new forms of state–business interaction, Russia's commercial elite continued to rely more on personal networks and informal relationships in dealing with the state than on formal rules and institutions.[54] The oligarchs' financing of political parties must be seen at least partially in this light. Party financing, of course, represented an attempt to promote policies favourable to their commercial inter-ests, but it was also, arguably, a form of protection money paid to the major parties in the Duma.[55]

The tycoons also faced a collective action problem. Those who ceased to lobby, bribe, and manipulate state institutions would risk losing out to rivals who continued to do so. Withdrawal from the oligarchic political game resembled a form of disarmament: if it were to work, then all the tycoons needed to make the shift together. Yet, Russia's oligarchs have never shown much capacity for sustained collective action. Commercial rivalry and lack of mutual trust have made it easy for the Kremlin to divide and rule the oligarchs, as has the tycoons' awareness of their own vulnerability to pressure from the state. Virtually any significant business in Russia has reason to fear close scrutiny of its tax affairs, its

[54] On this issue, see Andrey Ryabov, 'Budushchee Rossiiskoi vlasti', *Vedomosti*, 30 October 2003.
[55] I am grateful to Yulia Latynina for drawing my attention to this point.

origins, or its relations with officialdom. Indeed, criminal investigations are hardly necessary. Many of the most lucrative activities in Russia rest on licensing regimes—resource extraction, telecommunications, and banking, to name but three. In such cases, mere bureaucratic discretion can represent a deadly threat. Faced with an official campaign against a fellow tycoon, an oligarch's safest (and most lucrative) course is willing cooperation, in the hope of acquiring some of the victim's assets. The Kremlin's use of such divide-and-rule tactics tends, in turn, to reinforce the oligarchs' reliance on personal ties and particularistic lobbying— however much Putin himself may abhor such behaviour.

The Significance of the Yukos Affair

As of this writing (April 2004), the battle surrounding Yukos and its core shareholders is still under way. It is not clear what the fate of either Yukos or its owners will be. However, it is possible even at this stage to draw a number of tentative conclusions about the significance of the Yukos affair for relations between Russia's leading businessmen and the state. The course of the conflict to date has highlighted a number of well known problems with Russia's economic and legal-political institutions, none of which will be remedied quickly, regardless of how the Yukos case is resolved. First, the rule of law remains weak. Recent judicial reforms notwithstanding, the courts are largely subservient to the executive, especially the prosecutors, while the security services, the prosecutors, and the police remain highly politicized. Provisions of the new Code of Criminal Procedure have been blithely ignored, with prosecutors and police resorting to measures that are clearly illegal and that were unusual even in Soviet times.[56] Second, the Kremlin's taming of the media in 2000–2 has largely been successful. State control over many media organs and self-censorship on the part of others has meant that criticism of the anti-Yukos campaign has generally been muted, apart from a handful of Internet, print, and radio outlets. Third, there are no other strong state or private institutions prepared to challenge the federal executive. Fourth, property rights in Russia remain insecure, and the Yeltsin-era privatization settlement remains open to further, possibly substantial, revision.

The president and leading members of the government continue to declare that there will be no large-scale re-examination of the results of privatization.[57] And, of course, investors and businessmen continue to take comfort from such

[56] Examples include searching the offices of defendants' lawyers and summoning defence attorneys for questioning in connection with the cases they are defending.

[57] Reuters, 28 July 2000; *Moscow Times*, 3 November 2003; 'Putin v interv'yu inostrannym zhurnalisram prokommentiroval sobytiya po Yukosu i Voloshinu', politcom.ru, 4 November 2003; United Financial Group, *Russia Morning Comment*, 17 November 2003.

declarations, assuring themselves and one another that they can trust Putin to keep his word.[58] In fact, they have little choice but to trust the president: in the absence of stronger institutions capable of constraining the coercive capacities of the Russian state, there is nothing else on which to rely. However, few things could have demonstrated the fragility of the 1990s property settlement more convincingly than the fact that, after four years in power, Putin was still making reassuring statements about privatization—and that the business community continued to attach such importance to his every pronouncement on the subject. The backdrop against which statements confirming the privatization settlement were delivered was one of repeated de facto revisions to it.

The president appears to mean what he says, and with good reason: any hint of a serious campaign to revisit the privatizations of the 1990s could be profoundly destabilizing. Yet this did not preclude any number of 'one-off' actions against particular targets during Putin's first term. In each case, the essential strategy was to isolate the victim and emphasize those of his characteristics that made him an exceptional case. By focusing on the peculiar sins of a Berezovsky, Gusinsky, Goldovsky, or Khodorkovsky, the authorities were able to attack their chosen targets while reassuring the other tycoons—and, for that matter, the wider business community—that they had nothing to fear. At least, they had nothing to fear as long as they did not attempt to intervene. This approach proved relatively successful thanks in large measure to the fact that the targets of the Kremlin's wrath were not especially sympathetic victims, having secured their wealth and influence by rather unsavoury means. The oligarchs had little love for one another anyway and few non-oligarchs were eager to be seen rushing to their defence. Above all, however, Putin found it relatively easy to reassure the business community about the 'exceptional' nature of each successive campaign because, as noted above, the oligarchs and other investors were so eager to be reassured.

This reassurance, however, was always carefully qualified. At no point did Putin offer an unconditional amnesty for past violations. On the contrary, while repeatedly promising that there would be no witch hunts or political campaigns, he continued to leave open the possibility that past violations would be prosecuted. Some owners were, of course, more vulnerable than others. Putin's reference to 'five or seven' people was generally taken as a thinly veiled reference to the notorious loans-for-shares auctions of 1995–7.[59] However, the loans-for-shares deals were unique only in their transparency: the state was asset-stripped in broad daylight and the sums involved were widely publicized. There is no reason to believe that the insiders who privatized companies like Lukoil and

[58] See, for examples, Al Breach, 'The Post-Oligarch Era Begins' (Moscow: Brunswick UBS, 13 November 2003); United Financial Group, *Russia Morning Comment*, 28 October 2003 and 3 November 2003; *Moscow Times*, 3 November 2003.
[59] *Moscow Times*, 24 December 2003.

Surgutneftegaz (not to mention Gazprom) actually paid any more than the loans-for-shares tycoons; in some cases, they appear to have paid considerably less.[60] Revelations about the sums the state actually received for such assets would be sufficient to throw their owners onto the defensive. Even those who paid reasonable prices for their holdings would not welcome too much scrutiny. Metals tycoon Oleg Deripaska boasted that, having paid $3 billion for his companies, he had nothing to worry about. However, even he might not welcome an inquiry into how he had obtained $3 billion in the first place. Thus, all the oligarchs remained, to varying degrees, vulnerable to any close examination of the sources of their wealth.

After Yukos: Forward into the Past?

The Yukos affair gave Putin an opportunity to revise substantially the terms of his relationship with big business. Far from being the state's master, Russian private capital was to be its servant. Putin made it clear that the state expected big business to share the burden of tackling Russia's social problems and that the resource-extraction industries, in particular, would be required to bear a heavier tax burden than hitherto. The oligarchs, for their part, were at pains to demonstrate their loyalty to the Kremlin and their acceptance of the president's new line.[61] Where they had previously competed to maximize after-tax profits and market capitalization, oil companies were suddenly competing for official favour once again, at pains to proclaim their readiness to pay more taxes and to support all manner of social initiatives.[62] Lukoil declared with pride that it had abandoned many of its legal tax-optimization schemes and was actually paying more tax than was strictly necessary.[63] BP-TNK, clearly recognizing the need to adapt to the new circumstances, announced plans to move its core holding company on shore and to maintain its profit centre in Russia.[64]

The oligarchs' apparent docility is hardly surprising. In the absence of any serious political force capable of challenging Putin, big business had little choice but to accept the new 'social contract' with the state—indeed, the business elite seemed to accept it without waiting for the terms to be fully spelled out. Yet, the new bargain was no more reliable than the old. For the tycoons, the problem

[60] For a discussion of the loans-for-shares sales in the broader context of 'insider privatization' in Russia, see William Tompson, 'Privatization in Russia: Scope, Methods and Impact' (mimeo: University of London, October 2002), available at http://www.bbk.ac.uk/polsoc/download/bill_tompson.

[61] See, for example, the elite's reactions to Putin's mid-November address to the Congress of the Russian Union of Industrialists and Entrepreneurs; *Moscow Times*, 17 November 2003.

[62] For an overview, see the articles by Maria Levitov in the *Moscow Times*, 1 April 2004.

[63] *Vremya novostei*, 14 January 2004.   [64] *Vedomosti*, 28 January 2004.

remained the inability of the state to make a credible commitment. Indeed, the relative weakness of the oligarchs that the Yukos case exposed actually made it even harder for the state to commit to the terms of any implicit or explicit deal with the business elite; the case had highlighted just how great the imbalance of power had become.[65] In part, of course, this imbalance was conjunctural and reflected Putin's unchallenged dominance of the political scene as his first term drew to a close. However, there was also a structural aspect to the problem: the weakness of 'coercion-constraining institutions', which are an essential element of any system of secure property rights.

Secure property rights require a strong state, capable of protecting owners' rights and of providing impartial rule adjudication and enforcement. However, the strength of the state can itself pose the most serious threat of all to property rights, for those who exercise the state's monopoly of violence may be tempted to expropriate owners. A strong property rights regime thus needs a strong state but also strong institutions capable of constraining that state.[66] Russia still lacks such institutions. The absence of coercion-constraining institutions and the inability of the state to commit itself to rule-governed behaviour were highlighted by the fact that several of the criminal charges against Yukos shareholders involved matters that had previously been settled in legal agreements between Yukos and the state. On many of the counts, Yukos had compensated the state in agreed settlements for 'ethical and reputational' reasons, while maintaining that its actions were legal. The subsequent indictments showed that the state felt no obligation to uphold such settlements.[67] The prosecutors might have sought to overturn such agreements by alleging that they had been obtained by bribery or other improper means, but no such charges were brought against Yukos owners or the officials involved.[68]

In fact, Putin's attitude to property rights—or, at any rate, to the oligarchs' property rights—appears to owe more to Russian history than to the theories of his liberal advisers. Consciously or not, what the president offered the oligarchs was essentially conditional tenure. In the sixteenth century, the autocracy, facing new and potent military threats from the West, nationalized land in Russia and

[65] Gelbach (n. 53).

[66] Avner Greif, 'The Emergence of Institutions to Protect Property Rights', in Claude Menard and Mary M. Shirley (eds.), *Handbook on New Institutional Economics* (London: Kluwer, forthcoming).

[67] Such, indeed, was the case with respect to the Apatit privatization, which was the first case launched against Yukos's owners. See Peter Clatemen, 'Summary and Analysis of Report on Criminal Case #18/41–03', *Johnson's Russia List*, No. 11, December 2003 (http://www.cdi.org/russia/johnson/7462–9.cfm). See also the *Moscow Times*, 28 January 2004.

[68] At the end of February 2003, prosecutors finally opened a case against the head of the Federal Property Fund in connection with the Apatit settlement, but they had yet to raise any charges of corruption—only that he had acted *ultra vires* in concluding the deal. It remains to be seen whether this action will be extended to other officials involved in property deals with the oligarchs. *Vedomosti*, 1 March 2004.

allocated it to cavalrymen who were allowed to hold it in return for their service to the state. This solved the regime's military manpower problem and laid the foundation of the 'service state' in early modern Russia.[69] Putin's project is far less radical, but the parallel is nevertheless worth exploring. Putin's aim on coming to power was to restore Russia's economic fortunes and thereby establish the basis for her recovery as a great power. His embrace of the market was instrumental. The president was not a convinced liberal on principle but a nationalist who had been persuaded that market reform offered the only viable strategy for making Russia wealthy and powerful again.[70] Privatization, on this view, was meant to serve this larger purpose by putting assets in the hands of owners who could use and develop them more efficiently than the state—but who would develop them in ways that served the state's interests.

In other words, property was the gift of the state but it was not an unconditional gift. If the new owners failed to play the role scripted for them under this scenario, then they would have to be disciplined. Economically, this implies an insecurity of property rights that is likely to undermine performance, but politically, it un-doubtedly has a certain logic. Russia's capitalist class was created by the state and endowed with control over many of the state's most valuable resources. It is therefore expected to serve ends defined by the state and to accept that its exercise of certain rights—particularly the right to alienate assets—must be coordinated with the state.[71] Asked about the possible sale of a large stake in Yukos to a western oil major, Putin replied, 'As regards purchasing part of the Yukos company, again this is a corporate matter, but once again we are talking about a possible major deal here, and I think it would be the right thing to do to have preliminary consultations with the Russian government.' Seen in this context, there is nothing at all surprising in Putin's rather *étatiste* spin on the (apparently) liberal policy of reducing the tax burden on industry. The president declared that the main target of such tax cuts was 'to develop the economy and the social sector' and that 'entrepreneurs need help in deciding where to invest this money'.[72] Capital and labour are, of course, more mobile than they were in the early modern period, a fact which represents an important constraint on the imposition of 'capitalist conditional tenure'. Without reimposing Soviet-style controls on the movement of money and people, there are limits to how far the state can go in its demands on Russia's new capitalists. However, the Russian state may be able to go further down this path than many Western states could, precisely because so

[69] Marshall T. Poe, *The Russian Moment in World History* (Princeton, NJ and Oxford: Princeton University Press, 2003), 55.

[70] For a particularly eloquent expression of the geopolitical roots of Putin's economic liberalism, see his comments during his annual televised question-and-answer session on 18 December 2003, available on the presidential web site at http://president.kremlin.ru/text/appears/2003/12/57398.shtml.

[71] *New York Times*, 4 October 2003.   [72] *Interfax*, 30 March 2004.

many of the most important sources of wealth in Russia—its natural resource deposits—cannot be removed from the country.

None of this should be taken to imply that the era of liberal economic reforms has ended. On the contrary, a second Putin administration may well see a redoubling of economic reform efforts. The appointment of a strongly reformist economic team to the government formed in March 2004 has already served to reassure both the international community and investors that Putin remains committed to market reforms, and that the Yukos case is not a harbinger of *étatiste* policies to come. Moreover, if Putin is prepared to throw his weight behind a renewed reform push in the name of 'non-oligarchic capitalism', then the greater concentration of power in the Kremlin could make reforms easier to pursue. This would not, however, rapidly remedy the institutional defects discussed above, and it would be a mistake to believe that the appointment of a more reformist cabinet, together with a more market-friendly PR campaign on the part of the Kremlin, would preclude further cases like the one against Khodorkovsky. On the contrary, the logic of conditional tenure implies that, from time to time, the sovereign will seek to remind his servants of his rights over them. Certainly, Putin's behaviour as his second term began suggested that he had no intention of letting the oligarchs forget this basic reality: all the signs in early 2004 pointed to a decision by the president to avoid both a wide-ranging assault on private property and a *de jure* resolution of the issue that would settle the question of past privatizations once and for all. The legal vulnerability of the oligarchs' property rights, after all, was perhaps the president's most effective source of leverage in his dealings with them. Moreover, it is not at all clear that any particular outcome of the Yukos affair could resolve the tensions that underlay it—whatever the fate of Khodorkovsky and Yukos may be.

Putin appears to see no contradiction between this essentially qualified affirmation of property rights and the pursuit of market reforms, but others are not so sanguine. Former Deputy Prime Minister, Yevgeny Yasin, summed up the conflicting signals emanating from the Kremlin and the government as follows: 'We, those in power, want business to prosper. There won't be any de-privatization; everything will be fine. But when we want to attack someone, we will do so. We will crush anyone. You must realize that and be afraid'.[73] In other words, Putin wants dynamic capitalist development without having to deal with the political power of a dynamic capitalist class. On the face of it, this would appear to leave the president trapped 'between his need for economic growth and his need for political control'.[74] In his first term, a combination of skill and good luck enabled him to square the circle and pursue both with a fair degree of success. In the longer term, however, Putin or his successor will have to resolve this contradiction one way or the other.

---

[73] *Moscow Times*, 28 October 2003.
[74] Robert Cottrell, 'Putin's Trap', *New York Review of Books*, 50/19 (4 December 2003).

11

Putin's Reform of the Russian Federation

Neil Melvin

Introduction

The emergence of Vladimir Putin as president of the Russian Federation and the subsequent consolidation of Putin's position at the pinnacle of the Russian political order has been accompanied by a lively debate about the nature of the contemporary Russian polity. While there is a broad consensus that a significant change in the political life of the country has taken place under Putin, there is still a lack of agreement on how best to comprehend the nature and long-term significance of this change. Crucially, it remains unclear whether Russia under Putin should be viewed as a country that has turned its back completely on democratization. The uncertainty about the nature of the political system is reflected in accounts that highlight the mixed and contradictory elements of Putin's Russia. Writers have, thus, classified the Russian Federation as, *inter alia*, a 'hybrid' or 'managed' democracy, or even as being characterized by 'competitive authoritarianism'.[1]

Upon assuming the presidency in 2000, Putin launched a far-reaching process of reform in federal relations. The priority that the president attached to the issue of altering the centre–regional relationship suggests that these reforms should be viewed as a main pillar of Putin's broader agenda of change for the Russian Federation. A close analysis of the nature and direction of federal reform in Russia therefore offers an opportunity to examine an issue at the heart of Putin's effort to shape Russia's future, and thereby to gain an insight into the processes of political change under way in the country. Analysis of the evolving relationship between the centre and the regions under Putin is also important because the transformation of the monolithic Soviet-era territorial system into a federal style arrangement, with regions gaining significant autonomy from Moscow, was seen by many as one of the central elements of the process of political change that

---

[1] Timothy J. Colton and Michael McFaul, 'Russian Democracy under Putin', *Problems of Post-Communism*, 50/4 (July/August 2003), 12–21; Archie Brown, 'From Democratization to "Guided Democracy" ', *Journal of Democracy*, 12/4 (October 2001), 35–41; Harley Balzer, 'Managed Pluralism: Vladimir Putin's Emerging Regime', *Post-Soviet Affairs*, 3 (July–September 2003), 189–227.

emerged in the Russian Federation following independence. The institutionalization of bargaining between the federal centre and the regions on a host of issues,
based upon a recognition—at least implicitly—by both sides of competing interests and differing conceptions of the good, suggested a fundamental change in
the nature of decision-making in Russia. Further, devolution of authorities to the
regions, it was argued, provided a check on the ability of the centre to exercise
power as it had during the Soviet era. Taken together, these two developments
suggested that the 'federalization' of Russia constituted a vital element of the
broader process of democratization.

At the same time, many viewed the transfer of authorities to the regions with
some concern. The particular focus for attention was how to ensure national-
territorial integrity in the context of a devolving post-Soviet system. A number of
observers viewed with alarm the claims for autonomy made by regions, and
especially by republics; they feared these developments might lead to secession
and even to the disintegration of Russia.[2] At the heart of such concern lies the
political significance of ethnicity in the Russian Federation. The relationship of
the so-called ethnic republics with the rest of the country has been a particularly
difficult one. Chechnya has proved critical in this respect.

Establishing an acceptable mechanism for redistributing wealth between rich
and poor regions, and determining Moscow's role in this process, has also been a
divisive issue. Such economic questions acquired extra significance in the context
of the privatization policies of the 1990s. These provided new opportunities for
individual and collective enrichment at the regional level, using local resources
and property.[3]

The challenge that faced the post-Yeltsin leadership was, thus, to prevent
territorial disintegration, promote national cohesion, and encourage economic
development without sacrificing democratization. Putin's answer to this challenge
was to launch, early in his presidency, a reform in federal relations designed to
promote a recentralization of authority. The reform faced little effective opposition and Putin was able to claim the restructuring of federal relations as one of the
principal achievements of his first term.[4]

While Putin was keen to trumpet the success of his federal reform programme,
the changes in centre–regional relations raise important questions about the
nature of Russia's political system and the future direction of the country. Despite

[2] For reference to the English language literature on the possibility of the collapse of the Russian
Federation, see Henry E. Hale and Rein Taagepera, 'Russia: Consolidation or Collapse?', *Europe–Asia
Studies*, 54/7 (2002), 1101–25, n. 4, p. 1101.

[3] Gordon M. Hahn, 'The Impact of Putin's Federative Reforms on Democratization in Russia',
Post-Soviet Affairs, 19/2 (2003), 114–53.

[4] In his annual address to the Federal Assembly on 16 May 2003, President Putin noted that the
country's unity had been re-established de facto and *de jure*, and that state power had been
strengthened. The federal authorities were, as a result, now closer to the regions. Putin argued
that re-establishing a common legal space throughout the country had made it possible to begin active
work on the division of power between the federal and regional authorities. He noted that work had

the president's public justification for the federal reforms in terms of strengthening the rule of law and promoting political accountability, the main outcome of the changes introduced by Putin has been to enhance central control and to establish greater hierarchy within the federal system. In this way, reform has struck directly at key elements viewed as fundamental to the promotion of democratization in the country.

Putin's measures to alter federal relations have sought to challenge the asymmetry at the heart of Russia's federative system, and to rein in the regional elites from the ethnic republics. Not only have Putin's reforms undercut the autonomy of the regions while claiming to champion 'harmonization' and 'equalization', but the president has also sought to weaken the link between territory, ethnicity, and political power in Russia. This has shifted concern about the sovereignty and autonomy of federal units to one focusing on the problem of state capacity.[5]

The origins of this wide-ranging reform of federal relations can be traced to the late Soviet era. While Putin has spearheaded federal reform, the political momentum driving that process reflects a broad-based and deep-seated reaction to the rise of regional power and of minority ethno-nationalism in the late 1980s and 1990s. The re-election of President Putin by an overwhelming majority increases the likelihood of further initiatives being taken to consolidate the centralized and hierarchical system. Putin's announcement in September 2004 of a set of fundamental political reforms, notably the initiative to eliminate the direct election of regional leaders, casts considerable doubt on the prospects for federal democracy in Russia. Steps to downgrade further the political power of ethnic minorities, with the possibility of more radical measures to undercut the institutionalized position of 'leading' minorities, would probably meet greater resistance than that encountered by earlier reforms. Extending and consolidating centralized control, without provoking a re-emergence of ethno-political tensions in the country or undermining economic modernization, is likely to be one of the main challenges for Putin during his second term.

Federation, Reform, and Democracy

Some observers have suggested that the federal reforms introduced under Putin have served—intentionally or unintentionally—to roll back both democracy and

---

begun on making the regional power system more effective and better financed. The totally unacceptable situation that he saw in certain Russian territories that had put themselves beyond federal jurisdiction was at an end. Putin added that all regions of the country should now recognize the supremacy of the Russian constitution and federal laws and the obligation to pay taxes into the national treasury. In this context, he suggested that the process of integrating the Chechen republic into the country's political and legal space had begun.

[5] David Cashaback, 'Risky Strategies? Putin's Federal Reforms and the Accommodation of Difference in Russia', *Journal of Ethnopolitics and Minority Issues in Europe*, 3 (2003) (www.ecmi.de).

federalism and produced an 'accelerated counter-revolution'.[6] The reforms have recast centre–regional relations in a negative way—indeed, they have 'torn apart' the federal system. From this perspective, Putin's vision of future federal relations—with its stress on 'vertically integrated executive power' and the 'dictatorship of law'—coupled with structural and fiscal reforms of centre–regional relations, and a growing arbitrary interference in regional affairs, appear to support the view of federal reform as a core component of a wider push to establish a guided democracy.[7] The construction of a monocentric model of power in a territorial sense is seen as a part of the broader vision of a strong state where the influence of social actors other than the authorities—particularly, the influence of the economic and regional elites—is virtually eliminated.

The relationship between democratization and the reform of centre–regional relations is complicated by the mixed record of the Russian regions in the promotion of democratization.[8] Indeed, before the Putin reforms it was possible to argue that the federal centre was in many respects more democratic and pluralistic than most of the eighty-nine federal subjects.[9] Moves to strengthen the central state need not, therefore, necessarily represent a backward step in terms of democratization.[10]

Indeed, some authors have suggested that the federal reforms introduced by Putin have been beneficial to democratization and stability at the regional level. In this view, reform of federal–regional relations lies at the heart of an effort to strengthen the rule of law and to establish a functioning federal system. To achieve this, it is necessary to restrain regional arbitrary rule. The measures taken by Putin, notably legal harmonization, have forced regions, and particularly the republics, to become more democratic by weakening their executive power.[11]

---

[6] Cameron Ross, 'Putin's Federal Reforms and the Consolidation of Defederalism in Russia: One Step Forward, Two Steps Back!', *Communist and Post-Communist Studies*, 36 (2003), 29–47.

[7] Aleksandr Tsipko, 'Putin Rebuilds a Unitary State in Russia', *The Jamestown Foundation: Prism*, 6/11 (28 November 2000).

[8] The Council of Europe has noted the difficulties that faced national minorities in Russia's regions, notably Tatarstan and Bashkortostan. *Advisory Committee on the Framework Convention for the Protection of National Minorities: Opinion on the Russian Federation* (13 September 2002), para. 48.

[9] Indeed, some authors have noted that the measures introduced by the federal authorities to curb political opposition and critical media made them more like the 'guided' or 'manipulated' democracy that emerged in the republics and regions much earlier. Archie Brown, 'From Democratization to "Guided Democracy" ', *Journal of Democracy*, 12/4 (October 2001), 40. See also Vladimir Gel'man, Sergei Ryzhenkov, and Michael Brie, *Making and Breaking Democratic Transitions: The Comparative Politics of Russia's Regions* (New York: Rowman & Littlefield, 2003).

[10] Archie Brown, 'Evaluating Russia's Democratization' in Archie Brown (ed.), *Contemporary Russian Politics: A Reader* (Oxford: Oxford University Press, 2001), 565.

[11] Hahn (n. 3), 114–53.

Centre–Regional Relations in Russia

Under Soviet rule, Russia's regions had almost no autonomy.[12] During the Gorbachev era, the breakdown of traditional political and economic arrangements created new possibilities for the regions. Encouraged to seek more autonomy by Boris Yeltsin, and propelled by the rise of nationalist sentiment—notably in the ethnic republics of Tatarstan, Chechnya-Ingushetia, and Bashkortostan—regions began to play a more assertive role in the political life of the country.[13]

As a result, at independence the Russian Federation inherited the Soviet-era territorial structure but a very different situation in terms of relations between the centre and regions.[14] Although, to a considerable extent, the rise of regionalism originated in the late Soviet period, the debilitating character it assumed in the 1990s was greatly enhanced by the Yeltsin era's bargaining style approach to regional issues. Under Yeltsin, there was a further increase in regionalism, leading in some cases to the emergence of what one author termed 'regional warlordism'.[15]

The treaty-based principle for specifying authority relations between the central government and the regions, adopted by Yeltsin to counter centrifugal forces, was based initially on a universal approach to the regions. Comprehensive agreements regulated the relations between the centre and all regions. This approach was enshrined in the Treaty of the Federation, signed on 31 March 1992, and the 1993 constitution. The year 1994 saw the emergence of a new approach based on a series of bilateral treaties negotiated between the federal centre and individual subjects of the Federation. The system of bilateral treaties gave the president the opportunity to deepen his personalistic ties and, thereby, to consolidate his position in a time of weakly institutionalized politics. It has also been suggested that the treaties provided a pragmatic means to manage potential secession movements in Russia—notably in the ethnic republics—by allowing Moscow to negotiate accords based on the particular interests of each republic or region.[16] Eventually, nearly fifty agreements were signed, the most comprehen-

---

[12] In the final decades of the Soviet order, the Brezhnev era policy of stability of cadres did lead to the emergence of some strong regional leaders, but they remained tightly subordinated to Moscow. Vladimir Shlapentokh, Roman Levita, and Mikhail Loiberg, *From Submission to Rebellion: The Provinces Versus the Centre in Russia* (Boulder, CO: Westview, 1997), chs. 3–6.

[13] Shlapentokh et al., ibid., chs. 7–8.

[14] At the pinnacle of the asymmetrical Russian Soviet Federative Socialist Republic were sixteen Autonomous Soviet Socialist Republics (ASSRs). Below the republics were forty-nine *oblasts* and six *krais* (plus the two special status cities of Moscow and Leningrad); while lowest in the system were the five autonomous *oblasts* and ten autonomous *okrugs* (which were located within the borders of the autonomous republics and *oblasts* and *krais*).

[15] Peter Kirkow, *Russia's Provinces: Authoritarian Transformation versus Local Autonomy?* (Basingstoke: Macmillan, 1998), 139.

[16] James Hughes 'Managing Secession Potential in the Russian Federation' in James Hughes and Gwendolyn Sasse (eds.), *Regions in Conflict: Ethnicity and Territory in the Former Soviet Union* (London: Frank Cass, 2001), 36–68; and Graham Smith, 'Russia, Multiculturalism and Federal Justice', *Europe–Asia Studies*, 50/8 (1998), 1393–411.

sive being those for Tatarstan and Bashkortostan. Some observers have suggested that these agreements were less about minority rights and ethnic sovereignty than about the distribution of resources.[17]

While the bilateral treaties have been seen as an attempt to mitigate conflict, this set of agreements created an institutional and legal ambiguity at the heart of federal relations.[18] As a result of the treaty-based approach, federal relations were founded on a contractual rather than a constitutional basis. This approach also contributed to a steady fading of the centre's ability to shape events at the regional level and, in the late 1990s, facilitated the emergence of regional leaders as powerful national actors.

The federal centre was weakened by the economic crisis of 1998, and the regional authorities filled the vacuum according to their own priorities. Regional leaders developed a set of initiatives to counter the financial crisis. At the heart of these responses was a move to strengthen horizontal political ties amongst regions to confront a weakened centre. These initiatives also served to strengthen the sense amongst sections of the regional elite that by uniting they could play a key role in shaping the post-Yeltsin transition of power.[19] The growing self-confidence of the regional leaders in the late 1990s prompted the creation of the Fatherland–All Russia Party (*Otechestvo–Vsya Rossiya*)—which united Moscow Mayor Yury Luzhkov's Fatherland Party and the All Russia Movement of regional leaders, headed by President Mintimer Shaimiev of Tatarstan—to contest the 1999 State Duma elections. The party quickly became known as 'the governors' party' and in the summer of 1999 public opinion polls suggested that it would achieve an overwhelming victory in the elections. Fatherland–All Russia's candidate for president, Yevgeny Primakov, was widely seen as Yeltsin's most likely successor. The growing role of the regional elite led some to fear for the territorial integrity of the Russian Federation.

Putin's Rise and the First Wave of Federal Reform

The victory of Putin in the presidential elections of March 2000 represented a significant turning point in relations between the federal centre and Russia's regions. The emergence of Putin marked a defeat for the ambitions of leading regional leaders to propel Primakov to the presidency. Further, the new president was able, on the strength of his first round electoral victory, to reach a political deal

[17] Daniel Treisman 'The Politics of Soft Credit in Post-Soviet Russia' *Europe–Asia Studies*, 47/6 (1995), 949–76.

[18] Jeffrey Kahn, *Federalism, Democracy and Rule of Law in Russia* (Oxford: Oxford University Press, 2002).

[19] Lynn D. Nelson and Irina Y. Kuzes, 'Political and Economic Co-ordination in Russia's Federal District Reform: A Study of Four Regions', *Europe–Asia Studies*, 55/4 (2003), 507–20.

with the Communists in the Duma and on the back of the second Chechen war (launched by Putin when he was prime minister), to move on to the offensive.

Under the slogan 'dictatorship of law', Putin launched a series of initiatives designed to fashion a rigid 'hierarchy of power' between the different levels of government.[20] To achieve this aim, the president introduced a reform programme initially composed of six principal elements: reform of the system of presidential plenipotentiaries; the establishment of seven federal districts; reform of the Federation Council; strengthening the mechanism of federal intervention; legal harmonization; and changes in fiscal federalism.[21]

One of the main challenges faced by Moscow in asserting control over the regions was to find a mechanism to ensure regional compliance with the centre's instructions. As early as August 1991, Yeltsin recognized this problem when he established the post of presidential representative in each of the subjects of the Federation. But the presidential representatives proved to be ineffective. Most regional leaders were able to dominate the political and economic life of their region, and the presidential representatives were forced to depend on the goodwill of the regional executives. In 1997, realizing the difficulties that faced the presidential representatives, Yeltsin sought to strengthen their role by giving them increased responsibility for federal agencies at the regional level. This initiative proved ineffective and regional leaders continued to view Moscow as weak, and the presidential representatives as largely irrelevant.

President Putin sought to change this situation by a radical reform consisting of two interlocking elements. Unable to engage easily in a territorial reorganization of the Federation because of the legal and political difficulties involved in amending the constitution, in May 2000 the new president decided to reduce the number of presidential plenipotentiaries to seven and to place each of them in charge of one of the newly established federal districts (*okruga*). The seven new federal districts were based on existing military administrative districts and so simply overlay groups of federal subjects. The envoys were granted considerable, though ill-defined, responsibilities to oversee the federal agencies in the regions under their control and also to monitor the implementation of federal laws. At the same time, the Ministry of Nationalities and Regional Affairs—which had played an important role in federal relations—was emasculated. Following the creation of the federal regions, the branches of key federal agencies (notably the Prosecutors Office, the Federal Security Service, the Ministry of Interior, and the Tax Inspectorate) were themselves reorganized around these federal districts in order to minimize their dependence on the regional elite.

To complement and strengthen the structural reforms noted earlier, Putin introduced two measures designed to enhance the ability of the federal centre to

---

[20] Vladimir Putin, television address to the citizens of Russia on 17 May 2000, *Rossiiskaya gazeta*, 19 May 2000.

[21] Matthew Hyde, 'Putin's Federal Reform and Their Implications for Presidential Power in Russia', *Europe–Asia Studies*, 53/5 (2001), 719–43; and Ross (n. 6), 29–47.

shape developments at the regional level. The first was legislation to allow the centre to take action against regional executives and legislatures judged to be in violation of the federal constitution. The Federation Council initially vetoed the bill, but the Duma overrode the veto on 19 July 2000. Putin's second measure was a drive to ensure consistency or 'harmonization' between federal and regional legislation. This move reflected the view that greater legal uniformity was fundamental to any attempt to remove the unequal distribution of privileges enjoyed by regions.

Potentially, the most important element of the initial set of Putin's reforms lay in the area of fiscal federalism. During the 1990s, the wealthier regions had succeeded in retaining a significant percentage of their income. This reduced Moscow's role as the final decision-maker in terms of wealth distribution and investment across the country and led to imbalances between the so-called 'donor' and 'recipient' regions. In the first years of the Putin presidency, local offices of the federal tax collection service were finally opened in all regions and republics. At the same time, a reform of the tax code ensured that governors could retain only 30 per cent of the consolidated regional budget, whereas they had previously retained 60–70 per cent. Through this measure, Moscow gained control of most of the wealth of the few donor regions. Additionally, regions were prohibited from securing international loans without federal approval. Tighter fiscal monitoring by the federal audit chamber and measures to prevent regions servicing their budgets through commercial banks further curtailed the financial autonomy of the provinces.[22]

The first group of reforms introduced by Putin was critical in altering the nature of centre–regional relations. When Putin took office, the alliance of powerful regional leaders that had coalesced behind the Fatherland–All Russia party appeared set to challenge the position of the federal centre and to act as the kingmaker in the Russian presidential campaign. Once elected president, Putin's priority was to break the power of the regional elite at the national level.

The creation of the Federation Council by Yeltsin underscored the importance that he attributed to Russia's regional leaders, and the reliance he placed upon them. Putin introduced a new law that brought to an end the practice of ex officio membership for regional executive and legislative heads in the Federation Council. Instead, the two branches of regional government were each permitted to send a representative to the new Federation Council.[23] The removal of the governors

---

[22] In June 2004, Moscow won an important victory when the Constitutional Court upheld as constitutional the provisions of the Budget Code of 2000 that prohibited regions from holding their budgets in commercial banks. Instead, all budget accounts must be serviced through accounts of the federal or regional treasures in the Central Bank. The Code had been challenged by St Petersburg, Krasnoyarsk Krai, and Khakassia.

[23] The State Council, composed of eight regional leaders on a rotating basis, was established by President Putin on 1 September 2000 to assuage the regional elite about their loss of high-level political access following their removal from the Federation Council.

and presidents from the Council and their replacement with regionally appointed senators was designed to deprive regional leaders of a channel through which to exercise influence in Moscow and also to remove the immunity that they had previously enjoyed as deputies. While the bill initially faced some opposition in the Federation Council, objections were overridden by the Duma with little difficulty. The new membership of the Council was complete by January 2002.

Structural reforms to remove the regional elite from the federal level were combined with measures to reassert the federal government's capacity to control patronage and legal administration at the regional level. The grouping of the eighty-nine federal subjects into seven federal districts, each led by a plenipotentiary directly responsible to the president, allowed the centre to bear down on the regions in three ways: to bring regional legislation into line with federal laws; to re-establish central control over federal institutions at the regional level; and to impose tighter control over regional budgets. Despite the success of Putin's reforms in curbing the regional elite and aspirations to sovereignty in some of the republics, it quickly became apparent that these initiatives would not achieve all of the president's goals. As a result, Putin launched a second wave of reforms.

The Second Wave of Federal Reform

In his State of the Nation speech on 18 April 2002, half-way through his first term in office and two years after the initial regional reforms, President Putin assessed the restructuring of regional power and outlined the way forward. Satisfied that 'the organizational work' for establishing the seven federal districts had been accomplished, Putin urged the decentralization of further federal functions to the district level. He indicated that activities such as financial monitoring and personnel matters needed to be moved 'closer to the regions'.

During his speech, Putin also clearly signalled the end of the era of the bilateral treaties between Moscow and the regions that had been at the heart of Yeltsin's regional policies. Putin indicated that while the existence of such agreements was constitutional, they had led to 'an inequality between subjects of the Federation' and, therefore, an inequality between citizens. At the same time, he emphasized the need to delineate more clearly the distribution of power between federal, regional, and local level in order to 'raise the effectiveness of state policy and stabilize inter-budgetary relations'. Putin's proposal to strengthen local government was presented as an opportunity both to increase the public's control over local political activities and to improve the crucial connection between electors and the federal authorities.[24]

[24] Tomila Lankina, 'Federal, Regional Interests Shape Local Reforms', *Russian Regional Report*, 8/18 (29 September 2003).

Putin's speech outlined, in preliminary form, the two principal conclusions of a report that was being prepared by Dmitry Kozak, deputy chief of the presidential staff, on further reform in federal relations.[25] Kozak delivered his report on 1 June 2002. Following the Kozak Report, Putin submitted two pieces of draft legislation for the Duma's consideration in January 2003.[26] The initial piece of legislation was designed to restrict the conclusion of contracts—bilateral treaties—between centre and regions to exceptional circumstances. In this way, the Kremlin was able to justify as a priority for the new government in Grozny the drafting of a power-sharing treaty following the March 2003 referendum in Chechnya, while at the same time seeking to terminate all other bilateral treaties.[27] The second measure concerned local government reform. The main thrust of the legislation was to create municipal districts headed by appointees of the regional leaders. Local government would have a more stable and predictable financial base and large municipalities would be much more dependent on the regions where they were located.

The final major regional reform initiative to emerge during Putin's first term was the initiation of a process of regional mergers. The creation of the seven federal districts in the first round of regional reform had circumvented the constitutional and political difficulties of instituting a fundamental process of territorial reorganization. But the large number of regions in Russia and the wide divergence in their population and resources was still seen as a problem by the Kremlin. In response to this, Moscow developed an approach based on a gradual and apparently ad hoc process of voluntary mergers between adjacent regions— permitted under the constitution—beginning with the autonomous districts.[28]

In a pilot for the merger process on 7 December 2003, voters in Komi-Permyak Autonomous Okrug and Perm Oblast went to the polls in referendums on the unification of their two regions. The mergers received overwhelming approval. Following high-speed passage of legislation through parliament, the president signed a law establishing Perm Kray on 26 March 2004. With 'local' initiatives to merge receiving strong backing from Putin, there was considerable speculation that other regions would soon follow this path.[29]

[25] In the middle of 2001, Putin instructed Kozak to head a special commission to recommend additional structural changes in federal–regional relations designed to establish 'a single legal space for Russia'. The commission had two principal tasks: to delimit clearly the functions between the federal, regional, and municipal levels of government, and to reform the existing local government system. Nelson and Kuzes (n. 19).

[26] Indira Kvyatovskaya and Alexander Sadchikov, 'Regional and local government face changes in relations with Moscow', www.wps.ru/e_index.html (9 January 2003).

[27] Liz Fuller, 'Has Moscow Put Power-Sharing Treaty with Chechnya on Hold?', *RFE/RL Newsline* 8/15, Part I (26 January 2004).

[28] Vladimir Kovalev, 'What's Behind Russia's Urge to Merge?' *RFE/RL Russian Political Weekly*, 4/2 (16 January 2004).

[29] 'Putin Proposes Merger of Regions on the Fast Track ... As Cheliabinsk Politicians Discuss Merger with Sverdlovsk, Kurgan Oblasts', *RFE/RL Newsline*, 8/34, Part I (23 February 2004).

At the beginning of 2004, Deputy Prime Minister Yakovlev indicated that the federal government planned to take its programme of regional consolidation further and switch to centralized planning for regional development—notably in the area of transport issues—on the basis of a 'Spatial Development Concept'. He suggested that this change would mark a move away from the 'patchwork quilt' approach of economic planning and end the previous free-for-all in regional development.[30] Speculation about Putin's plans was further heightened with the publication in June 2004, by the Council of Production Resources of the Russian Academy of Sciences, of a programme of regional amalgamations, according to which Russia would be divided into twenty-eight administrative units, effectively eliminating the ethnic republics and territories.[31]

The second wave of federal reforms was designed to build on the initial steps taken by Putin. But this second wave marked a new phase of centre–regional relations, which sought to break with the Yeltsin-era conception of federalism. Instead, a formal, legalistic interpretation of centre–regional relations was developed which minimized the role of inter- and intra-governmental mediation and negotiation, and made federal relations a matter of 'jurisdiction instead of recognition'.[32]

Ethnicity and Territory

Alongside these bold measures to restructure federal relations came more cautious moves to reshape the relationship between ethnicity, territory, and political power in the Russian Federation. In order to help counter the problems created by the asymmetry among federal subjects, notably the disproportional political power of the ethnic republics, the Russian authorities engaged in an incremental refashioning of nationalities policies. The most controversial and dramatic measure was Moscow's policy towards Chechnya, namely the launching of the second war there. The need to combat secession and to reassert the supremacy of federal law was among the leading public justifications for the war, and remains the main reason given for the moves to reintegrate the republic into the Russian Federation.[33]

---

[30] 'Russia Cannot Live by the "Patchwork Quilt Principle": Federal State Planning is Vital'. Interview with Vladimir Yakovlev, www.wps.ru/e_index.html (15 January 2004).

[31] See http://www.nasledie.ru/oboz/01_04/1_07.htm for an interview with the authors of the report. Also http://www.aif.ru/online/aif/1232/02_06?print.

[32] Cashaback (n. 5), 3.

[33] Matthew Evangelista, *The Chechen Wars: Will Russia Go the Way of the Soviet Union?* (Washington, DC: Brookings Institution, 2003).

Putin has generally sought to downgrade ethnicity as a distinctive political factor in Moscow's policies across the Federation.[34] Behind this change lies an effort to decouple territorial and ethnic identities and to move the basis of ethnic claims, at least partially, into the realm of minority rights.[35] While the origins of this approach lay in the Yeltsin era, Putin sought to give initiatives in this direction renewed momentum.[36] The Law on National Cultural Autonomy of 17 June 1996 took a decidedly 'individualistic and associationist' approach to ethnicity.[37] In 2003 it was modified to fit in with Putin's *vertikalizatsiya* approach to federal issues, through amendments that produced a de facto nationalization of the national cultural centres—which ethnic communities had been permitted to establish as a result of the 1996 Law on Nation-Cultural Autonomy—and a limitation on their self-regulation.[38] The Law on National Cultural centres has been accompanied by careful steps to embrace the rights of persons belonging to national minorities.[39]

At the same time, the Putin presidency has seen a growing stress on the ethnic Russian character of the Russian Federation.[40] Reflecting these sentiments, chairman of the Duma Nationalities committee, Yevgeny Trofimov, spoke on 10

[34] This has also involved a downgrading of institutions with specific responsibilities for nationalities questions. The Ministry of Nationalities, Federal Affairs, and Migration Policy was replaced with a Minister for Nationalities Policy in December 2001 and this post was swallowed by the Ministry of Culture and Mass Communications as a result of the Putin Government reshuffle of March 2004. In September, however, a Ministry of Regional Development was established in response to the lack of knowledge in the government about inter-ethnic processes which became apparent, especially with respect to the North Caucasus during the events of the Beslan school siege.

[35] Cholaev notes comments by the Minister of Nationalities, Vladimir Zorin, that 'as far as possible, we will gradually move, so to speak, from an ethnic-administrative subdivision of the country to a non-territorial model. What this means is that if you are a Tatar, you should have the right to lead a full national-cultural life anywhere in Russia, not just in Tatarstan.' Zaindi Cholaev, 'A New Nationality Policy or a Setback for Russia', *The Jamestown Foundation: Russia and Eurasian Review*, 2/2 (January 2003).

[36] The framework for this approach was outlined already in 1996 in Russia's State Concept on Nationalities Policy (*Kontseptsiya gosudarstvennoi natsional'noi politiki Rossiiskoi Federatsii*).

[37] Bill Bowring, 'Austro-Marxism's Last Laugh? The Struggle for Recognition of National-Cultural Autonomy for Rossians and Russians', *Europe-Asia Studies*, 54/2 (2002), 231.

[38] The draft *On Amendments to Federal Law on National-Cultural Autonomy (NCA)* was introduced by the Government of the Russian Federation and passed by the Duma in the first reading on 27 June 2001, with the law signed into force by President Putin on 10 November 2003. A challenge to the restrictive provisions in the amended law regarding the number of national-cultural associations that could be registered in a region in the Constitutional Court was defeated in March 2004.

[39] The Russian Federation has ratified the Framework Convention for the Protection of National Minorities (FCPNM) of the Council of Europe and submitted an initial State Report to the Advisory Committee of FCPNM. See Advisory Committee on the FCPNM: Opinion on the Russian Federation and *Kommentarii Pravitelst'stva Rossiiskoi Federatsii k mneniyu Konsul'tativnogo Komiteta po vypolneniyu Ramochnoi konventsii o zashchite natsional'nykh men'shinstv v Rossiiskoi Federatsii*. http://www.coe.int/T/e/human_rights/Minorities.

[40] The 'unifying role of the ethnic Russian people on the territory of Russia' and their 'historic role in the formation of the Russian State' was already highlighted in the Concept of State Nationalities Policy of 1996.

February 2004 about his committee's work on a draft law 'On the Russian people'. He noted that Russia's official National Policy Concept declares that inter-ethnic relations would be largely defined by the Russian people, who are the foundation of Russian statehood.[41] The 'state forming' role of the Russian population has been complemented by an increased emphasis on the relationship of Russian Orthodoxy to the state, including moves by the Ministry of Education to promote the idea of Orthodoxy as a part of schooling. Steps have also been taken under Putin to strengthen the position of the Russian language.[42]

The Impact of Putin's Federal Reforms

An extensive reform of centre–regional relations was clearly a priority for Putin during his first term as president. It is difficult to assess the effectiveness of reforms in centre–regional relations because what precisely Putin hoped to achieve remains unclear. Although a variety of motives for the reform have been advanced in public statements, the principal aim of the changes appears to have been twofold. The initial goal for reform was to weaken the power of the regional elite.[43] The changes were also designed to establish direct presidential control over all the security structures and law enforcement agencies in the country and, thereby, create a system to bypass the presidential administration, headed for much of Putin's first term by Yeltsin-era hold-over Alexander Voloshin. In this sense, developments in centre–regional relations mirrored the general shift under Putin towards a militarization and politicization of the state through personnel policy.[44]

The overriding motive for federal reform appears to have been a sense that the federal centre, or more particularly the president, needed to increase control in the face of political opposition, including the growing assertiveness of the regional elite. In this area Putin achieved considerable success. His strategy was twofold: to push for legislation to prevent regions acting unilaterally while simultaneously exerting indirect pressure on regional elections to ensure favourable outcomes for the Kremlin. As a result, in the course of the two years following Putin's election, the regional elite were swiftly removed from the Federation Council and,

---

[41] 'Duma Committee Drafts a Law . . . That Puts a Premium on Ethnicity', *RFE/RL Newsline*, 8/ 27, Part I (11 February 2004).

[42] The Ministry of Education adopted in 2001 the Russian Language Federal Target Oriented Programme 2002–2005, which contains as its objective 'reinforcing the role of the Russian language in education'. http://www.ed.gov.ru/ntp/fp/rus_lang.

[43] Nikolai Petrov, 'Federal Reform, Two and a Half Years On', *Jamestown Foundation: Russia and Eurasia Review*, 2/1 (January 2003).

[44] Olga Kryshtanovskaya and Stephen White, 'Putin's Militocracy' *Post-Soviet Affairs*, 19/4 (October–December 2003), 289–306.

subsequently, rarely acted as a cohesive political force. By the beginning of 2003, the 'new' Federation Council had become largely compliant with president's legislative agenda.[45] At the end of Putin's first term, the influence and profile of the regional leaders had declined considerably from that of the late 1990s. Critically, by 2004, the regional elite were no longer in a position to play the role of kingmaker in the forthcoming presidential elections, as they had threatened to do in 2000. This marked a significant change from the Yeltsin era.

Along with constraining the regional elite at the federal level, Putin was able to re-establish a significant degree of central political control across all the territories of the Russian Federation. The seven new federal districts provided the foundation for a reorganization of key law enforcement bodies, including the Ministry of the Interior, the procuracy, and the tax police. Through such measures, the Kremlin was able to wrench the appointment of regional police chiefs, and other federal positions, from the grasp of regional leaders. As a result, the system of rotating public civil servants, that had been standard Soviet practice, was largely restored. This posed a real challenge to the web of close ties between the regional administrations and the security forces, the courts, and business that had emerged in the 1990s.

The creation of the seven federal districts in May 2000 also laid the basis for a strengthening of the position of those in the security forces (*siloviki*) in the structures of federal management. Five of the first seven presidential representatives were former higher officials in the police or were military generals. There is also evidence that a considerable number of those employed by the presidential representatives came from the security and law and order branches of government.[46] Putin's reforms seem to have succeeded in asserting increased control over the regional elite and in enhancing the position of the security services in the management of the Russian state. But it is far from clear that they were effective in terms of the official justifications for the reforms: to address discrepancies between federal and regional laws; to promote economic development in the federal districts; to improve coordination of the work of the federal agencies in each region; and to ensure a clear delineation of authorities between the different levels. Doubts remain, in particular, about the effectiveness in this respect of the federal districts and presidential envoys.[47]

[45] Danielle Lussier, 'Putin Continues Extending Vertical Power', *Russian Regional Report*, 8/3 (2003).

[46] Kryshtanovskaya and White (n. 44), 300. The findings of Kryshtanovskaya and White have, however, been challenged, notably regarding the role of former military and intelligence officials entering the ranks of the regional leadership, by research conducted by the Institute for Situational Analysis and New Technologies. Ekaterina Dobrynina, 'Chuzhie zdes' ne khodyat: Mify i pravda o rossiiskoi regional'noi elite', *Rossiiskaya gazeta* (17 March 2004).

[47] Peter Reddaway and Robert Orttung (eds.), *The Dynamics of Russian Politics: Putin's Reform of Federal Regional Relations*, vol. 1 (Oxford: Rowman and Littlefield, 2004), 277–301.

Analyses suggest that the envoys' initiatives met with varying degrees of success in each of the federal districts and in different spheres of policy within each district. Indeed, the achievements of each envoy depended to a large extent on the personality and skills of the individuals involved.[48] The envoys developed a variety of ad hoc approaches to pursue the overarching goal of strengthening the vertical structure of authority. Despite such creativity, the key problems of implementing change in the federal districts and imposing Putin's 'legal vertical' continued to pose a real challenge.[49]

Considerable questions surrounded the success of legal harmonization. While the presidential plenipotentiaries reported a steady rise in the percentages of regional laws brought into line with federal ones, many of the laws abolished were anyhow redundant. While overt opposition to the legal harmonization drive was rare, especially in *oblasts* and *krays*, the regions proved far from passive.[50] The republics of Tatarstan and Bashkortostan, in the vanguard of regionalization from the late 1990s, put up the greatest initial resistance.[51] By December 2003 Putin felt able to announce: 'a permanently-operating mechanism for bringing the regional laws into line with the federal laws has now been worked out in Russia'.[52] Significantly, on 31 March 2004, the Tatarstan Supreme Court finally ruled as unconstitutional both the republic constitution's provisions establishing Tatarstan's sovereignty and the requirement for presidential candidates to speak both of the republic's state languages, Tatar and Russian. In early 2004, Sergey Kirienko, presidential representative for the Volga District, reported that the process of bringing regional laws in the district into line with federal legislation was virtually complete (though he did note that there were still around 3,000 'discrepancies' in regional laws and 43,000 in municipal laws).[53]

Despite such changes in the environment of centre–regional relations, issues with the potential to inflame nationalistic feelings continued to haunt Moscow's relations with the republics—notably in the North Caucasus and the Urals.[54] In

[48] Nelson and Kuzes (n. 19), 507–20; Reddaway and Orttung (n. 47).

[49] Nelson and Kuzes (n. 19), 517.   [50] Ross (n. 6), 43.

[51] In December 2001, 72 per cent of Bashkortostan's laws were reported still to violate federal norms, a figure higher than in May 2000.

[52] 'Putin says federal laws holding sway again in Russia', *Interfax*, 9 December 2003.

[53] 'Putin says regions happy to bring their laws into line with federal ones', *ITAR/TASS*, 29 January 2004.

[54] Several authors have noted the increased prospects for instability in Dagestan as a result of the republic having to abandon its consociational political arrangements, which provided for guaranteed representation for most of the republic's ethnic groups, in order to comply with federal law. Edward W. Walker, *Russia's Soft Underbelly: The Stability of Instability in Dagestan* (Berkeley, CA: Berkeley Program for Post-Soviet Studies Working Paper Series, Winter 1999–2000), and Robert Bruce Ware and Enver Kisriev, 'Russian Recentralization Arrives in the Republic of Dagestan: Implications for Institutional Integrity and Political Stability', *East European Constitutional Review*, 10/1, Winter 2001, http://www.law.nyu.edu/eecr/vol10num1/index.html. The Kremlin's intervention in Ingushetia to ensure the removal of Ruslan Aushev as president, and his replacement with a pro-Kremlin Murat Zyazikov, has been identified as a key factor in the destabilization of the republic. Jeremy Bransten, 'Is a Chechnya-Style Conflict Brewing in Ingushetia?', *RFE/RL Feature Article*, 12 July 2004.

2003, the federal centre's efforts to override Tatarstan's ambitions to introduce a Latin-based alphabet led to tensions between Moscow and Kazan. Following the adoption of amendments to Russia's Law on Language, which struck directly as Tatarstan's legislation to introduce a Latin script for the republic, Putin was forced to announce the creation of a special commission to look into the matter as a means to calm rising passions. Despite the creation of the commission, the dispute continued to cloud Moscow's relationship with Tatarstan.[55]

In the summer of 2003, the Kremlin appeared to suffer a setback when the Russian Constitutional Court, following an application by Tatarstan and Bashkortostan, ruled that procurators did not have the right to file cases with courts of general jurisdiction questioning the constitutionality of regional constitutions and that judges in these cases did not have the right to rule on such matters.[56] Following Putin's legal harmonization campaign, the general courts were used to overturn hundreds of provisions in regional constitutions and charters that did not conform to federal legislation. According to the new ruling only the Russian Constitutional Court could make such decisions, a factor likely to slow down the whole process of harmonization.[57]

Questions have also been raised about the ability of the centre, through the system of presidential representatives, to coordinate the activities of and appointment of personnel to the territorial organs of federal power. In early 2004 there were as many as 450,000 federal employees outside Moscow, usually working within regional branches of federal ministries. The envoys' efforts to monitor the territorial directorates created tension with high-level federal executives in the Moscow ministries, which bore primary responsibility for the federal staff, but which were not directly accountable to the president as were the presidential representatives.[58]

An important rationale for the regional reforms was that the new arrangements would help to promote economic development. The creation of the new federal districts certainly provided a structural basis for initiatives in the economic area that exceeded the reach of individual regional leaders. The envoys were in a position to organize economic initiatives at both transregional and international level. At the same time, the Putin reforms weakened the economic institutions that regional leaders had established, notably the regional associations. The

[55] 'Tatar Constitutional Court Enters Fray over Cyrillic Alphabet', *RFE/RL Newsline*, 27 December 2003. 'Tatarstan Court Asks Russian Constitutional Court to Rule on Latin Script', *ITAR/TASS*, 3 March 2004.

[56] At the same time, on 31 March 2004, the Tatarstan Constitutional Court ruled in favour of a complaint brought by the Russian Deputy Prosecutor-General against the 2002 Constitution of Tatarstan, thereby striking down the provision requiring that the president speak the Tatar language and removing the word 'sovereignty' from the constitution. *Tatar-Inform News Agency*, Kazan, 31 March 2004.

[57] 'Bashkortostan, Tatarstan Weaken Putin's Reforms', *Russian Regional Report*, 8/13 (23 July 2003).

[58] Nelson and Kuzes (n. 19), 507–20.

federal districts were clearly designed to undercut the power of regional leaders, not to enhance it. Rather than building on existing economic linkages, Putin established seven districts that deliberately cut across regional associations among different districts.

A main element of Putin's regional reform drive was to delimit clearly the powers of federal and local authorities. Putin embraced local government reform at the beginning of his presidency. The final version of the reform, however, moved away from the initial promise of strengthening local democracy and extending the authorities of the local level politicians.[59] As with so much of the Putin agenda for regional reform, the principal aim of the new measures appears to have been to enhance control rather than to establish a more effective or more democratic system. Overall, the legislation in this area has reflected a legal and technocratic vision of the role of local government coupled to a centralization of fiscal and institutional prerogatives. The federal government has gained additional authority vis-à-vis both the regional and the local levels through the reformed system of fiscal federalism and its enhanced institutional and legal control over the localities.

In the 1990s, the municipal level often posed the major challenge to regional leaders within their own regions. It was, therefore, striking that regional governors, alongside representatives from the presidential apparatus and the federal ministries, played a leading role in the elaboration of local government reform. While the main thrust of this reform was to curb regional powers, key provisions strengthened the regional leaders' ability to select and remove mayors and control municipal spending. In this way, the legislation made local executives more dependent on the regional government. The enhanced role of the regional elite vis-à-vis local government has been viewed as part of a trade-off with the centre. The regional leaders accepted curtailment of their position at the federal level in return for a stronger role at regional level, thereby helping to enforce Putin's conception of the power vertical.[60]

The division of authorities between the centre and regions was not, however, settled by the new law on local government and the abolition of the bilateral treaties. On 1 June 2004, the State Council returned (for the third time) to the issue of the division of powers between centre and the regions—notably authorities of 'joint jurisdiction' outlined in the constitution—and put forward proposals for the transfer of five authorities to the regions. While Putin supported this initiative, he was careful to highlight that Moscow retained the right to 'temporarily' take back control if a region faltered in its responsibilities. In a move unwanted by the regions, Putin also sought to pass responsibility to the regions

---

[59] The new law on local government, approved by the State Duma on 16 September 2003, was scheduled to take effect from 1 January 2006.

[60] Tomila Lankina, 'Managing the grassroots: Putin's reform of local government', *Russian and Eurasian Review: The Jamestown Monitor*, 2/9 (29 April 2003), 6–9.

for funding and implementing part of his unpopular initiative to replace social welfare benefits for pensioners and veterans with cash payments.[61]

Intervention and Elections

Federal intervention in elections formed an intrinsic part of Putin's efforts to alter centre–regional relations. At issue was Moscow's ability to determine who would lead the regions. Following his election, Putin was quick to introduce legislation that allowed for the dismissal of regional leaders but proved reluctant to use it to remove popularly elected local leaders.[62] Even when the Kremlin was desperate to replace the widely discredited governor of Maritime Province, Evgeny Nazdratenko, Moscow opted to promote him upwards to a federal post rather than risk direct confrontation with an entrenched regional figure.[63] Efforts by the Kremlin to engage more actively in shaping regional politics were also dealt a blow when in July 2002 it proved impossible— following a Russian Constitutional Court decision—to prevent the president of Tatarstan running for and winning a third term. Indeed, following the Court decision, Moscow was required to alter federal law to indicate that all terms served by the regional governors prior to the passage of the October 1999 federal law on the organization of regional government did not count towards the two–term limit specified in the law. This allowed a group of powerful regional leaders to seek a third or even fourth term. Despite this setback, the Kremlin took a more active part in regional elections throughout Putin's first term.

During the first round of gubernatorial elections, in the winter of 2000, Moscow was unable to exert much influence on outcomes. Most analysts agreed that Kremlin candidates were successful in only four of the thirty–two elections. Nevertheless, it was during this cycle of elections that the Kremlin showed a new assertiveness by intervening to prevent the incumbent governor of Kursk region, Alexander Rutskoy, from standing for re–election.

Despite increased efforts by the presidential administration to shape regional elections between October 2000 and January 2002, the incumbency rate for regional governors and republican presidents remained high at 65.4 per cent.[64]

---

[61] Caroline McGregor, 'Regions in for a Dose of Kremlin Reform', *Moscow Times*, 2 June 2004.

[62] On the eve of Putin's second term, however, there were several cases of 'bottom up' moves to challenge regional leaders through the courts—including in Tver, Kamchatka, Ivanovo, and Saratov oblasts. Julie Corwin, 'Russian Prosecutors Take on Governors', *RFE/RL Newsline*, 8/95 (20 May 2004).

[63] At the end of 2003, the government was reported to be studying the possibility of simplifying the procedure for dismissing governors. 'Putin Expresses Openness to Improving Law on Ousting Governors', *RFE/RL Newsline*, 7/214, Part I (12 November 2003).

[64] Kathryn Stoner-Weiss, 'Soviet Solutions to Post-Soviet Problems: Has Vladimir Putin Really Strengthened the Federal Centre?', *PONARS Policy Memo 283* (October 2002).

By 2002, however, there were clear signs of the growing effectiveness of central interventions. The Kremlin succeeded in getting its gubernatorial candidates elected in eleven of the fifteen regional races, intervening particularly controversially to ensure the election of pro-Kremlin figures in Ingushetia and Krasnoyarsk.[65] During this period, there appears to have been a shift in the relative balance of power, with regional elections decided increasingly frequently by Kremlin influence in courtrooms and election commission headquarters. There was also a growth in the number of military and security figures taking charge of regions—with former generals taking office in Kaliningrad, Ulyanovsk, Voronezh, Smolensk, and Ingushetia.[66]

The fact that the Kremlin was able to displace regional executives in some republics—notably Komi, Sakha, and Ingushetia—suggested that the republics were losing their position as centres of regional resistance to Moscow. The republics of Tatarstan and Bashkortostan were seen as the last bastions of resistance to Putin's drive to impose control over the regions. There was a bruising struggle in the Bashkortostan presidential election of December 2003— including allegations of widespread fraud by the supporters of the incumbent—between the Kremlin backed challenger and Murtaza Rakhimov, the incumbent president. Eventually, the Kremlin agreed to drop its opposition to Rakhimov's re-election after having inflicted on him the humiliation of a second round of voting, and following suggestions that Bashkortostan had, on the Kremlin's instructions, surrendered control over regional gas enterprises to Gazprom.

Towards the end of Putin's first term, the Kremlin seemed increasingly able to shape regional executive elections to suit its purposes. If, during the 1990s, incumbency was the most significant factor in electoral outcomes, by the end of Putin's first term support from the president had become the key factor for election. While some incumbents continued to be elected—notably a group of regional leaders entitled to run for a third term—their victories were made possible by the agreement of the Kremlin.[67] These trends were confirmed in the contests held in March 2004 which saw incumbents generally succeed (Chita, Kaluga, and Voronezh) except where they were not supported by the Kremlin party, United Russia (Ryazan). At the same time, candidates supported by the Kremlin were not guaranteed success (Arkhangelsk, Ryazan), particularly if powerful national economic interests supported a challenger (Altay Kray).

---

[65] Pro-Kremlin candidates were elected in Krasnoyarsk, Buryatia, Smolensk, Ingushetia, Penza, Lipetsk, Tuva, North Ossetia, Kabardino-Balkaria, Dagestan, and Sakha. The Kremlin lost only in Kalmykia and Gorno Altay. Neutral results were achieved in Karelia and Adegey.

[66] Nikolai Petrov, 'Regional Elections under Putin and Prospects for Russian Electoral Democracy', *PONARS Policy Memo 287* (February 2003).

[67] On 5 September 2003, *Rossiiskaya gazeta* lamented the lack of alternatives in the forthcoming gubernatorial elections to the long-standing incumbents of Sverdlovsk, Omsk, and Novgorod because they controlled opposition in their regions. All three incumbents subsequently won re-election.

Concern about the limited ability of the presidential representatives to determine electoral contests at the regional level, particularly prompted by the failure of Moscow's candidate in the election in Altay Kray, led to a drive to further concentrate regional policy in the Kremlin—in the newly created regional development directorate—early in Putin's second term.[68] Improvement in this area was considered especially important ahead of the planned elections in almost a third of Russia's regions in the autumn and winter of 2004–5.

Power and Democratization in Russia's Territorial Politics

The territorial politics of the Russian Federation are most often presented in zero-sum terms, as a battle for power in which there are distinct winners and losers. In this view, Putin's reforms have clearly been designed to effect a transfer or reconcentration of power within the federal centre. There can be little doubt that in this sense Putin achieved a triumph during his first term. By the end of his initial four years in office, Putin's policies had largely ended the talk about the disintegration of the Federation. The political role of the regional elite at the national level had been curtailed and there was a move away from the personalistic, ad hoc, and imbalanced system of federal relations of the Yeltsin era. The federal centre was in a stronger position to influence developments in the regions, notably through the re-establishment of central management over federal personnel at the regional level, and a reorganization of fiscal relations. The president could justifiably claim victory in the 'war on governors'.

Despite concern about the aggressive reform agenda of the Kremlin and the growing role of military and security personnel in managing federal relations, there was little overt political conflict over the changes. Negotiation, coalition-building, and consensus, rather than confrontation, characterized the reform process. Putin made concessions and worked to build partnerships; and he focused on key battles. Further, the whole process of federal reform was conducted within existing constitutional arrangements. Indeed, on many issues there seems to have been a willingness within some groups of the regional elite to go along with the reform process. The reforms therefore had bottom-up as well as top-down elements.

While some worried that Moscow was regaining power through the federal reforms, there was also a sense that these changes were promoting change at the regional level, particularly in the ethnic republics.[69] Putin's reforms, especially

[68] Dmitry Balburov, 'Regional Leaders Can be Removed', *Russkii Fokus*, 19 (31 May 2004); and Kira Latukhina and Natalia Melikova, 'The Kremlin Compiles Lists of Good and Bad Regional Leaders', *Nezavisimaya gazeta*, 13 July 2004.
[69] Hahn (n. 3), 117.

the legal harmonization campaign, were seen to have improved constitutional democracy in most regions across a range of issues, including the separation of executive, legislative, and judicial powers as well as election laws, minority rights, and the demand for constitutional law. Together, these changes were viewed as contributing to a 'sunset of authoritarianism' at the regional level.[70]

When one looks beyond the narrow concern of rebalancing elite relations across the Russian Federation, the nature of Putin's impact on centre–regional relations becomes more complex. There is even some doubt that Putin was able in his first term to disturb the network of collusive political and economic ties between regional leaders and local business that provided the foundation for much of the struggle between central and regional elites in the 1990s.[71] Indeed, Putin may have offered the 'wrong solution' to the problem of regional resistance to his project of rebuilding the central authority of the Russian state.[72] While the president sought to extend control over the regions, his method was to add an additional layer to an already bloated Russian bureaucracy. Further, reliance on the *siloviki* to manage territorial politics was an approach fraught with risk. Military and security personnel generally make poor politicians and are unlikely to produce effective government and dynamic economies.[73]

While Moscow sought to restrict the resources available to the regional elite through fiscal policies, such measures risked killing off innovation and dynamism at the regional level—apparent in some regions, such as Novgorod in the 1990s— for the sake of control.[74] Towards the end of Putin's first term, Moscow seemed to be moving gradually against the business–politics nexus at the local level—notably in terms of the actions against Bashkortostan—but progress remained slow. What progress was achieved took place in a favourable economic environment; Russia was not challenged by the type of economic problems that promoted regionalism during the Yeltsin years. Faced with similar difficulties in the late 1990s, it is far

---

[70] Hahn, ibid. 125.

[71] Bartosz Cichocki, 'Does Putin Really control Russia?', *CSIS Prospectus*, 3/1 (Spring 2002); and Robert W. Orttung, 'Business and State in the Russian Regions', *PONARS Policy Memo 35* (November 2003). For a discussion of the emergence of these relations in industrial regions during the 1990s, see Kathryn Stoner-Weiss, *Local Heroes: The Political Economy of Russian Regional Governance* (Princeton, NJ: Princeton University Press, 2002).

[72] Stoner-Weiss (n. 64).

[73] Brian D. Taylor, 'Strong Men, Weak State: Power Ministry Officials and the Federal Districts', *PONARS Policy Memo 284* (October 2002). In March 2004, President Putin dismissed his representative for the Southern Federal District, Viktor Kazantsev, and replaced him with the former Mayor of St Petersburg, Vladimir Yakovlev. Kazantsev was the only one of the presidential representatives to be replaced ahead of the president's second term. Kazantsev, a former general, was removed, reportedly, because the president wanted greater attention to economic issues by his representative in the south. *Kommersant*, 18 March 2004.

[74] Nicolai Petro, 'Regional Democratization in Russia: Some Lessons from Novgorod', in Cameron Ross (ed.), *Regional Politics in Russia* (Manchester: Manchester University Press, 2002), 120–34.

from certain that Putin's federal reforms would have been effective in restraining a revival of regional activism.

Despite his success in changing the balance of power between central and regional elites and his clear dominance of Russian politics as he faced re-election in 2004, Putin remained, in important respects, reliant on the regional elite. The multi-dimensional aspect of power relations between centre and regions was most apparent in electoral politics. Although by 2004 the regional elite's direct influence on federal politics had declined, they were still looked upon as crucial players in the federal electoral process. The president continued to rely upon the regional elite to secure the votes necessary to elect the pro-Kremlin party, United Russia, to the State Duma in December 2003.[75] Regional leaders also proved vital for Putin in ensuring an overwhelming victory in the presidential elections of March 2004.[76]

Despite Putin's general success in reshaping centre–regional relations during his first term in office, some important constraints remained. The president was unable to push ahead with a full-scale reconcentration of political power in Moscow. Instead, he had to pursue policies designed to bring about a gradual shift in relations between central and regional elites and to effect a long-term restructuring of the Federation. Putin was unable to institute a radical overhaul of the regional leadership, and had instead to use incentives and leverage to remove unwanted regional leaders and to rein in those who caused irritation. As a result, regional elections became the principal battleground between the centre and the regional elite. In this way, powerful regional leaders such as President Shaimiev of Tatarstan, Moscow Mayor Luzhkov, President Rakhimov of Bashkortostan, as well as a significant group of long-serving regional leaders such as the governors of Omsk, Khabarovsk, and Sverdlovsk regions and the president of Kalmykia, remained in place. And despite the federal district system, they insisted on a direct relationship to Moscow unmediated by the president's envoys.[77] Nor were regions entirely passive in respect to the central agenda for reform. While they did not mount a direct resistance, guerilla-type opposition was notable in many regions, notably in key republics. The harmonization of Russia's laws was always just over the horizon but never seemed to arrive. Regions also adapted to the new environment and changed tactics in dealing with Moscow.[78]

[75] In this respect, the integration of a significant number of regional leaders into the United Russia party lists for the Duma elections was notable, as was the role of the regional elite in shaping the outcomes of contests in the single mandate races of regional elite. Robert Orttung, 'Are all Politics Local? The Decisive Role of the District Races in the 2003 Duma Ballot', *Kennan Institute*, 15 December 2003.

[76] The important role of the regional elite was apparent in the presidential elections of 2004, when regional leaders were instrumental in 'getting the vote out' for Putin. The power of the regional leaders was reflected in the wide variation of support for Putin, from 98.18 per cent in Ingushetia as well as over 90 per cent in many other regions (notably the North Caucasus), to 54.82 per cent in Belgorod. 'Huge Support for Putin', *RFE/RL Analytical Reports: Russian Political Weekly*, 26 March 2004.

[77] Nelson and Kuzes (n. 19), 517.

[78] 'Shaimiev, Rakhimov drop threats of conflict', *East-West Institute Russian Regional Report*, 7/9 (6 March 2002).

Putin and the Future of the Federation

The picture that emerges of regional reform is therefore a complex one. Following the Yeltsin years, there was clearly a need to introduce measures to establish a single centre of clear authority in order to take responsibility for ensuring effective state administration, establishing the rule of law, and determining the distribution of functions among the various levels of government. By the end of Putin's first term, regional leaders, at least at the federal level, were weaker than they had been under Yeltsin. But the power relationships underpinning the territorial politics of Russia proved to be multifaceted, extending beyond simple elite relations. The success of Putin's attack on the regional elite should not be confused with a destruction of Russia's federal politics.[79]

As with many other elements of Putin's Russia, an assessment of the federal reforms suggests paradoxical findings; the reforms can be read as both promoting and restricting democracy.[80] While moves to challenge the 'guided democracy' of many of Russia's regions have been viewed as a positive step, considerable doubts remain about whether the reforms involved gains in terms of democracy and effectiveness.[81] Beyond increased stability, there is little evidence that the regional reforms fundamentally altered the networks of political and economic relationships that underpinned the regional activism and the non-democratic regimes of so many regions in the 1990s.

Putin's reform agenda seems to have been primarily an ad hoc reaction to the political threat of the regional elite and a response to the opacity of federal relations under Yeltsin, rather than an effort to forge an effective, stable, and integrated federal system. The enormous cost in human suffering and economic damage of Moscow's policies towards Chechnya present a particularly chilling aspect of Putin's efforts to tame regional opposition. The contradiction between the 'political regularization' policy in Chechnya, based on a power-sharing treaty, and Putin's policies for the reintegration of the rest of Russia within the 'power vertical' was not lost in the other republics.[82] The ultimate failure to pacify Chechnya, even through military means, also cast a long shadow over Moscow's relations with rest of the country.

The gradualist approach that Putin adopted to reform of the federal system meant that the impact of his reforms was cumulative. A number of the reform

---

[79] Further, beyond the elite-level conflict, Mitchneck and her colleagues found that rather than confrontation there was evidence of considerable ties—indeed partnerships—between federal officials and regional policy-makers. Beth Mitchneck, Steven L. Solnick, and Kathryn Stoner-Weiss, 'Democratization Challenged: The Role of the Regional Elites', in Blair Ruble, Jodi Koehn, and Nancy E. Popson, (eds.), *Fragmented Space in the Russian Federation* (Washington, DC: Woodrow Wilson Centre Press, 2001), 129.

[80] Ross (n. 6), 44.   [81] Reddaway and Orttung (n. 47), 278.

[82] Gordon M. Hahn, 'The Chechnya–Tatarstan Connection', Carnegie Center Moscow (21 June 2004). http://www.carnegie.ru/en/pubs/media/70664.htm.

initiatives will not be fully implemented until well into Putin's second term. As a result, considerable questions remain about the ultimate end point of federal reforms.

Despite the considerable success that Putin achieved in restraining the regional elite, the fact that the president was forced to rely upon them for electoral purposes indicates that the president will have to continue to approach regional leaders with some caution. The failure of the Putin reforms to address fully the core of regional power—the relationship between regional-level political figures and local business interests—also suggests that more radical measures, such as the amalgamation regions or moves to appoint regional leaders, may face serious opposition from regional bosses.

Additional steps to centralize control in Russia will bring other risks. Further measures to weaken local autonomy and to dilute the political significance of ethnicity, particularly the link to territory, would raise questions about the ability of the reformed system of territorial management to accommodate the ethnic, religious, and regional diversity of the Russian Federation. Such steps would be especially difficult without the compliance of the regional elite. For this reason, Putin may aim to foster the consolidation of an integrated ruling elite across Russia, including key regional allies, rather than risk confrontation.[83] Putin's proposal in September 2004 to eliminate the direct election of the executive-branch heads in each region and instead to grant to the president the authority to nominate regional leaders may provide a means to begin to establish such an elite.[84] The fact that over fifty regional leaders were due to step down during the president's second term considerably strengthened Putin's hand in seeking to advance a further concentration of power in the Kremlin.[85] Under Putin's proposed new arrangements, incumbents would be eligible for reappointment by the president.

Following the Yeltsin years, there was clearly a need to introduce measures to establish a single centre of authority to take responsibility for ensuring effective state administration, establishing the rule of law, and determining the distribution of functions among the various levels of government. However, the steps taken by Putin to meet these challenges raise serious questions about the future democratic

---

[83] One observer has suggested that Putin enjoys a differentiated relationship to regional leaders: regional leaders on especially good terms with Putin; regional leaders with whom Putin maintains friendly relations but with reservations; and regional leaders whom Putin dislikes and avoids. A. A. Mukhin, *Piterskoe okruzhenie prezidenta* (Moscow: Tsentr politicheskoi informatsii, 2003), 17–25.

[84] Seizing the opportunity for introducing sweeping political changes presented by the Beslan school siege and other terrorist attacks, Putin announced on 13 September 2004 a set of reforms which in normal circumstances would have proved highly controversial. The reforms included a proposal for the abolition of the direct election of regional executives. In place of elections, Putin advocated the introduction of a law to grant the president the right to nominate regional heads. The president's nominees would be subject to approval by regional legislatures. 'Vystuplenie na rasshir-ennom zasedanii Pravitel'stva s uchastiem glav subektov Rossiiskoi Federatsii', www.kremlin.ru

[85] Nikolai Petrov, 'Constitution is A-Changing', *Moscow Times*, 29 March 2004.

character of Russia's territorial political system. The consolidation of a federal democracy is unlikely in the context of policies based on extending central control through federal political arrangements. Additional steps to centralize control will bring accompanying risks. Measures to weaken further local autonomy and the political significance of ethnicity would raise questions about the ability of the reformed system to accommodate the ethnic, religious, and regional diversity of the Russian Federation.

Putin's agenda of reform for Russia will also be compromised if modernization is sacrificed for centralization. It will be difficult to promote an economic revival across a country the size of Russia based upon a further tightening of control and reliance on the security services and agencies of law and order. But making economic and political space available at the regional level risks encouraging the reappearance of autonomous regional activity at odds with Putin's vision of the Russian state. Finding the balance between these elements will be one of the central tasks for Putin during his second term as president.

12

Vladimir Putin's Political Choice: Towards Bureaucratic Authoritarianism

Lilia Shevtsova

As in the past, Russia continues to defy forecasters' predictions and scientifically grounded scenarios. Many observers thought that Boris Yeltsin had successfully pulled Russia out of its totalitarian, imperial, and superpower past. The Soviet Union was no more and the new Russia embraced the market, held regular elections, and cooperated with the West. It seemed to follow logically that after the upheavals and revolutions of the Yeltsin years, his successor in the Kremlin would begin to stabilize the new order that had emerged, help society adapt to the new democratic and liberal rules of the game, and smooth the way for the population's adjustment to the new political and economic system under construction.

But it soon became clear that Yeltsin's legacy by no means promised any certainty of democratic consolidation.[1] Yeltsin bequeathed to Russia what could be called 'hybrid power'. On the one hand, this hybrid represented the same sort of personalized and monolithic rule, imposed from above and outside society's control, that Russia had known for centuries. On the other hand, it was legitimized by elections, since all other forms of gaining legitimacy, whether through violence, succession to the throne, or party ideology, had already been exhausted. Such a hybrid form of power could not be stable and was torn between irreconcilable monopolist-corporate and democratic-competitive tendencies. Theoretically, hybrid rule did not exclude the possibility of development in different directions: towards various types of authoritarianism (pure, selective) or towards institutional democracy. However, by the end of Yeltsin's rule the growing degradation of political institutions, widespread corruption and the assertiveness of the oligarchy, and the resulting growth in longing for order and a strong state limited the institutionalized democracy option.

---

[1] As Archie Brown commented: ' . . . [t]he Russia Putin inherited from Yeltsin was in substantially worse shape than the Soviet Union of perestroika years or, for that matter, the Brezhnev era.' See 'Introduction' in Archie Brown and Lilia Shevtsova (eds.), *Gorbachev, Yeltsin, Putin: Political Leadership in Russia's Transition* (Washington, DC: Carnegie Endowment for International Peace, 2001), 4.

In fact, the Yeltsin epoch in Russian political history failed to produce a political system as a network of independent and horizontally linked political institutions. The presidency or 'mono-subject' occupied all the political space, leaving no room or role for other political institutions. That is why we can only tentatively discuss Russian politics in terms of a political system. The lack of viable political institutions created a niche which has been filled by various informal links and practices (*zhizn' po ponyatiyam*, as such practices are called in Russia). Informal power relations, behind the façade of the constitution and the presidency, have become one of the most important characteristics of post-Communist Russian politics. A new conditionality has emerged: the more personalized power becomes, the more influential the informal networks. But in the Yeltsin era hybrid and shadowy power was not entirely consolidated; it exhibited incompatible trends and principles, and was capable of producing different developments.

Upon his arrival in the Kremlin, Vladimir Putin found himself faced with the choice of either taking the familiar road of traditionalist Russian power, and strengthening the monopolist-corporate aspect of the system, or of developing liberal democracy. Putin's first term in office, the way he began preparing his re-election, and the first steps during his second term suggest that he has already made his choice and has opted for the traditionalist road, even if he tries to present this traditionalism in new packaging.

Putin's leadership will most probably focus on a single aim, that of strengthening the state which subjects society and individuals to its will. What made Putin choose this road, and could he have instead taken the liberal democratic path of strengthening society? Can Putin still change the course he has set? And if he cannot now change course, what consequences will his choice have for Russia? These are the questions this chapter attempts to answer.

Putin's First Term

Three factors shaped Putin's leadership during his first term in office: the role he was appointed to play by his predecessor Yeltsin, the possibilities and limitations of 'hybrid power', and Putin's own views and political experience. Yeltsin and his ruling corporation appointed Putin to play the role of Stabilizer—someone whose job it would be to bring order to the chaos that emerged at the end of the Yeltsin years, and who would also guarantee the status quo and protect the positions of the ruling elite after Yeltsin's departure. But the logic inherent in the mechanism of governance that had developed in Russia in the 1990s affected the way in which Putin began fulfilling his functions as Stabilizer. Once established in the Kremlin, Putin was forced to submit to this logic, which, paradoxically, worked in many respects against the interests of the former ruling clan.

For example, in order to stabilize the situation and strengthen his own leadership, Putin had to not only distance himself from the 'Family', Yeltsin's inner political circle, but also to exclude it from power. In other words, according to the logic of Russian post-Communist power, the task of preserving the existing power system demanded that the new leader sacrifice the interests of precisely the ruling group that had brought him to the Kremlin.

Finally, Putin's past in the security services, his support for the ideal of a strong state, together with his belief in the market, all had an impact on how his leadership took shape. One could say that his spontaneously developed outlook of *market authoritarianism* became his basic philosophy and guiding strategy while he adjusted to his new role and began to form his own regime.

It was inevitable that he would encounter a number of serious obstacles in establishing his leadership. The balance of forces in the upper echelons of Russian society that had taken shape over the Yeltsin years became a seriously limiting factor. The main financial, administrative, and economic resources remained in the hands of Yeltsin's ruling circle and the big business figures close to this circle, who, already back in 1996, had defined themselves as 'the oligarchy'. Subsequent events were to demonstrate just how false this definition was by driving home the message that, in the context of the current Russian political structure, there was quite simply no possibility of big business having a monopoly on power.

The limited personnel pool that Putin had to draw on and its lack of management experience also had a limiting effect. Putin found himself constantly having to bargain and compromise with the old team and keep a number of its representatives (in particular, Alexander Voloshin and Mikhail Kasyanov) in key posts in his administration. Putin also had to take into account the fragmentation of Russian society and its political class. This obliged him to preserve the old leadership formula that consisted in having the president play the part of arbiter, standing above society and the political stage, regulating the main interests and tendencies from above, and refraining from definitively taking sides. This role can, however, be played in many different ways. Yeltsin played it as if he were a tsar, often passive like an old bear, watching political squabbles from afar and only intervening when it seemed to him that this or that political figure or force posed a threat to his power.

Putin began playing his part at the top in a different style, actively appealing to all political forces and attempting to be a leader with universal appeal. The mix of new state symbols approved during Putin's first term (the Communist red banner, tsarist double-headed eagle, Soviet national anthem, and post-Communist tricolour flag) reflects Putin's attempt to consolidate society by partially satisfying the interests of diverse political forces. In all, Putin initially continued Yeltsin's eclecticism, though the new order he established placed greater limits on the extent to which different political forces—communists, nationalists, imperialists, liberals, and democrats—could express themselves. But Putin's policy of trying to

do something to please everyone became an obstacle to his charting a clear course
of development for Russia.

Contradictions soon arose between the role of Stabilizer that Yeltsin had
conferred on Putin, and the role of Modernizer that Putin had begun to mark
out for himself shortly after his arrival in the Kremlin. This modernizing role
made it possible for Putin to look to more dynamic groups in society with an
interest in renewal and reform. In theory, the contradiction between modernization and stability can be overcome so long as modernization is about creating the
structural foundation for change and progress in society rather than merely
resolving local problems and catering to short-term interests. However, the
problem is that Putin's modernization drive is above all about preserving the
status quo. It seeks to preserve not those elements of the Yeltsin regime that
favoured oligarchic interests in the balance of forces, but those of personalized
power and patrimonialism. This keeps society locked in an incomplete transition
and indefinitely postpones resolution of the country's vital strategic problems. In
so doing, Putin's modernization project only serves to further intensify potential
instability in the country.

Putin was initially forced to follow a model of leadership bequeathed to him by
Yeltsin, and the system of 'hybrid power'. This was associated with many of the
traditional characteristics of personalized power in Russia: independence of
society; separation from reality; opaqueness, mysticism, and charisma; and an
autocratic style of rule. But it soon became evident that Putin's image, habits,
character, education, views, and previous life experience were beginning to push
him towards a different kind of leadership. Yeltsin was a monarch, albeit with
Soviet *nomenklatura* habits, while Putin tried to become a manager.[2] He seemed
consciously to be seeking a new kind of leadership image—that of a pragmatic
leader, a sort of CEO of Russia Inc.

As a representative of the new, post-war generation and someone with an urban
background, decent education, and even some experience of life abroad, Putin
represented a break with the traditional Russian and Soviet path to power in the
Kremlin. Leaders typically had first to climb the long and complicated ladder of
the *nomenklatura* hierarchy and their origins and background were generally
rooted in a conservative, often rural or provincial, milieu. As someone from the
middle echelons of the old Soviet *nomenklatura*, Putin's ascent to the Kremlin
overturned the old *nomenklatura* traditions of power reproducing itself from a
small select pool. At the same time, Putin's arrival was an attempt by the post-
Communist elite to find new ways of ensuring a line of succession to power; it
bore the marks of patrimonial and clan-based concerns.

---

[2] In this respect, it could be useful to study the differences between a manager and a leader when
analysing Putin's presidency. See John Kotter, *A Force for Change: How Leadership Differs from
Management* (New York: Free Press, 1990).

Also significant was the fact that Putin became the first Russian leader who had not fought for power and had not mastered the ins and outs of 'conquering' the Kremlin. This could influence how he goes about holding on to power: one cannot entirely rule out that someone who acquired power easily might find it just as easy to relinquish.

Putin's arrival in the Kremlin broke with the traditions for the succession of leadership in Russia, though it is not yet clear how this will affect the further development of political power in the country. The new leadership image displays features that reflect the new demands of the times as well as Putin's own intuition and experience, while continuing to conform to the requirements of personalized power. These demand the observance of archaic Kremlin rituals: following informal practices, cultivating servility at court, preserving the mystical nature of power, and maintaining a distance from society.

Putin at first seemed to try and get away from stereotypical Kremlin behaviour, allowing himself instead to be guided by common sense. At the beginning he quite often met people from outside the political circle and even invited former dissidents to the Kremlin. He was evidently attempting to keep open access to alternative sources of information and maintain contacts with a variety of social groups. But the Kremlin atmosphere soon came to dominate and he gradually moved to the traditional orbit of personal power, where the leader is shielded from society by an impenetrable wall of courtiers, guards, court analysts, and journalists.[3]

President Putin soon came to the conclusion that he needed to fashion his own system for ruling the country. He was unable completely to remove the Yeltsin 'Family' from the scene, but nonetheless began reshaping the mechanisms of governance, creating a so-called administrative 'vertical'. Putin's main focus was on re-establishing federal control over the state apparatus and the law enforcement and security agencies in the regions, limiting the political weight of the regional elite, and politically neutralizing big business. Under Yeltsin, the law enforcement and security agencies in the regions had answered to the governors and republic presidents. But Putin made them answer directly to the federal authorities in Moscow—one of the most serious steps he took towards creating his own power structure. Putin's new 'vertical' based on the law enforcement and security agencies went some way towards balancing the Yeltsin-era 'vertical' based on financial and economic resources. But Putin's 'vertical' was built above all on the agencies with the tools for repression in their hands, and as such it could be effective only in the event of a crisis or confrontation. In the event, the nature of the 'vertical' he had built pushed Putin towards authoritarian action.

[3] The memoirs of Yelena Tregubova, one of the Kremlin pool of journalists that covered the events of Kremlin life, paint an interesting picture. She recounts how Putin's entourage began strictly to regulate the flow of information about the Kremlin and president in a way that was never the case under Yeltsin. Even the questions that journalists put to Putin first had to be edited by the presidential press service. See Yelena Tregubova, *Baiki kremlevskogo diggera* (Moscow: Ad Marginem, 2003).

However, it would be an oversimplification to argue that Putin's rise to power in the Kremlin was accompanied by the seizure of power resources by the *siloviki*, as the representatives of the special services have been dubbed in Russia. This line of argument fits in neatly with traditional kremlinological analysis and provides a simple explanation of Russian politics. But it runs the risk of creating new myths. In fact, the *siloviki* in Putin's entourage have so far played the role of loyal praetorians; they have been instruments rather than the dominant power group. Moreover, Putin himself appears to have understood the situation and has counterbalanced his loyalists with other groups to avoid becoming the hostage of any of them.

Putin's support for market authoritarianism pushed him towards a clearly defined leadership paradigm, but there were also objective circumstances that helped shape his role. The 'hybrid power' that had emerged under Yeltsin carried within it the potential to move towards a more institutionalized democracy. That would have meant strengthening parliament, developing an independent judicial system, and giving public opinion a greater say. For this direction of development to have been followed under Putin would have required pressure from the political class and from society itself. During 1999–2000, there was practically no pressure in favour of liberal democracy. This signalled the absence of the kind of impulses for power to limit itself that had existed in Russia at the end of the 1980s and the beginning of the Yeltsin era.

Furthermore, Putin rose to power on a Kremlin provoked wave of support for a change of direction in favour of order and an 'iron hand'. What helped Putin establish himself in the Kremlin was the launching of the second Chechen war. Having become president on a tide of support for strong personal power, would it have even been possible for Putin to have suddenly taken a different direction, especially when no one was pushing him in that direction and when his policies enjoyed widespread public support? That seems doubtful.

What also played a part was that the democratic institutions that had developed under Yeltsin—independent media outlets, political pluralism, the parliament, and political parties—were being used by oligarchic groups to pursue their own narrow interests. As a result, any attempt by the new president to neutralize the oligarchs' political influence would have affected the way in which these democratic institutions functioned. To be sure, a leader genuinely interested in preserving a liberal and democratic spirit could have attempted to neutralize the oligarchy by strengthening the judicial system and legislative constraints (in particular, the law on lobbying and anti-monopoly legislation) and by making use of economic instruments, primarily taxation.

But Putin chose a different road. For him, restricting political freedom and political pluralism not only made it easier to bring big business to heel, it also fitted a vision of modernization in keeping with the traditional Russian triad— reform from above, reliance on the state apparatus, and the use of Western resources, without changing the principles and rules of the game within Russia itself.

The course of Putin's first term in office confirmed that his movement towards authoritarianism was pre-programmed by his set role as successor to Yeltsin, the limitations inherent in the system, the balance of forces that had emerged under Yeltsin, the demand for a strong hand and order that arose in society during 1999–2000, and, finally, by his own views on Russia and its development.

There was one other factor that could have exercised some influence on Putin—the liberal democratic minority in Moscow and St Petersburg and the presence of liberals in key government posts. Putin had some liberal experience of his own, having worked under St Petersburg Mayor Anatoly Sobchak, one of the most prominent Yeltsin-era democrats; in theory, this could have nudged him towards the views of the democratic minority. However, at this point the majority of Russian liberals were technocrats who supported the idea of a strong hand at the top, apparently in the hope that in a country without democratic traditions and with a strong conservative and left-wing populist majority, a leader with unlimited powers could become the main driving force for liberal transformation.

The technocrats of Yeltsin's government had nourished similar hopes when they had begun building the market while relying on Yeltsin's autocracy and making a deliberate choice to support only limited political pluralism in the country. In Yeltsin's case, the liberal technocrats had helped legitimize only the formation of Yeltsin's elected autocracy. Under Putin, however, the liberal technocrats, both of the old (Anatoly Chubais) and new generations (German Gref, Alexey Kudrin), legitimized Putin's change of course towards a more overt authoritarianism than had existed under Yeltsin. Subsequent events showed that by ceasing to pursue the development of independent institutions, the liberal-technocrats ended up placing in jeopardy the transformations they had themselves hoped to bring about.

But Putin's moves to centralize power, weaken independent political figures, and reduce institutional independence to a greater extent than had been the case under Yeltsin did not amount to the establishment of a dictatorship. The reduction in the autonomy of society went hand in hand with a reinforcement of the bureaucracy, particularly that of the federal state apparatus.

The state bureaucracy had emerged from the 1990s fragmented and disoriented and squeezed out of power by big business. But with Putin's arrival it began to regain its strength and consolidate. By the end of Putin's first term the old scheme that had existed before the collapse of Communism was back in place with the leader at the top, heading the state, propped up by the bureaucracy that had managed once again to make itself a key player in political processes. Big business was distanced from power, and the 'oligarchs' who failed to understand that the show was over—whether Boris Berezovsky or Vladimir Gusinsky, both influential political figures in the previous Kremlin court—were forced out of the political arena. But if big business often seeks to strengthen the personal power and role of the leader, the state bureaucracy, at least in Russia, has no interest in increased authoritarianism since it does better for itself under a manageable leader. This explains why the bureaucratic comeback that took place under Putin acted as a limiting factor on his personalized power.

The new political regime, with an increasingly powerful state apparatus at its core, has started to challenge Putin's leadership. The president's reformist agenda has become severely limited by the opaque and corrupted regime structures that he himself has created. Putin versus Putinism or the leader versus his regime— this development cannot be wholly excluded if the president fails to limit his role to that of Stabilizer. His goal of creating a strong and viable state also seems under threat since his political regime has associated itself with the state and openly tries to press apparatus interests as national interests.

By the end of his first term, Putin had discarded the main elements of Yeltsin's elected autocracy—a policy of mutual connivance, big business domination of politics, and constant personnel change. Among the main features of the emerging new regime are the importance of subordination and loyalty; the recentralization of state resources; the neutralization of the regional elite and the oligarchs; the formation from above of political institutions (especially political parties); and the increasingly corporate nature of different interest groups within the framework of organizations loyal to the state (the Russian Union of Industrialists and Entre- preneurs, the Chamber of Commerce and Industry, the Media Union, and so on).

Putin renounced Yeltsin's principle of tolerating the opposition. Yeltsin toler- ated the opposition so long as it did not become an influential anti-regime factor. But he lost no time in deciding to dissolve the parliament in 1993, once he saw that the opposition had begun to dominate it and was becoming a serious threat to his presidency. Putin, on the contrary, moved right from the start to marginalize the opposition. At the same time, he carried on a dialogue with this marginalized opposition throughout his first term, thus weakening its core even further. From time to time, for example, he met with the leaders of the opposition Communist Party and Yabloko, Gennady Zyuganov and Grigory Yavlinsky. This created the illusion that they were involved in the political process, while at the same time making it hard for them to move towards more open opposition. In general, the opposition came to play an ever more marginal role on the political stage. This was Putin's way of incorporating opposition and ensuring that it posed no danger to the leader and his regime.

Under Yeltsin, there had been considerable room in Russian politics for spontaneity and natural development. Putin decided that uncontrolled activity was dangerous and set about excluding it from the new political scene. The evolution of the 'party of power' reflects this process. Under Yeltsin this party, essentially a sort of 'trade union' of loyal bureaucrats created by the Kremlin to help legitimize the system during elections, went through various incarnations— Russia's Choice, Russia's Democratic Choice, Our Home is Russia. It was rela- tively independent and was even for some time guided by Prime Minister Viktor

Chernomyrdin. Under Putin, the 'party of power'—in the form of United Russia—was deliberately transformed into a Kremlin apparatus sub-department, completely under the president's control. As for the parliament, it lost whatever representative functions remained from the Yeltsin era and became a part of the Kremlin administration, essentially a rubber stamp for executive decisions. The fact that growing numbers of decisions passed through parliament under an 'accelerated regime', which ensured automatic approval without debate, suggested that the Duma had really lost its legislative function.[4] The result of this weakening of all the main political players was that the president was forced to take upon himself not only the strategic, but also the operational, management of the country.

What happened to power in Russia over 1999–2004 confirmed the conclusion that Igor Klyamkin and I reached in 1998, when we wrote: 'The underdeveloped democracy that emerged in Russia after the fall of Communism cannot be cast in concrete. It can either be jettisoned in favour of a new authoritarianism, or society will resign itself to the fact that democracy will inevitably be abandoned'.[5] So long as society and the authorities reach no agreement on a new power order in the country, the monopolist-corporate tendencies generic to the hybrid power system will inevitably seek to stifle democratic aspirations. By strengthening the monopolist-corporate component of the system, Putin provided the impulse for a qualitative change in the system of power.

Some observers have tried to interpret Russia's emerging change of direction as a deformation of the Russian political system. The issue, however, is not one of deformation (i.e. should the system formed under Yeltsin really be called a normal democracy?), but rather a question about the nature of personalized power itself: if not institutionalized, it inevitably drifts towards authoritarianism and perhaps even towards attempts to define itself in the form of a dictatorship. The essence of power remains the same—personalized and beyond society's control. What can change is the political regime through which this power directs society. Putin's regime represents a new modification of personalized power that differs from Yeltsin's 'elected monarchy.'

It would be a mistake, however, to think that Putin simply submitted to the 'iron law' of the system without doubt or hesitation. In fact, his first term in office saw him take various steps in different directions, as if trying to experiment and get a feel for how far the system would let him go and how easy it would be to manage. In this respect, Putin's construction of his 'presidential vertical' is interesting. Putin used this 'vertical' to restore greater control over power and society, but was nevertheless unable to form a completely servile regional elite.

---

[4] See Ch. 7 of this volume.

[5] See *Nezavisimaya gazeta*, 24–5 June 1998 and 7–8 July 1999. Igor Klyamkin and Lilia Shevtsova, *The Extra-Systemic Regime of Boris II. Some Particularities of Political Development in Post-Soviet Russia* (Moscow: Moscow Carnegie Center, 1999).

The only way to have made the regional elite submit completely would have been to opt for the iron hand approach. But the Kremlin either did not want to go this far, or was not ready to do so; more probably it simply did not have the capacity to drive through such a policy. In the event, the Kremlin not only wielded a stick but also dangled a carrot in the form of political barter (Putin's policy toward Tatarstan and Bashkortostan is a good example of this 'carrot and stick' approach), even if the number of concessions made by the federal centre dropped sharply by comparison with the Yeltsin years.[6]

Under Putin, the policy of imitation became a conscious choice. Putin evidently holds the belief that if Russia wants to become a modern country, it should look like a Western society. But at the same time, he clearly believes that Russia remains archaic and uncivilized and therefore must be kept under tight rein. It follows from this conclusion that institutions should be created from above and be kept under strict control. The result was that during Putin's first presidency the Kremlin launched its drive to create what many in Russia began to call 'managed democracy', although the result was to make Russian politics not only less democratic but hardly more manageable. Observers say that Yeltsin, the patriarch of Russian politics, who considered political freedom his great achievement, expressed considerable concern about the new situation.

Over the same period, 2000–2, Putin continued to pursue a pro-Western policy and economic reforms. Liberal technocrats such as German Gref and Andrey Illarionov remained in his inner circle. There was still some scope for criticism of the authorities and for political dissent. All this made Putin's leadership ambivalent and controversial—analysts joked about Putin sitting on two chairs and skiing with his skis pointing in opposite directions. Many observers thought that Putin was still hesitating about his priorities and final strategy. The ambiguity of his leadership (his pro-Western and pro-market views on the one hand and authoritarianism on the other) suggested that he might yet choose to follow the democratic path. Some liberal analysts in Russia hoped that Putin's sense of pragmatism and his aspiration to make the country part of the Western community would prevent him from slipping irrevocably into authoritarianism. They argued that attempts should be made to influence Putin and convince him of the need to build democratic institutions. But it soon became clear that pressure from the liberal minority was not enough to change the direction in which the political regime was evolving.

At the time, one might have gained the impression that Putin had succeeded in consolidating his own political regime by rejecting Yeltsin's systemic ambiguity. However, Putin created a new potential ambivalence by trying to pursue authoritarianism and a liberal economic agenda, simultaneously preparing the ground for a new Russian statism and following a pro-Western orientation. Besides, Putin created a future trap for himself by concentrating all capacity and resources at the

---

[6] See Ch. 11, this volume.

top and was forced to delegate control over these resources to the apparatus, thus increasing the leverage of the regime over his own leadership. He pushed ahead with economic reforms stalled under Yeltsin, only to see them blocked at the level of implementation by the apparatus he had allowed to consolidate power. Putin himself understood the constraining role of Russian bureaucracy and that is why he repeatedly highlighted administrative reform as a priority in all his messages to the Federal Assembly. But in the event he never dealt with the issue, apparently because he failed to find sufficient elite support and hesitated to appeal to society to back reform.

The Formation of a New Political Regime

The impression of ambiguity and hesitation in the Kremlin gradually began to fade. The parliamentary elections of December 2003 became the final accord in the creation of a new regime. The new Duma's composition reflected the tendencies that subsequently emerged. The 'party of power' (United Russia and the various smaller pro-Kremlin parties, including the Liberal Democratic Party of Russia (LDPR) led by Russia's main nationalist, Vladimir Zhirinovsky) acquired a constitutional majority and formed a huge parliamentary faction of 307 deputies. The Communist Party received half the votes that it had attracted in previous elections. For the first time, the liberal democratic parties, SPS (Union of Right Forces) and Yabloko, failed to clear the 5 per cent barrier required for getting seats in parliament, and, finally, the Duma now included an influential national-populist wing (LDPR and Rodina) that had attracted the support of more than 20 per cent of voters.

With the 2003 parliamentary elections, the Yeltsin era came to an end. Although many of the familiar faces and even political organizations that emerged in the 1990s remained on the stage, the evolution of power entered a new phase. The president no longer needed to spend his time and energy in dialogue and consultations with the main political players, for they had now all lost their political clout. Even once powerful regional leaders such as Moscow Mayor Yury Luzhkov and President of Tatarstan Mintimer Shaimiev, both re-elected yet again thanks to Kremlin backing, began meekly to obey the orders of formerly disliked federal authorities.

The 2003 Duma elections also symbolized the end of the whole post-Communist era in Russia's development, marked by the conflict between the authorities and the Russian Communist Party. Over almost an entire decade, the powerful and influential Communist Party had played the part of opposition to the Kremlin regime within the system, while accepting the rules laid down since the fall of Communism. The party's leader, Gennady Zyuganov, had twice helped smooth the way for the desired outcome in presidential elections by acting as a worthy opponent first for Yeltsin in 1996 and then for his successor Putin in 2000, attracting up to 30 per cent of the vote. The Communists' defeat in the 2003 elections meant that their party faded from the scene as the authorities' main opponent. But in spring 2004 it was far from clear who would take over this role and whether the new opposition would take shape as an opposition to the regime and leader or as one to the systemic rules underpinning the political regime.

The anti-oligarch 'revolution' that saw head of the oil company Yukos, Mikhail Khodorkovsky, arrested and imprisoned, dealt the final blow to the political ambitions of big business.[7] The oligarchy ceased to exist as a group with decisive influence on the Kremlin although big business continued to influence decisions on economic matters. The Kremlin's scare tactics worked and business leaders now learned to keep within bounds set by the authorities. Furthermore, the attack launched against Khodorkovsky not only produced a new political deal, but also triggered the rise of a new anti-liberal and populist mood in society.

Motivated by his anti-Communist sentiments, Yeltsin had intuitively tried to distance himself from the Soviet and *nomenklatura* past. Putin took the opposite road and began openly to revive elements of that past. A servile and blatantly cynical elite, traditional patriotic slogans and appeals for a strong state, suspicion of everything not seen as loyal to the Kremlin, and unbridled torrents of praise for the leader—these were all trappings of the still recent and not yet forgotten past. Putin initially seemed to take an ironic and amused view of these neo-Soviet trappings, but apparently he gradually began to see this Brezhnev-style revival as something inevitable. Asked how he felt about having his portrait on the wall in all state offices, in one of his TV interviews he came out for the first time with the quite serious response that the leader's portrait was one of the country's symbols!

In 2003 Putin began more actively taking the side of specific players in the regime—the bureaucracy and the law enforcement and security agencies—thus losing his role as even-handed arbiter. Furthermore, by neutralizing the country's political institutions and turning them into branches of his administration, he himself started to become a sort of dispatcher who inevitably had to bear respon- sibility for ensuing policies. Yeltsin was a polyphonic leader and this made it possible to see in him a reformer, revolutionary, stabilizer, and conservative. But Putin's authoritarian style led him to choose to play the part of guardian of the status quo, so narrowing the possibilities for taking on innovative roles.

To be sure, with presidential elections on the horizon, Putin continued to affirm his pro-Western and pro-market stance in setting the agenda for his next term, in an effort to appeal to the liberal democratic minority. The commission he set up under Igor Shuvalov to prepare the ground for administrative, housing, utilities, education, and health reforms came up with liberal proposals. Putin

---

[7] For a discussion of Khodorkovsky's arrest and its consequences for Russia, see round-table discussion 'Vlast' i biznes: leto 2003', Moscow, Fond Liberal'naya missiya, 2003; discussion also posted on website 11 August 2003; see http://www.liberal.ru.

himself continued to express a firm belief in the institution of private property. But his pro-Western and liberal rhetoric grew ever fainter and he was to be heard ever more frequently promoting a tough approach, the importance of a strong state, and the need to redistribute the excessively large revenues of big business. Sensing that the anti-oligarch mood had wide support among the masses, he began drawing on it more actively, perhaps without noticing that he was repeating the rhetoric of the nationalist-populist Rodina (Motherland) bloc, a political clone created by the Kremlin.[8] Having created a demand for national-populist sentiments, the Kremlin, with Putin at its head, rode the swelling tide rather than trying to swim against it. The danger was that in so doing, Putin could find himself trapped by the current.

The presidential elections of March 2004 gave Putin his own basis of popular legitimacy not, as before, one handed to him by his predecessor. In theory this should have increased his room for manoeuvre. In fact, his choices were limited by his own base, his team, his regime, and the fact that Russia had entered a new cycle of stagnant stability following frustration with the preceding phase of revolutionary breakthrough.

With his belief in traditional modernization and his leanings towards order, Putin made his choice in favour of the traditional state. But what is more significant is that the political class and Russian society, albeit for different reasons, both gave him their support. The political class supported Putin's return to the traditional state because this provided better protection for the interests of the ruling caste, which had found itself unprepared for life under democracy. A significant part of society—by no means all—supported Putin because people were tired of the fits and starts and erratic developments of the Yeltsin years and had begun to hope, as they had done a century earlier, that a patrimonial state would come to their aid and a Good Tsar would look after them. Putin's extremely high popularity ratings, which continued to remain above 70 per cent, seemed to suggest that all was well and the country was behind its president. Putin himself could easily have interpreted such ratings as a seal of approval for the direction he was taking.

How does one define the political regime that began to emerge by the end of Putin's first term in office? Analysts have long found making sense of power and leadership in Russia difficult because Russian political reality always manages to escape attempts to categorize it and draw comparisons and parallels with other societies in transition. In the 1990s, many thought that the concept of democratic transition made it possible to define the situation in Russia by plotting its position

[8] Some neo-conservative ideologues such as Stanislav Belkovsky, for example, have begun to demand that Putin be more overt and bold about restoring the past and speak of the need for 'renewal of imperialist values and a "soft-line" approach to restoring the Soviet Union', and 'a return to Russia's traditional religious and social–humanitarian values.' In order to make Putin's presidential victory 'real' they advised him 'to create a new Russian elite' offering themselves as a new team. Stanislav Belkovsky, 'Severe Defeat for the 90s elite', *The Russia Journal*, 22 December 2003.

on the long line marking movement from authoritarianism to democracy. In any event, there seemed to be grounds for defining Russia under Yeltsin as an immature and imperfect democracy.[9] Certainly, the fact that regular elections were held created the impression that the country was moving towards democracy. But by pushing in the opposite direction, the Kremlin forced political analysts to look for new ways in which to define the Russian system. The change of course towards authoritarianism took some observers by surprise, although it was in fact a 'surprise' that had always been predictable. Whatever the case, those who had been talking in optimistic terms about Russia's progress towards democracy now began saying with equal assurance that Russia was returning to totalitarianism and a police state. The urge to fit the Russian situation into a neat and clear slot once again took the upper hand.

Despite the distinct direction taken, it remains very difficult to characterize the emerging new regime. This regime continues to be hybrid. On the one hand, there is the obvious emphasis on personal power and restricted political pluralism, that is to say, there is a return to traditionalism. On the other hand, there is still a pro-Western orientation, an endorsement of private property, and a rejection of the usual Kremlin practice of consolidating power through mobilization—all of which goes against traditionalism. Moreover, Putin has gone further than Yeltsin in strengthening the market and drawing closer to the West.

It would perhaps be closer to the mark to call this a bureaucratic authoritarian regime. This is not a new concept and has been used by a number of analysts, including Guillermo O' Donnell and David Collier in their studies of Latin American regimes of the 1960s and 1970s that represented one form of modernization for backward and primarily commodities-based economies.[10] The Russian political regime, of course, represents a different social phenomenon and it would be inappropriate to draw direct parallels between the Russian and Latin American regimes, all the more so as they function in different geopolitical and historical contexts. The point is, rather, to borrow the concept itself, which allows us to define two of the components of power in Russia today: the emphasis on personal power and the leader's reliance on the state bureaucracy. It is the combination of these two elements that distinguishes Putin's regime from that of the Yeltsin years

---

[9] Many attempts were made over this period to define the Russian political situation using the concept of limited democracy. These included Michael McFaul's 'electoral democracy', Fareed Zakaria's 'non-liberal democracy', and attempts to categorize the Russian system as 'plebiscite' or 'delegated democracy'. Michael McFaul, 'The Power of Putin', *Current History*, October 2000. Fareed Zakaria, 'The Rise of Illiberal Democracy', *Foreign Affairs*, 76/6 (November–December 2002). These definitions implied that there was democracy in Russia, but that it was incomplete or had been deformed. All that was required was to remove these deformations and strengthen this or that aspect of democracy and Russia would then hopefully move towards full democracy. But in reality a different system had emerged in Russia, one that attempted to survive by imitating some (but not all) democratic institutions.

[10] David Collier (ed.), *The New Authoritarianism in Latin America* (Princeton, NJ: Princeton University Press, 1979).

in which the leader made what seems to have been a conscious choice to keep the apparatus from consolidating. The authoritarianism that has emerged under Putin is of a limited kind. It is limited not by democratic institutions or civil society, but rather by the resources the state has at its disposal and its inability to undertake repressive measures on a mass scale. In short, Russian power is embodied in mono-subject form by the president only in so far as the other players in the system have all been weakened. But the president is not all-powerful and can even be surprisingly weak in carrying out his role. The omnipotence of the leader produces impotence when he has to rely upon loyalists and the apparatus, not only when trying to innovate but also when seeking simply to survive.

At the same time, the 'bureaucratic authoritarian regime' concept has limitations when applied to the Russian situation. It does not make clear the relative weights of the two components or the overall degree of authoritarianism. Nor does the concept give a full picture of the direction development is taking, that is to say, how far Russia has gone in taking on a new system of values and to what extent it is still mired in the past. After all, what really makes the Russian situation unique, and is of greatest importance for politicians, is the phenomenon of still being immersed in a certain political legacy while at the same time turning their backs on it. This unique situation comes through in the yearning of the Russian political class for a strong state and for geopolitical status. It is also evident in their lack of experience of consolidation in peaceful conditions. In this situation, any definition of the Russian regime can only be approximate, and requires thorough examination of the specific features of Russian political reality.

The Future of Putin's Neo-conservatism

At the start of Putin's second term, analysts and ideologues close to the Kremlin or associated with the pro-Kremlin United Russia party sought to find a justification and ideological basis for the new regime. The term 'pragmatism', which had been used to describe the nature of president's course and his regime had become obsolete. The Kremlin team looked for an ideological package that would not seem hostile to the West and at the same time would not be liberal. It was in late 2003 and early 2004, when the term 'neo-conservatism' began to be used to characterize Russian political trends.

Conservatism is not necessarily always a bad thing; the whole question hinges on what it to be conserved. Putin's neo-conservatism (or neo-traditionalism), which has emerged as the main driving force in Russia today, essentially means not just keeping the country in a state of inertia. It also involves doing away with a number of the achievements of the Yeltsin era, above all freedom of speech and opinion, genuinely competitive elections, and freedom for opposition. What is happening is a return to the former state of affairs in Russia, characterized by the state imposing its will, not only on political life but also in the economy. Any conservatism in Russia will always be anti-modernist in approach because Russian history has never built up experience of society enjoying independence from state power, let alone of the state being dependent on society. A return to any of the pre-1991 traditions therefore represents regression for Russia.

Russia's neo-conservatism launched its offensive under the slogan of an anti-oligarch 'revolution.' This was an understandable choice, for the Russian oligarchs, through their cynicism, policy of plunder, and indifference to the needs of ordinary Russians, earned themselves the hatred of large sections of society. In a country where 5 per cent of the population managed to take control of the nation's main resources and join the ranks of the world's billionaires, while 35 per cent of the population (60 per cent according to some estimates) live below the poverty line, appeals to 'plunder what was plundered' are always guaranteed mass support and approval.

The oligarchic capitalist model itself could not be made either stable or effective and a way out had to be found.[11] The privatization of power by a narrow circle of leading business figures had led to the degradation of the state and society. Alternative exit solutions could have been found by creating independent courts, regulating business through taxes, bringing business into the open, and breaking the ties linking it with the bureaucracy that lay at the heart of both the corruption of the state and privileges enjoyed by businesspeople close to power. President Putin chose the simpler road of strengthening the bureaucracy, threatening all independent players with repressive measures, and pursuing the selective neutralization of business leaders who continued to interfere in politics.[12]

The arrest of one of the most influential oil tycoons, Mikhail Khodorkovsky, signalled the Kremlin's change of course towards greater bureaucratic control over the market.[13] It was obvious by this time that the Russian judicial system was being used as an instrument to carry out the will of the executive branch. The Khodorkovsky affair ruined the positive image that Putin had previously built up through his pro-Western policy. Things soon became worse when suspicions arose that there was more to Khodorkovsky's arrest and the attack on Yukos than had initially seemed the case. Not only did Putin's security men have an

---

[11] On the origins of oligarchic capitalism in Russia, see Grigory Yavlinsky, *Periferiinyi kapitalizm* (Moscow: Epicentre, 2003).

[12] See Chapter 10 of this volume.

[13] The attack on Yukos represented a turning point for many Russian and foreign analysts, making them doubt the positive potential of Putin's policies. 'Two Vladimir Putins—economic reformer and democratic backslider—have lived side by side without meeting,' wrote Michael McFaul. But the attack on Yukos in his view 'brought the two Vladimir Putins together.' McFaul concludes: 'Arbitrary rule by the state is not only undemocratic. It's bad for business.' Michael McFaul, 'Who is Vladimir Putin', *Wall Street Journal*, 9 July 2003. The Khodorkovsky affair led Thomas Carothers to conclude: 'Russia is not a dictatorship, but it is settling in for a long, grey period of semi-authoritarian rule.' Thomas Carothers, 'Hard Lessons for Arab Democracy', *Washington Post*, 25 November 2003

interest in removing Khodorkovsky from the scene, but so did his business rivals, above all Roman Abramovich, one of the most influential members of Yeltsin's inner circle. In any event, Abramovich appeared to benefit from the attack on Yukos. This cast doubt on the idea that the Kremlin genuinely wanted to end oligarchic capitalism in Russia. One possible explanation is that certain forces in Putin's entourage were trying to get their hands on a slice of big business assets under the cover of a campaign against the oligarchs. All this raises a question to which there is no answer at present, and to which there may never be one: to what extent was the president involved in this process?

In any case, the president's rhetoric, in which he insisted on the irreversibility of privatization in Russia and then cast doubt on this same irreversibility, led to fears within the Russian business community for its future and did nothing to encourage Russian investment in the country's economy.[14]

The Kremlin's campaign against the oligarchs had the inevitable result of encouraging the rise of strong statist ideas within the political class. In some groups this took the form of nationalism; in others it emerged as a new expansionism. Populism and strong state ideology have anyhow always gone hand in hand in Russia. In their most simple and concrete form, these ideas found their expression in the 2003 parliamentary election campaign slogans used by Vladimir Zhirinovsky's LDPR party—'We are for Russians and for the poor.'

New notes in Moscow's foreign policy had begun to sound even earlier.[15] Signs that Moscow and the Western capitals were disappointed with each other became clearly visible throughout 2003. The Russian authorities showed increasing concern about US presence in Central Asia and the Caucasus (in Georgia and Azerbaijan). The Kremlin's disappointment with possibilities for integration with Europe became more tangible. At the same time, Western circles also became increasingly disappointed in the partnership with Moscow. Russian observers began talking about a 'new isolationist' policy in Moscow.[16] A conflict of interests between Russia and the West in the former Soviet area seemed to have become inevitable. In its most acute form this conflict began emerging in Georgia after the political crisis there and the fall of Eduard Shevardnadze's regime. The partnership between Russia and the West had been based on the need to fight a common enemy—international terrorism. But what became increasingly obvious was the simple truth that unless it was also based on common values and principles, this partnership could be no more than ad hoc and temporary.

[14] 'The Yukos affair shows that the state's economic priority is not to fight corruption but to review the results of privatization independently from corruption'—such was the conclusion of a round table organized by the Liberal Mission Foundation in the summer of 2003. See 'Power and Business,' (n. 5), 30.

[15] See Ch. 13 of this volume.

[16] Dmitry Trenin, 'Rossiya vkhodit v "novyi izolyatsionalizm" ', *Nezavisimaya gazeta*, 8 December 2003.

This new geopolitical background only intensified the conservative line in Russian foreign policy. The result was a vicious circle in which the elite, having thrown its lot in with authoritarianism and a redistribution of assets, found itself also having to support the strong state change of tack in foreign policy, while the rise in anti-Western sentiment in turn fuelled the traditionalists' appeals for a return to the past.

Does all this mean that Putin has made a definitive choice in favour of an anti-Western and anti-liberal policy? The reality is more complicated. Putin is still attempting to play several tunes at once. Pro-Western views, albeit qualified, and support for the market remain part of Putin's outlook.

There is no doubt that Putin will continue to pursue market transformation during his second term, tackling above all the urgent issues of housing, utilities, and administrative reform. He might also take steps towards further banking reform, improvements in the quality of economic growth, and diversification of the economy through reducing reliance on the raw materials sector.

But the question is, how consistent a pro-Western policy can Putin follow if he has to rely on the backing of a conservative inner circle and if the team responsible for defence and foreign policy is made up of people who once spent their time fighting the West? As for market reforms, even if Putin's technocrats at the top attempt to maintain a liberal course, its implementation remains in the hands of the state apparatus, which is more interested in keeping state control over the economy and preserving the system of informal relations that is the breeding ground for corruption.[17]

Developments early in Putin's second term highlighted new problems not anticipated by the authorities. The Kremlin spin doctors had failed to foresee that manipulation of the Duma elections would end up undermining the holding of the presidential ones. With the political field so thoroughly cleared and the democratic parties defeated, the Kremlin suddenly had to wake up to the fact that there were no worthy opponents left to face Putin in the 2004 presidential elections. Battling for the Kremlin against funeral business owner Sterligov and Vladimir Zhirinovsky's buffoon of a bodyguard would have entirely discredited the whole election process for Putin. Unsurprisingly, the Kremlin spin doctors rushed to drum up more worthy opponents, and Irina Khakamada, Nikolay Kharitonov, Sergey Glazyev, and Ivan Rybkin entered the race. As a result of the Kremlin's game of imitating free elections, power started to lose its legitimacy and elections were turned into a farce. So long as the ruling elite remains averse to using force to keep its hold on the country, legitimacy through elections is its only means of ensuring continuity. In Gorbachev's time, his attempt to modernize the

---

[17] One Russian government representative, Arkady Dvorkovich, defined the role of the Russian bureaucracy as follows: 'The bureaucracy today is the main obstacle to economic development, and this because it is not competitive on the labour market...' 'Power, Business and Civil Society' (Moscow: Fond Liberal'naya missiya, 2003), 227.

Soviet system through the introduction of competitive elections triggered the collapse of the Soviet Union. In post-Communist Russia, the attempt to manipulate the election process can become a time bomb that may set off a delegitimization of power.

Another of the consequences of the Kremlin's policy that Putin will also have to face is that with no independent players left on the scene, he alone will be responsible for the country's entire development. No longer will the Kremlin be able to lay the blame on the Communists, oligarchs, or right-wingers. From now on, Putin will be held responsible for any failures, be they his own, those of his entourage, or even the errors of minor officials in distant Siberia. This is the logic of the 'vertical of power'—the leader, and not institutions, answers for whatever happens in the country.

Along with the issues of legitimacy and responsibility, Putin will also face the question of how to ensure the continuity of power, either by opting for a third term or by looking for a successor. Moreover, this is not an issue he can afford to put off until a later date. The political elite and Putin's entourage have to turn their minds to ensuring the continuity of power. There is already pressure on Putin to change the constitution so as to allow him to run for a third term. If he resists this pressure and refuses to go ahead with the idea, the elite will immediately start looking for a new leader, leaving Putin dangerously isolated. In any event, Putin will have little time for systemic reform because the way power in Russia is organized will keep him preoccupied with other matters to do with power itself, that is, how to keep hold of it or pass it on to a loyal successor.

The problems that Putin will encounter during his second term do not end here. He will find himself having to deal with a conflict, not particularly visible during his first term but now coming to the fore, between personalized power and the need to implement structural economic reform, which requires the creation of independent institutions. Attracting more investment, for instance, depends on ensuring the supremacy of the law and having independent courts that can protect ownership rights. In an authoritarian environment, where courts are controlled by the executive branch and where a phone call from the regional governor or a representative of the presidential administration suffices to influence their decisions, there can be no talk of protecting ownership rights and creating a favourable investment climate. In short, Putin's personalized power will come into conflict with the need for economic transformation. But even more serious conflict can be expected between the apparatus and the interests of economic reform. The composition of the Fradkov government, formed after the presidential elections of 2004, was an indication of the fact that the apparatus had prevented administrative reform. This left the president with an awkward and ineffective structure of governance that constituted an impediment to any radical change.

The clash between power and business reflected in the Khodorkovsky affair demonstrated that the Kremlin was intent on preserving informal practices and shadowy relations between the authorities and business circles that are hardly conducive to the creation of a stable economic environment with guaranteed property rights. The Kremlin's decision to try to settle this conflict by force had a destructive effect not only on the economy and the judicial system, but on the rules of the game by which regime and state operate, so helping to preserve patrimonialism.

The responsibilities Putin faces include not simply ensuring the country's development. He also has the far from simple task of marking the end of a historic cycle in Russia's development—the movement from one system of redistribution of assets to another. As historian Yury Pivovarov has rightly pointed out, 'the history of the Russian system is the history of the struggle between Power, which attempts to exercise some control over this redistribution, and the populace, which attempts to break free of this control and carry out redistribution in its own way . . . '.[18] Russia has entered a new historical situation in which there are almost no assets left to carve up. Instead, the time has come to legitimize not just private property, but also the way it has been distributed, which is rightly perceived as unfair. By putting an end to this constant process of redistribution, Putin would close one of the most significant chapters in Russian history and give an enormous boost to the country's development. Continuing the policy of putting pressure on business, however, would signify that he has no intention of breaking the chains that have traditionally bound together power and assets in Russia.

Evaluating Putin's Leadership

We can evaluate Putin's leadership in a variety of ways: from the point of view of how well he has carried out the role assigned to him by Yeltsin, or in terms of achieving the ideas and objectives he himself has put forward. If we consider what Putin has achieved in his role as Stabilizer, we can say that he has played his part brilliantly. He has brought order to the situation in the country and got most of the Russian population behind his policies.

Let us now take Putin's own stated goal of modernizing Russia as a criterion. Here, too, there are grounds for a positive evaluation. Putin has achieved continued economic growth, increased investment, and fairly good macroeconomic results. In any event, Russia is not threatened by economic crisis in the coming years even if oil prices fall, and the Central Bank's reserves of $72 billion and the stabilization fund (currently at $8 billion) would be of great help in the event of any unforeseen circumstances.

---

[18] Yury Pivovarov, 'Russkaya politicheskaya kul'tura i political culture', *Pro et Contra* (Summer 2002), 39.

And what of the cost of Putin's policies? The president has shown that he can achieve his goals without wasting too much energy and without losing the support of the political class and the population. Yeltsin was the one who provoked crises, overturned governments, and sparked conflicts. Putin is the opposite, a political minimalist who uses only limited pressure and also only in relation to a small circle of people. He forced only two people to leave the country—Boris Berezovsky and Vladimir Gusinsky—in order to liquidate television as an instrument for exercising pressure on the state, and in order to get rid of Berezovsky's reminders of what Putin owed him. Of all the oligarchs, Putin has sent only Khodorkovsky to prison and in so doing resolved, at least temporarily, the problem of ensuring big business loyalty to the Kremlin. In short, Putin has proven himself a politician able to manoeuvre with dexterity while being careful not to rock the boat. If we base our evaluation only on these criteria, then Putin fully deserves a positive assessment as a leader who has proved able to maintain stability in Russia.

But how solid is the basis of this stability? Putin's first term showed that power built on the 'transmission belt' principle only works in a system of unquestioning and total subordination, which, in turn, can be established only through fear and force. The moment the mechanisms of force weaken, or fear of the Kremlin dissolves, the 'belt' stops working. Even minor hiccups in its operation can throw the system out of balance, as all the components of the system are bound together in a vertically subordinate interdependence. What has saved power in Russia so far is that, despite having the outward attributes of subordination, it remains somewhat dispersed and unfocused. This means that if one structure stops working, it can be compensated for by another, or by a semblance of activity. The defects of the 'power vertical' have so far not been evident, but in the event of a crisis this form of running the country is unlikely to prove effective. This is why the Kremlin lost its bearings and could not decide on a suitable course of action during emergency situations, such as the Kursk submarine disaster or the hostage drama in Moscow.

The lack of independent institutions, capable of moderating the intensity of clashes between different groups close to power, leads to a situation where such conflicts become a source of constant tension. The fact that these political battles take place behind the scenes only makes the whole political process more unpredictable. Another factor to take into account is the move of large sections of the population 'beyond' the state, freeing themselves from direct dependence on the state (even during Putin's first term, 45 per cent of Russians surveyed claimed they could get by without state support).[19] The majority of those who have chosen to survive without relying on the state are unhappy with the way 'hybrid power' works. They could, at any time, go from merely subsisting outside the official

---

[19] Tat'yana Kutkovets and Igor Klyamkin, 'Normal'nye lyudi v nenormal'noi strane', *Moskovskie novosti*, 8 July 2002.

structures to turning against them, becoming an anti-regime factor and a challenge to the authorities. They could do so simply by voting against all candidates in elections or ignoring the elections altogether, thus undermining the principles of a model built on subordination.

The St Petersburg gubernatorial election, in which the Kremlin lobbied for its candidate, Valentina Matvienko, showed that even in a city loyal to the president, the population cannot be guaranteed to support Putin's choice. Matvienko won in the second round, but with difficulty and through increased pressure on her opponents. This election as well as that to the Duma in December 2003 underscored problems of turnout and mass voting against all candidates. These forms of voter protest reflect popular frustration with elections that bring no improvement to everyday life and signal growing popular disenchantment with politicians in general, including Kremlin appointees. Widespread disappointment with politics in turn undermines the legitimacy of elections and there are no other means of legitimizing power in Russia.

Reducing political institutions to no more than appendages of the presidency has the effect of increasing the influence of the apparatus on the decision-making process. Politics itself becomes self-sufficient and no longer needs society, which starts living its own life. Sooner or later this leads to a situation where society no longer needs state power. The collapse of the Soviet Union showed exactly what can happen when society and the authorities move in different directions.

The seemingly calm political climate in Russia is deceptive because it is largely based on imitation—imitation of order, imitation of democracy and independent institutions, imitation of strength, and imitation of responsibility. Imitation is a way of resolving the systemic contradictions between mono-subject power and democracy. Ultimately, an imitation of the presidency, the main political institution keeping order in the country, will also become inevitable. When Putin avoids responsibility in order to maintain his position that is a sign that he too has been infected by the virus of imitation. To be sure, the imitation game, as some analysts contend, can teach its participants new rules and principles. But in the end imitation has a much stronger negative impact, strengthening popular frustration and rejection of liberal democracy.

It is hardly reassuring that the institutions giving society its structure are dependent on the president's popularity ratings. Falls in these ratings would jeopardize the stability of the entire system. A regime based on a 'vertical' structure of power cannot ensure stability in a society that is fragmented and has become used to pluralism; all the more so since this regime does not have the tools at its disposal to ensure stability through force.

Can this kind of regime bring about modernization? Here again the answer is no. Given favourable economic conditions, such as high oil prices, this vertically structured regime may be able to achieve economic growth by renewing the existing infrastructure. But this applies only in an economy based on raw materials. A bureaucratic authoritarian regime cannot create the new sources of growth essential for transition to a more developed economic system capable of dealing with post-industrial challenges.

Continuing reliance on a raw-materials-based industrial economy in a society used to geopolitical ambitions and a feeling of responsibility for the world will only deepen the conflict in Russia between aspirations and capabilities. One cannot rule out that at some point the authorities could try to resolve this conflict by resorting to simple solutions, such as stepping up hostility towards the West.

To what extent was Putin responsible for Russia's turn towards traditionalism and conservatism, or was this turn an unavoidable consequence of factors beyond the president's control? Is Putin in his second term likely to help push Russia deeper into this conservative and traditionalist past, or will he help prevent Russia from sliding further towards a harsher form of authoritarianism, this time with a nationalist or imperialist face?

As we have already stressed, Putin was programmed from the outset to play a certain part, and it was difficult for him to go beyond the limits of the role he was given. This was especially difficult as he did not initially have either experience or a team of his own. This meant that even had he chosen to pursue real democracy rather than its imitation, he would have faced serious limiting factors. At the same time, however, the favourable economic situation and a high popularity rating did give him some freedom to manoeuvre and pursue an independent course. Yet the course he chose was that of building the 'presidential vertical'. Putin's own positions and views on power, the state, and the economy increased the weight of the other factors limiting liberal democracy. The security agencies and the state apparatus, for example, which had been in the shadows under Yeltsin, now came to the front of the political stage and began laying down their own rules.

We must give Putin his due, however, for being the first Russian leader to make a conscious choice in favour of the West—a decision that he turned into Russia's strategic choice. No Soviet or Russian leader had ever gone as far towards the Western community. But the lack of consensus on foreign policy issues and Russia's national interests, and the predominance of conservatives in Putin's entourage, prevented him from making this choice definitive and consistent. Even so, a new leader in the Kremlin would be unlikely to be able to reverse direction and revive an anti-Western mobilization regime and a cold war–like atmosphere. Russia does not have the resources for this and the Russian political class, nationalistic and imperialist-minded though it may be, does not really seek a new confrontation. Furthermore, a sizeable section of the population is unlikely to support attempts to consolidate society by gearing up against an outside enemy. Still, with no solid foundation for pro-Western views in Russia and no real understanding of the common interests shared by Russia and the West, there is fertile soil, not just for an inconsistent foreign policy in Moscow, but also for growing mutual suspicion and Russia's isolation.

Putin has preserved both liberal technocrats in government and a market reform orientation in policy, and will continue to do so. But in a context of

degradation of the judicial system, political control over business, and the formation in the Kremlin of a powerful bureaucratic 'oligarchy' looking to redistribute
assets, these reforms cannot give the market the impulse required for successful
development. Furthermore, it is the liberal technocrats in Russia, even more than
other groups, who bear responsibility for degradation of the democratic process,
because of their belief in the capacity of personalized power.

Putin, it must be said, has not and is unlikely to become a dictator, as some
predict. So far he has not given the security agencies total control. His realism,
sense of pragmatism, and natural caution may hold him back from going too far
in this direction. More significant, though, is the fact that Putin provided the
impulse for Russia's movement in this direction, and may not be able to stop it,
even should he attempt to do so.

The evolution of Putin's leadership also shows us how far political engineering
can be taken and with what consequences. It seemed that whoever could control
administrative resources, use all the capabilities of state power, and exert pressure
on the elite, the business community, and the security agencies would be able to
carry out any plans—create and bring down parties and trade unions, build their
own civil society, and control parliament. The first to try out such dangerous
but evidently intriguing political experiments was the notorious oligarch Boris
Berezovsky. In just a few weeks he put together a new 'party of power', Unity,
which became the dominant force in the new parliament at the end of 1999. A new
generation of spin doctors followed Berezovsky's example, creating new, often
virtual, realities without giving much thought to the consequences. But the
December 2003 parliamentary elections made it clear that the Kremlin cannot
control the results of its political experiments. There is no guarantee that the
Kremlin will be able to manage the 'vertical' it has created. Controlling an
imitation is very difficult, and sooner or later control itself could prove no more
than an imitation.

What does all this tell us about the type of leadership Putin embodies? There
are no grounds for concluding that Putin represents transformational leadership,
whose fundamental mission is not just to transform the state and regime but also,
as James MacGregor Burns rightly asserted, to raise it 'to higher levels of
motivation and morality'.[20] Putin's style makes him more of a 'transactional'
leader, more of a wheeler-dealer. At the same time, Putin has gone beyond the
bounds of 'transactional leadership', for he has not blindly followed the norms and
rules set by his predecessors—he has set his own rules. The problem is that by
cancelling out the democratic achievements of the Gorbachev and Yeltsin years,
Putin's new rules have taken Russia back, at least politically, to the point from
which it tried to move forward in the late 1980s. In short, Putin's leadership
contains traditionalist elements that negate the transformational paradigm.

---

[20] James MacGregor Burns, *Leadership* (New York: Harper & Row, 1978), p. 20.

After a decade of liberal reform, Russia is returning to a regime of power that seeks to keep society under strict control. The dramatic and hopeful years of spontaneous democratization and pluralism in Russia are over, at least for the time being. Russian society failed to produce the kind of pressures that would have ensured that Putin pursued the reinforcement of liberal democratic transformation. It will be up to Putin to define a new balance between centralism and democratic freedoms. He is unlikely to opt for pure authoritarianism, and even more unlikely to become an outright dictator. His regime will more likely be one of selective authoritarianism. We should not, however, be too hasty in our final evaluation of Putin's leadership. As Archie Brown has noted, 'Whether Vladimir Putin will be more than a transactional leader remains to be seen'.[21] The final evaluation of Putin's leadership will depend on whether he can keep the country from sliding further into the past and on how he assures the continuity or change of power in 2007–8. The way Putin handles the transfer of power at the end of his second term (if such a transfer takes place), and the forces that influence that process, will shed crucial light not only on the results of the democratic experiment in Russia, but also on the nature of Putin's leadership and his role in Russian history.

---

[21] Archie Brown, 'Introduction' (n. 1), p. 7

13

Putin's Foreign Policy Choices

Andrei Grachev

Western political analysts, intrigued by the question 'Who is Mr Putin?', thought that the most promising way to find an answer was to examine the new president's changes in foreign policy. The kind of relations Vladimir Putin sought to build with the outside world, and particularly with the West, might well provide the key, it was thought, to a better understanding of his domestic policy objectives. But even after the end of his first term, Putin's foreign policy remained ambiguous, leaving Western observers still trying to work out its underlying principles and priorities.

When Putin initially took over effective power in summer 1999—Yeltsin having appointed him prime minister and designated him successor—foreign policy did not figure prominently on his agenda. At this stage, and when acting president in early 2000, Putin was preoccupied with courting popular support so as to ensure a clear victory in the March elections. Even as the newly elected head of state, he remained concerned with domestic problems, especially with the need to rebuild the authority of the centre within the Federation. For the time being, the new president put foreign policy on the back-burner. For Putin, in contrast to Gorbachev, cooperation with the outside world and especially the West, did not form an integral part of the internal reform project. Faced with the disastrous balance sheet of Yeltsin's presidency, he felt obliged to distance himself from the Western world rather than to seek support and financial aid which had political strings attached.

In the peculiar political context of his unexpectedly rapid rise to supreme power, Putin felt compelled to build an independent political image for himself that was distinct both from his political 'godfather' Boris Yeltsin and from his powerful and experienced rival at that time, Yevgeny Primakov. Putin had to show that he was more responsible than the former and as least as competent as the latter. The circumstances surrounding his election, in which he had stood as Yeltsin's protégé, made him anxious to continue to build domestic legitimacy. The second Chechen war, in the wake of which Putin had come to power, served as an additional handicap to the kind of active diplomacy required to build equal and effective working relations with democratically elected Western leaders.

Reflecting on Putin's first term in office, one can distinguish at least three different phases in his foreign policy. In the first phase, at the start of his presidential mandate, Putin's policy bore some resemblance to Soviet diplomacy in the late Brezhnev period. The Russian president showed a rather reserved attitude towards his Western partners so as to point up a shift from the complacent stance typical of the Yeltsin years. Russia's defence doctrine was revised under the supervision of Putin's national security adviser and future defence minister, Sergey Ivanov. The notion of external 'strategic threats' to national security reappeared, as did the term 'potential adversaries'; both were clearly associated with North Atlantic Treaty Organisation (NATO). In those first months in office, Putin seemed to be much more at ease with the leaders of former client states of the Soviet Union—Castro, Gaddafy, and Kim Jong Il— than with his Western counterparts.

At this stage the mistrust seemed to be mutual. With a few exceptions, Western leaders observed with suspicion the accession of a former KGB officer to supreme power in Moscow. Condoleeza Rice did not hesitate to include Russia in the category of 'possible strategic rivals' of the United States.[1] Only British Prime Minister Tony Blair, who staged the first lavish Western welcome for Putin in April 2000, seemed convinced that the new Russian leader was open to engagement and influence.

Things started to change in the summer of 2001. During the first Russia–US summit, in Ljubljana (Slovenia), Putin launched a real 'charm offensive' against George W. Bush and apparently managed to gain his personal confidence. This seemed to confirm the extraordinary talent of the former Soviet intelligence agent to turn his political partners into close personal friends, a skill he was to display on a number of other occasions. After this meeting, Bush said that he had looked the Russian leader in the eye and looked into his 'soul'. But above all, the meeting demonstrated Putin's capacity to undertake a pragmatic analysis of the situation and to understand the futility, and probably the damaging consequences for Russia, of pursuing a course of confrontation with the United States.

The dramatic events of 11 September 2001 offered Putin an exceptional opportunity not only to justify a crucial pro-Western turn in his foreign policy, but also to offer Washington a long-term political deal on the most advantageous of conditions—not as a client in need of political patronage and financial aid but as a valuable strategic partner. However, those observers inside and outside Russia who hailed Putin's surprise decision to join the US-led anti-terrorist coalition, as a strategic 'choice for Russia's future', were probably engaging in wishful thinking. At that time, any choice other than this purely pragmatic political decision would have led to a dead end, and would have destroyed Putin's hopes of bringing Russia back into the mainstream of world politics.

Even if this decision made perfect sense in the circumstances, and corresponded to Russian national interests, Putin certainly deserves credit for the speed with which he reacted and for the personal courage he showed in taking a

[1] Interview in *Le Figaro Magazine*, 15 April 2001.

decision that went against prevailing opinion in the national Security Council, most of whose members recommended a wait-and-see position which would not have yielded the dividends of his bold move.

In the autumn of 2001, the spectacular phase two of Putin's foreign policy seemed to be producing the desired results. It allowed the Russian president to rise immediately to the level of the US administration's privileged partner. Moreover, Putin was able to position himself between the United Kingdom, the United States' closest ally, and most of the other European members of NATO, who could not offer the United States any comparable assistance in Bush's war against world terrorism.

However valuable, Putin's new status in his relations with Bush—as a kind of Blair mark two—came at considerable domestic cost. By insisting on such a close US alignment, Putin took the political risk of provoking a critical reaction from some of his generals. They were highly sensitive to the sight of US troops and experts arriving in Central Asia and the Caucasus, and setting up bases there. For the first time since his triumphant election, Putin saw some signs of opposition from the Communist party and some of the nationalist political groups, which, until then, had given him unconditional support.

One could say that in deciding to join the US-led anti-terrorist coalition (a choice apparently reflecting deep personal conviction), Putin emerged from Yeltsin's shadow and exhibited the qualities of a truly independent political figure and outstanding national statesman. Yet this period also saw the obvious tensions between Putin's internal and external policies develop into an organic conflict between two main policy directions—authoritarian at home and democratic abroad. As these contradictions became more evident, they provoked different interpretations within the major political family groupings about Putin's real intentions and about the ambiguities of his international position and image.

The balance sheet of phase two of Putin's foreign policy was a mixed one. By declaring himself a resolute opponent of global Islamic terrorism, Putin had indeed succeeded in obtaining de facto legitimization of his war in Chechnya, at least as far as US reactions were concerned. Nevertheless, most of his other expectations were not met. The Bush administration literally ignored Moscow's pleas not to withdraw unilaterally from the ABM treaty, and did nothing to slow down the eastward expansion of NATO. As a result, Putin was deprived of arguments he could use to defend his support of the United States and Britain in their military intervention in Iraq without a UN mandate.

That is why, after a period of serious hesitation, and to the great surprise of the Bush administration, Moscow's foreign policy took a sharp turn in March 2003, which marked the start of the third phase of Putin's diplomacy. Together with his colleagues from France and Germany, the Russian Foreign Minister Igor Ivanov signed a joint statement in Paris on 5 March. This formally challenged the US administration and announced that the three co-signatories would not allow the adoption by the UN Security Council of a resolution authorizing the use of force in Iraq.[2]

Joining the 'peace camp', headed by President Chirac, was a particularly difficult decision for Putin. In the heated political context of the preparation for war against Iraq, Chirac was treated by highly placed members of the US administration almost as one of the leaders of the 'axis of evil'. For Putin, choosing between the two camps inside the dramatically split Western family was a far more difficult decision than the one he had made to align with a consolidated West, mobilized behind the US president by its collective fear of a new and ruthless enemy.

To be sure, the Russians had much in common with the French, Germans, and Chinese. They were anxious about the arrogant kind of American unilateralism advocated by the neo-conservative ideologues dominating the Bush administration. All four states were enthusiastic supporters of the conception of a multi-polar world overseen by international law. Conscious of the fact that its veto right in the Security Council represented the last attribute of former superpower status, Moscow unconditionally supported the provisions of the UN Charter, particularly the stipulation that the Security Council was the only body entitled to take decisions concerning the use of force against a sovereign state. The effect of such issues of principle on Moscow's choice to align against the United States in the transatlantic debate was reinforced by the Kremlin's disappointment with its treatment by Washington following the events of 11 September.

This feeling of disappointment was not merely a momentary emotional reaction to Washington's behaviour. It marked the beginning of a deeper process of evaluation by Moscow of its long-term political goals, and especially of the means available to achieve them. In fact, Putin's decision to support the European position, as formulated by the French–German tandem, showed that he was parting with the illusions that had nourished his pro-American alignment. These were based on the supposition that the generous gifts he had offered to his 'friend George' in the wake of the dramatic events of September—intelligence on Afghanistan, access to strategic bridgeheads in Central Asia, logistical support for the Northern Alliance in its offensive on Kabul, and the abolition of former Soviet bases in Vietnam and Cuba—would be enough to secure a really new quality in Russia's relations with the United States. Accepting the role of a 'junior partner', Putin had assumed, would lead to Washington treating Moscow as a privileged strategic partner.

A disillusioned Putin saw alliance with Europe as a far more reliable way to ensure that Russia was treated as a respected and equal partner. Moscow was in a strong position vis-à-vis the Europeans since Chirac and Schroeder desperately needed Russian support for their position in the Security Council. This allowed Putin considerable freedom for manouevre and a chance to reorientate Moscow's

---

[2] See *Moscow Times*, 6 March 2003.

international diplomacy in a more balanced and traditional way, giving due weight not just to Western relations but to its links with the East—with China and the Islamic world. Given the dominant position of Europe as Russia's most important economic partner, the alliance with Paris and Berlin also underlined a shift in overall foreign policy priorities. It highlighted the Russian leadership's growing determination to move from the traditional Soviet model of diplomacy, obsessed with security and centered on the question of the military balance, towards an economically based strategy. And in economic terms, Europe was clearly the highest priority. In 2001 trade between Russia and the United States amounted to €10 billion, while the figure for the EU (€75 billion) was more than seven times that amount.[3]

Last but not least, Putin's decision to join the French and the Germans in opposing the Americans reflected domestic calculations. He saw the European alignment as a way of strengthening his internal position, a particularly important consideration in view of the upcoming parliamentary and presidential elections. By siding against the United States he could kill two birds with one stone. First, he could capitalize on the evident upsurge in popular anti-American sentiments provoked by the preparations for US–British intervention in Iraq. (Polls suggested that such feelings had risen to levels comparable to those during NATO military action against Yugoslavia in 1999.[4]) A pro-European move could improve the president's standing and help neutralize the nationalist-communist opposition. Second, the move served somewhat to rectifying his image in the eyes of the military establishment, which was generally convinced that the concessions made to the United States after the events of 11 September had been unjustified and had failed to yield dividends.

Even this phase in Putin's foreign policy failed to provide a satisfactory answer to the question about his real long-term strategy. After four years in office he had managed to build an international reputation as an able and imaginative politician. In an extremely difficult international context, and despite the continuing war in Chechnya, not only had he managed to secure and consolidate Russia's place in the prestigious G-8, but he had also succeeded in establishing close personal relations with a wide range of foreign leaders, representing quite different and often conflicting political positions. Having joined 'Old Europe' in its stand on Iraq, Putin had succeeded in maintaining close ties with European leaders who supported US policy—Blair, Berlusconi, and Aznar. He had also managed to escape the fury that the White House directed against Paris and Berlin. Putin, by contrast, was 'pardoned' by the US president.[5]

---

[3] Emmanuel Todd, *Après l'empire. Essai sur la décomposition du système américain* (Paris: Folio actuel, 2004), 206.

[4] *New Times* (Moscow), 13 May 2003.

[5] *Enjeux diplomatiques et stratégiques 2004* (Paris: Economica, 2004), 194.

Putin did not limit his diplomacy to building relations with Western states. When, in mid-2003, his plans of building a strategic partnership with the European Union (EU) ran into problems over Kaliningrad and conditions for Russia's entry into the WTO, Putin decided to remind Europe that Russia remained a Eurasian country. He flew to Malaysia to attend a meeting of the Organization of the Islamic Conference. Only days after he had finished listening impassively to Malaysian Prime Minister Mahathir's anti-Semitic tirades in Kuala Lumpur, Putin welcomed Ariel Sharon to Moscow and confirmed his commitment to the 'road map', collectively supported by the United States, EU, UN, and Russia.

Another diplomatic chessboard on which Putin played simultaneously, in professional grandmaster style, was the Chinese one. Concerns in Moscow and Beijing about Washington's dominance, and US criticism of both countries' failures to meet Western democratic standards, provided a natural impetus for Russia and China to cooperate on a variety of efforts concerning international issues. The Chinese had been particularly worried by the spectacular intrusion of the US military into the heart of Central Asia. With the clear intention of reassuring the Chinese leadership on this score, Moscow made special efforts to activate the Shanghai group, an organization concerned with all aspects of security in Central Asia, including militant Islamic activity in the region.[6] Putin also sought to capitalize on economic complementarities between the two countries. During his first term, China consolidated its position as top purchaser of Russian arms exports, including jet aircraft, missiles, submarines, and other military hardware. In addition, Moscow made play of its capacity to provide substantial energy supplies for the growing Chinese economy. In June 2003, Putin signed a strategic energy agreement with Chinese President Hu Jintao, who underscored the importance of the bilateral relationship by visiting Russia on his first trip abroad after taking office. The two states also announced plans to increase annual bilateral trade from $12 billion to $20 billion over the course of five years.[7]

This kind of political manoeuvring served as a temporary substitute for a real foreign policy strategy. Putin's choice to follow flexible tactics and adjust to the different expectations of his foreign partners, should be seen in the context of the constraints imposed by the domestic and international situation inherited from Yeltsin. Putin was limited by the tension between political expectations and material capabilities. On the one hand, there were widespread popular expectations that he would rebuild Russia's prestige and authority on the international scene. On the other, he had to cope with the economic ruin and internal crisis left by the chaos of the Yeltsin administration.

---

[6] The Shanghai Cooperation Organization is a group concerned with developing cooperation on regional security issues. It comprises China and Russia, and four former Soviet Central Asian republics: Kazakhstan, Uzbekistan, Kyrgyzstan, and Turkmenistan.

[7] *Asia Times*, 11 March 2004.

In addition to having to cope with such tangible political and resource restraints, Putin was also limited by the lack of a clear political 'project for Russia'.
He seemed uncertain about how he wanted to develop reforms to rebuild the state:
along historically proven authoritarian lines or along more innovatory yet less
surely tested democratic ones. This unresolved ambivalence in the Russian
president's domestic policy was reflected in his diplomacy. After all, if the priority
was to take the political system further in a democratic direction, then cooperation
with the West had to be directed towards building a strategic alliance. However, if
traditional priorities were uppermost, cooperation was merely a means of taking
advantage of a new kind of détente while Russia recovered from its transition
crisis.

For most of his first term, Putin chose to project conflicting images: one of a
modern politician and democratic reformer of a Western type, the other of a
mildly nationalist and conservative paternalist leader ensuring continuity between
the Soviet past and the post-Communist present. This intended ambiguity
seemed to work quite well, earning the president remarkable popularity in
different political constituencies. Western politicians and Russian liberals ad-
mired the president's reformist face, while the post-Soviet *nomenklatura*, Russian
nationalists, and large parts of the population who longed for the past, were
attracted by his other side. Both tried to convince themselves that the 'real'
Putin was on their side, and simply forced by circumstances to conceal his true
convictions. (It goes without saying that Putin's early professional training and
experience qualified him well for giving a convincing Janus-faced performance.)

Even though Putin made no spectacular political mistakes in the management of his foreign policy, there were some obvious failures. Some can be seen
as self-inflicted diplomatic defeats, stemming in part from an inflated sense of
Russia's capacity to influence its partners. They include the failure to secure
EU recognition of the unique status of Kaliningrad, to contain NATO's
eastward enlargement, and to persuade the US administration to preserve the
ABM treaty.

Other setbacks came in areas where tactical manoeuvre could not compensate
for the lack of well-conceived strategy. This was particularly the case in Russia's
relations with its 'near abroad', the Commonwealth of Independent States (CIS).
Having abandoned hopes of reinvigorating the CIS, Putin's conduct of diplomatic
relations with the former Soviet republics developed into exercises in 'variable
geometry'. Moscow applied a range of political standards and used different
political, military, and economic incentives and pressures in its dealings with
the various members of the Commonwealth.

An underlying reason for such variation was the fact that Russia's policy
towards these newly independent states was based on the tacit assumption that
their final international status still remained to be negotiated with Moscow. In a
number of cases the explanation lay in the incapacity of the Kremlin and the
government to formulate a clear policy. This left the conduct of policy in the hands

of the General Staff and military commanders, who were concerned above all with maintaining of Russia's 'strategic presence' in the former Soviet space. The most striking example of such 'delegated diplomacy' was in relations with Georgia. Here the sensitive issue of the presence of Russian troops and bases was aggravated by the close proximity of the 'bleeding wound' of Chechnya.

The ups and downs in Russia's policy towards Georgia, as with most of the other former republics now in the CIS, reflected the Kremlin's uncertainties on the domestic front. Moscow preferred to not to make any final decisions on how to conduct relations with its neighbours until it was in a position to make a choice between an assertive policy or the more moderate approach typical of relations within regional organizations like the EU; some combination of the two strategies was also an option. This hesitation reflected as much a lack of assurance on Moscow's part of its real capacity to impose its will as it did differences within the presidential team about the way forward, or general uncertainty about the possible reaction of Russia's Western partners.

Notwithstanding the mixed quality of the foreign policy record of his first term, Putin could certainly claim credit for the fact that he had succeeded in transforming his tactical approach into a real strategic asset, and had gained time without making any irrevocable policy decisions. He could claim that he had thus secured for Russia the chance to make a strategic choice once it had overcome its transition crisis and recovered its economic strength. Moscow would then be in a position to replace reactive diplomacy with a truly sovereign foreign policy.

The 'Putin Doctrine'

Putin started his second presidential term largely freed from the constraints of the first, yet also deprived of the alibis the earlier limitations had provided. His current foreign policy can no longer be considered to be the result of compromises, imposed on him by a fragile balance of domestic political forces, and by the pressure of strong external forces on a dependent Moscow. Russia is obviously no longer the 'sick man' of world politics. Over the last four years, Putin has gained considerable personal experience and is no longer dependent on the people and circumstances that propelled him to the Kremlin in 1999. The unchallenged nature of his authority was shown by the impressive victory of the pro-presidential party, United Russia, in the parliamentary elections of December 2003. It was confirmed and highlighted by his triumphant re-election to office in March 2004.

One can therefore interpret the current phase in Russia's foreign policy as reflecting Putin's conscious and relatively untrammelled choice. This is a conclusion reinforced by the considerable narrowing, in recent months, of the embarrassingly wide gap which previously divided the president's foreign and domestic policies. Even in the absence of any official document since the elections setting out the strategic orientation of Russian foreign policy, there are enough elements to identify and assess the essential characteristics of what may be called the Putin Doctrine.

To be sure, this line of policy reflects not only the evolution of Russian society during Putin's first term. In a more general sense it reflects developments over the course of the whole post-Soviet period and the experience accumulated by Russia in its relations with foreign partners. Remarkably, after a decade of dramatic transformations, the new Russia that is emerging seems to be closer to its historical traditions and to some features of the Soviet state than it was at the initial stage of reforms. These features include the return of nationalist sentiments and anti-Western reflexes; growing popular support for an authoritarian regime; mistrust of democratic institutions and procedures; and the obvious marginalization of liberal, democratic, and Western-oriented political parties and tendencies. According to Alexey Arbatov, one of the leaders of the liberal Yabloko party, which failed to secure representation in the new Russian parliament, the radically or moderately anti-Western forces that dominate the new State Duma will press the president to move in that direction.[8]

The autumn 2003 election campaign saw various parts of the Russian political elite trying to ride the rising wave of popular nostalgia for the past greatness of the Soviet state and so influence Putin's new diplomatic agenda. The leaders of the left-wing nationalist party, Rodina, took a 'patriotic' line, hailing the return of a 'strong Russia'; Anatoly Chubais, one of the chairmen of the ultra-liberal Union of Right Forces, promoted the merits of a 'liberal empire'. All of this was accompanied by expressions of apparent concern for the interests of ethnic Russians throughout the former Soviet space, which signalled a far more assertive approach to relations with the countries of the 'near abroad'.

The other new feature of Russian political life, and one that has undoubtedly influenced the reformulation of foreign policy, is a marked increase in national self-confidence. This is the result, on the one hand, of an impressive rise in registered economic growth, especially in the strategically vital energy sector. On the other hand, this new self-assurance reflects the Kremlin's belief that the new international context, particularly the scale of the Islamic terrorist threat, means that Russia is of new and greater value for the West. One of the leaders of the liberal Union of Right Forces, Boris Nemtsov, put it in the following way: 'Putin apparently expects that Russia's role in settling global crises will shield him from US criticism. The Kremlin hopes that the fight against terrorism will overshadow all other problems'.[9]

In terms of actual policy, the emerging 'Putin Doctrine' has been evident in at least two main spheres. First, in Moscow's behaviour towards the former Soviet republics, the new states that make up Russia's 'near abroad'. Second, it has come

[8] *Moscow News*, 5 January 2004.   [9] *Nezavisimaya gazeta*, 20 December 2003.

through in the changing tone of Russia's relations with the West, with important nuances distinguishing Moscow's policy towards the United States from its dealings with Europe. Given its bi-continental Eurasian presence, Russia cannot, of course, confine its diplomacy to North America and Europe. For the time being, however, its policies towards China and Japan, let alone the revival of any kind of global strategy, remain relatively undeveloped.

The 'Near Abroad'

The former Soviet space has a good chance of becoming the first testing ground for Putin's new foreign policy. As it has regained economic and political weight, so the former superpower has started to flex its muscles. It is probably just a matter of time before Moscow will find it appropriate to reassert its presence in a geo-strategic zone that many in the Kremlin certainly continue to consider Russia's natural sphere of influence. However, the basic question remains— what means will Moscow use to achieve its goals? Will it employ coercive, 'imperial' pressure and make use of local pro-Russian elites and Russian-speaking minorities. Or will it use 'soft power' giving priority to economic and financial instruments as well as the exercise of political pressure? In all probability, Moscow will use a combination of the two. 'We have no intention to subjugate the former Soviet space', declared Russian Defence Minister Sergey Ivanov in Paris in March 2004. 'Neither do we want to exercise military pressure here. Yet, from the point of view of security, our closest neighbours, the countries of the CIS, are of crucial importance for us.'[10]

The need to find policy solutions for problems in the south of the CIS is made more urgent by the fact that internal instability in some of the Caucasian and Central Asian states make them sources of real security threats for Moscow. Conditions in some 'failed states' open them to use as bases for international terrorist activities or as channels for arms and drugs trafficking into Russia. In other cases it is not a matter of direct security threats, but one of dangers posed to Russia's strategic economic interests, in the shape of oil and gas fields or pipelines. Moscow often feels it necessary to respond to what it sees as attempts by neighbouring states (Turkey, China) or by Western powers, above all the United States, to take advantage of the strategic and political vacuum created by Russia's retreat from the region.

One of the most troublesome cases for Moscow has been that of Georgia— Russia's traditional forward post in the Transcaucasus. Relations with the newly independent state, headed by the former Soviet Foreign Minister Eduard She-vardnadze, started to deteriorate in the Yeltsin era. This was of course the result of the first Chechen war and the obvious intention of the Russian leadership to exercise leverage over Tblisi by means of hardly veiled assistance to the separatist

---

[10] *Le Figaro*, 6–7 March 2004.

leaders of Abkhazia, Adjaria, and South Ossetia. In fact, Georgian–Russian relations were doomed to fall victim to an unfortunate combination of three strategic factors. First, the states shared a common border which was also the frontier with Chechnya. Second, Russia promised to withdraw its military bases from Georgia according to the Istanbul agreements of 1999 at the OSCE summit. Third, there were contentious economic issues, especially relating to the decision of Azerbaijani authorities and a consortium of Western investors to build the Baku–Tbilisi–Ceyhan pipeline to transfer Caspian oil to the Mediterranean, thus circumventing Russian territory.

With Putin's arrival in the Kremlin and the beginning of the second Chechen war, relations took a further downward turn. This was partly the result of Shevardnadze's attempt to trade off the rear bases of the Chechen rebels on Georgian territory (in the Pankisi Gorge) against Russia's support for Abkhazian separatists. Relations also deteriorated in part because of Shevardnadze's declared intention to bring Georgia into NATO. After the events of 11 September, Shevardnadze tried to neutralize Russian pressure and ensure US security guarantees by inviting US military experts to Georgia to help Tblisi in its struggle against terrorist infiltration. However, Shevardnadze failed in both projects and was eventually removed from the political scene, falling victim to the apparently spontaneous 'rose revolution'. The alleged role that the United States played behind the scenes in encouraging the Georgian opposition to topple Shevardnadze raised Moscow's hackles. Russia's foreign minister, Igor Ivanov, went so far as to accuse the United States of secretly helping to orchestrate the ouster of the Georgian president, naming US Ambassador Richard M. Miles as the main agent involved in the exercise.[11]

Georgia became a key test for the much proclaimed general cooperation between Moscow and Washington in an area which Russia continued to see as falling within its sphere of strategic interest. Washington took steps to increase its public support for Georgia. Donald Rumsfeld, the US Secretary for Defence, visited Tblisi and George W. Bush made a highly publicized phone call to the interim president Mikhail Saakashvili in which he promised to intervene, if necessary, to uphold Georgia's 'sovereignty, independence and territorial integrity'. In response to these US moves, Putin held a meeting in Moscow with leaders of the three Georgian separatist provinces.[12]

Russia's more assertive policy towards its southern 'near abroad' reflects the Kremlin's determination to protect its security interests and even to challenge US advances in an area where Putin welcomed US engagement in the aftermath of the 11 September attacks. And this shift in policy relates not only to the Caucasian section of Russia's 'soft underbelly', but extends to Central Asia. In December 2004 Putin and his minister of defence, Sergey Ivanov, opened the new Russian airbase in Kyrgyzstan, located only miles from the US facility which Washington

[11] *New Times* (Moscow), 15 December 2003.   [12] Ibid.

had established to support its military action in Afghanistan. Ivanov took the opportunity to remind his audience that, in accordance with the UN mandate, NATO military bases were deployed in Uzbekistan and Kyrgyzstan only for the duration of operations in Afghanistan and not for any 'further period of time'.[13] The fact that the Russian defence minister did not take the trouble to consult the leaders of the independent states concerned before pronouncing on such questions is symptomatic of Moscow's clear intention to reassert its leading role in the region.

The recent shifts in Moscow's policy in the south, and the new tone in its political dialogue with Washington, could intensify geopolitical rivalry between Russia and the United States in the Caucasus and Central Asia. As Russia resumes its traditional Eurasian game of recolonizing the former Soviet space, it could come into conflict with the Americans, especially if Washington confirms that it considers Central Asia and Transcaucasia, including the Caspian Basin, to be zones of 'strategic interest'.

In the troubled 'near abroad' of the south, Moscow has little hesitation about using military force to further its new and more aggressive policies. On occasion, it has borrowed the language used by the Bush administration, justifying the preventive use of force in the fight against international terrorism. With regard to its Western neighbours, however, Moscow has relied mainly on economic and political levers. To be sure, in the case of delayed evacuation of the former Soviet military base in Transdniestria, the Russian position has been as rigid as on the question of the remaining Russian bases in Georgia. But in its dealings with Kiev and Minsk, the main way in which Moscow has sought to assert its strategic influence has been to make use of dependence on Russian oil and gas and the growing participation of Russian capital in the privatization of key sectors of these states' economies.

It is quite significant, though, that Russia's concerns about its 'economic security', and ways of safeguarding it, are often voiced by representatives of the military. In an interview he gave to *Le Figaro* in March 2004, Sergey Ivanov declared: 'We are going to use all measures to ensure our economic security and preserve our economic and energy interests. This concerns the whole CIS and particularly Belarus.'[14] This was not the first occasion on which the Russian minister of defence had commented on these issues. In October 2003, at a press conference in Yekaterinburg, in the presence of the Russian president and the visiting German chancellor, Gerhard Schroeder, Sergey Ivanov stated that Russia reserved the right to intervene militarily within the CIS in order to settle disputes that could not be resolved through negotiation. At the same press conference, Putin declared that the pipelines carrying oil and natural gas to the West had been built by the Soviet Union and it was Russia's prerogative to maintain them in

---

[13] *Nezavisimaya gazeta*, 15 December 2003.   [14] *Le Figaro*, 6–7 March 2004.

order to protect its national interests, and this right extended even to those parts of the system that were 'beyond Russia's borders.'[15]

One example of this type of new 'economic diplomacy' was the decision by Gazprom, Russia's state-controlled gas company, to suspend sales to Belarus at domestic Russian prices from the end of 2003. The major Russian companies supplying natural gas to Belarus cut off shipments, accusing the authorities in Minsk of illegally siphoning off gas. At the beginning of February 2004, Unified Energy Systems of Russia announced an increase of 28 per cent in the price of the electricity it was selling to Belarus.[16]

Even the Baltic states, right up to their entry into the EU and NATO, felt the effects of Moscow's new and more 'muscular' policy. They were subject to the combined pressure of more active defence by Moscow of ethnic Russian minorities, its use of the smaller states' dependence on Russian energy exports, and hardly veiled threats from the Russian defence minister about reassessing Moscow's nuclear strategy. Ivanov hinted, in March 2004, at the possible deployment of tactical nuclear weapons in the region of Kaliningrad.[17]

Putin can count on solid support for a far more aggressive approach to asserting Russian interests in the 'near abroad' for at least two reasons. First, the results of the Duma and presidential elections strengthened his position and signalled, among other things, popular indifference to Western criticism of the human rights situation in Russia and Moscow's ruthless military tactics in Chechnya. Second, Putin's inner circle of *siloviki*, the majority of whom come from the former Soviet security and defence apparatus, clearly consider it both desirable and feasible, especially in the present international context, to transform the 'near abroad' into a bastion of Russian influence.

However, as a pragmatist, Putin will probably continue to avoid confrontations he cannot win. Despite Ivanov's 'muscular' rhetoric, there is very little likelihood of any direct military confrontation with NATO or the United States. Russia remains economically weak, a poor country with an extremely limited capacity to project military force beyond its borders. The performance of Russian troops in Chechnya has highlighted, in humiliating fashion, the sheer inadequacy of Moscow's military capacities. Equally improbable is the prospect of the construction in the foreseeable future of any effective anti–Western alliance. Nothing came or is likely to come of the 'strategic triangle' of Russia, China, and India, an idea first promoted by Yevgeny Primakov when he was foreign minister, and now raised by some nationalists, notably Dmitry Rogozin, a leading figure in the Rodina party which attracted considerable support in the December 2003 elections.

Despite the fact that he has described the collapse of the Soviet Union as 'a national tragedy on an enormous scale',[18] Putin does not believe in the possibility

[15] *Kommersant*, 19 October 2003.
[16] *New Times* (Moscow), 5 February 2004.
[17] *Le Figaro*, 6–7 March 2004.
[18] *Kommersant*, 13 February 2004.

of restoring the Soviet Union, still less the former Communist empire that extended beyond its borders. At times, the Russian president might well see himself as being in a situation comparable to that of Lenin after the signature of the humiliating Treaty of Brest-Litovsk with Germany in 1918. But Putin clearly understands that the former Soviet Union is gone forever. The only and very partial way in which the Russian president has sought to replay recent history has been his effort to try and reintegrate the former Soviet republics on an economic basis. In September 2003 Russia, Ukraine, Belarus, and Kazakhstan signed an agreement to establish 'a common economic space'.[19]

Russian Oil and US Bases

Economic factors have also figured prominently in Putin's conduct of relations with the 'far abroad' and particularly with the United States. Russia's oil wealth, together with its security resources, enhanced by Washington's war against terrorism, have both been major strategic assets in Putin's conduct of relations with Bush. In early 2002, for the first time in twenty-two years, Russia overtook Saudi Arabia to become the world's top producer of crude oil.[20] Russia's importance as a source of energy supplies for the world market rose considerably as a result of the discovery of significant new oil and gas reserves in the Caspian Basin. The serious rift in US–Saudi relations in the wake of the events of 11 September further increased the strategic value of Russia as future energy supplier. According to the US ambassador to Moscow, Alexander Vershbow, an America looking to reduce dependence on Middle East oil might be interested, within the next decade or so, in purchasing significant amounts of Russian oil.[21]

US government and corporate expectations of growing economic involvement with Russia, both through the purchase of energy supplies and by way of strategic investment, help to explain the hypersensitivity with which Washington has reacted to the 'Yukos affair'. It would otherwise be rather difficult to explain why, having weathered Putin's war in Chechnya and Bush's war in Iraq, US–Russian relations started to seriously deteriorate after the sudden arrest, on 25 October 2003, of Mikhail Khodorkovsky, the Yukos chief executive and main shareholder. The White House, usually careful when commenting on Putin's domestic affairs, did not hesitate to express 'serious concerns' about the campaign against the oil giant, contending that this could call into question Russia's commitment to the rule of law and could jeopardize the investment climate. 'Strategic cooperation remains important', declared a senior state department official days after Khodorkovsky's arrest, but the relationship had to be based in part on 'a sense that Russia is moving in the direction of democratization,

---

[19] *Enjeux diplomatiques* (n. 5), 194.
[20] Production reached 7.28 million barrels per day, ibid., 186.
[21] He spoke in terms of 'about ten percent'; see interview in *Moscow Times*, 15 November 2003.

of the establishment of a country based on similar values to ours. And that is where there are some serious question marks in the current situation'.[22]

The results of the Duma elections, which confirmed the strengthening of anti-Western and even nationalist sentiments within the Russian political elite, did nothing to defuse the tension that started to appear in official diplomatic and military rhetoric. US officials started to talk about the danger of a 'breach of values' in the partnership with Russia that could 'limit possibilities for the expansion of cooperation.'[23] At the same time, references began to appear in Russian semi-official publications to a 'crisis of confidence' that could signal the end of the 'new era' in US–Russian relations.[24]

A clear indication of the new climate in Moscow came in a speech by Minister of Defence Sergey Ivanov in October 2003: 'We cannot absolutely rule out the preventive use of force (outside Russian borders) if Russia's interests or its obligations as an ally make this necessary.'[25] This point did not find its way into any formal policy document nor was it explicitly endorsed by Putin. But the fact that the Russian president did not disavow the statement, nor explicitly temper it in any way, can also be interpreted as a deliberate warning signal to Russia's Western partners, above all the United States. The image Putin projected during the 2004 election campaign pointed in the same direction. Instead of participating in television debates with his supposed rivals, the president preferred to appear in uniform on the deck of a ballistic missile submarine to observe the largest military exercises in twenty years. Moreover, the escalation of tensions continued, at least at the rhetorical level. In December 2003, Sergey Ivanov announced that the strategic Topol–M missile force would be put on alert.[26] This measure marked a reversal in the trend, which had prevailed in the Yeltsin period, towards lower levels of military stand-off.

To be sure, such sabre-rattling statements, even when made by highly placed defence officials like Ivanov, do not necessarily denote an official policy change. The president himself, visibly comforted by his triumphant re-election to a second term, has gone out of his way to take a moderate line and has made a number of reassuring statements about the favourable prospects for Russia's cooperation with its Western partners.[27]

Perhaps because Washington was impressed by the scale of Putin's electoral victory, the United States toned down its criticism of Russia's democratic credentials. Soon after the elections, Elizabeth Jones, assistant secretary of state for European and Eurasian Affairs, noted that with 'a strong popular mandate and a sizeable working majority in the Duma, President Putin is well positioned to press

[22] *Interfax*, 30 October 2003.   [23] *Moscow News*, 15 December 2003.
[24] Vladimir Simonov, *RIA-Novosti*, 15 November 2003.
[25] *Le Figaro*, 25 October 2003.
[26] *RIA Novosti*, 22 December 2003.   [27] *Le Figaro*, 5 April 2004.

a programme of substantial economic reform. There is a direct connection between Russia's integration into the world trading system and internal reforms. Rule of law, respect for the sanctity of contracts, independence and the effectiveness of the judiciary, and curbing government corruption are all part of what is needed for Russia to become a major destination for investment.'[28]

Such politically correct public statements reflect the post–Cold War climate of relations that both Russia and the United States will probably continue to foster. Even so, moves by strategic and military planners have contributed to an increase in mistrust and mutual suspicion. For instance, announcements about the possible transfer of US military bases from Germany to Eastern Europe (Poland, Hungary, Bulgaria, and Romania) play into the hands of those nationalist and anti-Western forces in Russia which see in them confirmation of their theories about the threat of strategic encirclement of Russia by a hostile West. Some Russian specialists on strategic affairs have viewed with suspicion plans to locate military bases along the perimeter of Russia's borders, and especially at critical energy export points, whether on the Poland–Belarus border or near the Bulgarian port of Burgas on the Black Sea. They detect in such plans a malicious design on Washington's part to establish control over Russia's energy resources, the former superpower's last remaining hope for regaining its world status.[29]

The Russian military, on their part, presumably feel quite happy with such plans since they bolster their case for rebuilding Russia's capabilities to match a growing 'external threat.' For Russian liberals, who favour closer relations with the West, any hint of a return to the logic of a futile arms race augurs badly for the internal democratic reforms they support. As Alexey Arbatov, one of the leaders of the liberal Yabloko party (which failed to get elected to the new Duma), has observed: 'The West [meaning above all the United States] has not even made tactical concessions to Russia to secure good strategic relations for the years ahead. Western policy toward Russia has helped strengthen anti-Western, nationalist sentiments.'[30]

Between Europe and Eurasia

In the Soviet era, Moscow's efforts to court Europe usually coincided with downturns in its relations with Washington. During the cold war, political manoeuvres of this kind were usually ineffective and often, as in the case of the Euromissiles, proved counterproductive. In the new post-Soviet era, the European vector of Russian diplomacy has been driven by different motives and has opened up promising prospects for closer and more substantial relations.

---

[28] *Moscow Times*, 20 March 2004.
[29] Fedor Lukyanov, *Nezavisimaya gazeta*, 5 January 2004.
[30] *Moscow News*, 5 January 2004.

Russian policy towards the United States is driven partly by the nostalgia of Soviet-era veterans and partly by the ambitions and complexes of the new nationalists. Both groups dream of achieving a privileged partner/rival status for Moscow vis-à-vis Washington. The factors driving policy towards Europe are very different. Here the Russian president finds himself responding to his country's practical and real capabilities and needs. Having spent more than ten years of his career as a KGB officer in East Germany, Putin is clearly attuned to the 'appeal' of Europe. As a medium-sized regional power with limited economic and military (and demographic) potential, Russia is interested in a political alliance with Europe in order jointly to contain US unilateralism, especially in the ideologically domineering form practised by the Bush administration. In economic terms, Russia is increasingly becoming a de facto part of the EU's 'near abroad'. This process of integration is being driven by growing Russian gas and oil supplies to Western Europe, the ever-increasing dominance of the EU in Russia's trade balance, and Moscow's hopes of attracting major West European investment.[31]

Cooperation between Russia and the EU has also developed in the area of security relations. There have been discussions about establishing a permanent EU–Russia mechanism to complement the Russia-NATO Council established in May 2002. This is a project that represents a modernized version of the proposal for a collective system of European security put forward jointly by Gorbachev and Mitterrand in 1990, on the occasion of the signature of the Paris Charter for Europe. In its new form, this idea has once again become part of the official Russia–EU agenda.[32]

The prospects for Russia's long-term partnership with Europe do not seem to have been automatically improved by the end of the strategic 'honeymoon' between Moscow and Washington (even if there is no talk yet of this setback leading to divorce). From a European perspective, the apparent breach by Moscow of its notional agreement to abide by certain values only adds to the difficulties of selling partnership with Russia to publics already critical of Russia's conduct of the Chechen war. The problem of divergent norms may become an insuperable one if Putin's second term confirms the authoritarian evolution of the current political regime. There is far greater concern in Europe than in the pragmatic United States about the political direction of Russian domestic development. Washington has long been accustomed to overlooking the nature of the regimes that it finds useful to bring into various ad hoc coalitions against its declared adversaries.

---

[31] The 'strategic partnership' between Russia and the EU proclaimed by Putin and Romano Prodi envisages an increase of the EU share in Russia's trade balance, from 37 per cent in 2002 to 50 per cent in 2005. The energy sector represents 65 per cent of Russia's exports to the EU. See *Enjeux* (n. 5), 195.

[32] *Le Figaro*, 6–7 March 2004.

There are of course many issues on which Russia and the EU disagree. They include the conditions of Russia's membership of the WTO and Putin's proposal for a visa-free regime between the EU and Russia. Putin's choice of Mikhail Fradkov, Moscow's former representative in Brussels, as prime minister may be taken as an indication of the importance the president attaches to the need for the government to give priority to resolving outstanding issues in relations with the EU.[33]

The more fundamental problems in Russia's relations with Europe cannot be resolved simply by bargaining about export tariffs, internal energy prices, or agricultural subsidies. For the Europeans, strategic decisions on policy towards Russia depend on their willingness to bank on Russia's future development. Differences on this question could split Europe into 'old' and 'new', almost as dramatically as the war in Iraq divided European states in their policies towards the United States. The 'old' Europeans, above all the French and the Germans, relieved at having been freed from the Soviet threat, regard the new Russia as a promising factor that will allow an integrated Europe to enhance its strategic autonomy and even compete with the United States. By contrast, the 'new' Europeans, from the ex-Communist states of the east, remember the problems of their historic coexistence with their great Eurasian 'brother' and believe there are reasons for serious concern about the new Russia.

The results of the Russian parliamentary and presidential elections, and especially the way in which they were organized, along with Moscow's new assertive line towards its 'near abroad', confirm two facts in the eyes of the eastern Europeans: the rise of nationalist currents inside Russia and Putin's apparent authoritarian tendencies. They are not worried about dangers of a military attack. As former Polish Defence Minister Janusz Onyszkiewicz has put it: 'Direct armed engagement is not likely for at least the next decade. A greater concern is Russia's attitude toward the unstable and collapsing states on its borders.'[34]

For the same reasons, news about Russia's economic recovery in recent years as well as the favourable projections for its further economic growth is received very differently in the western and eastern parts of Europe. While western politicians and businessmen see the relatively high growth rates as an encouraging sign of greater Russian stability and predictability as an energy supplier and potential investment opportunity, their eastern colleagues note the growth of Russia's defence budget with some apprehension.[35] They are worried that Russia could 'revert to using its oil-and-gas concerns not as commercial enterprises but as instruments of foreign policy.'[36]

---

[33] It is likely that Putin's choice of Sergey Lavrov, the Russian representative at the UN, as foreign minister was meant to send a signal to Washington, albeit one of a very different kind from that given to Brussels by Fradkov's promotion.

[34] *Le Monde*, 25 February 2004.					[35] *Enjeux* (n. 5), 190.

[36] Janusz Onyszkiewicz, *Le Monde*, 25 February 2004.

The 'new' Europeans blame the 'old' for their naive stance of appeasement towards the unpredictable Russian giant whose 'innate' imperial reflexes they believe they know only too well. It was largely under the pressure of the 'new' Europeans that the European Commission published an unusually frank critique in February 2004 of different aspects of Russian policy, ranging from its 'more assertive stance' towards the former Soviet states to its failure to resolve the conflict in Chechnya.[37] This was probably an attempt to repair some of the damage caused by the total solidarity shown by the then chairman of the EU, Silvio Berlusconi, towards his friend Putin over Chechnya and the Khodorkovsky affair.

The controversy within Europe about Russia and its future course of development points up the basic dilemma facing Putin in conducting Moscow's relations with the outside world. There is no doubt that the Russian president has shown great dexterity in handling Russia's external relations in a very difficult period. Russia's weakness and the crisis of transition constrained Moscow from having much more than a reactive foreign policy. Using a chess analogy, one could give the president credit for the skill and effectiveness with which he has played his version of 'Putin's defence'.

What he faces at the beginning of his second mandate may well be a much harder test: an exercise in managing Russia's return to economic health and strategic independence. If Putin fails to resist the temptation to return to the reflexes of superpower behavior (even though Russia lacks the requisite might) or succumbs to the pressure of the patriotic and nationalist forces that have rallied around him, he will be held responsible for the reversal of Russia's journey away from its past. If, on the contrary, he manages to give Russia a new confidence and prosperity without transforming it into an actual or perceived threat to the outside world, he will help create conditions for its advance towards the future it deserves. In either case, he will have no one else to thank or to blame. Having secured absolute political power, the president will have to accept sole responsibility for the choice that is made.

---

[37] *Nezavisimaya gazeta*, 12 February 2004.

An Annotated Bibliography of Published Work by Archie Brown

Julie Newton

To read Archie Brown's complete works from the mid-1960s to the present day is a highly rewarding intellectual journey. Not only does that journey shed penetrating light on the nature of the Soviet Union, on that country's remarkable transition from Communism, and on post-Soviet Russia's ambiguous process of democratization, it also takes us back to the eighteenth-century Russian Enlightenment, advances our understanding of key concepts in political science, and throws light on issues in contemporary British politics.

This bibliographical journey demonstrates the 'historical benefits of reform over revolution'. It helps us to think precisely and clearly about democracy. And it alerts us to the long-term risks of neglecting the all-important task of building, and maintaining, the foundations of democracy in Russia.

The following annotations are divided into nine thematic categories, each arranged chronologically. Constraints of space have made it impossible to annotate all of Brown's published work.

Links Between the Scottish and Russian Enlightenments

This category includes Brown's earliest work on how the ideas of Adam Smith and other Scottish Enlightenment thinkers made their way to Moscow and to the St Petersburg Court of Catherine the Great via two Russians, Desnitsky and Tret'yakov, who studied at Glasgow University. Desnitsky proposed that the Russian Court implement a radical reform of the senate, turning it into an electoral body, and also advocated the rule of law, separation of powers, and just taxation. Had the Empress implemented the political changes that Desnitsky advocated—she accepted only the economic aspects of his proposals—this might have set Russia on the path towards constitutional monarchy.

'S. Ye. Desnitsky i I. A. Tret'yakov v Glazgovskom universitete (1761–1767)' (S. E. Desnitsky and I. A. Tretyakov in Glasgow University (1761–1767)) in *Vestnik Moskovskogo Universiteta (Istoriya)*, 4 (July–August 1969), 75–88

276 *Julie Newton*

'S. E. Desnitsky, Adam Smith and the *Nakaz* of Catherine II' in *Oxford Slavonic Papers*, New Series, 7 (1974), 42–59

Imperial Russia sent Semyon Desnitsky to Glasgow University from 1761 to 1767, where he studied under Adam Smith, John Millar, and others. Returning to Russia in 1767, he addressed Empress Catherine a 'Proposal', advocating economic reforms and the separation of legislative, judicial, and executive authorities. Desnitsky envisioned 'gradual development towards constitutional monarchy' along the British model (49). Although some of Desnitsky's tax proposals (based on Smithian economic ideas) appeared in Catherine's *Nakaz*, she could not accept the 'numerous suggestions aimed at reducing the power of . . . the autocrat herself' (59). This is the first piece of research to have traced the path by which Scottish Enlightenment ideas found their way into the *Nakaz*. The *Nakaz* did not have a big impact on the actual way in which Russia was governed . . .

'Adam Smith's First Russian Followers' in A. S. Skinner and T. Wilson (eds.), *Essays on Adam Smith* (Oxford: Clarendon Press, 1975), 247–73

This article examines Adam Smith's and John Millar's economic and political influence on Desnitsky, who was innovative-minded himself. But it also provides lively detail about the life of Desnitsky (and his fellow student, Ivan Tret'yakov) in Glasgow, and includes amusing details of a fight, when Desnitsky got angry and pulled off a Professor's wig, almost sending Desnitsky packing back to Russia. Adam Smith also comes alive in this article as a popular and enthusiastic lecturer, who inspired the two Russian students to try to spread his ideas in Russia. Catherine the Great thus became the 'third person in the Russian empire to be influenced by Smithian economic ideas'.

'The Father of Russian Jurisprudence: The Legal Thought of S. E. Desnitsky' in William E. Butler (ed.), *Russian Law: Historical and Political Perspectives* (Leyden: Sijthoff, 1977), 117–41

Today, as Russia struggles to institutionalize a 'rule of law', it is opportune to rediscover 'the father of Russian jurisprudence'. Returning from Glasgow University, Desnitsky promoted Russian legal reform. He called for a 'short manual of all-Russian law' to be published for 'the public knowledge of all', and proposed fundamental change in the university teaching of law. In Russia, such new ideas posed a 'radical challenge to the status quo' (140). Like his Scottish Enlightenment mentors, Desnitsky 'employed a comparative-historical approach to the study of jurisprudence and this, in turn, was rooted in a theory of development of modes of subsistence, to which political and legal developments could be related.'

Czechoslovakia, 1963–1968, and Eastern Europe under Soviet Power

These articles on Czechoslovak reforms were among the first in the West to detect and examine pluralist trends in Czechoslovak political development. Brown's analysis benefited from a 1965 visit to Prague on an academic exchange between

Glasgow and Charles universities. He made good contacts, notably with Zdeněk Mlynář, the leading theoretician of the Prague Spring, whose knowledge remained important to Brown years later. This early work on Czechoslovakia displays the meticulous research, dispassionate thinking, and broad analytical framework that distinguish this entire bibliography.

'Pluralistic Trends in Czechoslovakia', *Soviet Studies*, 17/4 (April 1966), 453–72

This article, published two years before the Prague Spring, assesses the nature and extent of change in Czechoslovak social, political, economic, cultural, and academic life. Of greatest significance for the future, the article predicts, will be further changes in the political arena. 'A wider section of Czechoslovakian society is beginning to air its views on political development. If governmental action is closely to correspond to these trends in opinion it is likely that . . . [there will be] a further divergence from the Soviet political structure . . .' (472). By 1968, those trends blossomed into the 'Prague Spring', which would have institutionalized that 'divergence' from the Soviet model, had it not been stopped by Soviet tanks.

'Political Change in Czechoslovakia', *Government and Opposition*, 4/2 (Spring 1969), 169–94 (reprinted in Leonard Schapiro (ed.), *Political Opposition in One-Party States* (London: Macmillan, 1972), 110–37

In analysing the dynamics of change, Brown emphasizes the importance of leadership in driving 'reform from above'. He demonstrates the underlying power of ideas, embodied by influential intellectuals and academic specialists, capable of radicalizing the leadership's political and economic goals. He also asserts that economic reform required political reform. And he points to the importance of political culture in analysing change and assessing trends.

'Changes within the Czechoslovak Communist Party, 1963–68' in V. V. Kusin (ed.), *The Czechoslovak Reform Movement 1968* (London: International Research Documents, 1973), 132–9

(with G. Wightman) 'Changes in the Levels of Membership and Social Composition of the Communist Party of Czechoslovakia, 1945–73' in *Soviet Studies*, 27/3 (July 1975), 396–417

This detailed analysis helps to focus attention on the wider significance of changing Party membership as a source of future problems for Czechoslovakia's Communist system. Ageing membership, youth apathy, and worker passivity are indicators of possible trouble ahead.

Political Culture and Comparative Politics

It is clear from his early work on the subject that Archie Brown's mid-1960s experience in Prague, meeting Czechoslovak reformers, led him to think deeply about the relevance of political culture. As he wrote in 1984, culture would become especially relevant—given the dissonance between official and dominant cultures in Eastern Europe—in the event of political or economic crisis. Five years later in 1989, events appeared to bear this out. Archie draws attention to the mutual interaction between political institutions and culture, and highlights the key role of political leadership and control over institutions in bringing about change.

Political Culture and Political Change in Communist States, co-editor with Jack Gray (London: Macmillan; New York: Holmes and Meier, 1977). Author of ch. 1, 'Introduction', 1–24; and, with Gordon Wightman, of ch. 6, 'Czechoslovakia: Revival and Retreat', 159–96; 2nd edn., 1979. Spanish edition, *Cultura y cambios políticos en los estados communistas* (Mexico City: Editorial Ell Manual Moderno, S.A. 1980)

The objective of this seminal volume is 'to relate political culture to political *change* or *continuity* . . .' in Communist states. It favours a 'narrow' definition of political culture in terms of 'subjective orientations' (such as beliefs, values), excluding behaviour. It also highlights the difficulties of official efforts to transform dominant cultures in Eastern Europe. The chapter on Czechoslovakia, co-authored by Archie Brown and Gordon Wightman, highlights the element of cultural continuity: after twenty years of Soviet-style Communist domination, Czechs described the inter-war period of pluralist democracy as the 'most glorious in their history' (164).

Political Culture and Communist Studies, ed. (London: Macmillan, 1984; Armonk, NY: M. E. Sharpe, 1985). Author of ch. 1, 'Introduction', 1–12; ch. 5, 'Soviet Political Culture through Soviet Eyes',100–14; and ch. 8, 'Conclusions', 149–204

This edited volume distinguishes between official and societally dominant political cultures, and stresses the long-term importance of the 'dissonance' between those cultures in Communist countries. Brown argues that 'official culture' *can* change in Communist countries, even in the USSR (183). He concludes that 'knowledge of "subjective orientations to politics" . . . alerts us to the potential for, or—as the case may be—some of the obstacles to, rapid change from an authoritarian to a pluralist political regime' (185). Nevertheless, Archie places predominant emphasis on the role of leadership and institutions, rather than political culture, when weighing the sources of such systemic change.

'Political Culture' in Adam Kuper and Jessica Kuper (eds.), *The Social Science Encyclopaedia* (London and Boston: Routledge and Kegan Paul, 1985), 609–11 (revised and updated entry for 2nd edn., 1996, 625–6)

'Ideology and Political Culture' in Seweryn Bialer (ed.), *Politics, Society and Nationality Inside Gorbachev's Russia* (Boulder, CO: Westview, 1989), 1–40

'Political Culture and Democratization: The Russian Case in Comparative Perspective' in Detlef Pollack, Jörg Jacobs, Olaf Müller, and Gert Pickel (eds.), *Political Culture in Post-Communist Europe* (Aldershot: Ashgate, 2003), 17–27

'Comparative Politics: A View from Britain', APSA–CP Newsletter, 16/1 (2005)

'Cultural Change and Continuity in the Transition from Communism: The Russian Case' in Lawrence E. Harrison and Peter Berger (eds.), *Developing Cultures: Case Studies* (New York: Routledge, 2005)

The chapter is critical of 'a cultural determinism which suggests that because of Orthodox religious tradition, autocratic Tsarist rule, and seventy years of Communism, Russia is doomed by history to be an authoritarian state'. The post-Communist era has, however, seen 'some revival of support for Soviet symbols and Soviet norms' and 'disillusionment with what has been presented to Russians as democracy'. The lesson is that 'democratic institution-building and a rule of law must be pursued for their own sakes'. It is not enough to assume that they will emerge as by-products of a market economy, especially given the nature of Russian-style capitalism.

Soviet Politics Pre-1985

Many of these works focus on the central role of the General Secretary in Soviet politics. The theme of leadership and institutional power in Russia remains a dominant one throughout this section and the whole of the bibliography. Brown made a major contribution to transatlantic and British scholarly debates about the nature of the Soviet system, political change, totalitarianism, authoritarianism, Communism, pluralism, and democracy. He also highlighted innovative developments in Soviet specialist writing on politics and international relations from the mid-1960s. This body of work on pre-1985 Soviet politics provided an indispensable basis for Brown's penetrating analysis of the nature and significance of Gorbachev's leadership.

'Policy-Making in the Soviet Union', review article in *Soviet Studies*, 28/1 (July 1971), 120–48

'Problems of Group Influence and Interest Articulation in the Soviet Union', review article of Skilling and Griffiths (eds.), *Interest Groups in Soviet Politics*, in *Government and Opposition*, 7/2 (Spring 1972), 229–43

This article welcomes Western scholarly efforts to elucidate the workings of the Soviet system by studying the role of competing groups. But it cautions against exaggerating the power of so-called 'interest groups' or suggesting that 'interest groups' enjoy (relative) autonomy in a country where the Communist Party holds a monopoly of power. It is more accurate simply to recognize the existence of a 'diversity of views in the USSR'.

Soviet Politics and Political Science (London: Macmillan, 1974; New York: St Martin's Press, 1976)

This book surveys Western literature on Soviet politics up to the mid-1970s and assesses its strengths and weaknesses. It analyses debates about 'totalitarianism', and points to the dangers of narrow single model approaches. The book focuses on Soviet political institutions, the role of interests and groups in the policy process, and Soviet political culture as particularly important areas of research. In the 1970s, this survey enriched the field with its self-critical stocktaking, the more so since neither the study of institutions nor analysis of political culture was at the time fashionable.

The Soviet Union since the Fall of Khrushchev, co-editor with Michael Kaser (London: Macmillan, 1975; New York: Free Press, 1976; 2nd edn., 1978). Author of ch. 10, 'Political Developments: Some Conclusions and an Interpretation', 218–75; ch. 12, 'Political Developments, 1975–77', 299–329; and 'Calendar of Political Events: October 1964–June 1977', 330–40

This comprehensive edited volume analyses developments from 1964 to 1977, covering political, economic, foreign policy, demographic, literary, and religious changes. Brown's two chapters on political developments see nationalism as the main source of tension that could lead to political change, followed by the threat to the Soviet power structure of social groups acquiring a sense of group (or class) consciousness (259). To these he adds demographic developments in the Soviet Union and the coming generational change in the Communist Party leadership. The 'growing pressures and latent tensions within the society' are likely in the medium and longer run 'to make progressively more difficult the conservative political management of Soviet society' (326).

'The USSR after Stalin' in *The Encyclopaedia of Modern History* (London: Hamlyn, 1978), 288–9

'Policy-Making in Communist States', review article in *Studies in Comparative Communism*, 11/4 (Winter 1978), 424–36

Brown welcomes increasing scholarly attention to conflicts of interests between groups within Communist states, but expresses concern about the narrowness of an exclusive emphasis on 'interest group' rivalry as *the* explanation of policy outcomes. He cautions against adopting a single explanatory model that 'prematurely rules out other elements and influences within the policy process and other conflicts within society' (427).

'Governing the USSR', review essay in *Problems of Communism*, 28/5–6 (September–December 1979), 103–8

This is a review article of *How the Soviet Union is Governed* (Jerry Hough's substantially revised and updated version of Merle Fainsod's *How Russia is Ruled*). It provides wide-ranging reflections about the problems of analysing Soviet political development and makes the case for multi-dimensional comparative approaches. 'While Hough's focus on political institutions and the policy process is entirely to be welcomed, it is a pity that he pays little . . . attention to the issue of continuity and change in political culture and to the successes and failures of Soviet political socialization' (106).

Authority, Power and Policy in the USSR: Essays Dedicated to Leonard Schapiro, co-editor with T. H. Rigby and Peter Reddaway (London: Macmillan; New York: St Martin's Press, 1980). Author of ch. 8, 'The Power of the General Secretary of the CPSU', 135–57

'Each General Secretary has wielded less individual power over policy than his predecessor, but *within* his period of office his power *vis-à-vis* his colleagues has grown' (136). In one of his first pieces on leadership, Brown throws comparative light on the rules of Stalin, Khrushchev, and Brezhnev. He investigates continuity and change in the sources of leadership power and discusses the constraints on its exercise. Brown points to a linkage in the post-Stalin period between a leader's style and his political longevity; if the chief executive 'leads from the front', he will have more power while in office, but his tenure is likely to be shorter than if he 'leads from the middle'.

' "Political Development" and the Study of Communist Politics', review article in *Studies in Comparative Communism*, 15/1 (Spring 1982), 131–40

The Cambridge Encyclopedia of Russia and the Soviet Union, co-editor with John Fennell, Michael Kaser, and H. T. Willetts (Cambridge: Cambridge University Press, 1982). Author of entries on History, 1953–79, and The Communist Party of the Soviet Union.

Soviet Policy for the 1980s, co-editor with Michael Kaser (London: Macmillan; Bloomington: Indiana University Press, 1982). Co-author of 'Introduction'; author of ch. 9, 'Leadership Succession and Policy Innovation', 223–53; of 'Postscript: July 1982', 267–72; and of 'Calendar of Political Events: 1971–July 1982', 254–66

Written just before Brezhnev's death, this piece anticipates how the passing of the old leader would set the stage for the most 'important political succession' process of the 1980s. A new Soviet General Secretary would be able to shape the forced renewal (due to age-induced attrition) of the top rungs of leadership and would have to respond to serious policy problems (223). Given the gravity of the issues, leadership succession in the 1980s was particularly crucial. Even though Andropov was the leading contender to succeed Brezhnev, Gorbachev's qualifications for the General Secretaryship had to 'be taken very seriously indeed' (269). Brown was the first to suggest Gorbachev as a likely future General Secretary.

'Andropov: Discipline *and* Reform?' in *Problems of Communism*, 32/1 (January–February 1983), 18–31

This article provides a detailed analysis of Andropov's background, political views, and policy initiatives, correcting the oversimplification which saw him as simply a former KGB chief. His agenda is one of discipline *and* reform, an uneasy combination in Soviet conditions. Discipline can hardly solve Soviet economic problems, the article explains; but reform without discipline could prove politically dangerous. Finally, as in other pre-1985 articles, there is informed speculation about the innovation-minded Gorbachev and his future.

'Pluralism, Power, and the Soviet Political System' in Susan Gross Solomon (ed.), *Pluralism in the Soviet Union: Essays in Honour of H. Gordon Skilling* (London: Macmillan; New York: St Martin's Press, 1983), 61–107. (Spanish translation in *Foro Internacional*, 23/2 (October–December 1982), 146–82)

This is a thoughtful contribution to the debate among Western scholars on how to conceptualize the distribution of power in the Soviet system. Brown cautions against the conceptual stretching of 'pluralism' or 'corporatism'. Referring to 'pluralism' in the pre-*perestroika* USSR in any form, whether 'institutional ' or 'bureaucratic', blurs distinctions between Soviet and Western political systems. Given the illegitimacy of group autonomy in the Soviet Union, one should not apply the term 'pluralism' to the Soviet polity. The chapter also analyses esoteric debate in the Soviet Union and the innovative contributions of Burlatsky, Shakhnazarov, and Kalensky.

'Political Power and the Soviet State: Western and Soviet Perspectives' in Neil Harding (ed.), *The State in Socialist Society* (London: Macmillan; New York: State University of New York Press, 1984), 51–103 (enlarged, updated version of contribution to Skilling Festschrift)

'The Soviet succession: From Andropov to Chernenko' in *The World Today*, 40/4 (April 1984), 134–41

When the geriatric Chernenko goes, Archie predicts, the number-two positioned Gorbachev 'looks strongly placed to succeed' him, but the latter would surely upset vested interests, if indeed he seeks economic reform. 'Much is at stake—not only the careers of individuals but the future of the Soviet system' (141).

'Political Science in the Soviet Union: A New Stage of Development?' in *Soviet Studies*, 36/3 (July 1984), 317–44

This article traces the history and development of political science in the USSR from 1965, when Fedor Burlatsky first attempted to promote it as a separate discipline. Generalizing about the nature of power or cross-national comparing of international political systems was new and contentious in the USSR. And yet, by the early 1980s, some innovative political scientists (*politologi*) came to see decentralization and even democratization as necessary reforms. Not only did their work mark a 'new stage of development' in the Soviet study of politics, as the article made clear, but it also sowed seeds for what grew into Gorbachev's 'new political thinking'.

'The Foreign Policy-Making Process' in Curtis Keeble (ed.), *The Soviet State: The Domestic Roots of Soviet Foreign Policy* (London: Gower, for the Royal Institute of International Affairs; Boulder, CO: Westview, 1985), 191–216

The Gorbachev Era

This category includes the double prize-winning monograph on the 'Gorbachev factor'—the primary factor explaining the systemic transformation of the USSR and the end of the cold war. Careful analysis of the evidence shows that such astonishing changes were not inevitable results of Soviet crisis or Western pressure. Indeed, contingency rather than inevitability, domestic politics rather than external pressure, explain the rise of this reformist leader. At first, Gorbachev (bolstered by innovative thinkers, many of whom were identified in pre-1985 pieces) sought to liberalize the system, but, as Brown shows, Gorbachev's ideas became more radical over time: by 1989, Gorbachev had consciously embraced political pluralism and was attracted by European-style social democracy.

'Can Gorbachev make a difference?' in *Détente*, 3 (May 1985), 4–7

Countering widespread Western scepticism about the prospects for reform, and the idea that a General Secretary could be the agent of it, Archie contends that Gorbachev *is* a reformer who *can* bring about change. 'Those… who think that, having reached that position, [Gorbachev] will be hamstrung, may be in for a surprise' (7).

'Gorbachev: New Man in the Kremlin' in *Problems of Communism*, 34/3 (May–June 1985), 1–23

In this detailed analysis of Gorbachev's rise to power, Brown argues that Gorbachev is an ideas-driven reformer who has the political power to make a difference, despite vested interests and bureaucratic torpor. The vast resources of the General Secretary suggest that Gorbachev has the political capacity to push through change.

'Gorbatsjov: een nieuwe leider, een nieuwe lijn?' in *Oost Europa Verkenningen*, 80 (August 1985), 3–9

'Gorbachev's Policy Innovations' in *Bulletin of the Atomic Scientists*, 41/10 (November 1985), 18–22

'Change in the Soviet Union' in *Foreign Affairs*, 64/5 (Summer 1986), 1048–65

A snapshot of Soviet change some fifteen months after Gorbachev's arrival to the top job, this piece urges sceptics to stop underplaying the extent and future of change. Not only does Gorbachev have the will and intelligence to pursue reform, he also has the political means to push it through, as demonstrated at the 27th Party Congress. Gorbachev's enormous powers of appointment allow him to fight bureaucratic inertia, and his political acumen helps him persuade others to accept deeper policy change.

'Political Science in the USSR' (updated version of 1984 *Soviet Studies* article) in *International Political Science Review* , 7/4 (October 1986), 443–81

This updated version adds the salient point that reform-minded *politologi*, having hinted at reform in the pre-Gorbachev era, represented a powerful source of ideas for policy change. Under Gorbachev, these innovative *politologi* would 'get a hearing'.

'Soviet Political Developments and Prospects' in *World Policy Journal*, 4/1 (Winter 1986–87), 55–87; translated into Spanish as 'Análisis y conjeturas sobre la evolución del actual curso político de U.R.S.S.' in *Afers Internacionals*, 11 (1987), 29–62

Reading this article today reminds us of Gorbachev's extraordinary political skill and intellectual will as he overcame conservative forces to get his reformist agenda adopted. It also a reminder of just how much was at stake during the political battles in 1986–7: 'It is… a battle of ideas. Genuine differences on where the Soviet Union should be going are being argued out....How it will be resolved...is of critical significance not only for the Soviet Union but also for the rest of the world' (57).

'Gorbachev and Reform of the Soviet System' in *Political Quarterly*, 58/2 (April–June 1987), 139–51 (republished in considerably expanded and updated form in Jon Bloomfield (ed.), *The Soviet Revolution: Perestroika and the Remaking of Socialism* (London: Laurence and Wishart, 1989), 63–84)

'Power and Policy: A Reformer in the Kremlin' in *The Nation*, 244/23 (June 13, 1987), 792–5

'What's Happening in Moscow?' in *The National Interest*, 8 (Summer 1987), 9–13

'The Soviet Leadership and the Struggle for Political Reform' in *The Harriman Institute Forum*, 1/4 (April 1988), 1–8

'Comment Gorbatchev a pris le pouvoir, 1978–1988' in *Pouvoirs*, 45 (April 1988), 17–29

'Khrushchev, Gorbachev and the Prospects for Reform' in Francesca Gori (ed.), *Il XX Congresso del Pcus* (Milan: Franco Angeli, 1988), 214–19

'Tat'yana Zaslavskaya and Soviet Sociology' in *Social Research*, 55/1–2 (Spring–Summer 1988), 261–6

'La Reforma Política en la Unión Soviética' in *Foro Internacional*, 28/4 (April–June 1988), 550–69

'Political Science' in Alexander Dallin and Bertrand M. Patenaude (eds.), *Soviet Scholarship under Gorbachev* (Stanford, CA: Stanford University Press, 1988), 33–39

This piece updates Archie's pre-1985 articles suggesting that innovative Soviet political science thought since 1965 had potentially important implications for change. It also provides excellent detail on key reformers involved in Gorbachev's government.

'The Soviet Political Scene: The Era of Gorbachev?' in Lawrence W. Lerner and Donald W. Treadgold (eds.), *Gorbachev and the Soviet Future* (Boulder, CO: Westview, 1988), 21–43

The piece begins with a detailed review of *perestroika* policies to date—economic reform, foreign policy innovations, and political change. Those changes enhance the potential for a radical overhaul, but a key question remains: does Gorbachev have the political means to realize that potential, especially in conditions of unremitting economic deterioration? It then assesses the factors favouring and constraining radical reform. Leadership is seen as the key, given that reform is not inevitable and 'change...can be in more than one direction' (41). The Gorbachev leadership can take credit for spawning a 'remarkably innovative and consequential' new era (41).

Foreword to Robert Desjardins, *The Soviet Union through French Eyes, 1945–85* (London: Macmillan, 1988), viii–x

Political Leadership in the Soviet Union, ed. (London: Macmillan; Bloomington: Indiana University Press, 1989). Author of ch. 1, 1–3; ch. 6, 163–217; and ch. 7, 218–31

This book analyses the phenomenon of political leadership in the Soviet Union from 1917 to 1988, focusing on the 1980s. Brown examines leadership and political change from the death of Suslov in January 1982 (which sparked the succession debate and removed barriers to reform) until after the July 1988 19th Party Conference, which marked a turning point in Soviet history by opening the way for competitive elections. Brown's penultimate chapter and conclusion focus on Gorbachev's leadership, his selection as General Secretary, and the origins of his reformist thinking. He concludes that while 'the concentration of a great deal of power in the hands of central leadership in Moscow' has brought Russia much historical pain, Gorbachev's consolidated power provides hope for those who prefer 'reform to reaction and evolutionary change to destabilisation' (1, 212).

Memorandum, 'Perestroika and Glasnost' and oral evidence to House of Commons Foreign Affairs Committee on 7 December 1988 (published by HMSO, January 1989)

'Gorbatschow und die politische Reform' in Karl Vak and Helmut Zilk (eds.), *Europa Aufstieg* (Vienna: Europa Verlag, 1989), 83–91

'Political Change in the Soviet Union' in *World Policy Journal*, 6/3 (Summer 1989), 469–501 (republished in abridged but updated form under title of 'Perestroika and the Political System' in T. Hasegawa and Alex Pravda (eds.), *Perestroika: Soviet Domestic and Foreign Policies* (London: Sage, 1990), 56–87; republished also in abridged form in Alexander Dallin and Gail W. Lapidus (eds.), *The Soviet System in Crisis: A Reader of Western and Soviet Views* (Boulder, CO: Westview, 1991))

Brown argues that Gorbachev has brought about systemic transformation from 'authoritarianism' to 'enlightened authoritarianism' to 'one containing . . . elements of political pluralism and of democratisation' (470). And though the economic situation is worsening, politics remain primary in the USSR. The real threats to Gorbachev's power lie less in the deteriorating economic situation than in centre–periphery tensions that stem from ethnic unrest and national aspirations.

'Reconstructing the Soviet Political System' in Abraham Brumberg (ed.), *Chronicle of a Revolution: A Western–Soviet Inquiry into Perestroika* (New York: Pantheon, 1990), 30–49 and 242–3

This thoughtful chapter puts the Gorbachev era into context. It considers the 'highly authoritarian' nature of the Soviet system that Gorbachev inherited, and assesses the changes brought by *perestroika*. It examines the impact of *perestroika* in four key areas—ideas, institutions, interests, and culture. Of crucial importance in the area of institutional change is the introduction of competitive elections for a legislature capable of holding accountable executive power. Recent experience of democratic ideas and institutions can change political culture, offering hope for a country with a long authoritarian tradition. But radical change is also associated with destablizing phenomena, such as revitalized national aspirations, capable of threatening the very survival of the Soviet state.

Dialogue with German Diligensky: 'Razmyshleniya o perestroike: kak izmenit' politicheskuyu kul'turu obshchestva?' (Reflections on *perestroika*: how to change the political culture of a society?) in *Mirovaya ekonomika i mezhdunarodnye otnosheniya*, 2 (February 1990), 51–8

'United States–Soviet Relations, 1990: Soviet Political Reforms' (evidence to United States Congress along with Professor Robert Legvold and Academician Roald Sagdeyev) in *Hearings before the Committee on Foreign Affairs, House of Representatives: One Hundred Fifth Congress, Second Session* (1990), 71–103

'Gorbachev's Leadership: Another View' in *Soviet Economy*, 6/2 (1990), 141–54 (reprinted in Ed A. Hewett and Victor H. Winston (eds.), *Milestones in Glasnost and Perestroika: Politics and People* (Washington, DC: Brookings Institution, 1991))

'Soviet Politics in the 1980s', review article in *Slavonic and East European Review*, 68/4 (October 1990), 725–30

Brown cites from one of the books reviewed in this article: ' "If in an ideocratic system the conservative's dilemma is that fundamentalism quickly degenerates into ineffectual, self-referential dogmas, *the reformer's is that his anti-authoritarianism subverts the authority of those who set the new line*" ' (726, emphasis added). This point, he notes, crystallizes Gorbachev's political dilemma after 1989.

The Soviet Union: A Biographical Dictionary (London: Weidenfeld & Nicolson, 1990; New York: Macmillan, 1991). Editor and principal author.

'The Soviet Coup: A Mixed Blessing', *The House Magazine* (The Parliamentary Weekly), 554/18 (18 May 1992), 12

New Thinking in Soviet Politics, ed. (London: Macmillan; New York: St Martin's Press, 1992). Author of ch. 1, 'Introduction', 1–11; and ch. 2, 'New Thinking on the Soviet Political System', 12–28

This book examines the intellectual sources of the transformation of the Soviet system in the *perestroika* period. Archie Brown's chapter analyses the substance and traces the evolution of the political ideas that inspired the transition from a highly authoritarian system to a politically pluralist one.

'The New Russia: Continuity, Dislocation And An Elusive Goal', *The House Magazine* (The Parliamentary Weekly), 556/18 (1 June 1992), 16–17

'New Ideas in Politics', *Discovery*, 12/4 (1992), 10–13

'The Leader of the Prologue', in Ferdinand Mount (ed.), *Communism* (London: Harvill, 1992), 293–300

'Gorbachev' in Joel Krieger (ed.), *The Oxford Companion to Politics of the World* (New York: Oxford University Press, 1993), 358–60

'The Succession and Reform' in Robert V. Daniels (ed.), *Soviet Communism from Reform to Collapse* (Lexington, KY: D. C. Heath, 1995), 47–66

Entries on Mikhail Gorbachev, Andrei Sakharov, and Boris Yeltsin for Seymour Martin Lipset (ed.), *The Encyclopedia of Democracy* (Washington, DC: Congressional Quarterly Books, 1995), vol. 2, 538–9, and vol. 4, 1101–2 and 1399–1400

Foreword to book by Andrei Grachev, *Final Days: The Inside Story of the Collapse of the Soviet Union* (Boulder, CO: Westview, 1995), ix–xiv

The Gorbachev Factor (Oxford and New York: Oxford University Press, 1996; paperback 1997). German translation, *Der Gorbatschow-Faktor* (Frankfurt: Insel-Verlag, March 2000)

Described by Sergey Peregudov, writing in the leading Russian political science journal *Polis*, as 'The most fundamental of all the books on perestroika', *The Gorbachev Factor* is indispensable for understanding how and why fundamental change took place in the USSR and what part the Soviet leadership played in initiating and directing that change. It also makes a valuable contribution to the literature on comparative leadership, democratization, and transitions from authoritarian regimes. Though not a biography, it traces the evolution of Gorbachev and assesses his legacy. Its core thesis maintains that Gorbachev, who was sincerely interested in reformist ideas, realized within three years that reform was insufficient and embarked on a total transformation of the Soviet system. The book also demonstrates that radical and peaceful change was impossible in the USSR (given the institutional nature of Soviet power) without a reform-minded, determined, and skilful leader in the Kremlin. There was *nothing* inevitable about Gorbachev's succession, the changes he launched, or the Soviet collapse that his reforms indirectly helped bring about. *The Gorbachev Factor* won two prizes: the WJM Mackenzie Prize of the Political Studies Association of the UK and the Alec Nove Prize of the British Association for Slavonic and East European Studies.

'Transnational Influences in the Transition from Communism', *Post-Soviet Affairs*, 16/2 (April–June 2000), 177–200

This article focuses on the process of transition from Communism in Central and Eastern Europe. It argues that these transitions constitute a 'Fourth Wave' of democratization, and were profoundly affected by changes in the Soviet Union. It underscores the major influence on East-Central Europe of transnational stimuli such as Western radio, foreign travel, idealization of the USA, the attractive pull of the EC, and positive perceptions of Western systems and policies. But the real trigger for democratization in the region was radical change in Moscow.

288 *Julie Newton*

'Mikhail Gorbachev: Systemic Transformer' in Martin Westlake (ed.), *Leaders of Transition* (London: Macmillan, 2000), 3–26

In early 1985, a former British ambassador asserted: ' "There's one thing we all know. The Soviet Union isn't going to change" ' (4). Four years later, it had undergone systemic transformation. Brown explains how, in 1988, Gorbachev 'moved from being a reformer of the Soviet system to a systemic transformer' (6), and how he evolved from communist reformer to social democrat, akin to Willy Brandt or Felipe González, who understood that the 'means are as important as the ends in politics' (18). Gorbachev was not the only author of change; serious systemic problems and pressure from below (from 'children of the 20th Party Congress' in 1956) both inspired and strengthened the cause of reform. On Soviet disintegration, causes include the coup plotters' folly, Boris Yeltsin's ambition, and the unintended consequences of democratization.

'Mikhail Gorbachev and the Transformation of Russian Politics' in *A Millennium Salute to Mikhail Gorbachev on his 70th Birthday* (Moscow: Valent, 2001), 100–6, and in Russian as 'Mikhail Gorbachev i peremeny v rossiiskoi politike' in *Mnogaya leta . . . Mikhailu Gorbachevu—70* (Moscow: Valent, 2001), 104–11

'Explaining the Peaceful Transformation', *The House Magazine* (The Parliamentary Weekly), 972/27 (7 December 2001), 20–4

Introduction to Mikhail Gorbachev and Zdeněk Mlynář, *Conversations with Gorbachev: On Perestroika, the Prague Spring, and the Crossroads of Socialism* (New York: Columbia University Press, 2002), vii–xxiii

Zdeněk Mlynář was Gorbachev's 'closest' friend (xiv). They had been classmates at MGU, and became friends for life. This book is based on recorded conversations between them. It demonstrates Gorbachev's intellectual depth and his undeniable social democratic proclivities. The *Conversations* are enlightening both as an historical document and as a compelling discourse on political philosophy. Brown's 'Introduction' criticizes those who condemn *perestroika* as 'a foolish attempt to "reform the unreformable" '. He argues that in the 'the highly institutionalized, well-established Soviet system, the only place a serious reform—which, then, had the possibility of progressing beyond reform to transformative change—could realistically begin, if it were to stand a strong chance of success, was within the Communist Party'. The Introduction provides valuable insights on two politicians who, despite having to operate within highly authoritarian regimes, managed to retain their moral compass.

Entries on Mikhail Gorbachev, Raisa Gorbachev, Union of Soviet Socialist Republics, Perestroika, and New Thinking in James R. Millar (ed.), *Encyclopedia of Russian History* (New York: Macmillan Reference, 2003)

'Gorbachev and the End of the Cold War', in Richard Ned Lebow and Richard Herrmann (eds.), *Ending the Cold War* (New York: Palgrave, 2004), 31–57

'The Soviet Union: Reform of the System or Systemic Transformation?', *Slavic Review*, 63/3 (Fall 2004), 489–504

The Demise of Marxism–Leninism in Russia (London and Basingstoke: Palgrave, 2004), editor and author of ch. 1, 'Introduction', 1–18; and ch. 2, 'The Rise of Non-Leninist Thinking about the Political System', 19–40

Seven Years that Changed the World: Perestroika in Perspective (Oxford: Oxford University Press, forthcoming 2006)

Russian Politics and Transition, 1992–2004

In the post-Soviet period, the leadership factor continues to be a main theme in Brown's work. If Gorbachev and the reformist wing of the *perestroika* leadership promoted democratization, the Yeltsin leadership neglected it. As the publications below point out, Yeltsin preferred political confrontation to democratic institutionalization. Excessive zeal (albeit rhetorical) for free-market economic reforms led to disregard for democratic, legal, or constitutional reform. These articles examine the sources and content of Russia's new hybrid polity—mixing democracy, autocracy, and kleptocracy—that Yeltsin created and bequeathed to Vladimir Putin.

The analyses of Putin's leadership stress the growing authoritarian element in Russian politics. Contemporary Russian politics bear the marks of merged Russian *and* Soviet cultures, with their traditions of 'order', strong leaders, *nomenklatura*, and centralized single-party control. Yet experience of democratization and free speech in the late Soviet and post-Soviet period period has also left its mark on the Russian people, although the weakness of political parties, of the legislature, and of civil society testify to the inadequacy of democratic institutionalization.

'The October Crisis of 1993: Context and Implications', *Post-Soviet Affairs* (formerly *Soviet Economy*), 9/3 (1993), 183–95

This detailed analysis of the 1993 bloody conflict between Yeltsin and Russia's parliament sheds light on the origins, course, and consequences of the crisis. It sees these events as a major setback for Russia's process of democratization: they championed violent confrontation over political negotiation; and provided an excuse to augment the executive's power at the expense of the parliament's capacity to function as a democratic 'check'—a change enshrined in Russia's post-crisis 1993 constitution, and in force to this day.

'Political Leadership in Post-Communist Russia', in Amin Saikal and William Maley (eds.), *Russia in Search of its Future* (Cambridge: Cambridge University Press, 1995), 28–47

This piece compares Gorbachev and Yeltsin as leaders and contributors to democratic change. Despite relatively favourable conditions, Yeltsin had made little progress in legal and democratic institution-building by the mid-1990s. Brown examines the ways in which the 1993 crisis contributed to the 'hybrid' political system that emerged under Yeltsin.

'Russia: The Long Road to Democracy', *The House Magazine* (The Parliamentary Weekly), 719/21 (20 May 1996), 12–13

'The Russian Transition in Comparative and Russian Perspective', *Social Research*, 63/2 (Summer 1996), 403–15

'Democratization and Political Culture in Russia', in *Democratization and Regional Co-operation in Asia* (Seoul: Kim Dae-jung Peace Foundation, 1996), 265–84

'Politika liderstva v Rossii'' (Leadership Politics in Russia) in *Vestnik Moskovskogo universiteta: Sotsiologiya i Politologiya*, 2 (April–June 1998), 59–77

Co-author of symposium, 'Russia on the Brink: Democracy or Disaster?', *Kellogg Institute*, 31 (Fall 1998), 16–22

'The Russian Crisis: Beginning of the End or End of the Beginning?', *Post-Soviet Affairs*, 15/1 (January–March 1999), 56–73

Pondering the central question posed in the title, this article sets the 1998 economic crisis in context. The real problem is the lack of progress in building democratic institutions and a law-based market economy during the 1990s. 'Both Russian marketeers and their Western advisors were . . . more interested in building a market economy than in building democracy. As a result of these misplaced priorities, they built neither the one nor the other' (57). The article makes a strong case for reforming Russia's 1993 constitution; and it asserts that a new leader, determined to build democracy, could make a real difference. There is no reason why it has to be 'the beginning of the end'.

'Russia and Democratization', *Problems of Post-Communism*, 46/5 (September–October 1999), 3–13

This article assesses Russia as a 'hybrid political system or mixed polity' (3). It goes on to consider the Primakov government's efforts to promote democratization in the face of the growing dangers to that process. The piece analyses the main sources of such dangers: 'golden triangles and diamond quadrangles' (the corrupting alliance among bankers, government leaders, and the new owners of natural resources and the mass media) and the population's resulting disillusionment. 'Russian democracy needs party consolidation and realignment, constitutional change, and the election of a president who (unlike Yeltsin) will give priority to political and legal institution-building and the rule of law' (10).

Memorandum to House of Commons Foreign Affairs Committee, printed as Appendix to the Committee's Third Report, 'Relations with the Russian Federation' (London, 2000), 176–8

'Is Russia becoming a democracy?' in *Beyond Transition: Ten Years after the Fall of the Berlin Wall* (New York: Regional Bureau for Europe and the CIS, United Nations Development Programme, 2000), 51–70

'Vladimir Putin and the Reaffirmation of Central State Power', *Post-Soviet Affairs*, 17/1 (2001), 45–55

Pithy and thorough, this article explains how and why Yeltsin's era was one of 'weak president, powerful interests' (46). It then turns to Vladimir Putin and examines the levers he is using to reaffirm that central state power—selective application of the law and administrative reorganization towards a vertical power pole. None of these augur well for the development of democracy, a law-bound economy, and genuine federalism. The only good news is that 'the battle for the mind of Putin is not yet over' (54).

Contemporary Russian Politics: A Reader (Oxford: Oxford University Press, 2001), sole editor and extensive contributor (thirteen introductory sections).

This unique volume usefully consolidates the best analyses of post-Soviet politics. It includes forty republished or newly written articles, covering twelve major dimensions of Russian politics, each with its own introduction by Brown as well as an introduction to the whole book and a long concluding chapter. It is both an advanced text and a valuable research resource (with many chapters written by Russian scholars) for those investigating specific aspects of Russian politics, such as institutions, leadership, economic reform, media, foreign policy, federalism, democratization, and more. Moreover, its thirteen separate 'Introductions' offer important insights from one of the most distinguished experts in the field.

Evidence to the House of Lords Select Committee on the European Union, *EU–Russia Relations* (London: Stationery Office, 2003), 1–13

Gorbachev, Yeltsin, and Putin: Political Leadership in Russia's Transition, co-editor with Lilia Shevtsova (New York: Carnegie Endowment for International Peace, 2001). Author of ch. 1, 'Introduction', 1–9; and ch. 2, 'Transformational Leaders Compared: Mikhail Gorbachev and Boris Yeltsin', 11–43. Portuguese edition, Editora da Universide de Brasilia, Brasilia, 2004

The second chapter helps to 'unpack' and better understand the role of leaders in Russia's complex set of five transformations: the political transition to pluralism, the economic switch to a partial market and capitalist system, the ending of the cold war, the freeing of Eastern Europe, and the disintegration of the USSR. It then contrasts the two leaders at three levels: styles, influences, and the interests and institutions that constrained or supported them. The chapter provides fresh insight into both Gorbachev and Yeltsin, based on new sources, including recent memoirs.

'Ten Years after the Soviet Breakup: From Democratization to "Guided Democracy"', *Journal of Democracy*, 12/4 (October 2001), 35–41 (republished in Larry Diamond and Marc F. Plattner (eds.), *Democracy after Communism* (Baltimore and London: Johns Hopkins University Press, 2002), 209–15)

'Russia as a "Normal" Object of Study in International Relations' in Bengt Sundelius (ed.), *The Consequences of September 11: A Symposium on the Implications for International Relations* (Stockholm: Swedish Institute of International Affairs, 2002), 163–72

'Vladimir Putin's Leadership in Comparative Perspective' in Cameron Ross (ed.), *Russian Politics Under Putin* (Manchester: Manchester University Press, 2004), 3–16

Works spanning the Soviet and Post-Soviet Eras, 1917–2004

These works merit a separate category for those interested in comprehensive overviews of the USSR and Russia. The encyclopaedias and short, comprehensive analyses are enormously valuable. Included here, too, are memorial pieces for a great specialist in the field whose invaluable work spanned both Soviet and Russian periods. Finally, this section houses Archie Brown's reflections on Britain's contribution to the study of authoritarian and totalitarian rule in the twentieth century.

The Cambridge Encyclopedia of Russia and the Former Soviet Union, (successor volume to fifth book on this list, Cambridge: Cambridge University Press, 1994). Editor, with Michael Kaser and Gerald S. Smith. Author of substantial thematic entries on 'The Khrushchev Era (1953–1964)'; 'The Brezhnev Years (1964–1982)'; 'Andropov and Chernenko (1982–1985)'; 'The Gorbachev Era'; 'After the Soviet Union'; 'Political and Social Thought'; 'New Thinking: The Domestic Context'; 'Emergence of "Civil Society" '; 'New Associations and Political Parties'; 'Post-Soviet Russian Politics'; and biographical entries on Mikhail Gorbachev, Boris Yeltsin, Eduard Shevardnadze, and Alexander Rutskoy

'Pamyati Aleka Nouva', *Ekonomicheskaya shkola*, 3 (1994)

'Professor Alec Nove, 1915–1994' in *Journal of Development Studies*, 31/2, (December 1994), vii–xi

(with Alec Cairncross) 'Alec Nove, 1915–1994: An Appreciation', *Europe-Asia Studies*, 49/3 (1997), 487–97 (reprinted with minor changes in *Proceedings of the British Academy, 94: 1996 Lectures and Memoirs* (London, 1997), 627–41)

A tribute to Alec Nove, this article describes the life and work of an extraordinary individual and scholar. As an analysis of Nove's judgment on the Soviet system and economy, it deepens our understanding of what went wrong with Russia's troubled transition to a market economy and democracy. Alec Nove had 'a remarkable ability to see what mattered and to make connections which others missed' (491). 'The pity is that the Russian government did not make more use of his profoundly practical knowledge' (487). The good news is that his knowledge, insights, and example remain timeless.

Entry on Alec Nove (1915–1994) for the *Oxford Dictionary of National Biography* (Oxford: Oxford University Press, 2004)

'The Soviet Union and Beyond' in Michael Howard and Roger Louis (eds.), *The Oxford History of the Twentieth Century* (Oxford: Oxford University Press, 1998), 176–89 (revised and updated for paperback edition published in 2000)

An enjoyable and admirable run through Soviet and post-Soviet political history, this chapter will interest specialists and newcomers alike.

'Communism' in N. J. Smelser and Paul B. Baltes (eds.), *International Encyclopedia of the Social and Behavioral Sciences* (Oxford: Pergamon, 2001), 2323–6

The British Study of Politics in the Twentieth Century (Oxford: British Academy in association with Oxford University Press, 1999), co-editor with Jack Hayward and Brian Barry, and author of chapter on 'The Study of Totalitarianism and Authoritarianism', 345–94; paperback edition, 2003

In light of the extraordinary transitions away from Communist authoritarianism throughout the Soviet bloc in the late 1980s and 1990s, it is useful to step back and assess the British contribution to the analysis of authoritarian and totalitarian regimes in the twentieth century. A substantial section is devoted to writing on the USSR, but attention is also given to delineating the concepts of authoritarianism and totalitarianism.

'The Communist Party of the Soviet Union' for *Supplement to the Modern Encyclopedia of Russian, Soviet, and Eurasian History*, vol. 6 (Gulf Breeze, FL: Academic International Press, 2004)

British Politics

This bibliographical journey ends where it started—in Scotland. Archie Brown is Scottish, of course, but *his* Scotland is one that remains united with the rest of Britain. The article on Scottish devolution explains why dispersing greater power to Scotland was essential for preserving the union.

'Postavení ministerského předsedy v britské politice' (The position of the Prime Minister in British politics), *Právník*, 6 (June 1966), 513–23

'Prime Ministerial Power', *Public Law* (London), Part I, Spring 1968, 28–51; Part II, Summer 1968, 96–118. (Reprinted in abridged form in Richard Rose and Mattei Dogan (eds.), *European Politics*, Boston: Little, Brown & Co., 1970; London: Macmillan, 1971; and in full in symposium published in Germany in 1974 under the editorship of Gerhard Ritter and Dieter Grosser)

'Asymmetrical Devolution: the Scottish Case', in *Political Quarterly*, vol. 69, No. 3, July–Sept. 1998, 215–23

The thoughts of a political scientist who has long studied the nationalities question in Russia, and who has written extensively on the Soviet Union's failure to preserve federal union, can shed much light on Britain's own nationalities problem. With Scotland in mind, Brown examines the nature of the problem: 'The essence is that we are talking about the institutional arrangements necessary to hold together a *multinational* state in an age when more states are splitting up than are joining together' (216). He argues that asymmetrical devolution of legislative power to Scotland is the only way of maintaining a multinational UK. He discusses Scottish particularities (such as its distinctive legal system) and compares and contrasts the position of Scotland with that of Spain's autonomous communities.

Other Writings

Articles published in weeklies, newspapers, and periodicals, including the *Financial Times*, the *Los Angeles Times*, the *Sunday Times*, *The Times*, the *Independent*, the *Guardian*, the *Observer*, the *Times Higher Education Supplement*, *The Scotsman*, *Scotland on Sunday*, *New Society*, *Newsday*, *Prospect*, *Global Business* (Tokyo), and *Oxford Today*, as well as reviews and review articles of more than 270 books, mainly in academic journals and the *Times Literary Supplement*.

Examples of substantial reviews and review articles

'A voice from the Kremlin' (the Khrushchev memoirs), *TLS*, 31 January 1975, 115; 'The torrents of the Prague Spring', *TLS*, 1 July 1977, 803–4; 'Adam Smith Verbatim', *TLS*, 23 November 1979, 46; 'The Soviet Union' (assessment of twenty five books), *TLS*, 25 January 1980, 95–96; 'Various shades of Red', *TLS*, 23 April 1982, 464; 'Change and Challenge' (review article on eve of Thatcher visit to Moscow), *TLS*, 27 March 1987, 313–14; 'Learning the arts of management', *TLS*, 9–15 December 1988, 1365–6; 'The statesmen and the putschists', *TLS*, 24 August 2001, 6; and 'Trust me, I'm a leader', *TLS*, 8 November 2002, 13–14.

Index

Index